YOURS PRESENTLY

RECENCIES SERIES

Research and Recovery in Twentieth-Century American Poetics

Matthew Hofer, Series Editor

This series stands at the intersection of critical investigation, historical documentation, and the preservation of cultural heritage. The series exists to illuminate the innovative poetics achievements of the recent past that remain relevant to the present. In addition to publishing monographs and edited volumes, it is also a venue for previously unpublished manuscripts, expanded reprints, and collections of major essays, letters, and interviews.

ALSO AVAILABLE IN THE RECENCIES SERIES:

Geopoetics: Geology, Materiality, Ecopoetics by Dale Enggass

Ingenious Pleasures: An Anthology of Punk, Trash, and Camp in Twentieth-Century Poetry edited by Drew Gardner

A Description of Acquaintance: The Letters of Laura Riding and Gertrude Stein, 1927–1930 edited by Jane Malcolm and Logan Esdale

All This Thinking: The Correspondence of Bernadette Mayer and Clark Coolidge edited by Stephanie Anderson and Kristen Tapson

"A Serpentine Gesture": John Ashbery's Poetry and Phenomenology by Elisabeth W. Joyce

Evaluations of US Poetry since 1950, Volume 1: Language, Form, and Music edited by Robert von Hallberg and Robert Faggen

Evaluations of US Poetry since 1950, Volume 2: Mind, Nation, and Power edited by Robert von Hallberg and Robert Faggen

Expanding Authorship: Transformations in American Poetry since 1950 by Peter Middleton

Circling the Canon, Volume I: The Selected Book Reviews of Marjorie Perloff, 1969–1994 by Marjorie Perloff

Circling the Canon, Volume II: The Selected Book Reviews of Marjorie Perloff, 1995–2017 by Marjorie Perloff

FOR ADDITIONAL TITLES IN THE RECENCIES SERIES,
please visit unmpress.com.

Yours Presently

THE SELECTED LETTERS

OF JOHN WIENERS

Edited by Michael Seth Stewart   Preface by Eileen Myles

University of New Mexico Press Albuquerque

© 2020 by the University of New Mexico Press
All rights reserved. Published 2020
Printed in the United States of America

First paperback printing 2024

ISBN 978-0-8263-6204-9 (cloth)
ISBN 978-0-8263-6635-1 (paper)
ISBN 978-0-8263-6205-6 (electronic)

Library of Congress Control Number: 2020947807

Founded in 1889, the University of New Mexico sits on the traditional homelands of the Pueblo of Sandia. The original peoples of New Mexico—Pueblo, Navajo, and Apache—since time immemorial have deep connections to the land and have made significant contributions to the broader community statewide. We honor the land itself and those who remain stewards of this land throughout the generations and also acknowledge our committed relationship to Indigenous peoples. We gratefully recognize our history.

COVER ILLUSTRATION Photograph by Elsa Dorfman, from the collection of Raymond Foye. Courtesy of Elsa Dorfman.
DESIGNED BY Mindy Basinger Hill
COMPOSED IN Garamond Premier Pro

CONTENTS

ILLUSTRATIONS

Eileen Myles

Which way do you know John Wieners? It is so weird to know him like this. In these letters he typed at twenty-one and twenty-two, he is ardent and precise, dark and ambitious—and by the end of the book what we get is a single stray postcard that arrived unduly late and forwarded by friends to Robin Blaser. Wieners's teasing and seasoned tone (of the sort one reserves for an old friend) is now what holds the message together, and that might be true as well of this collection.

John Wieners's letters form the charged invisible matrix of something else that distinguishes his work—a managerial self or genie, almost a sound one intuits that's always hovering at the edge of the work and through which John Wieners evinced his own "thereness."

The earliest letters here show the excitement of a poet becoming. We get the vivid naked tremulosity that would be shored up when he was a student at Black Mountain by the Olsonian call for "a living alternative to meter that varied like speech"[1] and when Wieners, embarrassed by the exposure inherent in his work, asked Charles Olson how he could stop writing "like this," we get John's account of Olson's response, which became his cri de coeur: "He [Olson] talks about *the intensity*, me John Wieners, the desire, the trouble in the poems, that the use of language is my image, on and on, talking as if I am a poet, possessing the talent to convert experience into form."[2]

Wieners was a changeable man, an adoring man, a calculating, generous, vengeful, and loving man. That's who I met in these letters. The famous and obscenely mean ones to Robert Creeley from the late 1960s are here, ones I've heard tell of for decades, and they are both awful to the core (fucked up and misogynist and racist as moments in these letters are throughout) and admittedly hysterically funny in exactly the scale of their assault.

Yet the John Wieners I'm most persistently intrigued by in these pages is just an expanded version of the one I already know. It's kind of Wieners in situ. There are so many lines I've underlined, gasping because, like Keats's letters, they hold the same breath and cadence and the sheer alchemical weight of the poems. In one letter he

---

1 See chapter 1, note 58.
2 May 24, 1957, letter to Robert Greene.

is talking about the agonies of his first great love, the famous Dana, the "Old Man" of the Hotel Wentley poems:

> So I still ache ache, and plan and resort to the old tricks.
> It just sounds like a Wentley outtake.

As a note, I'm presuming that any reader of this book is also a reader of Wieners's poems. I'd be fascinated by anyone who was not part of that small growing crowd, but let's go ahead.

(It is now at least three hours later.)

Now that is just the familiar parlance of the Wieners clock. But what is it? Is it a department store clock in Jordan's or Filene's Basement? Is it the subway?

His dark catholic warning tells us that one is always moving across an unknown game board, heading into who knows what, and all one possesses is one's capacity to know where "now" is, I think in terms of light and then the inky power that gets summoned from inside to notate and to give. It's a simple enough rule of thumb for life and it gave us John.

The way time tolls in his poems has its predecessor—which we have not yet seen—and John has already been in there waiting, feeling.

There's an attendant quality to his poems, almost sentinel—to magic, to sex, to possibility itself, to the sheer enormity of land and knowledge of it, and its interiors and the art within that, and the importance of who we are *within*. The oneness of community is just our witness to that shit.

In the early letters he makes a coeval call to James Schuyler, who is actually eleven years older than him, who he is hitting up for more work for John's magazine, *Measure*. I can't help thinking Schuyler would have snickered at Wieners's boyish ambition.

He explains excitedly to Schuyler (who I think hadn't drank the Kool-Aid) that "Projective Verse" had "set off a decade," "and MEASURE if my energies hold out, will end it. We must see ourselves as the new generation, initially our youth in these ten years."[3]

Wieners first hospitalization is noted in these pages, and the number of shock therapies (30), and insulin "treatments" (91) are reported as well in Seth Stewart's helpful and nonintrusive narration of which passage of John Wiener's life the next set of letters will be navigating.

So in lieu of a bio, this is it, the rarer one. A story told by himself and his relationships and I feel tremendous gratitude for how this account gives a fresh portrait of

---

3 June 11, 1957, letter to James Schuyler.

John for those of us who encountered him in our various, more distant ways or, of course, for those who never knew him at all. I relish this access to the growing man; I mention John Wieners's first hospitalization at the end of 1959 mainly because it's said in this book by those who knew him then just how violent and unnecessary that intervention was in the exact form it took. And rather than being a brilliant poet who endured a number of such hospitalizations on his way to getting worse, that initial stay may have marked and changed the very thing of him. A poet so very into making marks in time, on history, marking the things he'd seen on Earth and in dreams, *he* was marked disposable by family and state early on in a class-laden brutal way, and it did not simply begin something—but possibly it *made* something happen.

As a born Bostonian (and also as an Irish descendent of a paternal grandmother who was held in the 1950s by the same state institutions), I reacted to Wieners work before I even knew *how* it was working on me. His phrasing and his sound system so precisely arises from the specific map of language and land and time of itself, and I recognize it as the gesture(s) of an older cousin and gay cartographer of, for me, a Boston just before.

Scollay Square, the locus of strip joints and burlesque halls and tattoo parlors in the West End of Boston was demolished in 1962 (about my junior high), but it lived ripely in John's early time so he describes a Boston with an underbelly well equipped to hold poverty, deviant sexualities, and art (something I believe Creeley saw, too, in Boston and went on to say that was how he became a poet, finding himself one night on "another street"). Then the letters go on to describe the youth of a scene (after Boston and Black Mountain) in New York and in San Francisco, a scene that I myself landed on the tail end of. My tongue is hanging out at all this lore of "what it was like" firsthand.

There's no replacement for John's sneering at Allen G's fame and his own simultaneous desire for it, as would a sort of younger brother of the tribe. While relying on Allen too for real help and recommendations, the way we always do. And doesn't the hand always want to get a little bit.

The readings John gave in New York in the 1970s were redolent and tattered things, in a tiny shaky voice he commanded a room to lean in. By the 1980s we leaned in more for less, though the fabric of the event of John reading (with Allen still calling out, *read* John) included snide remarks about the people he was reading with that betrayed old friendships gone sour, the old rivalries and class resentments, and he stood at the podium reading the *New York Daily News* 'cause why not, and truly? I can't repeat enough what it meant in the years that John lived every time I spied him randomly on my every trip to Boston. In the overhang of the Harvard Coop there was John Wieners looking out on the square on a rainy day. In Filene's

Basement, at the height of its disparate riches, there would be John strolling among it all, dreaming and smiling slightly. Of the act of walking he said (and it occurs on fifty-one pages here, and generally once means more than once):

> It seems somehow moving helps, I mean literal action, such as walking. I'm a walking activist, that's what. But what d'ye do when you get old? Oh well, that'll take care of itself. One hopes, or imagines. Others have gone through it. That's the only grace, one figures.

In the mid-1980s I worked at the Poetry Project and John would frequently call, mainly toward the end of the day (when the light changed), and I never flattered myself that he was calling me. He would ramble a bit about captains and movie stars, and it seemed that there was a purpose in the call if only to touch a place that always was home, evidenced in this book by the many letters to Anne Waldman when she directed the project, often regarding how much she would pay him to read and the precise costs of his travel options:

> The Penn Central train from Buffalo to New York is 20.70 coach one way, $41.40 round trip, leaving 10:30 AM arriving GC 6:10PM. I shall go on Monday the 13th—Possibly the church could put me up for the evening. Yours in devotion Jean

If poems preserve, letters preserve even more with the apparatus of their pretense to reality: addresses, dates, and codified styles of greeting and closing. This book upends all of that in a multitude of ways. The bodies of JW's letters are a sea of strike-throughs. It seems part and parcel with his style, amending, deleting, wanting it all, the entire wash of history exposed even alongside the occasional erasure of his own last name. His letters variously close with "with love," "love and god," "yours, devotedly," "Yours sincerely Anne, with love," simply "yours," "your friend," but the deliberate strike through of Wieners own last name obsesses me. Largely done in letters in 1969 and 1970 (so he was thirty-five and thirty-six) it echoes the gesture of authors signing their own books by first crossing out the printed name—the intention being to make their signature be the only name. But what does it mean in a letter to a friend? John's own desire to lean in closer through effaced formality toward the addressee. At the end and throughout, this awesome poet sang a chimerical tune. John ~~Wieners~~ the legacy is there and then not, the history gone and shining as only the present does and can. He's your knowing friend, but what *does* he know? If there's anything newer than John Wieners's poems, it's the rolling body of language they come from. This is that pond.

ACKNOWLEDGMENTS

Selections from the letters have been published in *Poetry*, the *Battersea Review*, *Jacket2*, and the Lost & Found Poetics Documents Initiative at the CUNY Center for the Humanities. In addition to publishing "*the sea under the house*," the two-volume Wieners-Olson letters that initiated the letters project, the Center for the Humanities has sponsored and supported my research in a variety of ways over the years, and I am deeply grateful, especially to Aoibheann Sweeney, Sampson Starkweather, Ana Božičević, and Kendra Sullivan. This book has additionally been supported by the English Departments of the CUNY Graduate Center and the University of Alabama as well as the Poetry Center at San Francisco State University. Thank you to Mario di Gangi and Carrie Hintz, Joel Brouwer, and Steve Dickison for your help within those respective institutions.

This project originated in 2010 in Ammiel Alcalay's class at the CUNY Graduate Center; he has been my mentor through this process for almost a decade and has my eternal gratitude. A special thank you also to three comrades who helped me on a near-weekly (sometimes daily) basis: the generous and patient Raymond Foye; my dear accomplice Robert Dewhurst; and my kind Massachusetts guide Jim Dunn. I would also like to thank Basil and Martha Winston King, Diane di Prima, Micah Ballard, Eileen Myles, Gerrit Lansing, Dale Smith, Anne Waldman, Michael Rumaker, Duncan McNaughton, David Meltzer, Bill Berkson, Joanne Kyger, Robert Greene, Leni Sinclair, Elsa Dorfman and Harvey Silverglate, Joseph Torra, John Mitzel, Albert Glover, John Temple, Ralph Maud, John Wilkinson, Carol Weston, Amiri Baraka, Joan Richardson, David Greetham, Wayne Koestenbaum, Derek Fenner, Kevin Killian, Daniel Miller, Hoa Nguyen, LoVe Lee Day, James Coppola, Kokoe Johnson, Jaiar Mecxham, Nick Gamso, Karen Lepri, Bill Corbett, Maria Damon, Peter Hale, Benjamin Hollander, Michael Boughn, Jeff Gardiner, Jeff Davis, Simon Pettet, Miriam Nichols, Josh Hoeynck, Claudia Moreno Pisano, Iemanja Brown, Jared Margulies, Nat Raha, Sara O'Rourke, James Frase-White, David Grundy, Nikos Diaman, John Landry, Jed Birmingham, Patricia Hope Scanlan, erica kaufman, John Giglio, Neeli Cherkovski, Garret Caples, Jean Crozier, Ben Mazer, Don Share, Matt Hofer, Elise McHugh, Denise Edwards, Michael Bronski, Henry Pitts, Alice Sebrell, Jeff Arnal, Alan Skees, Sallye Rigsby, and my parents, Jerry and Ella Ruth Stewart.

The letters of John Wieners were gathered from the following collections: the Bancroft Library at the University of California, Berkeley; the Poetry Collection at the University at Buffalo (thank you James Maynard and Alison Fraser); Burns

Library at Boston College (Justine Sandaram); University of Delaware Library (Curis Small and Rebecca Johnson Melvin); the Lilly Library at Indiana University (David Frasier); the Special Collections Research Center at the University of Michigan (Kate Hutchens); Special Collections and Rare Books at Simon Fraser University (Tony Powers); the Smithsonian Institution; the Department of Special Collections at Stanford University (Tim Noakes); Archives and Special Collections at the University of Connecticut (Melissa Watterworth Batt); the Special Collections Research Center at Syracuse University Libraries; Special Collections and Archives at the University of California at San Diego (Heather Smedberg); Beinecke Library at Yale University; and the private collection of John Mitzel.

John Wieners was a devotional poet, his dedication to the poem total. He was central to many poetry communities: Black Mountain College, the San Francisco Renaissance, New York's East Village scene, the Beat poets, the bohemian demimonde of his beloved hometown Boston, the dispersed mimeo revolution, and the gay small presses of the 1970s and 1980s. Across several decades, Wieners was active as a poet, collaborator, correspondent, and editor; anthologized in the canon-making *The New American Poetry* of 1960; and revered by peers in each of his communities: "John Wieners' glory is solitary, as pure poet," Allen Ginsberg wrote, "a man become one with his poetry."[1] And yet, historians of the New American Poetry and its component schools often ignore Wieners's contributions or consign him to the periphery. How can a poet be renowned but unknown, adored but elided?

Wieners is largely disenfranchised from the various poetic establishments because he is, to literary historians, practically illegible. In those histories Wieners is often a footnote, remarked upon for his personality or sociological significance, not considered as an integral part of the narrative. He's hard to taxonomize: he was a queer self-styled *poète maudit* in the conformist 1950s; a protégé of political-historical poet Charles Olson who wrote audaciously personal verse; a lyric poet who eschewed the egoism of the confessional mode in order to pursue the Olsonian project of *Projective* (outward-looking) poetics. He was a Boston poet living on storied Beacon Hill, but not on Robert Lowell's Brahmin south slope—he was on the other side, with its working-class apartment buildings and underground gay bars. He was institutionalized, as were so many, but not at the expensive McLean Hospital, where the upper-class confessional poets went "gracefully insane"[2]; Wieners, like his friends Stephen Jonas and Joe Dunn, was placed in factory-system state institutions where treatment was brutal and cruel and anything but graceful. Because of these twists and contradictions Wieners has remained at the fringes of not just the canon but also the histories of those various subterranean schools that he inhabited. His story teaches us about the permeability and cross-fertilization of those circles, and allows us to read their histories in an entirely new light.

---

1 Wieners, Preface, *Selected Poems*, 16.
2 See Alex Beam's *Gracefully Insane: The Rise and Fall of America's Premier Mental Hospital* (New York: Public Affairs, 2001) for a history of Boston's McLean Hospital and its literary pedigree.

I chose to follow Wieners's itineraries through his letters in order to present his story in his own words, in such a way that it may be read as an autobiography offered to a dispersed readership. But letters offer more than autobiography, of course; a collection of letters is multivocal, offering a cross-section of the selves Wieners presents to the people and worlds he moves through, from the jokey beatnik machismo he puts on with Ed Dorn ("Eddie baby!") to the campy voice he inhabits with gay writer Michael Rumaker. The letters' "I" is an evolving performance that gives readers insight into Wieners's own self-fashioning, but also brings out surprising aspects of his correspondents' personalities. This is one advantage of the autobiography-in-letters: rather than the conventional memoir, which is written self-consciously with history—or some amorphous future reader—in mind, letters are written under specific exigencies at specific times, using languages the correspondents have established with each other. As such, the autobiography-in-letters offers many of the memoir's virtues while also preserving an embeddedness in contingency and community that memoir lacks. And so in the letters of John Wieners, assembled chronologically, we get not just the poet's life story but a vast array of life stories, as told to various friends along the way.

Wieners's story began in suburban Boston, where he was raised by working-class parents, and received a young education (he graduated at twenty) at the Jesuit Boston College. There he worked on the student literary journal and assiduously studied the classic poets, as well as a few favorite highly musical Modernist poets like Edith Sitwell and Edna St. Vincent Millay. He'd seen Charles Olson read at the Charles Street Meeting House during a hurricane in 1954, and after he finished his unsatisfying education at Boston College, he was determined to go study with Olson at the shambolic experimental Black Mountain College where Olson was rector, somewhere he could make a "living that counted."

He studied there in two noncontinuous semesters in 1955 and 1956, working with Olson, Robert Creeley, and Robert Duncan, and beginning life-long friendships with fellow students Michael Rumaker, Ed Dorn, and other young writers and painters. His letters home from this period offer a lively, poignant look at this strange and wonderful moment in literary and cultural history, with the presence, either as correspondents or supporting characters, of not just his fellow poets but also of artists like Franz Kline and Basil King; fiction writers like Fielding Dawson and Rumaker; young Black Mountain explorers engaged in the process of creating themselves.

For some critics, Wieners's association with Black Mountain presents an apparent contradiction: how could a student of Olson and his historical-political poetic project write personal, lyric verse like "I look for love. / My lips stand out / dry and cracked with want / of it"?[3] But Wieners did remain a student of Olson's project, a poetics grounded in an outward stance, an "open field" not just in prosody (opening up the line) but in subject matter, by opening the field of poetic inquiry beyond the self, and beyond the Romantic projects of mapping the self's interiors. For Wieners, the personal was not the *matter* of the poem, its substance and subject. Rather, it was a vantage to occupy, a center from which to understand, to call out to, the world beyond the self.

In 1957 he launched the first issue of his small magazine *Measure*, its name inspired by Blake's injunction to "bring out number weight and measure in year of dearth."[4] The name indicated, on one level, Wieners's intention to take a measure of poetry in the years since "Projective Verse," the 1950 essay he considered to be the great pivot of twentieth-century American poetry. Over the next five years he produced three issues of *Measure*, the poems presented simply and inexpensively in the style of the small-magazine movement of the time. The magazine was almost revolutionarily idiosyncratic, ignoring schools and geographies and juxtaposing poets provocatively by the logic of the poems themselves, according to Wieners's singular vision.

For Wieners, those *Measure* years, 1957–1962, were glorious and savage, spent in Boston and San Francisco and New York and Boston again, in and out of state hospitals and varying states of psychological distress. Wieners's best poems of the era are preserved in his majestic 1964 collection *Ace of Pentacles*, with its centerpiece 1962 poem "The Acts of Youth." This poem, which Olson called one of "the most beautiful and truest"[5] he'd ever read, begins in a place of great personal suffering—"with great fear I inhabit the middle of the night"—but by the end of the poem the voice has grown gloriously plural, with the closing "we rise again in the dawn. / Infinite particles of the divine sun, now / worshipped in the pitches of the night." The pronoun shift—from the lyric "I" to "we"—is a performance of its own, extending the poem's vision to include the whole suffering world. "I am brought to remember Orpheus," Denise Levertov wrote of Wieners, "who did not sing *about* hell: he was *in* hell, and sang there, leading the way out."[6] As he writes in "Children of the Working Class":

---

3 *Selected Poems*, 27.
4 "Proverbs of Hell," *The Complete Poetry & Prose of William Blake*, ed. David Erdman (1982), 36.
5 "the sea under the house," part II, 42, facsimile. This line was transcribed erroneously in this volume as "most beautiful and finest," necessitating a correcting note from Olson's editor Ralph Maud. See my essay for *Jacket2*, "The most beautiful and truest," for the story behind this error and its correction.
6 Levertov, "To Write is to Listen," 228.

I am one of them. I am a witness
not to Whitman's vision, but instead the
poorhouses, the mad city asylums and relief worklines. Yes, I am witness not to
  God's goodness, but his better or less scorn."[7]

The late 1960s was for Wieners a time of intensities, a summer of heterosexual
domestic bliss that ended in a crash, graduate study in Buffalo, travels to Europe and
out West, increased renown but also heightened psychological distress. His output
remained strong and the books—*Pressed Wafer*, *Asylum Poems*, and *Nerves*—reflect
a constantly evolving prosody, poetics, and worldview: Ginsberg, in his introduction to Wieners's *Selected Poems*, calls them "three magisterial books of poetry that
stand among the few truthful monuments of the late 1960s era."[8] The letters from
this period are insightful, erratic, and sometimes alarming, a living document of a
difficult time. The decade culminated with another institutionalization, this time
at Central Islip Hospital in New York. Central Islip was bleak; "wrong," he called it
in his journal. "The patients are half-drugged. They would be / better off dead, and
this kind of place / burnt off the face of the earth."[9] But even in this degraded world,
he kept up his writing practice, in letters, new work, and the journal, published forty
years later as *A New Book From Rome*. The letters from this time capture the poet
at a pivotal moment, as he struggles to restructure his mind after a decade of drugs
and state-sponsored medical abuse. "For the past 20–18 months I have been under
the delusion of being about 50 persons," he reported to Charles Olson. "I have given
them all up and am now ready for the next 50."[10]

Within a few years, he was cozily installed in his apartment on Joy Street, again
on the north side of Beacon Hill. He lived off a small disability check, in a modest
building managed by his brother. After Olson's death in 1970, Wieners continued
his trajectory toward the shared and the political, increasingly active in the early gay
liberation movement, the Stone Soup poetry community, the *Fag Rag* magazine
and collective, and the Beacon Hill Free School. In 1975 he released, via Good Gay
Poets Press, his densely packed experimental opus, *Behind the State Capitol, or the
Cincinnati Pike*.

During the 1980s, Wieners allowed the release of two collections of his work,

---

7 Levertov, "To Write is to Listen," 176.
8 Wieners, *Selected Poems*, 15.
9 Wieners, *A New Book from Rome*, 27.
10 Letter to Charles Olson, July 10, 1969.

Selected Poems: 1958–1984 and *Cultural Affairs in Boston*. He gave fewer public readings, preferring to write and spend time with just a couple of trusted friends. A 1997 article in the Boston *Phoenix* describes the excitement of an upcoming reading by the "mesmerizing apparition . . . Beacon Hill's own John Wieners, the oracle of Joy Street—one of Boston's best-kept poetic secrets . . .

> He is making a rare public appearance on this cold spring night, as the featured performer at a "Kerouac's birthday" reading sponsored by Stone Soup Poets and held in venerable Old West Church. The pews are crowded with local literati eager to pay him their respects; in fact, there are rumors that his performance—coupled with the recent release of his new collection of poetry and prose, *707 Scott Street* . . . augurs a Wieners comeback after all these years.[11]

John Wieners died at age sixty-eight, after attending a party with old friend Charles Shively. Not feeling well, he left the party early and collapsed in a nearby parking garage. He was found by an attendant and admitted to Massachusetts General, where he remained on a respirator while a concerned social worker and nurses doggedly tracked his identity through a prescription they found. They identified him through the pharmacy, enabling his cousin and friends to visit; Charles Shively and Jim Dunn were with him when he died.

In a 1974 interview, Wieners was asked, "For whom do you write?" He responded:

> For the poetical, the people. Not for myself, merely. Or ever. Only for the better, warm, human loving, kind person. The guy on the street who might hold open a door for you, left the bumper on your car, stops to give you instructions, spares some change, lets you in his bookshop. Friends I take for granted, like the future.[12]

Michael Seth Stewart
MAY 2020

---

11 Salmons, "He's Still Young," n p
12 Wieners, *Selected Poems*, 292.

My work on the letters began nine years ago, when I decided to research the letters between John Wieners and his mentor Charles Olson. Wieners's letters to Olson are housed at the University of Connecticut and Boston College maintains Olson's to Wieners. This project, which resulted in a two-volume chapbook for the Lost & Found Poetics Documents Initiative, *"the sea under the house": The Selected Correspondence of John Wieners and Charles Olson*, was so engaging and, as I came to see, important that I decided to continue collecting Wieners's letters and eventually his journals.

The earliest letters I found are from 1955, the first time he moved away from Boston. From Black Mountain College he wrote to his college friend Robert Greene that summer session and the following year, when he returned South for his second and last term at the school. Before Mr. Greene donated these letters to Boston College, the earliest letters available were from 1957, after Black Mountain had closed, so this contribution was extremely fortuitous and demonstrates the highly contingent nature of letter compiling. The available resources depend completely on who saved what, and what papers were sold to which libraries or private collections; this is why many of Wieners's close correspondents, represented here because they saved his letters, have no letters to him in their own collection. Other than his letters from Olson and some letters related to the 1957 launch of his magazine *Measure*, Wieners saved hardly anything anyone sent him. Collecting his letters involved making an extensive network of connections with scholars, librarians, and friends and colleagues of John Wieners. Many leads came from old friends mentioning offhand that there might be something in some other collection. My first year of research was an intensive, basic-training experience in textual research, networking, and archival detective work, discovering and refining my methods over time.

All editing decisions have been made with my central project in mind: to make John Wieners and his world visible. I want him to speak for himself through his letters as much as possible, assembled in such a way that the book functions as a John Wieners epistolary autobiography. The first question, then, is what method to use in transcribing and presenting the text, beginning with whether to present as the final product a critical or noncritical edition; that is, a "clear" text (based on critical decisions made by the editor) or an edition that tries, as David Greetham explains, "to reproduce a text already in existence"—in this case the letters—"and perhaps to use this text as a vehicle for annotation or interpretive criticism."[1] I have chosen the noncritical edition, presenting the letters, as closely rendered as possible, more or less as I found them in the archives.

The main advantage of the noncritical edition is that the changes—additions, deletions, nontextual elements like arrows or doodles—can be preserved graphically so that the reader can see the writing process unfold and be presented with an approximated re-creation of the text as it was presented to the editor. There is a spectrum of noncritical edition types, and the most attractive for this kind of project are the facsimile, which presents actual photographic reproductions of the original text, and the genetic edition, which preserves, via codes of varying complexity, the changes made to the original text. I decided on a genetic edition for this project, with a simple code system that will allow nontextual scholars to intuitively understand it.

Letters are usually revised as they are written, with words or entire sections struck out, new text inserted in the margins or connected with arrows and other notation. In my genetic edition of these letters, I am preserving all readable struck-through text (struck through in type), and italicizing any inserted or substituted text. Also, I have represented nontextual elements (arrows, etc.) either graphically or as footnotes. My decision is motivated by an ethos of preservation above all else, but just as important, with Wieners's strike-throughs and insertions left as they appear on the archived page, the reader is able to experience his writing and editing processes more or less as they happened. Countless times Wieners will scratch out a word, substitute a different word, scratch that out, and replace the original word, sometimes up to ten times, back and forth. Preserving this series, even if only with italics and strike-throughs, puts the reader in the position of reading over Wieners's shoulder, watching him vacillate as he composes.

Within the text of the letters, I use three systems of annotation, each serving a different purpose. First, each letter has a bold heading indicating the recipient, the date sent (or postmark), and Wieners's location at the time the letter was sent, if that can be determined. Occasionally the recipient's location is noted as well. Second, in order to facilitate reading these letters as a narrative, I have used headnotes at significant moments in the text, to signal geographical or biographical changes, note hospitalizations and major life events, and fill in gaps in the chronology to the best of my knowledge. I have tried to keep the headnotes as brief as possible, providing some context that holds the letters together. Whenever contemporaries like Diane di Prima, Basil King, or Michael Rumaker have published accounts of the same events or

---

1 Greetham, *Textual Scholarship*, 347.

periods of time as the letters, I've brought in short excerpts and references for further reading, in the interest of placing Wieners's experiences within their lived contexts.

While headnotes set the stage for the letters and provide sometimes necessary connective tissue, the footnotes are supplementary and address two different needs. First, many are metatextual, addressing textual ambiguities, providing necessary graphic information such as arrows or circles, and explaining creative spellings or providing citations referring to works in the bibliography. Many notes are textual "stage directions"—letting the reader know that certain text is written vertically along the side of the letter, for example—that are helpful but not so necessary as to require bracketed insertion into the text of the letter.

At the end of the book, there's a glossary of names, where I've given brief biographies not only for Wieners's correspondents but also major figures in his life such as **Dana Durkee**, his first lover, to whom we don't have any letters. Whenever people from that glossary first appear in the book, I've bolded their names.

Finally, footnotes are used to provide biographical or other identifying information for references within the letters. There are a range of available approaches to this sort of note, one being the sparse style of Sally Fitzgerald's Flannery O'Connor letters, which has only minimal information, usually presented as brief, italicized headnotes. This same effect, with fuller notes, is possible through the blind endnote option, as in the recent University of California Press edition of the Robert Creeley letters. The former works well for a collection like O'Connor's *The Habit of Being*, where most of the references are either to her own work or to well-established figures like the University of Iowa Writers' Workshop or the writings of Thomas Aquinas. But in keeping with my central mission—to make John Wieners, his lived experiences, and points of reference *visible*—I felt it was important to provide that information here, from references to old Boston and San Francisco dive bars and bookstores to poets and writers who are no longer widely read. My goal with these notes, as with the glossary of names, is to give the letters contextual support by illuminating often occulted information and allusions. Where a reference is widely known, such as when he talks about Edna St. Vincent Millay, I try only to give basic information and how the figure is connected with Wieners or his circles. The notes are by no means exhaustive.

"*a living that counted*"

John Wieners in the Italia – in
the Sixties sometime.
for Raymond of love. Ellie
76

FIGURE I   Photograph by Elsa Dorfman, from the collection of Raymond Foye.
Courtesy of Elsa Dorfman.

The letters begin in 1955, when twenty-one-year-old John Wieners arrived at Black Mountain College to study poetry with **Charles Olson**. The year prior, while a student at Boston College, reading Edna St. Vincent Millay and writing witty movie reviews for the student literary magazine, he'd read Olson via William Carlos Williams, who quoted "Projective Verse" at length in his 1951 autobiography. He went to see Olson read at Boston's famed Charles Street Meeting House, during a hurricane, and was electrified. His application to Black Mountain was answered immediately with an offer of free room and board (there were plenty of empty rooms at this point, and "board" would prove scant at best). It was at Black Mountain that Wieners found what he called "a living that counted."

His new classmate **Michael Rumaker** described Wieners in a letter to his boyfriend:

> This boy Wieners has been a lifesaver this spring . . . He's the darling of Olson's class, for the poems are really terrific, very beautiful, fresh, and revealing. He is one of those true gay fellows who can get away with murder—because everyone loves and enjoys him—I think it is that sense of utter abandon in his nature, a sense of light irresponsibility, suggestive of so much magnificent freedom, which makes him attractive to everyone. He even looks like a poet.[1]

* * *

Robert Greene
Thursday, the 20th [Spring 1955]
[Black Mountain, NC]

Read slow, this is a bombshell.
Dear Bob:

This will be short and confused, but have and wanted to tell you about this place, and this shall serve as asking you to write when you have time, to tell me 1) re: Veronica 2) future plans 3) Joe's marriage 4) summer still at Vermont YES YES YES 5) how

---

1 Michael Rumaker, *"like a great armful of wild & wonderful flowers,"* 15–16.

does Dana look, and all other news but especially bout plans, and if you say Army, I will, yes, all over you.

The student body numbers at the most 15. Excellent living conditions. No cubicle, etc. but a wing of a little Dutch house, called Mountain Stream, with a mountain stream running beside it for 24 hours. Three rooms, a kitchen, a piano, etc. **Joe and Carolyn [Dunn]** in one, no one in the other if I can help it, and me in the back, under trees, with a little screen door, and three screened windows, one window with only a screen. I take theatre, lithography, and writing under Olson who is the only Man to have said anything NEW or FRESH about Poetry—since before Pound, and before Pound, Ernest Fenollosa, in his essay "The Chinese Written Character as A Medium of Poetry"[2] and before Fenollosa, John Keats, not in his own poetry, but in his letters, when he attacked Milton and Wordsworth for their Egotistical Sublime, as he called it. His doctrine was the only new thing said (Negative Capability)[3] for many, I do not know how many, hundreds of years. Look, read, and read, and try to refute this. Poetry for 300 yrs. up to 1910 and Pound, was nothing but imitation of old forms, from Shakespeare, and Elizabethans to Pound to Olson, who has added more. His essay, Projective Verse in Poetry: New York, 1950 Issue no. 3. the first thrust.[4] And he has gone on from there.

Naturally, this is the only place of its kind in this country, no one has any major interest but in what they create. The pace of life is something I have never known, and which you probably touched, mind you, only touched, at Middlebury, with their hundreds, at the most here, with wives, and for kids, it comes to 25, and with 600 acres. at least 13 buildings, many unused and in disrepair. Classes are as follows: Writing: Monday and Wednesday nite—8 on, usually to end at midnight,

---

2 Ernest Fenollosa (1853–1908), American professor and historian of Japanese art. His essay on Chinese written language was first published by Ezra Pound in 1919, and its insights—especially on the poetic primacy of the image—became central to the development of modernist poetics. Fenollosa writes, "The moment we use the copula, the moment we express subjective inclusions, poetry evaporates. The more concretely and vividly we express the interactions of things the better the poetry" (*The Chinese Written Character*, 57).

3 In a famous letter from 1817, John Keats (1795–1821) describes his concept "Negative Capability" as the state of mind "when man is capable of being in uncertainties, Mysteries, doubts, without any irritable reaching after fact & reason." (*Selected Letters*, 41) Poet Micah Ballard's monograph on connections between Keats and Wieners, *Negative Capability and the Verse of John Wieners*, was reissued by Bootstrap Press in 2017.

4 Charles Olson's manifesto "Projective Verse" was first published in 1950. It calls for "composition by field," a rejection of closed forms that insists, in the words of **Robert Creeley**, that "form is never more than an extension of content" (*Collected Prose*, 240). As Wieners describes it in his 1955 journal, "a line should run according to a man's breathing, and this is determined by the emotion of the poem, or from his heart, and the syllables used in a poem, by a man's need. This is open verse, and mind-music, as Steve Jonas is constantly spouting" (*Stars Seen in Person*, 44).

once at Peek's a tavern four miles out,[5] and last Mon, having coffee in one of the rooms until 1.

Theatre—Mon, Tues, Thurs, Frid, mornings—9:30 on usually to noon.

Lithography[6]—Tuesday nite—8:30 to 10:30.

Naturally my whole interest is in Mon, and Wed, and the wild stimulation that follows. [...]

Please write soon, I would like so much to see you again, but write.
  Love,
  J

Shall wait a week, and then send some subversive magazines to your house, if you have not answered, addressed to;
  Robert Greene, Atheist.

I will, too.

Black Mountain College
Black Mountain, North Carolina

I shall be home in June for a week, and then come back here until September and then Boston again, or maybe shall stay here until December, that is if Dana would

---

5 Ma Peak's was a blue-collar, country bar three or four miles from Black Mountain College. Basil King remembers a night when Wieners showed up at his room "all gadded out in high heels," wanting to go to Peek's:

And John came in all dolled up and he said, "Take me to the bar!" And I said okay. We went down there. We were seated to drink. Then John all of a sudden gets it in his head to go over and sit on one of the farmer's laps. The guy pushes him away. He goes to somebody else, and he cuts a piece of meat and tries to feed it to them. It's just crazy. How do you talk about somebody who will do this? And there was a woman who ran the place, who was friendly toward Black Mountain people ... She came over to me, and she said you got to get John outta here, Ma Peak's gonna call the sheriff, who was her cousin. I got him out of there, by then he was disheveled. And we started to run and then both of us realized that if we were running and they caught us they'd kill us, or they'd do something to us. So we stopped. And I saw the sheriff talking to Barbara. What possessed me, to this day I do not know. I walked over to the sheriff and I said, "Excuse me sheriff, could I talk to you?" And he didn't answer and then I waited and he looked at me like okay, say something. And I said, "Is your mother alive?" He said yes. And I said, "John just lost his mother. He's not like this all the time." The guy melted. He put us in the car and he drove us back to the school. We did things like that. (Basil King, Unpublished interview with Robert Dewhurst, January 2, 2012)

6 American artist Joseph Fiore (1925–2008) taught the lithography class which, like all the arts classes at Black Mountain, was open to students of every discipline. Fiore also taught drawing at the school; his class is vividly remembered in Fielding Dawson's 1970 memoir *The Black Mountain Book*.

only come and live in a little house, by the side of a field. If he won't, I shall live in Boston much against my will, for the winter months, and then come here again, with money this time, that is, if they will have me.

John Homsy[7] and Dana are coming back with me in June, to spend a week here, maybe you could come too, if you have not gone to Middlesbury, it costs nothing.

Show this to people, as I can't keep repeating myself in letters.
Thanks.

Robert Greene
Thursday [Spring 1955]
[Black Mountain, NC]

Dear Bob:

Well, Bob, it's begun for me, or rather a part of it, only a line of it is done. I brought seven new poems into class Monday, and after I finished reading them, I heard someone clapping, and I looked up and it was Olson. There was no real criticism of them until last night, when the class asked me to re-read them, and after they were, to begin ~~their~~ *a* critique. Nothing really important was said, but then it was Olson's turn. He admonished the class for being too modern to enjoy these poems. He said that one had to applaud after hearing them, as they were bursting from their seams language-wise. He also suggested that I submit one of them, the longest one, for publication, as the poem says everything about the subject that can be said, that I had held nothing back, and on these grounds alone, it should be published. After class he told me how lovely parts of them were, and all of this from a man who really is first-rate in poetry today. . . . I will leave this for a while, but I first want to tell you some of what I have been doing. In Lithography, I have completed a drawing on stone, from which I shall print 12 copies. Would you want one? It's real shat, but you could use it in the bathroom, and it is an original litho, this is the process of Toulouse Lautrec. Mine is quite quite abstract, but if you want one, just ask. O.K.? In theatre, I appeared two Sunday nights ago in a scene from STREET SCENE by

---

7 John Homsy was an old friend from Boston, mentioned briefly in Wieners's 1955 *Untitled Journal of a Would-Be Poet* (collected in *Stars Seen in Person*).

Elmer Rice with a girl called Mona Stea. I was Sam Kaplan to her Rose Maurrant. She was excellent, and I could have been better, but it was a wonderful production, and much enjoyment. I am now doing FAUST with me as Mephistopheles, and we are also rehearsing Ezra Pound's translation of Sophocles' THE WOMAN OF TRACHIS.[8] There will be dance, drama masks, music, etc. in the production.

About French, a Robert Hellman[9] is coming here for the summer from the U. of Iowa, and last summer, he gave a course in Proust and Rimbaud, and intends to offer another course in French Lit. this season, so I will definitely be able to enjoy a little of francais.

It was very good to hear that you had enjoyed some or achieved some satisfaction from working on Bellay's poetry. And the question you put forth is a good one. Don't you think that one Learns because he has to, not that he wants to. We know many things, but to keep knowledge we must learn it and keep on learning, thus it is not so much a perfection of self, but a damn necessity of self. We have to learn, not to be educated or articulate or successful, but simply because there is something there that makes us learn, and thus we should only learn that which we are forced to. This is not progressive education. I mean when you have the essentials, whether you want them or not. This is simply something above the essentials, then again, the things we are learning now are really essential to ourselves.

About movie fare, it was funny to hear you speak well of Heart of the Matter when sister had wrote that it was corn corn etc. but her main complaint was the lack of spiritual struggle.[10] As for me, I would love it, I think. Also the End of the Affair[11] is out in Ny, with Debbie Kerr and Vannie Johnson. What ridiculous ads if you've noticed. I think Time gave it a shoddy write-up. The movies I have seen are two: the bill of fare here is impossible. The Revenge of the Creature:[12] sequel to the original Creature of the Black Lagoon, which I had seen up in Boston, and whose sequel I couldn't miss. It was riot. Lori Nelson gets seduced by a half-fish-man. But naturally is saved. The other film was On the Waterfront[13] (now my 3rd time) but I was

---

8 Pound's translation of *Women of Trachis* was published in 1957 by New Directions.

9 Robert Hellman taught writing at Black Mountain. His story "The Quay" appeared in the first issue of *Black Mountain Review*, in 1954.

10 The 1953 film *The Heart of the Matter*, based on Graham Greene's book of the same name, is the story of a Catholic man who has an adulterous affair and is tormented by guilt. Wieners's sister Marion (1925–1992) was a nun for many years.

11 Another Graham Greene story about Catholics committing adultery, *The End of the Affair*, stars Deborah Kerr (1921–2007) and famously closeted matinee idol Van Johnson (1916–2008).

12 *Revenge of the Creature*, a 3D sequel released in 1955, stars Lori Nelson (b. 1933) as an aspiring ichthyologist.

13 Crime classic *On the Waterfront* was released in 1954.

stinking, so it didn't matter. The afternoon of that day, I was walking to the Studies Bldg.[14] and met **Ed Dorn**, poet published in Origin,[15] and he and his lovely lovely wife invited me to Peek's for a beer. They brought their baby, who was brought up in a bureau drawer in a chicago tenement. And at midnight we returned, bare-footed, hysterical, the baby had been taken home earlier, after having devoured a package of pretzels and two packages of peanut butter and cheese crackers. But they are fine people, she being a divorcee who left her husband taking two other children with her, Fred and Chansonette,[16] to live with Ed and sleep on dirty sheets on a mattress in their living room, the same house that Joe and Carolyn share. As she said, I left convention and a PHD for him, but he's so beautiful, I love him, etc. He really isn't but she loves him, etc.

I close now for a day or so in the rain here, it's like Monsoon country.

Monday.

Still raining, steadily since Thursday, I laid out in it Saturday night for fifteen minutes in a big raincoat. Laying out in the grass with the rain coming like hell. I then went down and danced for hours, like Zelda Fitzgerald,[17] on the deck of an old studio, to jazz and the rain through the leaves. I would be so happy here, but I can't stand it

---

14 In 1940, Black Mountain College moved from its rented Blue Ridge campus to the Lake Eden location, and the Studies Building was their first building project. Abbreviated from a more ambitious, four-wing design by A. Lawrence Kocher, it is a 200-foot-long rectangular building, its stone ground floor topped by two stories of wood and concrete with room for sixty-one studies and two faculty apartments, a Modernist block perched at the lake's edge. The Studies Building still stands, used as administrative offices by the Christian Camp Rockmont, where it is known by campers and employees as "the Spaceship."

15 *Origin* was founded in 1951 by Boston poet and publisher **Cid Corman**, who brought Olson on as a contributing editor; their important letters, chronicling the creatively agonistic process of production, were published in 1969 as *Letters for Origin*, and six poems from Olson anchored the first issue. *Origin* was foundational to avant-garde poets, including Creeley, **Denise Levertov**, and Louis Zukofsky, who published his opus *A 1–12* through Origin Press in 1959. Having begun its life as a Boston-based magazine, it was at the core of Wieners's "personal cosmology of contemporary poetry, but also to his sense of Boston itself as a central (not peripheral) site of contemporary practice," Robert Dewhurst writes in his essay "Measure: A Quarterly to the Poem, 1957–1962." For the young Wieners, *Origin* was "a crucial chain-link in the history of this tradition" (8), and inspired Wieners's own efforts to create a poetry magazine after its "final" twentieth issue of series 1 in winter 1957. *Origin* resumed in 1961 and continued, with periodic interruptions and changes in location, through 1984. Cid Corman was planning a sixth series when he died in 2004.

16 Fred and Chansonette Buck, children of Ed Dorn's wife Helene, lived with them at Black Mountain for a year, an experience both Bucks wrote about in their work. Fred (1948–2018) was a postal worker, photographer, and poet in Gloucester, and Chansonette is a teacher, poet, and painter in Berkeley, where she earned a PhD studying twentieth-century poetry and poetics.

17 Wieners and his college friends were, like many young people in the mid-1950s, obsessed with the 1920s bohemian subculture, with the glamorously troubled Zelda Fitzgerald (1900–1948) holding particular imaginative sway, having died in a sanitarium fire in nearby Asheville.

without Dana, and this morning I received a long overdue letter from him, answering important questions I had asked him (like what are you going to do this summer, will it be work in the Fire Dept, why can't you come to BM and me for the summer) and he answered the questions with answers like YES or NO and I DON'T want TO. So there is nothing for me to do now but stay here, work hard hard harder, but it is so hard to be in a beautiful place, and the person you want most won't come, for some reasons I am afraid to think about. So it's done, and I can do nothing but stay here, and hope he realizes that this is his chance for salvation, and he is putting it aside for dollar bills and security. What do I do in a case like this? I have written my heart out asking him in all kinds of hysterical ways to please come in June, and the worst thing is that he could come if he wanted to, but won't now. So I am not going to answer his little note, so awfully cruel, the cruelest thing he's ever done, and just go on by my old self and fill up as many pages in as many books as I can. And hope maybe in a year or so, or years, Dana and I might see each other again. I will not be home to Boston in June, probably not in September, and yet I do not want Black Mt, without him, but as you can see, Boston offers so much, and yet it cannot teach me, nor criticize me, or help me in what I have to do. I know I could go home for good in June, and work with Dana during the summer, and maybe in September we could come back here. But it is up to Dana to suggest how and when we can meet again, as he evidently now is content to stay away from me. Thus whatever I could suggest to him would really help matters none. He has to find out himself and help me and want me, and his letters had none of these thoughts in it. And we could die tomorrow. But this is no reason to depress you, happy as you must be with the thoughts of Middlebury and the apparent luxury you are going to have. It is wonderful.

Last night too, I read three of my poems before the entire college, and enjoyed it. When I get things in order, I will send them out for publication.

It was beautiful what you said in one of your letters about the end of one era, and because we are still young enough, the beginning of another. I think so, and it will be an era as rewarding and young as this last one, but let's hope not as hectic. It was a wonderful era, we've had two or even three together you know. The Freshman-Sophomore, The Lax and nearly sterile transitional period of Junior-Senior, when resolutions were formulated, and then at the end of The Senior, the blossoming of the Third, leading into a culmination for me, at least, of Grove Street, which is as far as you can in the poor wild Boheme stage. Now the other, the beginning of the work, and the distance and the isolation of ourselves from each other, and then I hope will be the coming together and the exchange and the enjoyment of what we have profited.

It's silly to end this note with all the paper full, but I am going to.

And I hope you are growing too, but I know you are.

Thanks for asking me back, and I will be soon.

your friend always, and all eras.

John

Write whatever you want to about Dana. The Greeks were right when they said that Eros tossed a man down to his inferiors.

PS. I received the Stylus.[18] How shocking, not only the cover, but that absolute hussy drawn by something called Adams. Luman's poetry, not much I think, nothing there that has not been said a 100 times before. Why the hell bother to say it again, if you can't do it in a new way, and the sonnet form, and etc. with some of those horrible rhymes is not a new way. Song in Defense of Myself had a charm, but so reminiscent of Housman,[19] and the ode, has passion, but don't you think it gets smothered and becomes unreal in that artificial form? L.

I think this era, is the hardest I have been through, as I am now totally alone, for the first time, and very nervous about the possibility of a life alone, old, drunk, etc. And yet what else can I think of when this thing is being smashed, a thing that was always warm inside of me, and now it's as if I am paid back for all the warmth. You know that old cliché, you have been too happy, or we have been too happy, the gods will punish us surely. But still as Blanche said, sometimes there's God so quickly.[20] Right now, there is nothing but John Wieners and white paper, and it is killing me, but still I must be a . . . . Fill in the dots. This letter to you has released some tension. I also can play 2 songs on the piano with 1 finger. My Buddy and Stormy Weather, also a little of Heart and Soul, so things aren't as bad as they seem.

---

18 *The Stylus* is the Boston College student literary magazine on which Wieners had worked with Greene.

19 A. E. Housman (1859–1936), gay English poet and scholar whose traditional verse was heavily associated with the Edwardian period.

20 From Tennessee Williams' *A Streetcar Named Desire*. After Mitch kisses Blanche DuBois, having declared their need for each other, she replies, "Sometimes—there's God—so quickly!"

Robert Greene
Tuesday, May 24th. 1955
[Black Mountain, NC]

Dear Bob:

Of course, I have to answer your letter right away, even now when I should be writing, and the main reason is because I feel so elated by it, and also by another writing class last night. I brought in two poems, a love poem, which begins, "I have wanted to write a love poem like the river merchant's,"[21] and another, an address to Hart Crane, and Harry Crosby, two suicides.[22] I did not work hard on them, especially the suicide one, as it was written while I was stinking on Friday, and written while I was in tears up to my knees. I brought them to class last night, read them in my turn, there were so many manuscripts we all read them one after another, and then waited, me sure that they were a failure and a dis-appointment to the ones of the week before. They talked for an hour on two poems of Mike Rumaker's, and then a boy asked to read mine again—and then he commented that he liked them, and I asked a question: I would like to know how I can stop writing poems like this: Olson laughed and laughed, he said you never can, and you better not. He asked me what I meant, and I answered with: preoccupation with myself. The class then launched into them. In a second, failure is turned into success, at least for other people. Olson then began answering my question. I don't remember what he said in quotes, but he talks about the intensity, me John Wieners, the desire, the trouble in the poems, that the use of language is my image, on and on, talking as if I am a poet, possessing the talent to convert experience into form. We went to Peek's afterward, and I could hear him talking up the other end of the table about the emotion in the poems. When we went up to pay the bill, he came over and thanked me for the night. I was writing to Dana this morning, at about 10:30 and he came in, and talked with me for two hours, talked not in the way that if you work hard you will be a poet someday, but that if you work hard you will be a better poet than you are now. He asked me to write 5 different poems on the same subject: "the river merchant" it's an allusion to Pound's translation that we loved so much in Boston.

He left and I walked to the mail, hoping to hear, and I got your letter, I never

---

21 Ezra Pound's "The River Merchant's Wife: A Letter," published in his 1915 book *Cathay,* is a translation of Li Po based on the work of Ernest Fenollosa. The poem to which Wieners refers, "Ode to the Instrument," is included in his August 11, 1955, letter to Michael Rumaker.

22 "Hart Crane, Harry Crosby . . ." was published as a broadside by the Detroit Artist's Workshop in 1965, and was the lead poem in Wieners's 1984 book *Cultural Affairs in Boston.* A copy of the broadside was in Olson's personal collection (Maud, *Charles Olson's Reading,* 318).

expected to hear you talk this way. What you say, I know, is true, that Dana just loves me for this reason: that I can give him back love from someone he respects, but I must never give him more love than he gives me, I must never lower myself by loving him too much, I must be neat and clean, I must be a poet—all these things I have to maintain for Dana's love. When I wrote those letters to him, throwing down all pretense, telling him I should give up writing, anything, BM, to be near him—I got back letters with no love in them, demands that I must stay at BM, he was going to BC for the next 2 yrs, lectures, sermons, all types of near-pleas to get back up and treat him as I had always done, holding him off, yet still giving him enough love, but not all of it, even though he does want it all. Of course, it is doomed because I know all the reasons now, and nothing can last unless you don't know why it is lasting. So I still ache ache, and plan and resort to the old tricks.

(It is now at least three hours later) While I had been writing this to you, Ed Dorn, the poet I mentioned came in and we talked re the party that C. Joe and I gave in the lobby of our house last Saturday night. A big scandal occurred in which a young girl, 18, from Cherry Lawn School, visiting here for two days, to determine whether or not she should attend BM in September was either raped, statutory, or willingly, I don't know, by a [redacted on manuscript in black ink], a student here, so things were coming to a head, as this [redacted] has caused trouble before, namely with Ed's wife Helene, and also with Carolyn. He is a repressed homosexual, with this great male mask, the worst kind,[23] Ed and I talked for an hour, and then we went to the yard of our house, and Helene, Ed and I had tea, and were joined by Olson who came back again with a fresh manuscript in his hand. It was a poem he had just written, called A Post-Virginal, for John Wieners.[24]

You know how I feel. How does it happen, what has it happened, I'm not even trying to find out. I just know now that as long as I live I will be a poet, that my life, way of and function of, will be the writing of poetry, as long as it lasts. Yesterday over the cliff, today on top of it. When I finish this letter, I will write a few words

---

23 In *Black Mountain Days*, Michael Rumaker refers to this incident in his "1955" chapter:

> There was the pretty, underage girl who came as a prospective student and who was promptly propositioned by several of the hungry males, one of whom was alleged to have succeeded with her. When the girl's father found out, he created a row over it and threatened to prosecute with charges of statutory rape, but was persuaded by Charles and Wes not to, and the incident, much to the relief of everyone involved, except of course the father and daughter, was hushed up. (488)

24 Later published as "The Post-Virginal," the 1955 poem is a meditation on the nature of form in Olson's other "P.V.," 1950's "Projective Verse": "Form is not life. Form is creation. It changes the condition / of men. It does not disturb nature. Nature, like god, / is not so interesting. Man // is interesting" (*Collected Prose*, 354).

to Dana and then spend as long as I can stand it, writing it, because as they say here when you're in heat with the poem, write write and hurry. It doesn't last, and it's too good to waste while it's lasting.

I have only read your letter once, so whatever I say has to come from that, and I don't want to stop writing to you to even re-read it.

I know what you say about Dana is true, but still in him is the ability to fill parts of me up. He is coming down here June 13th, *for six days only!* I guess, and my original plan was to leave BM with him in June and work in Boston for the summer, and then the two of us come back for a long long time. The school will advance loans to me until December, I am sure, but this way, I could earn my own way and then stay here through the winter and all next year. Don't worry, this place has its limitations, and I see them, but still, I am getting the time and THE CRITICISM, and the encouragement every time I want it. I cannot get these things in Boston to my satisfaction as you know, but still I do not feel I can go through the daily business of existing without Dana. This is where I am weak, and if we broke it off now, I know it would be better in terms of my development but I am too weak, something I never thought I was, at least in terms of this kind of need. I thought I was weak in my intensity towards the poem, but here I am strong, but there will be dry days, months, maybe years without the actual accomplishment of the poem as I guess I have now, and who will keep me alive then?

Dana does not want to come here, but I know that by pretending that I intend to stay here without him, and *pretending that* this is the end, at least I will say this, he will come down. He does not think I will go back to Boston with him, but while he is here in June, I will be cold, uninterested, back on the old role, and he will then begin to make gifts to me, and the one I want is his coming here in September.. If I asked him to, he would not, but if I pretend no, stay where you are, Dana, all I want is my poetry, he will do whatever he can to stick with me. (I think this is the best course to follow)

I want to say one more thing in my mind. I will write again after the heat is off, but this I want to say. Don't let pity destroy you, pity kills your action to the degree that it's passive. If it is not passive pity, O. K. But the complacent, the serendipity, (serene-pity) that Pound coins in his latest Canto, the 85th is a disease.[25] We must

---

25 Ezra Pound's Cantos LXXXV–XCV were published by New Directions in 1956 as *Section: Rock-Drill.* The name "Rock-Drill" was meant to suggest the hammering out of Pound's ideas, and was inspired by the title of Wyndham Lewis's 1951 review of *The Letters of Ezra Pound* (Carroll Terrell, *A Companion to the Cantos of Ezra Pound,* 533). For the irreverent, very queer *Boston Poetry Newsletter* that Wieners printed up and distributed with his friends the summer of 1956, gay Ezra Pound devotee Stephen Jonas wrote a poem called "Cock-Drill."

have the simpatico, this is the only way we achieve relationships with beings, I know, but the other kind, is the suffocation of yourself, in the face of the intolerable misery of the world, the feeling that I can do nothing but cry over them, without trying to correct or even kill. *This isn't necessary to say—I don't know why I spent so much time on it. A first impression.*

Enough, I guess, I will re-read your letter over and over. It is wonderful to hear it from you. I think it marks a break maybe, I am not sure. but please don't regret writing it. It is the best thing you could have done for me, it establishes you in my vision as also (what words can I use) a dynamic in my life. Do you see? Not just a boy in the past, but an energy of my present thought, a factor in my life. I had forgotten since I got here, and maybe before that, that you should be a voice in my mind. Now it is here again, just another wall we have broken down or built up for ourselves, I don't know which. Built up in the sense that we think even more strongly of and for each other. I hope this doesn't sound like the pledge of eternal friendship, that you spoke of, I don't want it to sound like that.

I will write again soon, in a week probably, but you write when you want.

Letters from Marie, Florence's wedding invitation, and Bilver Monday.[26] Marie's was so wonderful and so upset because she had kissed you and held onto you tight in the car, and was afraid that you would think her a frustrated cheap 17 yr. older. She is unbelievable, she won't live long like herself. I don't think one can do it. She has to change or die/ Maybe not, maybe she is a miracle.

Don't tell her I told you. Love, ~~Vienna~~*John*

Robert Greene
Friday June 1955
[Black Mountain, NC]

[This is a nearly un-intelligible letter.]
Dear Bob:

This paper was put into the typewriter to start a new poem, but I answer your letter first, an enjoyable one with the news of the clan. I did write to Marie, a little drunk and sentimental, but a true letter. Entertainment-wise, this land has been hectic,

---

26 Mutual friends of Wieners and Greene from Boston. In his 1955 *Untitled Journal of a Would-Be Poet* (published in *Stars Seen in Person*), Wieners describes carousing with Marie (no Florence is mentioned) and a Bilver Plack, with whom he works at translating Rimbaud (48).

especially with this Ed Dorn and Helene, so much fun and sharing so completely what I love. I finally did Balling the Jack for the school the way I used to do it, but never as wild as now, what with all the tricks I have picked up from Roxanne.[27] Underneath the moon in front of the studies building before 10 or 12 students after Ed Dorn had finished his number in a white shawl, we had danced in a circle for an hour, singing all the stupid songs, screaming, not even drunk, just tired, as Pearl Bailey says. There is a boy here called Mike Rumaker, short story writer, from NYC, Helene's from Duluth, Minn, Ed from Matoon, Illinois, they met in Seattle I think, and she was then married, but such a lovely girl, like a Madonna by some artist I forget, all bones in her face, soap and water face, long straight brown hair, educated by nuns, although non-Catholic, low voice, soft, Ed is a little looney, seriously, with big eyes, and when he answers a question, it's like you jerked him with a string. They are coming to Boston in September, for two weeks, and he is applying to Harvard for a fellowship in history, she has been to Boston once, loves it. They don't sound at all here like they are, because these things I say can all be applied to other people, you just have to see them together, they really are like no one I have ever met before, and this truly is something to say about them. They had us to supper twice, as we are penniless, living on crackers and second-hand tea-bags which we hang up on the wall to dry to use a second time. He asked me to Peek's for a beer at 2 in the afternoon on Memorial day, and at midnight we returned to the campus, we had brought Joe Dunn (Carolyn was furious) Harvey Harmon[28] from L. A. with us, and were joined later in the afternoon by Herb Ross, my ex-roommate from Philly, and the girl who has come down here to live with him for the summer, Jackie Kline (names, names) also were joined by Seymour Whittaker, a mountaineer. We ran up a bill of 14.05 which we haven't paid for, and ended up playing pool in Asheville 20 miles away. We thought Big H. (Helene) would be mad but we serenaded her under the window when we got back with, I can't give you anything but Love, and she took us inside, and listened with great glee while we spent an hour telling her what we had done. Ed supposedly was to come back and get her at four, but she took it all

---

27 "Ballin' the Jack" was a popular early twentieth-century song and dance first performed publicly in the *Darktown Follies* review at Harlem's Lafayette Theater in 1913. Known for its high-energy gyrations, "Ballin' the Jack" was performed on film by Judy Garland and Gene Kelley in *Me and My Gal* (1942), Danny Kaye in *On the Riviera* (1951), and Dean Martin and Polly Bergen in *That's My Boy* (1951).

28 Harvey Harmon was a student at Black Mountain College. Martha Winston King, in one of her memoirs of the time, "Seventy Years Ago in the South," remembers him as "pale and romantically listless," a sort of gentleman scholar who "used to sit in the bathtub for hours with his books and his papers piled on a plank that fit across the tub" (n.p.). He and wife Lorraine moved out to San Francisco during the great migration of Black Mountain alumni after the school closed. It's unclear who the other "names, names" are in this section, beyond Herb Ross. King mentions a "Herb (x)—a theater student from Pennsylvania" in "Three Months in 1955."

wonderfully. Their son Fred, is amazingly bright, smokes cigarettes, as all the kids do here, even Katy Olson, age 3, and occasionally gets drunk with Ed and keeps on shouting Ipsalante, Ipsalante, the town in Michigan where he was born.[29] All the kids here usually go stark naked, and possess the most unbelievable imaginations. They all see snakes and bears, have lynching parties, dinner parties of their own, swear. We cleaned out three sewers yesterday, and when Katy asked; what's that white thing at the bottom, Pops, Charles looked at her calmly and said, that's a pile of shit, my dear, and she went away satisfied.

How Freeman Frank and Bettina[30] ever got to each other I don't know, but I did nearly die. Was it an engagement party or what?

Monday

Wasted three days really, but all action seems so worthless when 3 weeks from now, I do not have the faintest idea what I will be doing, North or South, alone or loved. I do not have the strength of those words, Bob, at least now. I am out of heat, and my day, nearly my entire day is spent in planning, wondering whether or not Dana will come here for the week of June 12th, as he has promised. A promise has always been a very solemn thing between us, and yet, he has broken three since I came here, and most likely he will break this. Today is his birthday, and I sent off this morning a Birthday Parable, or allegory, and of course, all I did was ask him to come here for that week. I gave him till Friday to contact me, and yet I have let myself need this, and I suppose, it's only because I have little chance of getting it, that I feel I need it so much, but it is getting better, and if no word by Friday, I will send one last letter, a very dramatic one, spewing it all out, getting it out of my system, and freeing myself of him for once and always. Yet I hope I get his letter by Friday and all that will not be necessary.

Re my activities: We are very poor, in fact, I do not have a single penny left. Our food provisions add up to this, 1 quarter box of pancakes, 1 box of Hominy Grits, 1/2 can of corn, 2 frankforts, and 20 crackers. These are mine, and I must spread this to last until the opening of the second quarter, June 20th. This is another reason why Dana's coming or not coming is crucial, but I shall survive.

I have hustled my way around the campus, and had dinner out twice last week, breakfast once, and lunch twice, plus gifts from unknown admirers of ice-cream cones, cigarettes and beer. I now roll my own cigarettes out of pipe tobacco, and they are ghastly.

---

29 Fred Buck was born in Ypsilanti, Michigan, in 1948.
30 Mutual friends from Boston.

I have another dinner date tomorrow night, at two girls' place, and their boyfriends. Tuesday is the best night for dinner, as we go to town that day for provisions. So I will have a lovely meal that night, and then I will start on the Faculty. I have made good friends here, one girl knitted me a pseudo-loin cloth out of cellophane, leaves, wood, yarn and old newspapers. This coming Thursday and Friday night, we present Pound's Women of Trachis, it is not really Pound's but a translation of his from Sophocles. My litho came out fine, but I will not mail it, and if Dana comes down, it will be given personally *to you*. You see, I will come back to Boston for the summer, if he comes here, and I will work and save and come back to BM for the next year. You can live on $6.00 a week here, royally [. . .]

* * *

Back from his first term at Black Mountain, Wieners was in Boston at a very exciting time. The cold first months of 1956 saw Boston flush with new energy: **Jack Spicer** had arrived in December for a short stint, joining his old Berkeley friend **Robin Blaser**, who was working at a Harvard library and thriving among the Cambridge Poets' Theatre crowd. **Frank O'Hara**, too, was in Boston, spending the spring 1956 semester studying at Harvard. These new arrivals invigorated native Boston poets Wieners, **Stephen Jonas**, and Joe and Carolyn Dunn, who

> led lives so louche as to approach a form of magic . . . uniformly charming,
> witty, and lovable, they sought poetry by following Rimbaud into a
> systematic derangement of the senses, a regime which left little time or
> inclination for ordinary jobs or schedules.[31]

Together they formed what **Gerrit Lansing** called the "occult school" of Boston poetry, fascinated by the occult but also occulted, hidden on the back side of Beacon Hill while Robert Lowell, Sylvia Plath, Anne Sexton, and their ilk were garnering attention in the more upscale parts of town. It was a Boston renaissance that was invisible to many Bostonians, though right under their noses; their "newsletter" came with the injunction "Post whatever pages of it poke you in the eye in the most public place you can find—i.e., an art gallery, a bohemian bar, or a lavatory frequented by poets."[32] These letters from Wieners's first days back in Boston (initially from his parents' house in Milton) capture a spirit of joy and adventure that would permeate the next year of their lives, as he struggles to maintain community, searching Boston for apartments with Dana, writing and reading with friends. For the visiting Spicer

---

31 Ellingham and Killian, *Poet Be Like God*, 70–1 (hereafter referred to as *PBLG*).
32 *PBLG*, 75.

it was a very trying time—Blaser wrote to **Robert Duncan** that "Jack isn't at all well here. The total absence of his admiring juniors leaves him pink and shell-like"[33]—but for the others it was a generative time in their shared youth.

* * *

Michael Rumaker
[Aug 11, 1955]
[Black Mountain]
[Milton, MA]

Thursday

Dear Michael:

I got up five minutes ago, washed, went down to see mail (almost psychotic, my need for mail) and opened yours, read, and am excited. How stupid of me to end up with the word 'clever.' Those things in the story that excite me, (and I call them that), but I agree with you. Of course they are not clever, but creation.

I came running up here, all excited to write to you, and I begin and go dry—so to warm up, I will start with my own poems. As you can see, machine is beautiful, better now than ever. And yesterday was first day with it, so typed up all poems written since leaving BM. They come to 11,[34] but like you, I do not know. And the reason for me is, I write them so crazy. I feel hot, or chaotic, so begin writing, and by the finish, it has come out, the thing inside, but they are all written on the moment, and when that ends, usually about 30 mins., I figure, I put it aside, not forgotten, but really unable to touch it again, until I am forced to, or the deadline I have set in my mind has been reached, and then I take them all, and spend an afternoon or a day, tightening, working out lines, watching words, matching words,—all sort of mechanical and I could do this, over and over, if I have hit a poem that still excited me—like the 'wreck' poem, or poems OTHER people seem to be interested in—thus, even those ones from BM have been tightened and mostly always—shortened, brought down to essentials. I hope. I will send the poems off to Olson, probably tonight, also some to you, O. K. and the copy of the 'wreck' which I am happy to give.

Back to what you have said—true; / maybe we are talking about same things, but the crux to remember is that if you feel someone has to go, let them, all the way,

---

33 Quoted in Jarnot, *Robert Duncan: The Ambassador from Venus*, 157.
34 "11" is circled.

even though reality might stand in this way. Now what is reality—my using it here I guess means, making people real as they are expected to be, following the laws of real, as we know it, or as the readers know it, or as you know it—rather than letting Billy suddenly (this is nuts) sprout wings and fly. I think I have said it, there. If I wrote, and I dried in the writing, then I would take this way OUT, and it would be easy for me, and maybe this is fault. I think you have told me your 'raison d'etre' of writing, and I agree with you. Yeah, you are more than right—'that kind of fantasy is backboneless to me, doesn't give the imagination a chance to set its teeth into: to something solid: this earth, what's in it.'

I wish we could touch like that,[35] sexually, but until this other one dies in my eyes, even after, I am no good, I am afraid of taking off my clothes in front of anybody else—HEY—maybe that's why homosexual love or homosexual sex is SOMETHING—because it's not a blending but a give and going back, each remaining separate, yet, god knows, in contact. And thus, the act is not selfish, as I have been told by the 'soul-saving' set, when they tell me, "there is no union, only a giving, so one may take." Who wants to unionize. I give all of me, dangerous or not, when the pull is there, when I KNOW all of me is wanted,—yet I don't give up me: and for a prize, I get something else added ontop of me, whether it be a body or an emotion. *I get supplemented.*

All that really matters is that the dry spell has broken, and always will break, you want it to that much, so I remember, you writing that you got up every morning, hoping something begins and nothing does, but you must know (you probably do) that the mornings may stretch into months, without it, still it's there in you—all you need is patience, in those times only, on the hot days, patience with nobody or nothing. viz. Brancusi quote—you remember—85th Canto, I think, something like, those days when I would not give 15 mins. of my time to anything under heaven.[36]

I know who this unrequited love is of yours, the one watching the dancers, I can't see it myself, and I hope you do get tough; so there looks like nothing there, but don't get hard, hardness means, I suppose, no holes to let it out, use it and then you escape

35 Circled, arrow down to "give and going back."
36 In the 85th Canto, the first of the "Rock-Drill" section, Pound is referencing avant-garde sculptor Constantin Brâncusi (1876–1957) when he writes:

"One of those days," said Brancusi,
"when I would not have given
"15 minutes of my time
"for anything under heaven." (579)

from the dying you. You know I say these things, as much for myself, as for you. I do feel though that all of us, in this, can hear this stuff from each other, it's our duty to each other, remind each other to keep holes open, mostly through our finger-tips.

Now some news about my plans for Sept. Tomorrow, Dana and I resume apt. hunting on Beacon Hill, something high up, with lots of space and windows. Looked at something in a god-awful tenement, with an hallway, indescribable—5 flights up, 5 rooms, $55.00 a month. It is too much to pay, so we are eating the landlady down, a Mrs. McGonagle, who is fine as she don't care what us boys do at night, in fact wants us to make so much noise so as to evict the widow downstairs and her four children. If we can have it at $45. we will take it, and the rooms are wonderful, big and a lot of walking space, and room for guests, which I enjoy, especially if from BM. If you can do it for a week, Mike, do it—bus fare from Boston to NY is $5.75, and a midnight train—roundtrip—is less—the Owl, a vacation special. You know, Dana will drive all who can fit, and who want to, back from BM to the North. So far, Herb Ross asked and Joe and Carolyn said—as far as NY, that is, if they don't get an extension of loan. Things are indefinite there. I know, so make no plans, simply realize that a car will be available for four or so, if they want it.

I am like at the end of a poem, so goodbye for a while and write as <u>soon</u>[37] as <u>you</u> want to.

Big polio epidemic here, 80 cases a day, and I have a stiff neck, so begin building an oxygen tank for my arrival.

My love,
John

YOU CAN'T KILL THESE MACHINES[38]

Only a paper moon hanging
      over
a smashed up body by a squeezed car,
chopped bones and their moaning as sweet music plays
body and soul   on the road with blood
        on our arms.
A hundred feet up the street his watch
and further a door handle, some chrome

---

37 "soon" is circled.
38 "You Can't Kill These Machines" and the following poem, "Ode to the Instrument," were both published in issue 10 of *Floating Bear*, in an issue devoted entirely to Wieners's poems. See Di Parma and Jones, eds., *The Floating Bear: a newsletter, Numbers 1–37, 1961–1969.*

while somebody sits on him to keep his head whole
              somebody says his sides are coming out of his shirt.

You, dying under this moon, what would it be for you
on an old road with nobody to hold you,
blackd eyes and mashed hands.

They can carry this other body off,
                           out of my eyes,
pick up, put in his sides, piece his watch,
but your hair gold in the headlight
chin also
high cheek clean in the beamlight,
                             this is not in my eyes.

Silver silk is the skin I love to
                  and thru
the bedroom went the whispering and laughing and lighting
of matches.
        Don't let the matches
go for it comes, fear of
shall it be alone or together we get it
some starry blue night
on what highway?

As long as my blood grows cold on the skin I love to
and your good leg is on mine
and a hundred feet up the ditch
somebody else brushes off our mouths,
who cares.

      A copy for Michael Rumaker   from John Wieners
                           who was there[39]   August, 1955

---

39 Rumaker recounts the occasion of the preceding poem in *Black Mountain Days*. After a movie night in
town, he was riding back to Black Mountain with Tom Field and Wieners when they came upon a tragic
and bloody car wreck. Former army medic Field tended to the young driver splayed on the asphalt, "John
whispering to me how much the victim, with his blood-streaked blond stubble of hair, resembled Dana;
he shuddered, imagining if it had been Dana sprawled there in the road . . . Back in his room, John later
that night wrote a poem about the incident, naturally threading Dana into it, which he showed me next
day and gave me a copy of" (492–93).

ODE TO THE INSTRUMENT

I have wanted to write a love poem like the river merchant's,
and call: I miss your arms under my ear,
small words like sad song, running wine,
there are cold sheets.

I write the news:
we found and ate red plums today, rain, the rivers are full.
I saw your name in a book.
On the deck where I danced one morning

                                                            I heard you

in the frogs with rain on leaves.
Saturday night I laid down in it,
then walked back wet hoping you were home

                                                            to dry me.

Bring curtains for the bedroom.

Why shouldnt it be where?   again.
It is thirteen days now
they bury men on the third.

                              No words are better than bitter word
                              bitter word is you live.

When we step on moths,
do they feel the rip,
I mean does it last?

I wanted to send a love poem.

All I stamp is me with no chains on
asking
how do I go through tonight?
When you're little you can go sleepy bye bye
and no big feet follow.
But I have put away, I am a man
from laying out my face
in the rain
in the hours where you were.

If you are coming down on the Blue Mountain Skyway,
please mail it soon
and I will come out to meet you
        as far as Philadelphia.

for Michel, if he will pardon the sloppiness,
and take it to say Thank You.
              John

ON THE FIRST PAGE[40]

Out my window
runs the Neponset, a river enough to be written,
(but bloody from my baby wounds)
Phlox flowers, purple for any passage
or page or poem or whatever
(planted because Mrs. Reddington had yellow phlox)
Green grow the oak trees, giant leaves for publication
(beatings from their branches is not in content or text)
Christmas star, christmas trees, mistletoes and holly
but mother under everything in festival paralysis)
Old linoleum
        (she laid on that also
only it was daddy who kept her there those times)
My sister (but she cries at night)
My mates, play and otherwise,
Yes I can sing of tornado nights on fire
With black passion and no dawn
mouths that bleed from kissing.
Oh it was love love love
on our bedroom bathroom living room walls
(but that house full and go boom in the 39 winds)

It seems there's nothing to sing out
this boyhood window

---

40 "On the First Page" was published, dated 1961, in the Wieners collection *Cultural Affairs in Boston* with only minor edits (a couple of punctuation changes; the break between lines 16 and 17 is after "with" in *Cultural Affairs*) except that the line "My voice" has been omitted in the published form.

> except her
> across the street in the blue bushes
> my lady of the gold cloak
> stringing silver bow and arrows
> wanting eyes
> waiting for me as for no other.

My voice:

> Mother at your feet is kneeling
> One who loves you is your child
> Mother your altar boy is singing
> In sob syllables of sugar breath
> Mother cross my hands and hope to
> > Death,
> appropriate me from the living.

Wieners, 55

Michael Rumaker [Philadelphia]
December 2, 1955
[17 Irving St. Apt. 9. Boston]

Dear Michael:

Finally I <u>can</u> write to you, for now 1) this 2 mos. hocked typewriter is back in my cold study 2) the 3 mos. shade of inactivity, boredom, squabble and doubt is over. I have come alive again, Mike, for the first time since leaving Black Mt., that is, really alive, now over a period of one week duration, while before it was only spurt, die, spurt, cry, and the spurting was short and far between the dying, etc. Dana and I live in five rooms on the 5th floor of a slum, but it is long and light, with steam heat and an extra bed, for week, weekend, or overnight guests. This means you! But more important, I am coming to New York on Friday, Dec. 9th, through Sunday, Dec. 11th, with the Poets' Theater.[41] No, not acting, not writing, only some sort of

---

41 The Poets' Theatre (1950–1968) was founded by a group of Cambridge poets who all, except for V. R. "Bunny" Lang, were attending Harvard at the time. The group, including Molly Howe, Lyon Phelphs,

stand-in, errand-runner, lackey, usher-type post, but all very exciting for me, and the REAL reason for my activist state. The show is Finnegans Wake, adapted for speakers and chorus by Mary Manning, etc. etc. and to be presented at the Poetry Center Saturday, Dec10th, and Sunday matinee, Dec11th. Herb is acting the role of Finnegan, and he too will be in the city, // we hope, staying at the Dunns, address, I think, 407 W. 23rd St.

I have begun a one-act play, finished it too,[42] am still on unemployment, or didn't you know, since Sept. 20th. Dorn was right, that one never starves in this society. I get 19.00 a week for signing my name, and that's all, but now, the irony, when I have only two weeks to go, I begin to feel like writing again. NOT a word from me, Mike, all these months, and yet I suffered no great agony. I went to movies, fought, drank, read (a little) etc, but god, what a feeling to be like in the mts. again. It comes on me, usually late at night, like now. That is why I WANT TO SEE YOU. I want to talk, just to be around and active with you, sit in Central Park in big over-coats early Sunday morning, walk to the bookstores, ride the bus up Riverside Drive maybe. I know it's short notice, but I will manage a place for you to stay, if you can make it. I have not written to Olson, but have read two letters he sent to other people in Boston, one to a young insane friend of mine, a religious (he preaches on Boston Common) near-fanatic, who sent Olson a 20 page poem[43] about his insanity, his family tree, his memories of his shuffled childhood, his internment 5 doors from his mother in the same asylum, and Olson showed to [Robert] Creeley and they are publishing it all in Black Mt. Review #7, since 6 had gone to press, I hope with the PIPE[44] in it.

The drive from BM to NY with Olson and Creeley last Sept was the most memorable experience ~~of yours~~ *I had* except for certain nights at BM. I suppose I am being sentimental and pleading, but just to walk around a bit together in the cold would be fine!

And of course, to see Finnegans.

Richard Eberhart, and John Ciardi, was committed to "experimental plays not likely to obtain commercial production, and to encourage poets to write for the stage and to educate them in the techniques of the theater" (quoted in Melvin Maddocks, "The Poets' Theatre gives itself a curtain call, *Christian Science Monitor*, October 22, 1986") and performed plays by John Ashbery, Lang, Frank O'Hara, and Archibald MacLeish. Famed performances included Richard Wilbur's translation of *Misanthrope* and Mary Manning Howe's adaptation of *Finnegan's Wake*, both in 1955. Of special interest to any students of the Theatre and mid-1950s Boston is Alison Lurie's *V. R. Lang: Poems & Plays With a Memoir* (Random House, 1975).

42 *Asphodel, in Hell's Despite* is a one-act play whose production history features prominently in Wieners's correspondence with **Irving Rosenthal** in 1961. See Wieners's letter dated November 9, 1961. As he mentions in this letter, the play was written in a flash in 1955.

43 Wieners is referring to **Edward Marshall** and his poem "Leave the Word Alone."

44 Rumaker's story "The Pipe" appeared in *Black Mountain Review* no. 6, *Evergreen Review* no. 9, and in his 1967 collection *Gringos and Other Stories*.

I was down to NY one weekend lasting five days a month ago, but didn't go near the Cedar's[45] or see anyone, except Dunns for 5 mins. as I felt, as explained above.

About trip up, Creeley spent most of it sleeping but Olson and I talked in Back seat re everything from landscape to poetry, *or rather he talked.*

There is so much to talk of, and it can only be done together in person. Also I will have a food allowance from the Poets' so we can share that, thus if you are broke, and you are, no doubt, this would help. Bring manuscripts you think we or you would like to show, and I will bring some, too.

You show yours and I'LL show mine.

Another quick and forgive me, dear Mike, for not writing before. I know since you have gone thru it all ~~before~~ *you understand (the only word I can find)* while I was at the top, you down, re avoidance and contact. PS. Don't worry about building up a reserve for the weekend, as it will be quiet, and I will make no demands.

   DANA TOO   My love,   JOHN

Michael Rumaker
New Year's Day, 1956
[Boston]

Dear Michael:

I have just returned from a movie-house called the Rialto,[46] which is the refuge for a good percent of the old, the poor, the cold, the drunk, the perverted of the city.

---

45 The Cedar Tavern (1866–2006) was a bar and restaurant that served as locus for downtown New York culture, especially to the Abstract Expressionists and Beats who gathered there when it was located at 24 University Place, between 1945 and 1963. Condominiums now stand in the Tavern's place.

46 The Rialto Theatre, originally known as the Star, was a fixture of Boston's Scollay Square. Separating the West End from the rest of Boston, the Square served as the beating heart of Boston's working class until 1961, when its lively and livable streets were classified by government agencies as "slums" so that they could be destroyed. In the name of urban renewal, some 27,000 families were displaced to substandard housing elsewhere in the city, and the area was converted into a concrete expanse of buildings known as the Government Center. In his vital history of Scollay Square, *Always Something Doing*, David Kruh describes the neighborhood from its Puritan origins through its demolition. One of several legendary theaters in the Square, the Rialto was nicknamed "The Scratch House." Kruh explains:

> Open all night, at only a dime for admission, it became a de facto boardinghouse for some of Boston's homeless. If you were brave enough to go inside for a show and unlucky enough to sit in the wrong seat, you soon found yourself scratching your way through the matinee. A regular spraying of the theater didn't seem to do much to rid the seats of vermin, although the perfume smell of the spray did manage to cover up the smell of the people who slept there. (117)

They go there to keep warm and the management keeps the place cold. I have walked home in the cold, my ears freezing, and my coat like a piece of paper around me, and I thought, what if I had no place to go, no place but the Rialto.

Now as I sit here, I can't imagine the cold any longer, it doesn't exist, I'm not in it, my ears are thawed, my coat is on the couch, yet I feel guilty because the old men are still out in it. I feel guilty because I don't do any writing and justify my existence. Every day of my life, half of it is taken up with when will I begin. I blame Dana for it, I blame Boston, the neighborhood I live in. I think of myself holed up in some romantic little room, alone, on a schedule, but I know too well I can't ever accept that kind of life. This letter sounds like it comes from one just beginning, and yet I'm not just beginning. I been on this thing for years, and nearly all of those years I have wasted, I mean, the time of those years. It's so strange. If I sat down and went back and wrote those years, day by day, down, and read them in a book, I would say: what an exciting life, ooh, what I wouldn't give, that's what I want—still all this crap, this anxiety and worry, over waste mainly, is the biggest waste. It drives one out for distraction, never to more work. You think I wasted so much. I can just kill a few more hours, and that's what you do, kill it, bury, smother.

I long to be back in Black Mt. I worked harder there. I think of myself there in pain, I seek out pain for myself,

why need thee weep?   thus the affinity to torching it up, I can't face the music, but let's face it, John, the stuff is pretty sweet to the men sleeping in the Rialto open all night.
I know the cure:
get out of here. get into something vital, leave it, and then weep all night because I left it behind me. One great lifetime of self-pity and the poetry to come out of it, what will it be but dirge, lament for John, that's the kind of poetry I want to write, UNTIL I come up to the real stuff of pain like cold on the ears. I really think physical pain is the hardest, the mental brings tears, but the other blood, and that's what I need in my veins. Now right now, I am not in pity, I am just trying to see me, and deep down a resolution is coming, of course, New Year's, but it does want to put me out into the cold and remember it, and remember that I get cold very seldom, and the rest is unimportant.
So the bed's unmade and Dana isn't fleshy anymore and I'm not at Black Mt. and I want Olson to teach, etc. etc. still I'm warm, I'm Bohemian, I write, I'm young, and I am going to remember that the cold is hurting people, whether I make a poem or not, still that poem can help somebody's cold. A new anti-histamine.

Michael Rumaker
[March 2, 1956]
[Boston]

The new March, '56

Dear Michel:

I am writing this, because it is three in the morning, and I feel I have to write, but am dry of "inspiration," yet the mind is going. Why I am dry of the poem is, yesterday, I sent off to Olson, the play, all the poems, 3 or 4 finished ones, since October!, a batch of un-done ones, and the great impetus of getting all these things ready for him produced in me 2, maybe three, I think of the best things I have ever done.

I don't know what they are. Poems—or prose—or super-real or what. I can't hardly remember writing them, I mean, what was in them, only that I desperately wanted to speak to him. And I am still in the euphoria of accomplishment.

Olson once said to me that most Americans bored him, because they refused to deliver the goods of soul. It is true. I didn't know it at the time, but now I do, having read more of the contemporary . . .

So I am going at people like Cocteau—The Diary of an Addict, or the formal—Opium, the diary of an addict. [47]

Appolinaire;[48] selected writings—ed and trans. by Roger Shattuck, one of the "Cambridge poets" hereabouts, real base and academic stuff the introduction, but Guillame? himself is very exciting. It is a New Directions book. Another one of Cocteau's is "Call to Order" critical essays up to 1926 with a fine one in it re Picasso, who himself is a delight.

I turn to these men only for the reason of exasperation with that which is at hand, namely the Donald Hall's and the Richard Wilbur's[49] surrounding me in this sterile Boston, or rather, it is Cambridge area.

---

47 Jean Cocteau (1889–1963), French writer and artist. *Opium: The Diary of His Cure* was written in 1930 as he weaned himself off the drug.

48 Guillame Apollinaire (1880–1918), French poet and art critic whose writings were indispensable in the formation of Modernist poetry and painting, especially a field he called "Orphic Cubism." His *Selected Writings* were edited and translated by Roger Shattuck (1923–2005) for New Directions in 1948. Wieners would later address these writings and art explicitly in his 1958 poem "The Windows."

49 Donald Hall (1928–2018) and Richard Wilbur (1921–2017), American poets and critics, both Poets Laureate of the United States; their well-crafted verse was unavoidable in the 1950s and 1960s.

Also the little (125 pages) of Jane Harrison's prolegomena[50] has been opening the new world.

And Lawrence[51]—The fantastic Kangaroo, the most exciting novel I have ever read, oh that is so inadequate. I say, I experience all of Kangaroo because of Lawrence—that it // the experience of "Kangaroo" has been great, quantity-wise.

Also of course, the approaching of June, the realization that I shall soon be a part again of this budding thing, this thing on the black mountain, not Olson alone, but what he grows there, out of the dirt in his fingernails, as I say in a poem to him 'The Big Man on the Mountain.'

the blood of him his wheeze on me
his dirty fingernails
with violets in their dirt
I pick and hand to you

My own life is good. The last week working nights until seven in the morning, that is, writing, then sleep, and take my morning walk under neon lights, going the other way from the boys and girls returning from the typewriters. The life, of course, which excites me, the life of counter current.

But if I get to the black mt., I have to have money, so the last two days I have tried to find work, and so depressing, if I let it, which don't, but still an agony, I have to go through. To counter-set it, I went on a binge tonight at the library, with abt. 10 books, all exciting, which I dip or rip into middle, end, beginning.

Tomorrow the pavements.

June the world.

---

50 Jane Harrison (1850–1928), British classics scholar and feminist pioneer whose 1903 *Prolegomena to the Study of Greek Religion* was central to modern Greek mythology studies. Primary to her study was a foregrounding of ritual as a way to understand myth, an approach whose absence Wieners will later lament when reading Samuel Noah Kramer (see his letter to Charles Olson of September 22–23, 1957, in Wieners and Olson, *"the sea under the house"*). Olson dedicated his poem "A Newly Discovered 'Homeric' Hymn" to "Jane Harrison, if she were alive" (*Collected Poems*, 363).

51 D. H. Lawrence (1885–1930), English writer whose prose, poetry, and critical writing were essential to Olson and, through his influence, Wieners. In his essay "D. H. Lawrence and the High Temptation of Mind," written in 1950—the same year as "Projective Verse"—Olson calls Lawrence a master of "moral perceptions" that are "so instantaneous as to be immeasurable in time" (*Collected Prose*, 135). Robert Duncan recalled of his Black Mountain cohort, "this small group of writers, what we all shared was that we were followers of William Carlos Williams, who read him in the light of D. H. Lawrence" (*A Poet's Mind*, 257). Lawrence published the Australia-set novel *Kangaroo* in 1923.

ii

But I want

very much to hear about you, and whether you have made yourself well again.

And of course, the writing, maybe some of the poems, if any, you have done, you could send, as I possibly could help on them, that sounds pompous, but at least, I cd. make a critique on them, but I wd. like to get something, which I wd. return, so don't worry abt. making a special carbon. Just something to make you alive to me again. I am a funny one for that. With you least of all, though. All the others are dead. Tom,[52] a little breathing, and Dorn much more, but still not alive, so I can't write to a dead man. I wish I could write to him, and he wd. send pictures of Fred, or Helene—no no—that is so sentimental of me, but still, whether they have changed.

Your mention that he might come east is exciting. to get settled. Maybe he is only 250 miles away, as I write.

The more I read of Lawrence, the more I see Lawrence in Dorn. I think of them together, often. The walk Dorn had, that walk as if he was going through underbrush.

Well, now I wait for Olson, maybe no answer until I see him in June, and I hope he is there (any inform. you have re this I would love to hear) but I think from the nature of stuff I sent, I will get an answer. It was immediate, and I hope, lift him under the arms, like he said of one of my poems, once did.

The BMR? When? I never know on this St. Williams Island. Are you sending others out? I sent two early RHYMED and traditional trashy poems to the NYer and 4 days later, had a rejection slip. That is all. But I do want publication, somehow, maybe, it's only the need of the winter, which the high mt. air will cure.

I have talked enough, yet still I can't sleep, I am doomed to another dawn, but I send this now, so I can have your answer, I hope soon/

Thank you for the pleasure you gave me in your letter re "Asphodel." I think what it did for you, your letter of joy did for me.

What I tried to do was to show that LOVE survives in hell's despite, in the lovers' despite, in the audience's—that with our hate, it is love, with our selfishness, it is love, with each generation, each recurrence of the pattern, each dialogue, each triteness and lust, it is still there, as DH said, the call, and the answer. In the 2nd

---

52 American artist Tom Field (1930–1995), an army medic in Korea, studied painting under Joseph Fiore at Black Mountain from 1953 to 1956, after which he moved to San Francisco and worked among other Bay Area artists generally ignored by the New York–centric artworld. With Alberto Saijo, Lew Welch, and **Philip Whalen**, he founded a Zen Buddhist community called Hyphen House.

version, this is clarified and a happy note, is that BM or rather Herb wants to do it this summer, from which I will learn so much, and which will be exciting.

My love to you, very warm now,

John

* * *

Wieners spent the summer of 1956 at Black Mountain College, his second and final term there. The school had dwindled to ten students, living on meager rations but always working together, producing at the end of the quarter a ramshackle production of Robert Duncan's play *Medea at Kolchis*. It was the first time Duncan and Wieners spent together—he'd been away during Wieners's first term—and they had an instant connection. They were both openly gay, both inspired by the Orphic mysteries and the romances of Mary Butts and H.D., as well as the projective poetics of Olson. It was another pivotal season for Wieners, a crucible of "dreadful freedom"—as he reports back exhaustedly in this next letter to Robert Greene, "I can't believe that I am only 22."

* * *

Robert Greene
Thursday, August the 9th, 1956
[Black Mountain, NC][53]

Mon Cher Robert:

Just came back from the sunlight, blinded from reading your lovely letter in it, and felt I had to write again to you. I realize how much has been denied me by not knowing French, and something just has to be done about it, if only to take those silly extension courses again next year. The summer feels from here that it has been good to you. For me also, all or nearly all the anxiety has been lost, and even when it hung the heaviest on me, it must have strengthened as it bore me down, because, so many are unable to last here. We have had one party (I talk social, because it is such an integral part here) and after that one party, as I think I told you, one boy left, in complete frustration and loneliness, and another had himself committed to the bughouse in Asheville. Another had left the week before, and Herb leaves tomorrow.

---

53 This letter is written on the Black Mountain "Curriculum of the Soul" stationery, cream paper with ancient glyphs.

The principle of the place is to push one to his limits, to force him to earn his own way, in all phases, and the result is: that the man either runs away, breakdowns, or survives endures to do his best work. And the principle is none other than that of "freedom." No one really knows just how far they can go, so they go too far, one, if he is driven that way, goes too far. And I endure. Along with about six or seven others. That's all. And the crazy thing is, that it doesn't matter, what with the peace one finds after. And the pace, "the beautiful monotony" of the place. The french poetry course sounds as if it could not be better. Appollonaire even in translation is an excitement. Michaux I have only heard of but he was featured in that issue of <u>Origin,</u> I showed you with Rene Char.[54] He also paints, and check on this. I find out from a new student here that Michaux[55] has given up his poetry, and only paints now? It wd. be interesting to find out why.

That wonderful touch you mention of knowing personally that men discussed in class, has always been the thing I think I enjoyed the most. And Lennie could always convey that illusion, as if they had just written the poem last night and read it to him over lunch that afternoon. That was the "glamor" of his teaching.

French theatre I am completely ignorant of. Yes, Cocteau's "Infernal Machine" is translated. Never read it, but BU, I think, did a job on it last year.

Francoise seems like a personification come true. But more that, Robert, if she comes into that world of "friend"

(Duncan just walked by, he serves as cook for three of us now, since **Basil [King]** left) Olson's new book, "The Maximus Poems 11–22" came out last month, and he read it to us entire, which was a charge. Five times through. I felt I had to run home and begin pecking on the typewriter.

BMR # 6 has been out two months, and they all have stuff in it, even Rumaker has a long story in it. He's the boy from Philly, with whom I spent two days, and who has just left here after his week's vacation. When he was in classes, like last week, one lasted (Olson's) until ten minutes to three in the morning. From

---

54 Rene Char (1907–1988), French poet sometimes associated with the Surrealists, whose works often concerned the Hermetic traditions and were translated by several of the New Americans. His poem "The Lace of Montmirail" was translated and published by Cid Corman in *Origin* no. 11.

55 Henri Michaux (1899–1984), Belgian-French poet and artist known for his India ink and sepia drawings and paintings.

9 on. # 7 will be out this winter and Marshall will be in it, alongside such people as Herbert Read,[56] Edward Dahlberg,[57] and W. C. Williams.[58]

When you are thirty-five, your time for being very young, you will feel, ends when you touch 29. I do know what you mean. I can't believe that I am only 22.

It was a new birth, and I can't say anything about it at all for once, because you said it so beautifully.

I go out for breakfast now, with only three weeks remaining here. I approach my leaving here with great joy and great fear, but I would not have it any other way. Dana writes once:

"PS. Let's buy a dog" and we will, Robert, we will. I feel I have just gotten off a tight-rope wire over Niagara Falls, and go down now for the honeymoon. I hope I do not hex myself by my optimism.

love
John

Robert Greene
Thursday, Aug. 12, 1956
[Black Mountain, NC]

Mon cher Robert:

After the long silence—no excuse—but I hardly think outside the immediacy of this place. Thus each day ends with a tired groan.

---

56 Herbert Read (1893–1968), English art historian, critic, and philosopher.
57 Edward Dahlberg (1900–1977), American writer originally from Boston. At various times a soldier, day laborer, expatriate in Paris, and anthropologist, he taught briefly at Black Mountain College. In "Projective Verse," Olson credits Dahlberg as the one who "first pounded into my head . . . ONE PERCEPTION MUST IMMEDIATELY AND DIRECTLY LEAD TO A FURTHER PERCEPTION." Their passionate and contentious correspondence was collected in 1990 for *In Love, In Sorrow*, edited by Paul Christensen (Paragon House). Herbert Read (1893–1968), English art historian and literary critic.
58 William Carlos Williams (1883–1963), American poet whose *Paterson* (released in five books between 1946 and 1958), an epic "poem of place," informed and inspired the work of Olson and the other poets coming in and out of Black Mountain College. His notions of measure were key to the BMC poets; he sought to break the iambic line and establish a living alternative to meter that varied like speech. His concept of measure as the Modern alternative to meter was certainly on Wieners's mind as he chose *Measure* as the name for his magazine.

I take 4 mornings 4 afternoons (sometimes) and 1 evening with Duncan on Meaning and Content (the poem) and Basic Technique (the poem) and Rimbaud (The Illuminations), also 1 morning spent in his reading from The Poets—Thomas Hardy, W. C. Williams, and Yeats, so far.

Happy to hear you on Appollonaire. Tell me more about Hoag?? and the others you are doing. Of course, by the time you get this, the session will be ended. Shattucks translation, I hear, of him, is quite juiced up, while Mme. Varese's[59] on Rimbaud, is quite dried down/ I can't get R's Madame X. out of my mind, she who set up her piano in the Alps.

Heard from [Frank] O'Hara with all kinds of leads for the fall in NY, but I will be most happy to return to Dana. I don't feel any diminishing of feeling for the same, but as usual, you musn't tell the old dear, even tho he knows. Duncan met him, liked him, and of course, Duncan and I are fine friends. I always make one. Dana was with George when we met one morning, and afterwards, Duncan asked me who the dishrag[60] was! NP—For four weeks here Gilbert sent no money, and it was near starvation. No butts, no food, oatmeal for days, and finally, I was forced, along with my kitchen-sharers, one of whom left after the last party, to boost groceries from the A&P. Which practice has stopped, since Gilbert sent down the money in post-dated checks. Also Atty. Rosenberg came thru.

My own actual production has been slow—but I feel I have already learned more essential ingredients (substance) in 4 wks. here, than 4 mos. of reading in Boston. Next year, or beginning in Sept. after we get settled, I will bring it to use.

I had no trouble adjusting to the tenor of life here, although some do break, when faced with the "dreadful freedom" we all face today, though lesser extreme out there than here. After our 1st and last party, the above mentioned Basil King left, in complete frustration and loneliness another boy [several words redacted in manuscript] had himself committed to the bug house in Asheville, and the week before, a boy called Graystone,[61] a painter, left for the same reasons as Basil. But we keep getting new students all the time.

Herb Ross leaves too Aug. 10, without his degree, and without producing my play. That was part of his graduation plan,[62] but the faculty did not feel he was ready yet

---

59 In the first section of Rimbaud's *Illuminations* (via the 1946 Louise Varèse translation), "As soon as the idea of the Deluge had subsided," among many apocalyptic reactions, "Madame*** installed a piano in the Alps. Mass and first communions were celebrated at the hundred thousand altars of the cathedral" (5).

60 Arrow from "dishrag" to "George."

61 Grey Stone was an eccentric young man, even among Black Mountain's quite eccentric student body. He shows up in Martha Winston King's invaluable memoir from the period, "Three Months in 1955: A Memoir of Black Mountain College."

62 Like everything else at Black Mountain College, graduation was unusual. After meeting with his primary

for it, so he was told he wd. have to wait, maybe six months, and WORK. He leaves, though, and I guess they all feel, GOOD. Even Herb does.

I meet with Olson twice a week—one night on manuscripts (I get a poem out a week) and one night on Myths and Fairy Tales. In fact, both teachers have centered for the summer, around.[63] In Duncans today, we traced Snow White back to Persephone, Eve (the apple!) and Oedipus (he was abandoned, remember, like her, and was ordered put to death, like Snow White.

Olson read us Alcestis[64] yesterday. If you don't remember, we had it, I think, in Soph. Greek. I didn't remember until about 20 lines down in the translation, which is intolerable.

For relaxation, this week, I made a large (3' by 3') collage or montage of Great Greta Garbo. I cut out various poses of same and transposed them onto other situations for ex. GreatGG over a gold cross, GG on a Grecian column, in a wheat field, in an exploding atom, in a river, etc. Also I acquired a lovely small red and gray painting, framed, which I carry back home.

[. . .]

Robert Greene
Sunday, august 19 *1956*
[Black Mountain, NC]

Mon cher Robert:

Just to write and say it is the night of the full moon, and here today, all day, everyone feels it. I don't know why. Eloise stays in the house and says she wants to see no one, Duncan is afraid to go home and write because of what might happen in his play, Olson won't answer his door, Eric stays in bed and reads. I didn't look for these things, but earlier I couldn't explain my own mood either. I walked all day, in here, out there, anywhere, filled with some kind of worry, old fears about the future, and then I wondered why all these others were acting so closed in. I blamed it on the grey Sunday, until I went out a few minutes ago. It is 8:30 PM and the roads are

---

advisor and agreeing to a program of study and work, the student would meet again with the advisor for examinations. Rumaker went through the full process with advisor Robert Duncan (detailed wonderfully in *Black Mountain Days*), but Wieners was only at Black Mountain for two nonconsecutive terms, already having graduated college, so his evaluations came directly and informally from teachers Olson and Duncan, as they would for many years.

63 Ditto marks from "around" to "Fairy Tales."

64 In the indispensable *Charles Olson's Reading* (1996), Ralph Maud notes that Wesley Huss had given Olson the 1953 Penguin Classics edition of Euripides' *Three Plays: Hyppolytus; Iphigenia in Tauris; Alcestis*, tr. Philip Vellacott (272, n.12).

nearly as bright as daytime, and I look up, and there's the answer, with an orange ring round her, the full moon. What else can I use to explain it, this caged atmosphere. I want to go, be off, see something different, but all one can do is wait for it to pass. I wonder if tonight you feel, think back when you read this, anything similar. You must be under the same moon.

Much has happened since I last wrote. I definitely stay until the end of the month, as I have been given a lovely part in Duncan's new play.[65] It is Arthur, the author, a combination of W. B. Yeats, Pound, Olson, a man filled with fanaticism, fantasy, old dreams, and ONE new hope. What a part!

[...]

This is poetry for the theatre. That is why this summer, I know, has been so important for me. Whole new areas have opened up, where I was ignorant before. It is a most rewarding thing to know, that as the years go by, the thing one has chosen, or been chosen for, in life, has been the right thing. The longer I stay the more reward I get from the poem. It is like a re-charge of the energy I got over five years ago, when I said, "Poetry will be my flag." That is why I can never feel quite as alone again, because I have this mysterious gift, force, which won't leave me alone, and which like love inside of me, won't die. Christ, it makes one feel awfully humble. Not that I have created anything comparable, but as Olson says, I am in the Process, and possessed, in love with the word, so there ain't nothing else to do. And I had such doubts last spring, what with other matters.

I have written Dana twice, and he has answered once, not the last one. So I guess he still has decisions to make. I think he thgt. the summer with me would make his decision for him, but now as the time draws near for me to come home, I feel he might have doubts again. Or maybe it is just the full moon, that makes me think this way.

The boys I mentioned to you that left have all returned, what with even two new students. Basil came back with a new car, a convertible Willys Jeep and we went off

---

65 Eloise Mixon and Erik Weir were students at Black Mountain College. Mixon was a poet and actress "who had not yet written a poem," Duncan remarked, but who had "natural measure in the syllabic line ... in workshop exercises [at BMC] Eloise's performance was considerably 'better' than my own" (Ellingham and Killian, *PBLG*, 85). Mixon moved West after Black Mountain, and Duncan wrote her a part in each of his plays after *Medea at Kolchis: The Maidenhead*, the play Wieners is discussing in this letter (Ellingham and Killian, *PBLG*, 85). In his 1963 preface to *Medea*, Duncan writes that BMC theater instructor Wesley Huss asked him, in the summer of 1956, to present a new play, and he decided to work on the story of Medea as "a pubescent girl" with "obsessive passion pre-figuring the woman's wrathful jealousy" (Duncan, *Collected Early Poems and Plays*, 593). He envisioned Arthur (the role in which Wieners alternated with Louis Marbury on the production's two nights) as "a last remnant of Pre-Raphaelite kings living on in the art-nouveau last stage ... There is no scene in which he is not playing the mask of the poet" (594). In the Black Mountain production (August 29 and 30, 1956), Eloise Mixon played Edna, Erik Weir played "The Doctor," and the old woman Garrow was played by Wes Huss.

(four of us) to the drive-in last night and saw <u>Trapeze</u>, which I enjoyed thoroughly.[66] We had been drinking, and on the way home, Basil who is filled with all kinds of drives,[67] began to speed, very fast, up to 70 mph, and sometimes on the wrong side of a three-lane highway. What could we say. Speed had possessed him. Ahead of us, a car put out from a cut-off, and Basil couldn't slow down, swerving out to the middle lane, sideswiping into an oncoming car, sending us off across the street to the <u>left</u>! <u>up</u> an embankment, bouncing from two wheels to two wheels, right up thirty feet to the top, where we hit a telephone pole, and came down, still he couldn't stop, and smashed into a street sign at the bottom, kept going, until the car stopped. No injuries to none of us, except Basil spent the night in jail, is out on $300 bond, and appears in court tomorrow morning on charges of drunken driving, and reckless driving. We three also must appear as witnesses. And Dana can tell you my premonition about death on the highway, still I was not afraid, and was, I guess you could call it transfixed, through what seemed to be three separate accidents. But of course, I know I can come home no other way but on the train. A car wd. be impossible

---

66 *Trapeze,* Carol Reed's 1956 film about circus performers, starring Tony Curtis and Burt Lancaster.

67 In his book *mirage: a poem in 22 sections*, Basil King remembers this occasion as the night after he'd found out his hero Jackson Pollock was killed just a week before, on August 11, in a single-car crash:

It was 1956
I owned a Jeepster with a plaid top
and white sidewalls
it was 1956
I remember John Wieners
I don't remember who else
we all went to see Trapeze
in a drive-in
we'd been drinking
and I know I drank during the movie

On the ride
back to Black Mountain
I drove through the stop light at Oteen
in my drunkenness I went across
the dividing line, up the hill
towards the Veterans Hospital
swerved to the right
missed the fence
came down the hill
and swiped the back
fender of a car
The state trooper
asked me to walk the white line

John told the trooper
"He always walks that way" (55)

unless I knew the driver, and a bus is like a large coffin. I sound like such a lily, but I just have to admit this re meself.

Duncan just came back and he sits one foot away. He has just read the beginning of his third act, where the heroine, who will die because "she cannot celebrate tomorrow." The play is called MEDEA; part 1, The Maidenhead. DESIRE and the agony caused by same. He just left to write more. If ever you see a man possessed when writing, it's him. He will be back, all nerves and shakes, after he writes the next scene. And the tremendous life of this existence. And the power is shared. His gift carries over to me. Olson's does too. And by my youth, I transfuse something to them.

The new Origin #XIX came out yesterday, featuring German poetry, and a woman called Astrid Claes,[68] who I have never heard of, and who you probably never have. But on the back cover, there is a note by the editor saying that Miss Claes wd. like to dedicate her work to the friend of her friend,

Richard Alewyn.[69] ! ! !

I close Robert now, to transmit some of this tension to whatever I can write. I think only two more weeks before all this ends, and I think again only two more weeks before I begin again my actual life, the life of love, . . and the waiting is done.

As Eliot writes in his four quartets:

"What we call the beginning is often the end
And to make an end is to make a beginning.
The end is where we start from . . .

We shall not cease from exploration
And the end of all our exploring
Will be to arrive where we started
And ~~the~~ know the place for the first time.

(This is the last stanza of the poem)
And all shall be well and
All manner of thing shall be well
When the tongues of flame are infolded
Into the crowned knot of fire
And the fire and the rose are one."

Love and see you soon,
John

---

68 Astrid Gehlhoff-Claes (1928–1911), German poet and prolific translator.
69 Richard and Veronique Alewyn were mutual friends from Wieners's pre-Black Mountain Boston days.

In this first letter to Olson, Wieners reports on his exciting life in Boston, busy with the Poets' Theatre and work with his friends, trying to maintain the creative energy of Black Mountain. He is fighting, he says, "to keep meaning and intensity (its so easy to fall back)," and one way of doing this is a new magazine, one that will continue the work begun by Olson in 1950's "Projective Verse." He tells Olson that the magazine will possibly fail, "but the effort must be made." He has already written to Villiers, the UK press that Boston poetry stalwart Cid Corman used for his small magazine *Origin*. "Projective Verse" had "set off a decade," he writes to **James Schuyler**, "and MEASURE if my energies hold out, will end it. We must see ourselves as the new generation, initially our youth in these ten years."

~~*

Charles Olson
Jan 8, 1957
[Boston]

Dear Charles:

I write 2 days after a 23rd birthday. I write after such a long time. I write out of what <u>most</u> of the time appears a desert (with snow). I write to enclose Laurence.[1] And to wish I was there and able to endure.

I won't send this tonight but add to it once or twice more so I can tell you what I have been reading and also to get some Robin Blaser poems to send you. He and Steve Jonas are the only two left and we try like ladies bridge to meet one night a week to read what if anything has been written. [Edward] Marshall has taken to coming back for weekends to see [Steve] Jonas but I haven't met him yet and if you still need a copy of that manuscript (per **Jonathan Williams**) "Tug of War" maybe he would have it tho I think he sent you the original and only.

Last night I met Paul Goodman.[2] He was at a Poets' Theatre play of a friend of his and at a drunk cellar party, rather an antique shop party he talked so that after a while I only stared at his grey swamp water eyes—jelly eyes—blob eyes. Maybe that is why I am writing tonight because I didn't like him much, his glory in some

---

1 Wieners is referring to D. H. Lawrence.
2 Paul Goodman (1911–1972), bisexual American anarchist, writer, poet, and psychotherapist, a cofounder of Gestalt therapy who had a tumultuous, short tenure at Black Mountain College before Wieners arrived.

story of a duncan lover, "stealing" same which I tried to keep cutting off but he had to glory more so I finally said "Well, Duncan got the Venice poem[3] out of it, and that's worth more than any Goodman a Jerry put together," which sort of shut him up on other matters which were the "poor" students at BM and leaders and disciples and chumps and Hail and beware I thought jelly eyes. And later the playwright said Paul, you really are the American writer, living, and someone said—yelled— Shah-hit! And I've tried to write a poem about it but couldn't so I write a letter.

My own writing has been slow—almost nonexistent but in my mind every day like other things come back every day, the same people, so I write mostly I guess "journal entries" which unfortunately always have to do with me and I doubt very much whether I have found "the black that is blacker than black" tho I desire their skin since New Years. And of course I have the problem that without the agony of love to write off I have very little else. I went to Yeats but it doesn't show. And of course I have the excuse of this job which takes up so much time. To make the living that doesn't count. I try to forget none—nothing—of Black Mountain, a living that counted. When I came back, Joe Dunn said pick a card (this after I decided to stay here) and I picked a sword in the ground? which Spicer said: a test of strength which failed, the sword was that way.[4] But I know this is my way to stand it and the fighting to keep meaning and intensity (its so easy to fall back) makes strength. It's in Blaser's face, a jaw that says hit it and you'll be the hunted. And the ladies bridge helps, and letters. and sometimes the surprise of Boston, what we are in. And of

---

3 Robert Duncan's "The Venice Poem" was written in 1948. In his essay on the "symphonic form" of the poem, Robert J. Bertholf describes its creation:

> Duncan was having an affair with the poet Gerald Ackerman. Paul Goodman came to Berkeley, met Duncan and Ackerman, and then left town with Ackerman. Duncan was distraught with passions of rage and jealousy, caught between knowing his feelings toward Ackerman were authentic but suffering the inauthentic feeling of betrayal.

4 Just a month after getting this letter, Olson would have his own negative encounter with Spicer's Tarot. At a gathering in San Francisco after Olson gave a series of talks on "propositions of projection and composition by field in the light of Alfred North Whitehead's *Process and Reality*," Spicer sat at the enormous man's feet and began to spread his Theosophist cards. This was "the biggest *faux pas* Spicer could have made," as Ellingham and Killian recount. He "was done in by a fact he could not have known, that Olson had foreswarn Tarot completely some years back, after a frightening experience in which the cards had eerily, accurately predicted—to the day—the death of his own mother" (*PBLG*, 87). Olson's response to the reading was to "'crush Jack totally'... Later, Spicer revealed that Olson had rebuked him for attempting to 'make something happen' in San Francisco through incorrect technique. 'Your poetry is bullshit, just like your rituals, just like your cards,' Olson allegedly snarled." Spicer replied through a poem, "A Postscript for Charles Olson," which argues that "If nothing happens it is possible / To make things happen. / Human history shows this" (88).

course the knowledge of what and how <u>you</u> are right now. The <u>example</u>, I mean, of you under the conditions which for all I know maybe couldn't be better, for you.

Jonathan says Mexico in the spring. His stay here made a good night. So now at five after 2AM, the same.

Wed the 9th

So I get home today and see your card oh Swannanoa[5]—my heart's in the highlands and on me birth nite. You shall have them coming. Boston today is warm and the snows fill up the gutters. I helped a showgirl across the Chelsea Street circle—a harbinger? and today I bring from the library

The Journals of Cocteau

Mary Butts[6] Speed the Plough

Yeats' Letters on Poetry

    to Lady Dorothy[7]

R. Radiquet[8]—Count d'Orgel

and the Midnight Court from the Irish

of Bryan Merryman[9]

Thursday PM

We live across from a schoolyard. Where the girls from the 4th grade do the bumps and grinds. Cy Scollay's[10] within a stone's. And there is a sign posted:

---

5 Black Mountain College was located in the Blue Ridge Mountains' Swannanoa Valley.

6 Mary Butts (1890–1937), British Modernist writer whose memoirs, stories, novels, and journals speak to the mystery of Old England. A student of occultist Aleister Crowley, she was credited as a coauthor of his *Magick (Book 4)* in 1912; her friend Jean Cocteau illustrated her 1928 book *Imaginary Letters*. Like most Modernist women artists her work fell largely into obscurity, but she was admired by Wieners and the other poets in Robert Duncan's circle. Butts's collection *Speed the Plough and Other Stories* was published in 1923.

7 Wieners is referring to the correspondence between Irish poet and scholar W. B. Yeats (1865–1939) and his student Dorothy Wellesley, Duchess of Wellington (1889–1956), first published by Oxford University Press in 1940. As in the correspondence of Olson and Wieners, Wellesley's ongoing discussion with Yeats is a meeting of master and disciple, and the letters always return to the mysteries of poetic creation: "My head is full of new verse," she writes to Yeats, "singing, pounding even in my ears, but practical affairs must be dealt with . . . but perhaps no inspiration is ever lost, but recurs months, perhaps years later. It seems to me that poetry is begotten of a tune" (Wellesley, *Letters on Poetry from W.B. Yeats to Dorothy Wellesley*, 31–32).

8 Writer Raymond Radiguet (1903–1923), with Cocteau as his mentor, cut a Rimbauldian swath through Modernist Paris in his brief life. His novel *Count d'Orgel's Ball* was published in 1924.

9 Brian Merriman (ca. 1749–1805), Irish poet. His 1,000-line-long *Cúirt An Mheán Oíche* (The Midnight Court) is considered one of the great comic poems of Irish literature, a satiric twist on gender roles and sexuality that uses the mode of the vision poem.

10 Scollay Square.

> What Kind
> Of Man
> would allow his dog
> to Befoul
> the Children's
> Playground?[11]

And I am sure that you will be as disappointed as I am with most of what I send you. The effort is harder than ever and I look back on past <u>lines</u> with envy. But the desire accordingly is stronger than ever. So all will right.

The poem about father on the beach was done today so that's a good sign. And your post card has sent off a chain reaction. Last night I was in bed from 10pm to 2pm today and dreamed every possible dream in the book. I wish there was made The Book of Dreams. Also I wish there was more of what is being done NOW within my grasp. Before there was Origin to catch up on and even last summer—pace makers—but there ain't none here and whatever territory Steve is in or Blaser's in is there's too much for me. Where are you in? You can be used Am I right in this? Looking for spaces to inhabit. Like Laurence has enough space, opened same so that there is free room for any inclined there. And I'm not a rock-driller unfortunately, besides afraid of Pound affecting-infecting my own too much. What I might do is go back over all the near two years stuff to find business to exploit. For what strikes again. Because its always fight. Eat or starve, green grass or wither. And the trouble with what I send you is swamp—misery, it becomes a thick bore-bog and there are lights but too deep in the mush. So maybe retreat a bit. Get off the gold moon. To maybe something dry like this <u>Pa</u> poem. Untheatrical despite the sets.

Anyway now (post postcard) it's a good time with much blizzards and everybody cursing and falling down in the slush except Dana who has snow tires and me who has[12] and
some dogs in the neighborhood.

Remember me to Betty[13] and the other Charles and I hate to end because there's no one else to talk to.

---

11 A box is drawn around the text.
12 Arrow from "has" back to "Dana."
13 Elizabeth "Betty" Kaiser (1925–1964) studied voice and music at Black Mountain College, where she fell in love with Charles Olson; they had a son, Charles Peter, and moved to Gloucester after the college

So I won't for a bit. This is the 2nd letter I've written at all since Sept. The others in answer to Mike who wrote good news re the tarnished place & the Windhover Press.[14]

Will the week there mean lectures? But there's no sense in asking questions because I don't want to set up an obligation on you. They're on me from you and that's enough.

I never thought of you as a MOLE. Paul Revere sees your lights out at sea.

Enclosed also find a letter to go out tomorrow to Villiers. The only reason to give for it is something has to be done here, so I sponsor this without friends. Do you think it worth the go? Blaser, Jonas & I will call ourselves the editors but if it contains—becomes actuality, it will contain only what Arc did & some, Spicer & Marshall and the 'locals.' Will you give some. The stuff has to be published but of course don't bank on it.

BOSTON: a blast from—etc., the contributors listed below that. "The opinions expressed in this magazine do not necessarily reflect those of the city." It depends on what Villiers sends as estimate—and then raising money on a complete typesheet of the first issue—also selling space to the bookshops, galleries, Poets' Theatre, and society poetry supporters. With individuals taking care of distribution if possible in different cities

Villiers was the choice because it must be cheap.

I understand Arc[15] was only an "anthology" and Origin's gone and what else but BMR? Besides I have to use this excess energy on something besides roamin' those roads.

Whatever you have to say will be heeded. And as it stands needed. Maybe it's a waste because it won't go but the effort must be made. And it can be right if a firm grasp—the one voice—is kept. Mine now and mine when. The doubt then expressed was from a few thoughts on 4 Winds.[16]

Again 2:05 and again until tomorrow.

---

closed. She died in a car accident in March 1964 outside Buffalo, New York, where Olson was teaching at the time.

14 Windhover was a small press based in Short Hills, New Jersey, which printed several books for Jonathan Williams's Jargon Society. Another Windhover Press was established in 1968 in Iowa City, also publishing many mid-century American and British poets.

15 In spring 1947, Philip Lamantia and Sanders Russell edited *Ark*, a political literary magazine out of San Francisco. Robert Duncan, Kenneth Rexroth, and Paul Goodman were among the distinguished contributors. Only one issue was released.

16 *Four Winds. A Quarterly of Arts and Letters* began in Gloucester in June 1952. Edited primarily by poet Vincent Ferrini (1913–2007), to whom Olson addressed the initial "letters" that became *The Maximus Poems*, the magazine lasted four issues (three, with one a double issue).

Well it took more than tomorrow. It is Jan 16th and the routine of being pulled back & forth to work and bed has taken its great time. 7 days there last week. Still since I began this I began and finished on & off subways, quiet afternoons at Desk I, - Yeats' <u>Letters on Poetry to Dorothy Wellesley</u> which have given me some of what those two had. And the poem <u>A Message</u> was finished 5 mins. ago while the book was finished an hour ago, both giving me great joy. The book of course led me to her poems and his intro. in Oxford Book of Med. Verse—1935 plus the selections, which I find hard to read, unaccustomed to the verse. You lose your eye & ear for rhyme, steady feet, etc. But I shall enjoy Yeats all the more now. And I have the <u>Words for Music, Perhaps.</u>[17]

Mainly since your card, a very happy time.

And I have gotten the bills you forwarded. They are from a book club I joined there called The Art Book Guild, but whose books must still be at BM. If they are, I will send postage, if you could forward. Enough business.

We have been living at a literal ten degrees below zero for 3 days and I thought on Cambridge Street this morning—'Oh for a beaker full of the warm South.'

I do hope you can write and will say what you have to re the enclosed. I hope there's light from me. I don't think of any but the last 2 as finished.

"Mrs. Yeats had said: 'Come back and light the flame.' ~~the day he died~~

I want to write again and hope it is all right with you with or without poems.

> My love
> John

This is positively the last postscript but re-reading this letter as a <u>one</u> when it has been done in so many parts is not a very pleasant record to face.

Pardon the crap about Goodman. He is as befits now nothing but a voice at a drunken party.

Also I've wanted to ask this often but do you think anywhere is a copy of a poem you once wrote which has "For J.W." on it? Eighteen months ago. It matters more now.

The magazine too, without a push behind me, I doubt will ever get off paper. Or on it. Enough reflection.

> I wait for a word.

---

17 W.B. Yeats' collection *Words for Music Perhaps and Other Poems* was published in 1932.

Charles Olson
February 8, 1957
[Boston]

Dear Charles:

I wasn't going to write again until you got back from there, but yesterday I heard from Villiers and they w/ print a mag. the size of Origin, maybe some, 10 pages shorter (all the better), 300 copies of same, for $163. So I am excited, and it is deep water for me, and so what, it can be done, because there isn't much space, but there is a freedom permissible where else? And where do I get the money. 16! people at $10. a head and you have it. I can hustle that much in this city, plus selling in so many ways natural to me/

What do you say. There is an excitement in my air, and I have written to Spicer, Rumaker, Dawson,[18] Vande Wiele,[19] asking for their ears. if only to listen for me. And distribute.

And it won't be politics, I have no reputation to lose, nor none to make. And I am ignorant which is good.

And I write to you, so you can say, not junior league,
 with your eye upon it,
clean, a ball to your bat.
A phrase of Blake: Bring out number weight & measure in a year of dearth.

I ask of you what you have, the poem.
Say, FIRST ISSUE.

Blaser

J. Williams

Spicer

Duncan

Marshall

Olson?

---

18 Fielding Dawson (1930–2002), American fiction writer and friend of Wieners's from Black Mountain. A New York native, he was also known for his painting and collage work, as well as his longtime work teaching maximum-security prisoners. His *The Black Mountain Book* is an invaluable, lyrical memoir of his time at the school.

19 Gerald Van de Wiele (b. 1932), ex-Marine and art student at Black Mountain, handsome abstract expressionist who went on road trips from Swannanoa to New York with Wieners and fellow art student Basil King to explore artist lofts and studios.

Dawson

Jonas

Rumaker

and let it stand on a height of the best of all of them.

I will send the entire copy out by April 1st, with 1/3 of money. then two months back&forth on galley proofs, and another 1/3, and on June 1st, I w/ have 300 copies in my living room, not to stay, dated, Summer, 1957.

I fit here, this use of energy, and feel behind me all the little creeps who sat down and decided they would publish a little magazine. No matter what, I have their strengths.

Whatever questions you have, ask them, and I offer you all the white space you want to walk in.

Don't rush on an answer, as SF is probably in your mind, but it's gonna be there on June 1st.

REVIEWS? This can be wide open, and that don't mean 'deviated'!

My love,

John

On the 20th of Jan. the snows Began to Melt

I saw a woman stagger on the train
With orange flowers in her hand

ON JANUARY 20TH THE SNOWS BEGAN TO MELT[20]
I saw a woman stagger on the train

---

20 This poem appeared with a few changes ("on this" is removed, "hold" is changed to "holds," and different lineation) in *Floating Bear: a newsletter*, edited by Diane di Prima and LeRoi Jones/Amiri Baraka, in issue 10, which was devoted exclusively to Wieners's early poems. They were gathered, di Prima says in her introduction to the *Floating Bear* anthology,

> from manuscripts that he had left around at different people's houses where he had stayed at one time or another. The really early stuff, from his Black Mountain days and right after, he had left at Frank O'Hara's house years and years ago. Frank just laid the manuscript on me. John also stayed at LeRoi's [Jones/Baraka's] and left stuff there, and when I came out to the West Coast, I was given poems that he had left at **Wallace Berman**'s pad . . . There's a huge stack of unpublished John Wieners floating around somewhere (ix).

With orange flowers in her hand
And I could not make up my mind
To be the woman or: orange flowers

carried underground on this
            suddenly before me a boy
came on
            and he hold in one hand
a bed,
            my mother
            would say,
of red
            gladiolas
a blur of carnations and yellow

A color to soak the black off death
& I know
            dying or dead
            women who receive these
                                    see
blinds slashed,

like me in the tunnel under Charles St.
hot as a bee is, seized on their smell.

                    ~~*

With the urgency and energy that characterized all of the small magazines and mim-
eographed newsletters of the late 1950s and 1960s, Wieners was working on issue 2 of
Measure before one was off the press. His confidence was growing, the project a true
reflection of the poetic world that Wieners inhabited. In this next letter to Olson,
he reports proudly on *Measure*: "It is all mine, ME the first two letters." Of course,
concomitant with youthful confidence is youthful cockiness, and the letters reflect
this as well, most strikingly in upcoming letters to **Barbara Guest** and Philip Whalen.
By the end of the summer, Wieners would ask Robert Duncan to "have patience
with me," admitting he "might have started M too young. Let it thicken with me."[21]
But in just these two first issues Wieners was able to generate a great deal of new

---

21 Letter to Robert Duncan, July 26, 1957.

energy and work, giving many writers their first publications, including Kerouac's first poetry publication. Like *Black Mountain Review* and *Origin*, *Measure* offered a space for the widely dispersed New American poets to come together.

One of Wieners's chief concerns for issue 2 was expanding the field of poets beyond his Black Mountain and Boston friends, and so these letters from the spring and summer of 1957 are to an ever-expanding roster of poets in New York, San Francisco, and abroad. *Measure: One* was a sterling calling card, and through its published authors and his other new friends, he befriended others. He'd met **Allen Ginsberg** (whom he teasingly called "Ginsbergmessiah") on a trip to New York, kicking off a lifelong friendship, and through Ginsberg's prodigious contacts Wieners was able to bring in newly famous Beat writers like Kerouac, Burroughs, and Whalen—and through Frank O'Hara and **Donald Allen** he plugged in to new channels of the New York and San Francisco poetry communities.

In a 1982 class at Naropa's Summer Writing Program, Ginsberg remembered meeting the younger poet during this time:

> Wieners had come down from Boston and showed up in the Cedar Bar, with Ed Marshall, another poet, whose work is in this Don Allen anthology, *New American Poetry*. They were both gay. They were both from a sort of gay hustler's benzedrine maybe-a-little-bit-of-junk scene ... we were meeting in the ambience of Frank O'Hara. Frank O'Hara knew Wieners' poetry and thought it was very good, and Frank was sort of the arbiter of taste, a social arbiter.[22]

Wieners's letters to these young poets and writers, expanding out from old friends to new rising stars, offer a unique snapshot of these now widely known figures at a specific moment in their lives: they were all desperate for a break.

~~*

Charles Olson
[March 3, 1957]
[Boston]

Dear Charles:

I write wondering whether you are back, and to say that I am ready for you. The first spin is over, with the 1st issue paid for, or nearly will be, if I let myself believe it.

---

22 The transcript of Ginsberg's class was posted at the Allen Ginsberg Project as "Allen Ginsberg on John Wieners—part one" on what would have been Wieners's eightieth birthday, January 4, 2014.

I don't/work as though I had not a penny and every pitch is the important one. All kinds of squabbles already from the far country-side/ but none in this house. It is all mine, ME the first two letters, and the sure ty coming from the ears I ask to stay open. So I assume the responsibility and the labor.

Mine the arête.[23]

But of course Marshall et you and Michael providing the fluid. OK now the space is yours. And I tell you some random thoughts. The second issue MAGIC poems on the tarot? *the book of* dream stuff, archetypes drifting their long "garments," what else? So it doesn't go to press until July 1st, could you make some notes on magic? *Etc*

Then again, some translations of Frobenius?[24] Or is that walking in snow tracks, what about reprinting that article passed that spring from The New Age? And Larry Eigner[25] writes that you thgt. Origin 20 wd. have "a précis" of the history course you taught at BM?[26] So why not here? He wanted it, and others do. Me.

Some notes on BM? if you wanted to step into that. What you and Duncan were brewing last summer. You see, all I want to do is open to you that this space is open, that there is no limit, I put none and want you to know none. Instead of filling it up with scrappy little verse from BM alumni and Ginsberg's finds, two from you, one from her, three from etc/

make each issue a contribution/ I hate wedge, but that. Something that wasn't there before.

---

23 In "Maximus to Gloucester," Olson writes, "the only interesting thing / is if one can be / an image / of man, 'The nobleness, and the arête.'" *Arête* can be translated from Greek as "'goodness, manly excellence,' (similar to 'virtue')" (Butterick, *A Guide to the Maximus Poems of Charles Olson*, 608).

24 Leo Frobenius (1873–1938), German ethnologist and archaeologist whose ideas on culture were foundational for the thinking of Ezra Pound, who corresponded with Frobenius in the 1920s and 1930s and used his theory and stories of Africa in *The Cantos*.

25 Larry Eigner (1927–1996), American writer. Born and raised in Swampscott, Massachusetts, Eigner was nonambulatory, born with cerebral palsy, and his poetry and essays explored the universe from a unique perspective. He established lasting friendships through correspondence with many of the New American poets. Robert Grenier and Curtis Faville edited a four-volume *Collected Poems* (2010), reproducing Eigner's one-keystroke-at-a-time typescripts and making available his extraordinary achievements.

26 Wieners is referring to the course at Black Mountain in spring and summer of 1956 from whose notes would come Olson's *A Special View of History*, published by Black Mountain student Robert Hawley's Oyez Press in 1970. In her introduction to that edition, Ann Charters explains that Olson's ideas on history (and the stance one takes toward it) are integral to understanding the Olsonian—and Black Mountain—project, the same work that Wieners would continue after his terms there. Charters writes, "THE SPECIAL VIEW is a tangible fragment of the Black Mountain experience: It was at Black Mountain preparing THE SPECIAL VIEW OF HISTORY that [Olson] fully realized that *a man's life is an act of giving form to the condition or state of reality* (concerned obviously as a moving thing himself) *at the exact moment of his birth*—So therefore error or truth in the execution of that imperative is the whole shot!" (11).

With this kind of hammer in my hand, I get the fluid recharged over & over to attack fresh the problems of no money, no outlet, etc. And I hammer coin and outlet. Even POST VIRGINAL did it, and what Jonas showd me last night, and Marshall every weekend. So when you get the rest and time, drop what you think, and of course, as soon, the verse/s. The first copy must leave here April 1, and green, I gotta make the page. So at your leisure, or I could make the copie, and send you back the original, if you prefer.

I wd enjoy it more than you think.

Very fine, all this work, with sinus in the air.

Thanks for the scalpel to the poems

I had my session in the tarnished places too, last week in NY amidst dirty sheets, and has taken me three days to move at the local speed again, which somehow means faster, despite their expressed. Marshall though a grand delight, taking me on tours of his new-found knowledge, as YOU SHALL SEE.

Come on now with your load,

of love

John[27]

Allen Ginsberg [Tangiers]

April 15 [1957]

[Boston]

Dear Allen:

I wanted to wait until No:1 had happened, and done with money and contents before I wrote. It is & printer writes 'shd be a sellout if only by subsequent demand. But little doubt of it.' Advises I increase No:2 to 500 since it is to MAGICK: a handbook of dreams, the black & white voices of the enclosed and others: with a finger in the myth." That's on the back of One. I like layout if it don't turn out the queen, crocheting.

I am following up all leads in your letter, which boosted me greatly, and will write and get K's poetry from the man/ Perkoff sent a batch/ cd. only find one, he's

---

27 In the bottom left corner of the letter, Wieners has drawn a layout of the *Measure* cover with captions "BOSTON: ONE," "SUMMER 1957." He has written vertically along the left margin: "aquarterlyto&be-poem&/YARDSTICKTOTHEVERTICAL"

slow/ clogged in the stanza but nice jumping from 1 to another. Attempt at ritual, or something.

I am interested to have AGins in No:2 if you send it, give me a load to choose from, something contemporary with you now/ maybe a statement on the state of affairs? (That don't sound good)

And I will write to the others, I will try, if I find the money to increase the 48 pages to 63. A great deal of mss. But it's a lark to find out how few people can write and though flooded with crap, my own stuff seems to benefit, I do.

And I want you, after you get One, to let loose on its lacks, I am hot of course, to tell you what's in it, but want it to surprise, as it will, if only for freedom there. There are other queer shoulders at the wheel, or well. I will mail copy as soon as it reaches here, which shd. be early June, so if you change let me know somehow and it is for you people the thing is made. To put the excitement for you? I need it every day/ the push to say/ it's being done/ against the rest of the doing. And where? How often is it discovered, do I find anyone making it, the junkies just want to become vegetables, but maybe it's only this town.

I got Corso's book and like much/ and the queer poem better now, seeing it laid, and also Bird.[28] The one I read was unfixed, I imagine, and if you want to, contact any of these people per me, that I am open, for I give 35 hours a week to making bread for Mr. Fireman and myself, which leaves after 5 for Measure, which is shit of a way of life. Pound said the business is not something you do on weekends/ but after Sept. he goes to the breadline and I have the 40 hr. day back.

No gripes though as this year is the best one yet.

Olson back at BM, after SF and a week of lectures. He opens No: One: then Marshall et al., with Duncan ending.

I hope Tangiers is good for the line and that you can choke me with a load of your stuff/ and direct those you yourself are hot on to my stoop. But don't feel this

---

28 Jack Spicer's "Song for bird and myself" appeared in *Measure* issue 1. It is a dark poem, to say the least, beginning with the lines "I am dissatisfied with my poetry. / I am dissatisfied with my sex life. / I am dissatisfied with the angels I believe in." Robert Duncan's reaction was to be "angry at his doing that Bird thing. Most angry because his lack of Measure misused the given experience, which had yielded otherwise a beautiful poem" (August 25, 1957). Spicer was characteristically waspish about *Measure*, from its "littlemaggotish name" to Wieners's selections: "Wieners had had the nerve to reject Spicer's Boston piece, 'Poem to the Reader of This Poem,'" Ellingham and Killian explain, " . . . and to ask instead for 'Imaginary Elegies,' the suite of poems Spicer had written for Robin [Blaser], which he regarded as his best so far—and far too good for the upstart, no-nothing Wieners, who 'only understands Black Mountain poetry and Cole Porter'" (*PBLG*, 94).

last one a necessity, as if no word by, say, May, I will go after them myself. Am hot to give Lamantia[29] a space, a feeling I have here.

Thanks for what you have done already.

Yours,
John

James Schuyler
April 22, 1957
[Boston]

Easter Monday

Dearest Jimmy:

I still have sleep seeds in my eyes and behind them there are whirling things. This is ~~not~~ just a well from your letter, how much of a boost it gave me. I have spent the last few days addressing those announcements to every library that spends over $20,000 on books/ and the knowledge that there might be others / and you have their names makes me very joyous, sent their names. I am glad because if nothing Measure in intent is out to make ~~the~~ *a* measure for those who need it *us*. We're the ones who need the lift. The others got TV. We need elevators. Highheels?

Well, I have the drafts of letters I was going to write you about your poems. They are the last ones in the folder. The two I intend to use 'I think that we *(rich)* should get down on our knees and thank God we have money.' That poem has all sorts of Magicks in it. A nice statement. The magic of objects in it.

I have broken two typewriters. Of course if all the others reply to those announcements, there will be no copies left. The printer writes me I shd expect a sellout on NO: 1, if only by subsequent demand. But little doubt of it! Also to increase No: 2 as 'esoteric numbers' sell well.

I am most enthusiastic about you sending me your new poems. And I will wait until then before I return those of the first batch I won't use.

I wd. like to be in New York again. In fact I am awake from a dream in which a NY painter Michael De (something) was in my bedroom in Milton explaining a large painting of his that hung on the wall. He had once had a very intimate relation

---

29 Philip Lamantia (1927–2005), American poet and publisher born in San Francisco. According to his biography in *The New American Poetry*, he was "hailed by André Breton as an authentic surrealist poet; first appearances in *View*, 1943–45; broke with surrealism by 1946. Since then mostly underground, and traveling" (Allen, 440). His long-awaited *Collected Poems* was published by the University of California Press in 2013.

with F O'H and was waiting until I got packed because we were going to the Silver City together. But I dont remember any hint of a coitus between us.

He was tall, say and thin, with an Adam's apple and thin neck and Italian. Something I don't usually dream about as sexual figures. So it's very strange. A male muse? Anyway he had knowledges and I felt I very much wanted to go with him. In fact anxious because I was taking so much time in picking out the right clothes.

I will follow up this very morning with announcements to those you list. I wd. rather they had it than the University of Tulsa,
Yesterday was abcess tooth day but I am recovered. And wd. struggle up from a novocaine haze to address 10 more libraries and then back to coma.
[...]

Just a ps) I can't find the pen—

What Olson does demand of us is that we go back blind / have no rules but as he says those the poem under hand demand.

A very basic thing and the subject/ content of those poems becomes more immediate to us. Thus a poem on boredom—wd. have contained in it perceptions that all we are running over—we vitalize thru the process of running to catch up with what is going on at the act of writing. It cd take us over the precipice—vide Le Fou[30]—it cd take us to Babyland. Cd fuck up the sentence as we know it, as **W. S. Merwin** will never know it.

Bring an excitement form wise—not just word-wise excitement but the twist of the hip—even the way we walk will be put in the poem - it gets that basic. Should if we let it. Thus those damn readers get their money's worth. They meet us. Watch us dance.

———————

I am very happy right now.

Charles Olson
Thursday, April 25 [1957]
[Boston]

Dear Charles:

I'm on my third machine. Having busted two, the last two borrowed. So I got this tonight to send off the two enclosed and let you see.

---

30 *Le Fou* was the title of Robert Creeley's first published book of poems, in 1952.

Disregard the Holliday bit, as it went in as I was typing.

They are the strangest poems because they switch in my affections. Right now it is the short one I want to be a part of again. But they do have excitement and show a way for me, nothing excluded, in fact, the

white hand on

white stockings

said it so that I wanted to get these to you quick. As everything else about us.

I have not done a thing with the poems you blueinked, except that I go to that tunnel every morning & night, and at night I think of me in it, and the flowers and the boy advancing. You see if I start this, then I don't make Measure for a while

BUT WE HAVE PANSIES.

And the black magic is simply something I latched onto thinking you all wd. pick it up/ not my own, in fact no one's, as no one picks it up, objects in fact/

but another thing, I wd. like to have some Rumaker dreams, and have pushed him so that there will be. Great ones, if the letter that arrived with yours is any inkling. Oh, has he churned hisself. Black waters, so that I am filled, run over with them, am in accord with all he says from his self.

Do you know where the fairies have come from? Jonas. In fact, I send it along, as it is in the first issue, and it scares for what they can do by implication to you people. but I hope you say OK. Language. And I threw out the dedication, as we can't be that inread thing, I don't think. And the ending's nothing, except for Mr. Luce.

NO: ONE being printed, with the proofs shd. have been here three days ago. No word from Marshall, through the address which I list below is the same one I think you used except I put on Rm. 23. I have nor have any of us (jonas) heard from him since late February. Which is very strange.

I agree completely with the note, except that no one writes it. In fact, I find,

so few can write. I am flooded with stuff which becomes an awful weight, because I have to write back kind encouraging letters. There is always enough to encourage. But to write one as Marshall does, or as SPRING over and over again does, is very rare. In fact nowhere.

I still work a full week with 'the dear Harvard boys' which or who literally drive all the queer staff crazy, so much intrigue and foot tapping and shaking shadows on the walls and dropped trousers/ that we dash frantic all afternoon from one level to the next saying here comes scuffed loafers, or Miss Mulatto went in again, that each month gets more crowded, and they should have stuck to Weld Hall.

Achilles Fang[31] wrote also what do I think of the idea he does 'a small paper on Pound and Mussolini (20pp) . . . But I do not see any earthly use in such stuff.' Nor do I. Of course, we'd sell out and be assured for life, insured, but I think to have Fang wd. be good.

How it came about, was I met him in Grolier's[32] and he suggested to make the magazine, I include one big name a month, whether I like the poetry or not. I told him I wd. lose my enthusiasm, and he said nonsense, only one page.

So two nights later I wrote
're our conversation in Grolier's how would
you like to be the 'name' in No: 2.'

'You may get some translations from me after this summer' which I think would be good enough. I wd. like to hear what you think of this. I will see him next week and tell you then. Also that P & M is a temptation. As he might make it exciting. Then again it wd. be cashing in on something I don't give a damn about. But mss-wise I got some more Marshall for No: 2. And Jonas says he has two on the Tarot Deck (The Hanged Man) and (The Tower) and I thgt. I would write to Robert Creeley and ask him for some.

I also think if you want to do it, and send me a wide poem, I wd. send it first to Villiers and say can you print this as is, because I did go back to all those you mentioned to see the job, and they do cut it off/ but with enough voice at them, it does not have to be so in the future. Or they could be printed sideways/ the whole damn book. Then again, I know you have Evergreen #3 after you,[33] and that means

---

31 Achilles Fang (1910–1995), sinologist and editor whose legendary (among Pound scholars) 865-page Harvard dissertation was a study of every single allusion in the *Cantos*, which he did not publish for fear of offending Pound by pointing out errors with sources. He was a close correspondent of Pound's during the latter's incarceration at St. Elizabeth's. Asked for his opinion on including Fang's proposed essay in *Measure*, Robert Duncan replied, "This Pound-Mussolini thing is a dead horse. There is no issue in making Measure an agency for Pound" (Unpublished letter to John Wieners, 1957, John Wieners Collection at Syracuse University).

32 Founded by Gordon Cairnie (1895–1973) in 1927 using his own thousands of volumes as the stock, the Grolier Book Shop is a legendary Harvard Square haven for poets and writers that was operated by Cairnie until his death. From 1974 through 2006 the Grolier was owned by Louisa Solano, before being sold to Nigerian poet and Wellesley professor Ifeanyi Menkiti.

33 Donald Allen had written to Wieners in March, "I very much hope you will send me some of your poems for consideration for Evergreen Review. I think we'll be able to publish one or more in our third (next fall) issue, along with Denise Levertov, O'Hara, etc" (Unpublished letter from Donald Allen to John Wieners,

money, etc. so I would go there for as much as they want Still the hungry says there must be <u>something</u> left over.

I am timid to put my foot in [illeg] we plan this fall, Mike pulling out, and so many faces looking in the window at you, but Dana wd. never take Mexico (yet)
If you come to Boston, be assured any time this summer that you can have the use of this apt. all set up, for a couple of weeks, Dana putting out fires again on the North Shore, and I cd. live with parents or anywhere for as long as you want it here. It's two nice high ceilinged rooms, with kitchen and bath, and I guarantee you no interference of any sort, except the woman upstairs has heavy heels on the stairs in the morning. We live in a house built 1790, they tell me, and its all furnished.
And we cd. have a poetry reading both Boston & Cambridge, big ears here now. 2 (nearly three years) a long time to spread the word, but it's spread. and I'd get you a 100, at least. Though Dana says we've got to go to NC on our way out. So. ~~I have gone~~

Donald Allen
May 16 [1957]
[Boston]

Dana wishes a full month.
Dear Don:

Just to get things back to you quick. PLEASE care for the Olson as you say a copy aint nowhere, and I love it more than the rests, almost.
The THIS is accurate, setup etc, except in the fancy printing the left a 1/2 space after commas, and I tried this with no luck, *so* . . .
Also enclosed my copy of Olson's biography copied from source.
I have already written him re Evergreen 3 and I have a letter done today, so I will add news in yr note, at least jubilation over interest. Though thinking on, I don't know what his reactions are. *(Mine)* → Much respect for you doing it, not that in five years, he wont be there anyway.

March 11, 1957, Donald Allen Papers at the University of California at San Diego). Neither Wieners nor Olson appeared in *Evergreen* issue 3.

He also has a completed unpublished book on the later Shakespeare, (plays), from which he read one chapter in class. Excitements there, no doubt.[34] You have read his essays, I suppose, and Projective Verse, which really set new things, I am sure, in the Trail Blaser's air. Though Robin went one up, when he wrote O 'breath as texture' rather than Corman's 'sound' alone. So O came back strong with long excited letter, which will serve as another Maximus; at least Max gets in notes to Robin.

His Address is simply:
Charles Olson
Black Mountain College
Black Mountain, North Carolina

Also I have the old Twice-a-Years, oh fuck it, I aint no lending letter (library and I sound too fevered to go on.
                    Very nerve-wrack time, Steve [Jonas] being evicted, and having to appear in court Sat morning, his neighbors signed a petition on the 'music' he not owning a phonograph for 3 mos. And they trying to break into his apt. last Mon or Tues/ with a 2x4, smashing two panels, so now he bringing counter suit for attempt to do bodily harm etc (damages not to exceed 5,000 dollars) all this & eviction/ with Blas suffering appendicitis attack tonight/ and who knows what they'll find wrong (he dont eat) but yeast pills and bennies. So to stay/ one has to move
                    scratch the scalp
attempt to take giant steps, the cracks are that
wide
in the pavement.
                    But we'll all go to court Sat and stand there with Dr Fineberg across the room muttering, I'll get you out you black bastard, and red-headed George Murphy muttering,[35] they're the last of that bohemian crowd left over from last year, oh yes, we have grand plans for Mr Jonas, well,
                    we'll see
there'll be paideuma
        in the sky
bye and bye.[36]

---

34 In a footnote to Olson's essay "Quantity in Verse, and Shakespeare's Late Plays," editors Donald Allen and Benjamin Friedlander note, "Although his published output offers no hint, Olson worked assiduously in the 1950s to produce a book on Shakespeare—ten chapters are preserved in Olson's papers at Storrs. Out of that attempt came the essay at hand, 'banged out' in 1956" (*Collected Prose*, 431).

35 Apparent nemeses from Boston.

36 *Paideuma* is a term from Leo Frobenius that Pound uses to describe "the tangle or complex of the inrooted

Thanks for the subscription, gave me a lift, and write as you can from
Yaddo of the lovely ones,
Yes Frank has two full pages, from Second Ave. in Measure 1.[37]
      Our best,
            John

Charles Olson
May 16 [1957]
[Boston]

Dear Charles:

Just wanted to get this off to you. How this whole 'culture' wears on one (me). If I
did not have the knowledge of me at BM, could entertain the fantasy of shoving it
all and going off to 'the fabulous island' (Tiamat?) For even that sheepdip (BM's)
cant do it. We come soiled & needy, from our mothers the white living rooms and
it is piled on before our eyes/
                        are open, turned into consumers, customers at
a bad bargain basement. And of course, Measure means a kind of personal whip at
it and me. Now this sds. guilt-ridden etc. but not so—its that
                  when the talisman comes under the hand/ then one sees the
past filth of things of full ears & 'entertainment.' Too much lying back in the silk
cushions. And only when one is shook to see the struggle / just what's up and how
most of the time we aint up at it. Spend the day in a frenzy of waste.
Oh, I suppose they all saw this. Wordsworth too late and soon only I ask myself the
way out, like the bull.
                  How Measure obligates (the 10.00 more than before) and it
means I must reaffirm myself, you know, keep the blue eye
blue. And then again/ only
by staying in its midst and letting
the heart get a good, only by walking a sure foot
down the primrose path / only it aint inertia or sin
letting the energies be misdirected to the / or whatever, the passing
parade (no band)

---

ideas of any period." Pound insists, "The Paideuma is not the Zeitgeist"; rather, it refers to "the grisly roots
of ideas that are in action" (*Guide to Kulchur*, 58).

37 Wieners published "Section 9" of *Second Avenue* in the second issue of *Measure*; O'Hara's book-length
poem was released in full by Totem Press in 1960.

And the law you're under/ or were maybe gone now per Blaser's letter. Only I think often of where you can go and as you do, others take their lead. Let that be stated. I take the lead from footprints. Now anyways. That is why what you do this year will be a lead for many—what a burden, you dont want but such at is—MEASURE, a true wedge for us all to beat our space on- hobnail boots. Well, we do go on. And that's the wonder that each month seems to be greener, a new bush, than the last.

Yours,

John

[…]

Charles Olson

[Late May, 1957]

[Boston]

Dear Charles:

An instant reply (which I have been trying to write since I got yours at 6: now 8:15) That you seized on something wasnt there.[38] Blaser had showed me your letter (there was no one else to) and one has to share that kind, no? He even photo'd it to keep the pink paper in the house. Per it, I knew thou to be free. No more chain on the chain on the eagleleg. *This what I meant. And where shall he roost?*

And the statement: 'where you can go' really a question. For it has been with me, this where?—I entertain daydreams. nightdreams. Gloucester in the hand to give you! Last night, you in a gray silk suit, sitting, very long legs, and someone on my right (smiling, encourage, Duncan?) as I climbed onto your knee Danny Boy. Now that is the most embarrassing six words I have ever had to write. You were smiling also. Though later angry! though I dont remember naturally why.

Then last week, there was a cottage in Provincetown, a galleyinn where Dana & I usta go. And your new wife was there, a woman I had never seen before. You will laugh, but she was very motherly, and plump, hausfrau, hair pulled back in a bun, black hair, and full cheeks, loving, I kissed her on the cheek, she was making dinner

---

38 Wieners is responding to the May 15, 1957, letter in which Olson demands:

Please write instantly what you mean by
"And the law you're under / or were maybe *some how* per Blaser's letter"
please expatiate. Wld like very much (wld help) to know what you think I was on, & the other statement "where you can go" ?? WOW. Tell me. I'm—lookin'! (*"the sea under the house,"* v. 1, 32).

for us. Dana & I & Elizabeth (her name) and you came in from town/ and we sat down to eat, talking of old things at a wood table, the sea at the other end of the room, out the windows, and the waves breaking in the warm sound like they do at Provincetown under the house.

SO DAD, take it as you will, its there, Im afraid. But all right, I know, meant to be such, in fact, filling me with a surety.

Since last September, the two of us planned SF, after graduation, etc. A season in the firehouse. Then Measure happened. Now I dont want to bring it out to their laps. I want it somewhere like Boston, with an aura around it, what Boston has to them (all).

It has come to me that it is the internal 'city' that counts. The many mansions of/ and in me moviehouses. I dont need SF anymore. Nor have you ever.

In the silent films they used a technique called THE IRIS SHOT. Birth of a Nation!
    'Mothers & children weep while a Great Conquerer rides to the sea'

And the screen is black except for that woman & hers (1914) huddled left nothing else, then it widens & we are on a hill, its a mountain, and in the great valley below, as big as fingernails ride 5000 horses. The camera dont move, IT OPENS. And the cavalcade, even the lead(er) what is uncovered. And somehow I heard the sound. Nothing moves really, but the children getting in closer, lifesize, the bugs below moving out
                    Then the fist closes down again & we are left, as opening, with ma & kids.

COULD coming here be an IRIS PERISCOPE for you? That the countryside will be revealed. Except something must be offered. And to pull out in September, is nothing, a hack, as the goldgal says. It's a terrible problem pour moi, as has been all in which you are concerned. The each decision has brought knowledges (the consequences of each) I wd. be impoverished without.

You in New England will (would) cause a 'great stir,' that Maximus walks on his literal ground. In San Francisco, another displaced person. Then there's Mexico & Wenner Cren.[39] But not Maximus' land. Where the source is (not the honey nor the bees) that's where he's gotta go.

---

39 In 1952, the Wenner-Gren Foundation for Anthropological Research had awarded Olson the grant that made his Mayan research possible.

And source means return? The internal. Texture is determined by.
Structure.
    What ground its laid/
                    The sea under the house.
Now you mean by law weightier things than I did, with the legal.
    Your phrase in last letter I took my lead from:
           'Law/Property.'
But you come
try us.
And I realize the pressures on you, so I leave the lead
'the thread from the right shoulder. And from the forehead' 's YOURS.
But what we have here is also

[…]

I wish I cd. say what I think you was on, have only the result, here, since 1950. PV: that has been a law one learns like walking, with all that goes in learning such a process/ all fours, till finally you get to the knees on the other side of the room, AND HANG ON.
Deadline for 2 is middle June—if anything comes
Duncan: "Do try to get from Charles his
satyrs poem for #2."

Robert Duncan
May 21 [1957]
[Boston]

Dear Robert:

Could you please pardon haste here? I just want to get off to you how Measure 2 stands, or has its back up, but not against a wall, good?

A digression first? Yr statement on the personal ever since first quoted to me by Robin has of course been a thing in my mind (also I remember now at BM) Poetry not a statement of, or expression of self, but a participation in (is this right) the/ or/a created world.

Now this is hard on me, because I carry the personal so around me (not any longer the loveburden) I wrote O tonight, there is a larger desire to participate in, (but there was nothing I cd do about same until it had removed itself, this immediate desire) but I still have the personal/ personae?

That I believe & must state it somehow the objects of my world/ the belly grinders, etc compulse me to write of them, that we only have our own eyes, what their structure forces them to see, how some lights are shut out.[40] This all ties in with me as editor, that I cannot afford any partial vision, any personal one, and thus yrs against Spicer I believe in / BECAUSE I have seen it in action, know the (can I call it evil) source, the misery it feeds on, how it creates the situation to feed on, how it becomes homeless without same. And that it comes down to nothing more than ego, or self, & exploiting of same. 'Bandwagon,' beat yr own drum, etc. And if your own sounds hollow, then find a head to beat.

A heart.

An actual blood sucking, but this leads as in the case of Jonas' later poetry here to a participation in larger matters, that He (jonas) despite trapped always by this intramural play with whomever he is in contact with, has managed to create, rather, dredged up 'the mystical recurrence of things.'

Back to Jack: There is no excitement in form. His Song for Bird in Measure I is the most boring of all, in fact none other bore, even O'Hara, in his chi-chi, has a quality (you'll see) but Spicer lays on the page, no care, it aint ideas he thrills to, I feel its feelings only, where he has participated HIMSELF in like feelings. Rexroth[41] who's done more work, but who now really is nothing more than a performer. I think maybe none of us shd have success. That our word is waited for.

'the beginning again and the beginning again and again'
That never are we/ have we made it.
So much tho I have had to be taught. This business that this world owed me.

---

40 In a letter dated May 24, Duncan responded:

I'd say Wieners keep the objects of your world—just look at 'em straight on. Belly grinders, when all is in focus, is as real as trees. This focus, (a turning between subject and object; right declaration of where and when; exact placing and timing) needs more practice with belly grinders than trees?

What I sense as needed in your work is some not making too much of a good thing. Even perhaps an artificial impoverishment of wit (your mind is so ready with material) to begin with? (Unpublished letter from Robert Duncan to John Wieners, May 24, 1957, John Wieners Papers at Syracuse University).

41 Kenneth Rexroth (1905–1982), American poet, writer, and activist central to the San Francisco Renaissance. Considered the "Godfather of the Beats," he organized the 1955 Six Gallery reading where Allen Ginsberg first performed "Howl."

I OWE IT everything.

Well, these statements have demanded themselves, so they end.

[...]

Barbara Guest
May 23 [1957]
[Boston]

Dear Barbara Guest:

There is not enough. I have gone over them 3 times after receiving them & now again—different. This time their qualities are here for me much more. But I want more. Maybe this cannot be. That you are not structured such.

I give you your intent.

Also this is a liberty I take for you didnt ask anything still something compels me to write this out. BECUZ you've read me, I believe. Not sure of this, but believe so. Thus something has been created. Enough on cause.

It is the intent that these are intimate poems. Addressed to the cause of them. I suppose the 'prose' piece makes it more w/ with me. For the form of it. And the technique.

You arent particularly careful in it. As I sense in the others you care too much what happens—too conscious this is the poem underhand. We're young. We shd. take every chance in the world w/ the form. The painters do.

I also feel you & me weaned on different people.

Now today May 24

the prose piece comes thru so clear that I wd want to use it if you can send me more to fill out a bit. Not this/ but others of yours. If not at this time, I'll keep it & wait UNTIL YOU DO THEM. I am interested. Qualities I sense that are nowhere else.

The first 2 lines of Geliebte Frau and then are we eating lettuce, nein NO! for me.

PS: Also the 'to echoes in marble & grass' If that means what I think I love it but I cant be sure because you have just given me nouns could mean anyplace/where? Place it for us. This is not advice to rework these simply for when it happens again. How dense of me. You must have Verlaine[42] and I dont know him at all.

---

42 Paul Verlaine (1844–1896), French Decadent poet.

I have the sense that you and I are defeated before we even begin, that you will resent this, but I take the chance in case in case you dont.

Have you read Charles Olson's
PROJECTIVE VERSE essay 1950
Appeared first No:2 Poetry: NY (not london!) Jim Schuyler has my only copy—which he w/ return soon if you wd like, I wd gladly send same. Just for stimulus only. It's terrible to the touch, the paper it's on. Also WCW reprinted first 1/2 in his Auto-biography.

May I tell you what I think deters/detours?
Obvious invention.
            'singsonging'
I dont understand 'which you seek to transgress'
The ocean? She's gonna wade it?
Again/ we all 'breathe/ most necessarily'
                        There is such precise vision in all three. That these kind of vaguenesses interfere.

Now you are not at the place & time for the outside to be interfering like this letter/ but if you can, I wd. enjoy reading more and also knowing more who you are in communion with/ spirit-wise. Who are those ones you feel know the same ground as you. That is the exciting thing about the little you sent. The feeling here that you have your own ground. And I want to know more of it. I dont want to send you off to Magic but for a great many reasons Mary Butts—some novels—you wd love.

June 30

So you can see where I been these weeks: nowhere. New York once, for abt 24 highwalking hours.

Don Allen writes that you have done some beautiful poems/ Well, you just got to send them. And Jim, if you wd get after him, has done some very interesting ones, I will print in Measure II. You will forgive the delay, but I have been in a terrible funk, emphasis on terror, which tonight I begin to struggle out of it. And if it wd be not obligation on you, it wd give me great pleasure to have your new things. Have you also read:
Earnest Fennolosa's
Essay on The Chinese Written Character as A Medium of
    Poetry: trans by E Pound.

Jim will have a copy of this, or can be had from the Square Dollar Series[43] for $1.00. I can get you this. If you send me a Schuyler 'Truth Dollar.' Whatever, I have thgt about you often. A friend who read your three, said you are an excellent metricist.

        'I say to you, Ursula,

        There are immense problems,'

not for Measure fortunately, which goes ahead under encouragement from the entire countryside. No II upto 64 pages (wow) etc. But not a single woman yet, except two small poems of VR Lang.[44] So there is space.

My best to you,
    John W.
And be more prompt than
this one.

                          James Schuyler
                           June 11 [1957]
                            [Boston]

Dear Jimmy:

    Let me just say this off the top of my head, that you are going to have a tough time making it alone / verse-wise, there. Now, I dont mean you wont have ears, and people liking what you do, but you will not find many truly digging what you are trying to do. Frank & who else? They might like the feeling : quote, but why you write this way (knowing there is no other) they'll plague you, cause you self-doubt, being weaned on Poetry: Chicago. So this initially is to urge you to develop all you can yr resistancies, even—when you think you have made a real hit: send off to Olson,

---

43 The Square Dollar Series was founded by T. D. Horton, a disciple of Ezra Pound's who set out with bookseller John Kasper to print "little known works which Pound said were essential for every student," sold for a dollar each. Fenollosa's essay was one of six titles they published (Stock, *The Life of Ezra Pound*, 430).

44 V. R. "Bunny" Lang (1924–1956), American poet. At the heart of Boston, Chicago, and New York's poetry scenes—most famously mentioned in her friend Frank O'Hara's poems—until her early death from Hodgkin's, Lang was a poet who was known for her electrifying personality. She published widely and wrote two verse plays, both staged by the Cambridge Poets' Theatre, which she'd cofounded. Her work was collected in Alison Lurie's *V. R. Lang: Poems & Plays With a Memoir* (Random House, 1975).

for he is most open to any effort. Robin Blaser did just that, and rec'd back reams of stimuli. This is, only in case, you want to go back, to Tiamat, the easy couches.

USE, the man said, of yr self, as object, of the others as objects/ no hurt ego in the way, well, you dont have to worry here. That is more my kick.

I am most excited over what I call: yr market poems. That Christ, yes, this can be our gallery, will have to be.

That you are committed, involved & I suppose that is why the advice, because the involvement is such, you wd. go anywhere, where you think the green field is, & I dont want you in the wrong pastures.

PV set off a decade (1950 and MEASURE if my energies hold ~~on~~ *out*, will end it. We must see ourselves as the new generation, initially our youth in these ten years, &

if we survive,

after 1960, then we will be at the point of departure. As Pd, Wms, Marrianne have all departed bringing up their own wonderful gifts.[45]

Now is the time for the dredge, the pooling of energies, where we can learn to be sure.

Olson is one of our fathers, and those others are our grandpeople. It is a continuity. And that bastard strain of Wilbur, Booth, Hall, on and on and on, they are everywhere, a reversal, a falling away from the 'new' going thing. They must be ignored, as one wd imposters at a clan gathering.

This does not mean any sacrifice of individual quality, kicks, diseases, etc, simply that we are in agreement, these are here simply to be used, allowed in to lead us on. They the determinants. The individual perceptions, how yr eyes are like no one elses, and never should you look for someone else's eyeshade to wear.

Of course, it means continual work/ it sleeps, stays down, away from us, if we sleep. And so much has been done already, even the grandpeople still at times set the pace. It means exhausting all that they have, and still having enough to go on. That is why Olson cursed once, he only had his sixty or so yrs. Of course, he wrote first poem in mid-thirties, (his) so that is why he feels behind. Also of course, why he has/ does take such giant-steps. To catch up.

---

45 Wieners is contrasting Modernists Ezra Pound, William Carlos Williams, and Marianne Moore with "that bastard strain" of Richard Wilbur, Philip Booth, and Donald Hall, all institutionally affiliated poets heavily represented in the 1957 anthology *New Poets of England and America,* edited by Hall and famously exclusionary toward poets of that Modernist lineage.

[…]

PS:

How HUDSON FERRY on re-reading now 3rd or 4th time has all the qualities. That you need not worry about anything/ but sufficient work. That you strip until you think you'll have nothing left, but three lines, that you be tight, and when you see it, set it down, even if this 'it' is yrself, it does not need be 'objective' as Big Daddy tells us.

But in the act of it, pin down, and watching so all the loose material be cut down away, as Ginsberg aint learned yet, in his compulsions, that too much is there that dont matter to anyone but him. And that's wrong, becuz, stating them is not enough sometimes, as he does, that those myriad things dont even matter to him, because he has not taken the care to 'order the 'experience' to its own rules, its own syntax, jumps,

allow me to faint dead now. go home.

> *When*
> *can I expect more?*
> *As you do them, maybe?*
> *I cd. handle better than batches—*
>
> *oh—you make the rules—*

Philip Whalen
June 29 [1957]
[Boston]

Dear Phillip Whalen:

I'm sitting here, saying: Lets get this show on the road. Three weeks I've been away from Measure, for no reason I can find but it got too big for me, too many of you. So there has been a flight into Egypt, or the Rialto Theatre, somewhere, a lot of places, I wont remember.

You are the first/ on my return. And the hardest. The book opened that way. I very much would like to use a great deal of what you do in Measure. A going thing. From issue to issue, as you do it. However it comes to you. Not only the poem. But say reviews, bitches, COMMENT. Put the man in. I'll leave the comeback on this to you. But there is space for you & the others, as I tell them. We will last. A necessity here.

I have just re-read the poems, for I wd say, the fifth time. Over the weeks, much on my mind. But nonetheless, I cant bring myself to say: yes, they go. It's me you gotta make happy. And I aint. Not with yours, or the four Allen sent me, or most of Mr Snyder. Now what right have I got to say that. Me, I never, at least for months, wrote a poem that makes it as well, as ANY of these. That has the wealth these poems, esp. yours have. I'm not a critic. And they're not anywhere so near so I can even say what I dont like. If they were bad, yes, it wd. be easy, I cd. fill this space up what where you shd. go, what's not there, etc. but I cant. Because the poems don't allow it. The intrusion of my 2cts.

I know the process & I'll call it, the agony. How this, the poem, is the reason for all of us. I wish Measure I was in, & I cd send it, and it wd. say those things that please me in the poem, or at least expose myself. I intend to print a lot, that dont please me personally, & even if I never dig your work, which isnt so, as I do: SMALL TANTRIC SERMON & THE ROAD*RUNNER/ and a great many parts of both Sour-dough Mt. and esp. The SlopBarrell.[46]

So take this, as an effort on my part, I am not entirely equipped for, or equipped for, at all, at least this kind of letter. Being of no help at all/ only stating the wish that you will send for the two or three years left Measure, your poems as you do them. And I will print those ones I see fit, for Measure. And use you as much as you give yourself into my hands. Right now, I aint making it, with any of you. I hope you can see me thru this, that I am only asking more of you. Since I believe it's been demonstrated, there is. Right up to that fucking limit. I gotta end this, or Ill call you up on the telephone. Will you come back with your new stuff, no matter what?

> *My best to you,*
> *John Wieners*

> *I wd. use.*
> *And yours to me. (sure). And the 1st half of "Invocation & Dark Saying"*[47]

---

46 "Small Tantric Sermon," "The Road-Runner," "Sourdough Mountain Lookout," and "The Slop Barrel: Slices of Paideuma for All Sentient Beings" were all in Whalen's *Collected Poems*, published in 2007 by Wesleyan.

47 "Invocation & Dark Sayings, in the Tibetan Style," also in Whalen's *Collected Poems*.

Michael Rumaker
[July 2, 1957]
[Boston]

Dearest Mike:

Just the shortest possible to say: all is well, & that we leave prob. Sept 15, so if you smell an apt, do something, three rooms at least, oh fuck, we'll find it ourselves.

MEASURE I finally arrived, first copy, the rest coming by boat, shd be here anyway, & I'll send one. Measure II thus held up, so it goes out finally end of week, with you, & Creeley & Duncan. Charles (short poem) Kerouac poems, one great one by Duerden, Richard.[48]

Anyway, I am working, and writing poems like crazy, which if I myself ever got them typed up, would send you.

64 pages in Measure II, but I feel I told you all this before.

Reading: Sons and Lovers.[49] (still)

Dips into new edition of Rimbaud: Illuminations, also my heart is quite light and Boston has exposed herself, itself more to me in the last month than my entire life here, her people, alleys, dawns.

So I feel I'm up her skirt, and altho the dark terrifies, the night does, there is so much to touch, eat that I never knew before. The mornings on milkcartons down on Washington street, or from Balas's roof,[50] the junkies, and bums MINE, me swinging with them, as one, worth what one pays in physical losses. Thieves. We are them.

Let me get back to business, just wanted to send love and do hope we cross somewhere, it will be good to share what we both have come unto.

L—
John

---

48 Richard Duerden (1927–2000), American poet and publisher involved in the San Francisco Renaissance. Duerden's work was published in Donald Allen's *The New American Poetry*.

49 D. H. Lawrence published *Sons and Lovers* in 1913.

50 Tom and Jan Balas were old friends of Wieners from Boston who later moved to San Francisco. **Diane di Prima** remembers Jan as "very, very beautiful, very wasted, very patient and good. John Wieners knew many women like this and always sort of identified with them" (*Floating Bear*, 571) Both Tom (a very talented painter) and Jan (a poet whose work Wieners published in a special issue of *Floating Bear*) eventually cleaned up and led long lives.

Michael Rumaker
July 6 [1957]
[Boston]

Dearest Michael:

This will probably turn out to be a short note, but I want to write. For the past three weeks, I have been very sick, & I want you not to tell anyone there that, for I been flying high on wings not my own, anyway I dont think it wd be good for Measure if they knew I at times went on wing so far removed. Dana after graduation is back on the FireDept in Swampscott, so that means a great deal of time not here, and w/o my knowing it, this disrupted my work of the last three months so much I went out the window, so I wd stay up on pills for 40 or 50 hours: NOT doing a bit of work but wandering everywhere in the city, dredging, crawling in the gutters baby. Have been to my job abt 2 days, dont even know if I still got it, but think so, since they know I'm getting thru in Sept. they will have some patience with me. Anyway you go so low, you do hit bottom, and that is where I was yesterday: but dont think I'M silly, I got yrs yesterday and one from O, which lifted me enuf, so today I am somewhat restored, and after a bath & some food, I will try to return. Also got involved with a group of on again off again addicts, who have some glamour I am prone to.

Magick book not yet off, yet this too you must keep to yrself. It all works out tho, as Olson sent short poem which fits so beautifully. Marshall also called this morning, will see him tonight.

I dont know what else to say, but that we still plan to be there, leave here mid-september, and if you wd not find it an intrusion, cd find you in NM whenever, as we will go to Taos, & you will be somewhere near by. Anyway, Dana even knows nothing of this, w/o him I wd be completely lost, a fucking straw on the tide. With him I have a home, a pattern which allows work.

This letter will come as a burden to you, but I am alright now, so dont worry, & I plan complete retreat until I can leave this dying city. One thing, I do feel it most important that no one there know of this, believing they wd lose faith in Measure. Its first issue has not yet arrived, thru no fault of mine, as I have $$$ enuf to print 2, simply printer slack, but two weeks ago promised 1st copy here "shortly" whatever that means. This also has been a thorn, since I promised so many the 1st of JUNE. I will send it to you right off, and you'll know that things are alright here then.

I intend to stay completely away from any stimulant, and to bring myself up to the job underhand, it's just I wanted you to know my silence. Things are not well with you either *(I feel)* & I think NM a good idea, the city can be of no use to us. A place where we cannot see the process, which does not allow us part, so we go to those means which allow us, fake means to take part. The trip west will be good, slow, & of a purgative nature.

Yes, I use only Part I, I thgt that set.

It opens the magazine, darling.[51] Do write as you can, it is this renewing of old bonds that causes rebirth. A rebirth only in the sense that the sun is one. This dont mean obligation on anyone's part, but that we shd not despair at complete loneliness, becuz there really cant be any for us. Ultimate loneliness, yes, but not complete. Not full, only that the lower forces do invade with a sense of completeness, they dont really have.

I have made a copy of yr picture, and will return original as soon as . . .

Thank you for yr letter and do hope its soon we share only a meal together.

> *Love*
> *John*

I aint sad

Literally there are 50 letters to answer! Also there about 100 subscribers to Measure. Some tho for only single copies.

> *The Origins only cost $1.50*
What can I buy you. Poetry: Chicago,
for the other 50¢

> Robert Duncan
> July 26 [1957]
> [Boston]

Dear Robert:

Long delay due to making MEASURE II presentable also more to the truth: opening of Boston's secrets in a way not known before. In fact. I am / have been for the last

---

51 Wieners is referring to Rumaker's essay "The Use of the Unconscious in Writing," which led off *Measure*'s second issue. Olson called the piece "an ex. of true magick." Olson compares Rumaker's observations regarding the symbolic process in composition, where "beauty, like the sacred, is dangerous," with Jung's, concluding that "the process is symbolic (good enough, no need to argue—transfer of force 'a throwing together') but the material of the process is image. Which is what, as you know, I have always felt had to be insisted upon" (*Selected Letters*, 247).

month flooded with 'a disordering of the senses' that makes me believe in the Elect ('The secret's stashed & only I know where it is') both the damned & saved. Rimbaud: I alone have the key to this savage sideshow.[52] Boston is that now. A show of junkies, cocksuckers, outriders, THIEVES. But to get to business. All personal revelations can wait until October. Dana & I leave here at latest Sept 15. Measure One IN but bulk still arriving by boat (he says). All paid for & 1/2 sold out. City Lights[53] w/ stock 10 in SF. Its main joy to me is that room is left for II to show improvement. Not CONTENT*wise but editorial surety. And I w/take whatever chances with it in future open themselves to me.

[...]

> *much love*
> *John*

August 6

Much changes in my own life. Fired from Lamont.[54] Good. Measure can roll. I got to raise more money, & time now to do it. Start again from the beginning, as if making new.

Bulk arrived & all mailed out this afternoon. Say what you will, I will dig it the most, no matter if you only bitch. There's no reason why I dont bring in a whole new crazy crew in III, if only there were some kind of crew around. Bruce Boyd?! Arthur Kloth?![55] Barbara Guest?

---

52 French poet and *enfant terrible* Arthur Rimbaud worked out his notion of the poet as seer in several letters to friends. In one letter, to Paul Demeny on May 15, 1871, Rimbaud wrote that any true poet must "know himself completely," and to become "a *seer*":

> The Poet makes himself into a *seer* by a long, involved, and logical *derangement of all the senses*. Every kind of love, of suffering, of madness; he searches himself; he exhausts every possible poison so that only essense remains . . . He arrives at the unknown, and when, bewildered, he ends up losing his understanding of his visions, he has, at least, seen them! (*I Promise to be Good*, 33).

The prose poem "Side Show" in Rimbaud's *Illuminations* concludes with the line "I alone have the key to this savage side show" (23).

53 City Lights, an independent bookstore in San Francisco, founded by poet **Lawrence Ferlinghetti** in 1953. After publishing Allen Ginsberg's *Howl and Other Poems* in 1956, Ferlinghetti and clerk Shigeyoshi Murao were both arrested on obscenity charges. Murao's charges were dismissed, and Ferlinghetti was acquitted in a landmark trial.

54 Wieners worked at Harvard's Lamont Library from the winter of 1956–1957 until he was fired in late summer. In a later poem, "Dormant Lamont," Wieners looks back at this time in his life: "Poverty passes away, forgotten in splendor / of morning light, seen through a library windows' crevices" (*Selected Poems*, 257). However, as he indicates in this letter, the job afforded a great deal of time for reading, especially in the Woodberry Poetry Room, which already had one of the best collections of small poetry magazines in the nation. Wieners's study of these magazines informed and influenced the editing of his own small magazine, *Measure*.

55 Bruce Boyd (b. 1928), an important member of the Venice West community of Beat poets alongside Stuart Perkoff, who was included in Allen's *New American Poetry*. Arthur Kloth was a Berkeley friend of Jack Spicer's who, according to Ellingham and Killian, wound up relocating to New York.

Again, my apology on the omission. It negates so much, also highlights my own inertia. This is not directed to receive a denial of latter from you. I know.

HD's Sel Poems, now out.[56] What dya think? It wd be great to bypass it completely & still do The THREE BOOKS. Tho the last poem in Sel Poems is such a hit. Review worth it, just to quote it entire in Measure. Sorry on long delay, but have not been swinging on much of anything of late. Do write & send yr friends to the City Lights, tho more important, I lose money on bookstore sales, 40% discount, & Measure costs .60¢ to print. So have them send bucks here.

Please push Helen Adam so I can USE her in Measure
& have patience with me.
might have started M too young. Let it thicken with me

Michael Rumaker
August 17 [1957]
[Boston]

Dearest Michael:

Your red letters have been the utmost joy to me: the spontaneity of them, the actual taking that wide trip alone right in yr mouth, so there is a great tipsy joy/ delight even in the disgust, man, their almost good enuf to print, but you dont—no, we won't even go into it.

Anyway, thanks also for turning me onto Connie O,[57] as I sent her MEASURE, then one high afternoon, two days ago, I just walked into Beacon Press / and there she was at THE desk, and all was of the greatest order. I never sensed before her actual high-borness. An embarrassing thing to come back at her, probably, so dont, but I sensed it off so much of her. And SHE liked Measure, which was a surprise, when I knew that yr fuckin glassunicorntown wd. not. Of course, it's not yr town. I do hope you write what you once mentioned: thing on the myth of SF.

For you: dont be put off by surface qualities of M: One, as I repeat, it has a breadth to it. And not queer, as some think.

---

56 In 1957, Grove Press published the *Selected Poems* of H.D., her only American collection until New Directions' *Collected Poems* in 1983.

57 Constance Wilcox Bunker (1919–1975), Olson's common-law wife when Wieners first arrived at Black Mountain. Michael Rumaker describes Connie as sensitive and elegant, with "dark eyes that had an edge of sadness and inward contemplation . . . a delicate bird" (*Black Mountain Days*, 17). She left Black Mountain with her daughter as Olson's relationship with Betty Kaiser became apparent.

That has no weight here, the queer. There is so little actually to choose from, if say, Olson doesn't come thru/ or if one believes in making *it* on strengths not already used by other magazines.

Stop the defenses, John, it's not needed. Two will be different. Of more substance, I think. No MARSHALL, who is now asleep five feet away, do you have & will you be willing to give over to me the 8 pages of copy you made from his TUG OF WAR? He found 3 himself of what I think was a 20-page poem.

Also, could I have all mail after September 15 forwarded care of:

Rumaker

1130 Sacramento

San Francisco 9, that is, upto the 1st week in October or maybe a week later/ but other than this; collecting it out of box, I wd put no obligation on you. If you say yet, do you have a reliable box? As checks arrive say twice or so a week, only $3.00 ones, but what makes M. *real*?

And then: there wd be an absolute deluge of bookclub circulars, bills, maybe a few books, other mags, & letters, a few. You really are the only one I can think of with trust. Somehow I wd rather keep my personal away from Robt. Not that I have any reason to say that. but our judging days of each other are done. And his of me are not, or mine of him. Joe & Mary F [Fiore] were here, but did not see them, Connie said they spent week at Wellfleet, and wdn't it be great if she wrote? I am after Connie too, but I doubt she will. She started going around, taking books off the shelves for me, & sent me out on wings. She said: drop in here anytime; I said, if you are sure it's not an imposition: she said: dont be silly, imposition's a pleasure.
I got fired two weeks ago from Harvard, and god, I am writing or just stopped two days ago, like I never have before.
[...]

Charles Olson
Wednesday Aug 21 [1957]
[Boston]

(isn't it wonderful the mail's so quick)
Dearest Charles:

The PM shadows make wings on my floor: because the pleasures from Measure are PM, &

so many after the exhaustion of the last two weeks, which I have worked as never before at the poem/ failed to come thru with the light word, the dawn

But it's 5 pm and the word makes activity in the room.

YES, of course come in this Sunday night & bunk over. We'll talk & etc (depending on you & yr weight then stay here as →*love* lord of the house & have Kate[58] in for breakfast [. . .]

Marshall was here last weekend/ and is due in again for this one, but I will find out tonight when definitely, he'll be here. (You can be here alone Sunday or have him—Blaser—Jonas in to see you, whatever) I myself found much wrong with ONE, & hope Two of a wider reach.

Also our itinerary at Sept 16 takes us down to some Civil War battlegrounds/ so maybe we can meet again at Black Mountain;

that doesnt mean I'm gonna let you off seeing/ me here.

What shd be in Measure is the short swipe: the rabbit punch, so I do hope (god how much) you use yr dump truck, back it up here

I got poems maybe so UP; anyhow they're where I've never been before.

In fact I been as free poem-wise/ time-wise   cock-wise

She runs for me in August.

You certainly is a traveling man. Marshall moving back here is set to do his escape from hell, the word on his season, there. So maybe you is the bug for his ear, in there.

My love, & welcome home.

JAWN

Please use me NOW anyway I
can be of help—

---

58 Kate Olson (1951–1999), daughter of Olson and Constance Wilcox.

Robert Duncan
Aug 22 [1957]
[Boston]

Dear Robert:

When the phone rings & it says Hello John this is Charles, *it's a special night, wow—* he's in Gloucester and will stay until middle of Sept, then back to BM for business, then I imagine, becoming a NEer; so I leave town: but it is happiness he's here and also a pain, that one *must* take him on his terms and that there is so little time. But I will spend a few days in The Fishousetown: and work on the structure of Measure: what he is already riding on he said was the City-State issues, but I think too those other demands disperse him.

Yr letter is of such importance that I wd like to print it totally in Measure. Do you think this alright? of course, I will be there by the time III has to go off, so if there are deletions etc, you can tell me. It fits better in Four, with Ginsberg's which is of such a different order, namely only a definition of self, his is, his image of himself as Napoleon poet: while yrs is concerned with the process, how we must use ourselves. *The state of the poem—*

I think personally for you, that you/ we must go where our <u>likes</u> *in yr sense of conviction* are, where we are freest formwise, where the wings can have their full spread: that is what I look for: breadth of a man's reach, how much his eye can hold, the 'direction of will' so if I was say: a lover of poetry only, Measure wd offend me, but if for my practice, I realized the moist ground of the thing, (which Spicer, is not particularly fertile) then I wd say; I must put my hands in this, altho it looks like shit,

it is where this new grows, & where I must, if I am to survive. I have no choice but go here. Measure is edited simply by my conviction: and it is and always will be: a thing of process also, that it is opened onto new territories by nearly every one of yr letters, that others must see as you is I think reason enuf to print yrs of the 18th.

The beginning of 3rd paragraph was simply to say: dont push yrself to a ground, where the stench is so bad, you will die, where yr Green Lady has no field to ride. For you have been able to match the both grounds in yr stride: & this of course is what makes you of Measure to all of us.[59] Those who cant shd be included in Measure, I

---

59 In his last letter, Duncan had urged Wieners to "use MEASURE to shape what poetry will be.

I don't need to tell you this—one thing is clear to me, and that is that your sights are set on THE WORK; that you lose interest when the focus is set upon writers trying to make a place for themselves.

agree, simply because our country at times is pretty stark, savage neonwise (Helen has the moon) languagewise—but Spicer's Bird is a rare one for him, he wont find that one homing unless he admits it might be over in our land. & of course, he fails on both sides/ but less in Bird than in any other of his I read, still Psychoanalysis I think his best. Then Bird.

Spicer shdnt really come in because he is limited on both counts: his structure wont allow in what his (ego) dont 'like.' Olson shut out, Creeley, anything BM; but anything that gives pleasure or pain to him: where he can identify, yes—that's for me, that's poetry; that's why we dont talk abt poetry anymore, it is so filled with this kind of sick bird, looking for songs to accompany them down to hell, men's rooms/ or into the arms of 'Jesus;' looking for messages with the sound they have on their own personal 'phonograph records.' I dont think we shd put up with their opinions, weights, etc. any longer.

That it must be the poem, the 'health of it' we are digging,
They're sick: (the word) their use of it abuses—also their "love" & conviction (they have them) is abused, but we cant be infected.
Again it is by our language we show, make manifest everything. That it is in our hands: that we constantly fill it w/ life, jumps, / creating the patterns in it, we see around us: and these patterns are not rymed couplets or always correct grammer, or measured lines, sometimes even obscene patterns, that shd not be doing what they do, have no right, sucking the life off others: all these we have to include.//
Also the neat formal ones. But everyone thinks there wd be no place for that in Measure / did they read Dorn, / or that we're queer, did they read Olson/ that there is not enough substance/ did they read Duncan/

Olson said in that letter to RB:[60] 'And the problem, anyway, is reality and language, any use of it—' wait, I'll go on and give the rest of it: it's that important if the attack there gets too strong on M:

'And the problem, anyway, is reality and language, any use of it—a use of it, not just a poem. Lord! If we wrote a poem except both (a) to write a poem and (b) because we cant help to, and breathe!

I shall continue to send you (as I do to Black Mt. Review) the central work. With the joy, for me, that you demand it. Let's ride the outer edge of the risk; the central work does. It's the peripheral (like my Green Lady in Botteghe Oscura) that rests in the sure thing of the accomplished (Unpublished letter from Robert Duncan to John Wieners, August 18, 1957, John Wieners Papers at Syracuse University).
60 The remainder of this letter is quoting a May 3, 1957, Charles Olson letter to Robin Blaser.

Wow. I sure say breath, like testing whether a person is alive, on a mirror, does it show, I mean not the mirror, it is now opaque, there is fog on it, this girl does breathe! Aint it the greatest?

Esau's hand, as well as Jacob's, as well as : hair on it, or not, but that the word or not the word in that moment—"space"—is right. C'est pas le mot juste, c'est le mot shaggy ou glossy, le polysyllable ou le monosyllable.'

[. . .]

Charles Olson
Tuesday Aug 27 [1957]
[Boston]

Dear Charles:

I meant to write yesterday (Kateday / but 5–10 mins after leaving you, I was in Criminal Court, waiting to make perjury for a friend who got tossed into a pit, etc. by thugs & I was 'eyewitness' supposedly.

Then came home & there was a letter from Marianne Moore: & I quote from it for you.
"I really benefit by:

I have no longer any excuse (Charles Olson)
for envy. My life

has been given its orders; the seasons
seize

the soul and the body and make mock
of any dispersed effort.
also: Spring: we salute you
  season of no bungling* (without capitals at the first of the line."

(she goes on)
"A (moral) sea-roll in the gait is better for seamen than for poets but I
like: 'Put crumbs on the outside of the window

Let them
(Jack Spicer).   come outside."

In any case, I enclose a dollar for a copy of the next issue."

Etc

(Then Ps)
"I think (I think
spring bungles more than any other season; but the concept is sound.)[61]

So all reports on Variations sound success: no negative ones/ yet all have dissonant
voices on other contents. Where one praises/another damns.

After the letters; I wrote some; then mailed them and then spent four hours at library:
tracing Amphetamine sulphate & dextroamphetamine sulphate:

Benzedrine & Dexedrine which I hope I can make a poem out of.
Also Wallace Gould's[62] APHRODITE which I got from A Rexroth Review on
the micro-film while tracing Benzedrine in the NY Times. He said only WCWms
& himself remembered who Gould was.   GOULD writes a long prose line
(BUT not cumbersome or syntactic particularly, retelling the whole herstory of
Aphrodite in the 1st PERSON
      'I raised my hands to my hair to pull it. I drew
all my heat to my eyes.
I glared, glared at the very godhead.
'Lowering my head, lowering it lazily, I met his glance. I peered
   out through my hair, which, disheveled,
hung to the floor and lay there, curling, lazily even, or fancifully thus,
much like many a golden serpent, gorged. The eyes of the godhead glittered.'
Also amphetamine has one of its roots named after the Temple of Ammon: Jupiter's.

---

61 "Season of no bungling" is the last line of Olson's poem "Variations Done for Gerald Van De Wiele,"
which was published in *Measure* issue 1.
62 Wallace Gould (1882–1940), American poet whose *Aphrodite* was published in 1928 and praised in *The
Dial* by William Carlos Williams. In 1917 he wrote *Children of the Sun: Rhapsodies and Poems*, a volume
dedicated to the work of American artist and poet Marsden Hartley (1877–1943), painter of (among other
places) Gloucester's Dogtown, memorialized in Olson's "Letter 7" of *Maximus, to Gloucester*. Hartley
responded with a glowing essay calling Gould "The Poet of Maine."

Then I came home, much un-Zeus-or Jupiter like & fell asleep until noon today.

But your thoughts/words on the practice have been beating in my head these two days. And I grope, for you shall see from these poems enclosed, what I attempt I make at the line, & it springs directly from PV: from yr practice, which[63] even two years ago you had doubt on:

After the Post-Virginal. When you said backyard of Mt Stream (Spring '55) that you wondered abt PV. But it *becomes* a bore only in the hands of those who ill-use/ abuse it, that anything does!

a dress, a song or a way of wearing the hair, once it falls into the hands of anyone but him who first made it. Others may learn from it, but they have to make their own way / whale's width.

The derivators, imitators do that/not at all: what Pd calls:

diluters.[64]

After the "1) Inventors (they found a new process"

in the 5 & 10¢ store

'found' in the sense of country, nation?

"2) The masters (who combined a no. of such processes)" & governed.

Let Measure stick here/ be glued in this NE where it all began, we think. I gonna put #3 back at 48 pages just to be sure.

I'd rather have his Number 4: "Goodwriters without salient qualities ... Ie men who wrote sonnets in Dante's time, men who wrote short lyrics in Shake's time."

than have it stuffed with 'men who came/ (come) after the 1st two kinds of writer, and cldn't do the job quite as well.' What we got now: both country & poem.

Well, enough quote job. Let me just apologize if I have put too much pressure on you, (that I was taught quantity) & the letters some day after daying, Olson prose like in Origin! etc. Olson this, weight they want. & from what other hands?

But this kind of talk is added pressure, simply that 'you dont know until the

---

63 Handwritten arrow from "which" to "PV."

64 In *ABC of Reading*, Ezra Pound identifies six "classes of persons" who create literature. After the Inventors and the Masters, he lists "The diluters. Men who came after the first two kinds of writer, and couldn't do the job quite as well" (39).

involvement of writing it.' And this enuf reason for any man to hold off: until he is sure he can swoop in & smack that whaletail into the surface.

           Somehow I guess initial point of this was: dont allow yrself to go dry in the face of what 'diluters' have done to yr practice. That since it is yours, it does not bore us. (That PV is not a bore, nor Maximus,) that Eigner is not, nor Dorn: *who have learned from it.*
      That since we possess ourselves, there is no problem, but the one of being involved in writing it. And the hangup at BM holds you from this, & not a very perceptive pressure at this end <u>does not</u> let down the channelgate.
           Out to see again! So for my own mind, let me remove obligation commitment here until YOU are <u>free/out</u> to make same.
      Tho when I have been most committed against my will (I thgt at the time) it has been fruitful.

Well, I enclose my own. I shd wait until I can read them aloud & if you'd rather do that, we can. Form-wise they will bore: but if you do read them: plow thru abt 3/4 & I think they get better: maybe beginning with the Rimbaud one.

(I remember they disconnect the phone here <u>Sept 3</u>, but not me until Sept. 15. So if you pick the day (anyday) then I can come there, or you here, & if you have a big breakfast, I will- or may I- take you to lunch?
      Copley Square's the only place left, or Roxbury Crossing.
        Love
[…]

                         Michael Rumaker
                       August 28 [1957]
                          [Boston]

Drest Michael:

How long has it been, & now they're done, 1hr ago I decided to go & have sex to celebrate but I didnt know & now I'm back: 6 AM

    With a beautiful Boston AM, one of the few left, I thgt at least there wd be something on the strts. But all I got is Fats Waller
Godarn gal: yr socks dont match/

baby what happens, yr socks etc.

So Charles is here:

26 Fort Square, Gloucester.[65] Please keep this address quite to yrself, as I'm not sure I'm even supposed to give it out, but I know he wldnt mind to you. He now is in Maine for a week with Kate & I also have you to thank for setting me into Connie, she is such a delight, altho wont see Charles; so I was runner last Monday morning of Kate from her at South Sts. to him at North Sta. Kate is beautiful, blond streaked hair & skin like toffeecream, etc. One front tooth out. Connie's face is a little looser, but her mouth & eyes & hair are lovely, that open face is still upto yrs: also there seems a more relaxed way abt her, at least I am more so with her.

If you ever get drunk & want to call, her number is North Scituate 2162 W—*telephone*
Bull Rush Farm
No, Scituate, Mass.

Again: Gloucester is on the North Shore, & Scituate is on the South.

I am sorry abt the poems: there is no pleasure left in them for me at all, only a lot of wasted labor as I see it now. Still they get better as they

progress. They are a series: something like a HORN SET IN BOSTON, or

It's parttime, kiss off Boston, etc. I dont want to go, but before I go behind bars, etc. I better [..]

Also the Spicer he said: ' personally authentic, witty, delicate.' All makes me think Charles gives little care to 'form' tho that doesnt hold as he is hung up now: that the diluters of PVerse have made his practice a bore. That only the formal interests him or the wide long line, as 'wide as a whale's tail'

But this has been building in him a long time: I can remember him expressing dissatisfaction with PV Spring 1955. Then too, he has always been partial to long line. Wldnt you say. The Causes?

Maximus loaded, with them.

---

65 Olson rented his Fort Square apartment from 1957 till his death in 1970. Peter Anastas writes that Olson "demonstrated that by living in a book-filled $28-dollar-a-month cold-water walkup at 28 Fort Square, on Gloucester's waterfront, one did not need to possess material wealth in order to pursue a rewarding life" ("Olson Is Gone, But We Are Here).

It is his breath. But I too think when D Allen begins using broken lines, it's time to stop. That the diluters, bore, because they mis-use, abuse, like somebody who sings a song meant for Gert. Lawrence,[66] that only she cd. do, they cant, they bore us.

Thus the same in craft. And why the maker's use of it is of matter.

As you can see re enclosed, I am still a diluter, trying to break out. But at odds, just where.

And O says you dont know until you get involved in writing. He's gone to Hellman's but he plans to have me up when he gets back, I hope it works out,

tho I feel very uncomfortable at No Sta, at a loss for the 1st time, but it is Measure maybe stands between, that I cant take his non-submission of material, very graciously. That I will try, & let him work it out, OK, when you think how little were in the 1st 2 BMR's even. BUT CHRIST, HE'S THE ONE WHO TAUGHT US QUANTITY.

That goddam BM business stands in way too, & he has to go back Sept 15–21 but we'll go too; I am getting to be a shrew, & I wonder how close I am to insanity.

And Marianne wrote nice comments abt O & small little remarks. But also $1.00 for second issue, so I am very pleased, there. & Duncan is much involved, and [**Michael**] **McClure**, has changed his mind, I hear, & we plow on.

When I see you, all this crap will have gone out of my system/ purged by trip across. USA. And I will come clean, onto those glasshills.

Thanks for so much, that I feel you are a force behind, & positive thrust for Measure, for Wieners,

and photograph enclosed. I had copy made, but will have to wait until later, for loot, & time to do it.

No loss, I dont feel.

---

66 Gertrude Lawrence (1898–1952), English singer and star of musical theater, originator of the lead role in *The King and I*, a lifelong favorite of Wieners.

Charles Olson
Sept 22 & 23 1957
[New York City]

Dear Charles:

Just back from 8 hrs with *near* every book S Noah-Kramer[67] ever wrote, at NY PLib. Except he aint no noah. I cant understand why the Sumerians did so little for him, that he can impose on them: find as fault their lack of 'epistemology' cause & effect, 'logic.' Of course, this is mainly From the Tablets of Sumer (Falcon's Wing Press 1956) & it is a write down. The one done 12 yrs earlier, which I hope I'll get tomorrow, for the texts (translations alone), *better*. that's the only value of his labor, what he makes available. Not one phrase from the man himself. Which is harsh, but 8 solid hours, is too long to be kept waiting. When I should have looked only for their words.

I remember some of the loveliest poems being told by you before. When Inanna lost it in the garden.

The main purpose of this is to serve as cover for the enclosed, which is the prize. They told me you wouldnt have reproductions in the house, but I want you to see this anyway. So lucky to have it *at* all. The original is possibly a 1/5th larger. Beside it/ the only other of his I could find: THE PRESENTATION IN THE TEMPLE. Would you say that is a capella in the upper left corner of PARADISE?[68]

I spent last night again on da capo & it is much better. But still want to wait a few days before sending. I want you to know how much I feel *you* laid on me (out for me) last Tuesday *& Wednesday*. The Rimbaud *of mine is* not improved turning into ~~paragraphs,~~ *form like Illum*. but da capo has come full swerve *from this* ~~that's~~ it's more packed/ but no immediate hooks for any reader, *I fear*.

I have thgt. too along the way, that Orion: O'Ryan[69] is of the secret of secrets. I want

---

67 Samuel Noah Kramer (1897–1990), Ukrainian American scholar whose work in Sumerian mythology was integral to Olson's sense of history. In 1949, Frances Boldereff had given Olson a copy of Kramer's "The Epic of Gilgamesh and Its Sumerian Sources," and he was "launched on the path that, after eighteen months of further work, would result in the essay 'The Gate and the Center,' his first formulation of the postmodern, with its thesis: 'the archaic sought'" (Maud, *Charles Olson at the Harbor*, 81).

68 The reproduction Wieners enclosed was probably of Giovanni di Paolo's 1445 painting *The Creation and the Expulsion from the Paradise*. Di Paolo also painted *The Presentation in the Temple*, which Wieners discusses with Olson in a letter dated September 30, 1957.

69 Olson's poem sequence *O'Ryan* was published in two editions in 1958 and 1965 by Joe Dunn's White Rabbit Press. "O'Ryan 8" describes a young man "all lit up / like a pinball machine // a son of the working / classes" (*Collected Poems*, 327). Poet and scholar **William Corbett** recalls a visit in the 1960s to Olson in Gloucester in which he commented on *O'Ryan* and the striking image of the pinball machine, at which

you to know this, that whatever I might stumble on shall not be revealed. I agree, you pass it through the work, until someone else ~~makes~~ *breaks* its surface *or //* thru their work *//* ~~then no one~~ *into the source.* ~~else shall be turned on the stars~~ *until then no one else shall be turned your stars* (i.e. *per me).* I can find nothing encouraging out about Capricorn, & wonder how I should have adopted him, so strong. Only the horn, and the Blood that breaks thru. Like Dionysius.' No ATTENTION AT ALL TO RITE IN Kramer! Which is what I want. Dates, and objects, and how often and many. Like we have it so clear from the Indians, the little I know. Orion can lead you. (I only read #2); leads you into as much field . . . "Capricorn is part of the earthly triad; it is the place of the creation of Saturn (with Aquarius); it governs the thighs and knees." I wd rather be under Aries' horn,

(OH YES: it is covered wagon:)   Perseus and mother put into chest and thrown into the sea, the children (Zeus, etc) of Uranus imprisoned in the body of their mother, the earth. That is an actual: ←*chronos*

        reverse-apochtastasis[70] (?) fact

          (happening).

Or am I taking it wrong. That being locked
up with them, does not prove they are carried
in us. Except we know they are. I wrote something
long time ago, (12 mos.) about the way I hold my cigarette like She does. ~~over~~ *to
Page II*

And I will send that. Once I can get a corner *out* there. Also on the Boston train from Gloucester, I wrote like crazy, which I'*ll* send. Maybe the cigarette one tonight. Just throw it away afterwards.

Did you know this? I dont see how *so confidently now* but it does bring Pharmakos: Fool together, a little.

"Hebrews knew him as Kesil, the Foolish or Self-Confident, or as Gibbor, the Giant, identified with Nimrod and tied to the heavens for impiety."

"Olson clapped me on the back and exclaimed that I had seen the poem's center" ("A Letter from William Corbett").

70 *Apocatastasis,* the Greek concept of restoration or restitution, as in the reappearance of the sun and moon after an eclipse (in Plato's *Dialogues*) or the reconstitution of the body after death. Olson will refer back to apocatastasis in a "birthday poem" for Wieners in his January 15, 1958, letter (*"the sea under the house,"* 2:6).

And "Peruvians believe a criminal held in by two condors"[71]

This morning with the dawn I went out and begin walking up
Fifth Avenue from Washington Square, where they yelled at me: " Oh Ham-let!
Oh phelia "

but I went on from one window to the next, passed along. Until I came to Tiffany's
#727, and they have *a* relatively small window for jewels, etc. Only each one had
every detail like an undeveloped negative drops OF THE ZODIAC. It filled six
windows. It is simply that, I think. A process used on ~~an~~ *some* original MAP, but I
am going back tomorrow, Monday. And try to talk me into one, which I will send
to you. It was as laid */more than eye wants /*out *like* Roxbury-Malden ~~in~~ Earth's orbit,
ecliptica, and precise drawings of every constellation, the 1st and 2nd magnitudes
carried jewels (well, the first one of any sort of the sky I have ever seen.) That the
face on the prow of ARGOS is you*!* The mouth no, not as much.[72]

The sun does enter the world again under our sign, but Aries it says 'early mythologies
identify the Ram with Zeus, with AMMON, the ram god of Egypt.'[73]
    And look, why RA died. But you told us that before. I have my parents, both
kinds. It's the Grand ones I'm looking for, that it is the time now for them to begin
to *hide* or as Miss Stein:
    "When I grow up, you can be the old Grandfather and ~~come~~ live with us!"

This is all there is on alan as I first got it. But I find now: the Hebrew means (tho
out of use): small-eared dog.
    "alan Tinguian (Philippine Islands)"[74]
"Spirits, half-human, half-bird with toes and fingers reversed. They are sometimes

---

71 Wieners is quoting from a 1953 book on UFOs by George Hunt Williamson, *Other Tongues—Other Flesh.*
   In it, Williamson writes that the giant Orion, also called Kesil, was envisioned by ancient Peruvians as "a
   criminal held in the heavens by two condors" (382).
72 The prow of the *Argo*, Jason's ship in Greek mythology, was crafted from the magical wood of the forest
   Dodona, and was capable of speaking and prophesying. After its mission, the ship became the constellation
   Argo Navis.
73 In the first book of H.D.'s magisterial *Trilogy*, after repeated prayerful *amens*, she plays with the associations
   of that word by invoking "Amen-Ra, / *Amen*, Aries, the Ram; // time, time for you to begin a new spiral."
   After reminding readers of H.D.'s abiding fascination with astrology, the readers' notes of the first New
   Directions edition add that "Aries, which in Latin means 'the ram,' is a constellation containing the stars
   of the spring equinox, and is the first sign of the Zodiac. Early mythologies identify the Ram with Zeus
   and with Amon, Ammon, the ram God of Egypt" (H.D., *Trilogy*, 180).
74 The Alan is a monstrous spirit from the mythology of the Tinguian tribe of the Philippines.

mischievous or hostile, but are usually friendly.*(?)* They are described as hanging, bat-like from trees and as living in forests. In Tinguian mythology and folk tales they appear as foster-mothers of the leading characters and are pictured frequently as living in houses of gold."

Also now that I think of it, ~~that~~ *our* goat must come in with some blood *on his hoof or horn* from the sacrifice of the king → *of Saturn* the very ~~day~~ same day → *or one before*. Again, tho, I mix the movement of the stars, with myths surrounding them. That the bird <u>alan</u> might have something hidden in the <u>salaman</u>-der "sometimes a bird, living in fire"

And Rigel (you again must know) sometimes is The Foot in the Mud also known as The Double Axe.[75] That I just see this: "In astrology, Capricorn {→ *I somehow see him (Le Fou) as unable to fall—unless he cuts his own foot off*} is a feminine nocturnal sign, movable, cardinal, and melancholy, and in nature, cold, dry and earthy. The mansion of Saturn and the exaltation of Mars"[76] (All those adjectives, I mistrust it.) *Plus I don't like "her" clothes*. But there are leads.

I will keep you posted. When they reach a 'completion.' And wonder if you ~~know of drop that~~ *shall* ~~drop~~ thgt abt SHE WHO ITS AT WILL, → *with its drop = there will be only yr handwriting = which is not fair to you* ~~and there will be nothing of you in Measure #2, which is not fair to you as much.~~
~~Is there any doing that could strengthen Dscentus Spiritus i,~~ That lost business on Capricorn might——*turn/up?* but you probably think I'm trying to angle in ~~on that.~~ *yr friends* ~~So dont feel you needs answer.~~

I have wondered often if I revealed a different Jaw

I never will // altho there is great joy when I feel [come?] to the same "(wisdoms)"
- I.e. alone
The "dead" hits

---

75 Another reference to Williamson's *Other Tongues—Other Flesh*, which says that "in North Africa, the stars in Orion emerge from a muddy well, and Rigel, the last star to rise above the horizon, is the foot in the mud. To the Greeks, in addition to being the Mighty Hunter, Orion was called the Giant, the Warrior, the Cock's Foot, and the Double Ax" (382).

76 "Capricorn is the mansion of Saturn, and the exaltation of Mars" is a quote from Boston editor Arthur Gilman's essay "Astrological Terms and Divisions of Time" accompanying the 1879 *Poetical Works of Geoffrey Chaucer*, 1:cviii.

PS to Measure, to them. Possibly you back (up the Spiritus to #2 . Length I dont feel matters.
Either end.

Please pardon the mess—it is such a displeasure to read. But I am in PO across from Penn Sta. On the way out.
    Last night the living nightmare, so today trembles.
    from Union Square, the rain on the newspaper stand
    we sat in it.

There was a stakeout to bag junkys. And, I amble in after typing this. Alan's red shirt was my banner. I joined the confederates again. No one was busted. // Much love

In the fall of 1957, Wieners made the journey west, joining friends from Black Mountain and Boston who had already moved, or returned, to San Francisco, that "glassunicorntown," as he derided it even as he moved and creatively thrived there. With Dana, he first stayed with Michael Rumaker, then moved around among his new circle of friends, most notably for stretches with **Joanne Kyger** at 707 Scott Street and **Robert Lavigne** at the Hotel Wentley.

During this time, he wrote to Ed Dorn, "We are desperate men, and the rest bore." But even among the desperate poets **Anne Waldman** would call the "Outriders," Wieners was always one of the farthest out—Dorn and Creeley held various teaching positions throughout their careers, Olson taught and, although always poor, still received grants and accolades from time to time—but except for his four years in Buffalo, when he worked as a grad student-teacher in the poetics program, Wieners had no affiliations, no means of support except for family and friends.

As Wieners's quest for derangement of the senses, and general love of the underground, led him into harder drugs and rougher living situations, the letters of this chapter become more bleak. As he tells Rumaker in one, "It's a fuckin fun city and I hate it," and indeed, as he moved from the relatively innocent marijuana, Benzedrine, and Valo (inhaled off the amphetamine-soaked cotton balls inside a decongestant spray) to cocaine and heroin, Wieners became more desperate and fractured, even as he produced the work that would establish his reputation. These next few letters, written to Robin Blaser while traveling cross-country, retell the speed-based events of his last letter to Olson, except now the tale is more overtly paranoid, Wieners's followers and spies stepping out of their shadows.

* * *

Robin Blaser
Sept 26 [1957]
[On the Road]

Dearest Robin:
    Please excuse handwriting as we are batting along on Highway <u>64</u> into Memphis—

From NYC last weekend I tried to call you 5–7 times as I left my <u>only</u> suit hanging on back of <u>Balas'</u> living room door. Along with Khaki Jacket.   It is navy blue with thin pinstripe.

Amidst the welter of your days, would it be <u>too much</u> for you to box this and ship c/o Rumaker. I wouldn't ask but there is no one else. As it is I fear it already sold in the hunger of their days. Tom will remember once you mention it. If you cant reach him home—try Alan—RI -2–1960. You see if he is evicted the clothes may get lost.

New York is desolate. With non-commitment (?) the virtue. The movies requiring or worth more of a man's attentions. Thus I missed the intensity of you and me. Also I ran into the police & narcotics squad and I was followed for one day and 1/2 by a force of them until I left town. <u>So</u> if there are questions there from strangers about any of us, be wary.

The story: I spent the dawn one morning walking up Fifth Ave window shopping / writing down addresses of shops I wd come back to Monday. Monday from 4 to 6 AM I spent in Union Square but noticed the same cabdrivers circling wherever I was. Eighth Street, Sheridan Square, Washington Square—the same faces. I didnt worry. But early dawn Monday (having waited out a rain-storm in a newspaper kiosk, I looked across and saw 2 figures make some panicky shadows <u>in</u> the shadows of the Union Square Savings Bank. Well one of them after a while crossed over directly to me while the other slid down the shadows & disappeared. The one coming to me a Kerouac-type with a pipe in his mouth. He didnt say anything but walked by me & into park. I did not turn around. After a while I walked down towards a restaurant, had a cup of coffee, & walked back in front of bank. It was daylight now and I kept walking uptown. But changed my mind & walked into the street heading back where I came from. And I saw this car which had been turning the corner—stop. I walked in diagonal, a car came on. I went very fast until I came to a monument & then turned back quick—again catching the car following me. I ran into the park, the car pulling up into parking space.

Then I realized I had done nothing but <u>perhaps</u> witness a score, or just attracted some attention by the red jersey, or benny state I was in.

In the park, a man was doing these frantic exercises, supposedly, as I approached. Morning sit-ups etc. But thinking back, I think he too was a cop. For I decided I wd. find out what was going on. Also I did not want to lead them back to O'Hara's. For one hour, like a sucker, I played cops & robbers up & down NY streets. Certainly making them think I was some sort of connection // but also I began to see some of their methods. They all dressed as middle class workmen. Lunch bags, soft hats & zipper jackets. They also all carried newspapers. And would not meet my eyes which taunted = I dare you. Finally I got so tired ~~and~~ *I* took a couple more turns and came home. O'Hara & Joe LeSeur went to work, I packed my bags and, having talked it over with Frank, was convinced it was only my own paranoia, that simply to "go about your own business", was the best way.[1] And this seemed right for the next two hours I saw

Robin Blaser
Sept 27, 1957—
[On the Road]

Returning to life after "kicking

benzedrine (none for 4 days)[2] and coming down a hill to "rolling" green plains of OKlahoma.

Left in the river only drying stones stuck—cohere in the sun. America despite your nostrils and outhouses with the picture window. I am exhilarated by the wind tillers and the fields of sun flowers / daisies. The day's eye falls and we speed on Route 66 to reach where it's setting. New York we leave behind. Its movie house poets and its Federal men who follow us on the streets, all the streets and avenues, pursued by G-men who would pin me down behind bars, take America out of my eye, take this open car and imprison us all.

They have set snares for me and I escaped. They set men on me at corners. Who unwrapped in his hands round boxes to trap me. Or passed me and tapped on my

---

1 Frank O'Hara's longtime roommate Joe LeSueur recalls Wieners's epic day at the library, which came while he was staying with the two:

John went to do some sort of research at the Forty-Second Street public library while we went to see *The Curse of Frankenstein* at Loew's Sheridan. That evening John, high on Benzedrine, came home and told us about the horrifying, hallucinatory experience he'd had at the library. Later I said to Frank, "Isn't it funny, we go to a horror movie and don't feel a thing and John goes to the library and is scared out of his wits." (Gooch, *City Poet*, 301)

2 Wieners found sources for amphetamines soon after arriving in San Francisco. Rumaker recalls it was Wieners who first encouraged him to try them:

John with a sly grin and slow care removing the white Benzedrine pills from his pocket and lining them up reverentially on the oak table top for all to see, like communion hosts. Pointing with a smile of revelation as in a hushed, hieratic voice the quartered segments of each pill became in his eyes, and ours, "the cross of Saint Francis," that mystical connection underscored when he told us, his eyes widening in revelation, that the St. Francis pharmacy across from the hotel of the same name was where he got his legal and illegal scripts for bennies filled, mostly 500 at a time. He'd been converted to them some time before and now wanted to convert the rest of us, "Especially you, Michael," he breathed softly, looking pointedly at me. "This is mostly for you because I know you'll get it the most." (Rumaker, *Robert Duncan in San Francisco*, 56)

wrist. Circled my nights in taxis, an eye on me in Alan's red shirt. I have escaped. I race across country. all roads west. My driver is blond. The country flat. They called me by my first name, they sounded their horns. For the time being, they are outsped. New vistas ~~are~~ open. New plains. Ugly in their flatness. ~~But~~ Here white cottonballs line the highway & the sun has hardened my skin. My eye cleared of soot. America's cities. America's laws. We pass yr diesel ~~engines. Leave soot for the slow runner's eyes~~

The flunky with his wounds and scarface did not stop me. The spy they dressed up like my mother did not hold me. The man stalling for time in Liggetts did not trick me. The beautiful boy his suitcase empty (he shook it ~~as~~ so the stolen goods rattled) did not make me follow up 5th Avenue. I hopped a bus on 22nd Street and a girl kept rubbing her knee on mine. Her handbag was open. I saw the same faces circle me all day. My last day east.

So by evening at Penn Station they had all re-assembled ~~and~~ *some* made quiet obscene noises as I walked thru them. One asked me ~~how~~ when was the train I'm supposed to go to Newark. Even a 16 yr old they ~~are~~ had bought red shirts like the one I wore the night before in Union Square. And he had a pastie on ~~his~~ *the* needlemark in his main line. And his eyes whimpered for my mercy. I went by. I sang: I know that you know. But I know you too. ~~All in~~ Every store I went in, if I stayed more than 2 minutes, one of them came in and slipped the clerk a note.

The man you are waiting on is a suspect
Do nothing to arouse his suspicions but
please watch his movements.

I wanted to scream in a Marlborough book store. It got so bad I thought they were taking pictures. I couldn't laugh anymore when I passed them on street corners. I was biting my lip. They almost had me. They had changed shifts. If only I could make a train out.

Now nothing but this fabulous 6 foot wide highway—from Oklahoma City to the sea to the ashes of Lawrence.[3] We follow the natural run of the river, we follow the railroad, follow the sun, ~~Dana said~~ *the driver says.* [two lines scratched out]
          It is sunset, [two words scratched out] and speeding
                         thru plains

---

3 The ashes of D. H. Lawrence are interred at his ranch in Taos, New Mexico, in a shrine his widow Frieda had built for him. According to Frieda, he is literally in the shrine; she said that she poured his ashes into the cement altarpiece. The altar is enormous, white stone with DHL carved onto the front, and beside it sit Lawrence's denim shirt, cowboy hat, and typewriter. Several years later in a letter to Denise Levertov, Wieners remembered this trip from 1957 with Dana, writing, "We looked into the blue box underneath his typewriter. I was terrified to see his blue denims folded up in there. I don't see why, now" (March 24, 1964).

where we cannot be followed.
It is open westward, ho

Philip Whalen
Oct 3, 1957
[San Francisco]

Dear Phillip: YES. (You dont have to go further.)

Arrived 4 hours ago—and yours/here. Like a city. Entire unto itself. Know ~~that~~ *first* off that Take #4 on 12: VIII: 57 goes into #5 THE DOMESTIC (scene). OK OK—but the poem demands we wait. You are carried here in all yr. flesh. // And now in all honesty, the humility you open in me from Harangue:[4] (two "r"'s?): its alright w/me if there's 3. That ~~one~~ what can anyone say in the face of that poem. I wish Measure could come out tomorrow so that those words, strain, the man breaking thru might be "issued abroad"—the hilltops etc. And this not because it is to JW but that. Across the kitchen table: Tom Field says "God they're both beautiful. I'm gonna write Whalen too" and Ebbe B.[5] says: "I cant say anything, it's that there for me." Not that

Charles Olson
[Oct. 30, 1957]
[San Francisco]

I have to write you—looking at G de Paolo's
(Paradise[6]   - that I did not know these

---

4 Whalen's "Harangue From Newport, to John Wieners, 21:IX:57" is an epistolary poem, an extension of their *Measure* conversations. Describing the ordinary ugliness (a landlord with a growth on his nose) and beauty ("chunks of agate-jasper on the beach") of his life, Whalen writes, "I should write you something that would / Scare you, make you laugh, / or generally turn you on. / WHAT / I'm doing now: Trying hard to be visible, to be / Totally conscious of this time and place, / of you / And every sentient being." He closes sweetly, by exclaiming that "you not only see me clearly, // (A MIRACLE!) // You understand everything I say" (*The Collected Poems*, 86).

5 Ebbe Borregaard, poet and erstwhile publisher at the center of the San Francisco Renaissance.

6 Giovanni de Paolo (1398–1482), Italian painter whose *Paradise* (ca. 1445) was part of an altarpiece with *Expulsion From Paradise*; both Dante-inspired paintings hang in the Metropolitan Museum of Art.

last 2 nights why I liked it (was drawn to
it so.
    And The Pentagon officers have
    let me know since x–xxii (during
    that AM <u>why</u> to so many scents on
    my part and the structure of the diamond
    held up to the light during these nights
    tell me.   Tell-us   they signed
    things.
    I want to write more often. But no time
and all is scattered so but Giovanni made me
I have long scroll poems I hope to send shortly.

   Just want you to know it is very close I am to
you. The alphabet, the cards, and my
mother.
    I didnt like the address here
but 16 & 16 are 32.
          and a Leaven-worth
what causes us to rise, the bars on the jail
ourself. You in the square fort.
Please keep clipping.
         No-names. ~~just~~
to practice rites, take a 1/2 tube-stick to your hip
& move towards your brother. Tomorrow I pick
up a book: The religions of Near East. Sumerian,
               AKKadian
      texts ea. by Isaac Mendel-
  The Library of Religion Series #4.   sohn.
    The Liberal Arts Press—153 W. 72
        NY 23, NY
The beautiful → green knob of the hill. they find each other

                                  our
I had to open this, because I find out I dont live at 1632 Leavenworth, but 1362,
which is another matter, indeed.

Well, it is a nearly unbearable town, and they can flutter their wings all they want to,
they cant wipe that away. If it werent for Mr. Rumaker, I dont know, and he hopes
to get out by January 1.

Dont believe a word you read, if you read them. And it aint only my jaded Eastern eyesight. I suppose if we lived in North Beach? But the place,[7] they are all under siege, suspicion and punctured vanity (s) fill the air with a very unpleasant sound.

Anyway you hold the fort, as I do Boston, and I wish I could put down some notes on City (is there one?) for you so you would say something for M- but I am barely able to write to my mother.

This isnt even a Renegade town, anymore. And the International Settlement[8] is closed down. Well, we'll go to the Black Cat[9] on Halloween.

Love,

yours,

John

I've often wished I answered you that beautiful night you asked me
—who can you trust—

I meant to.

Charles Olson
November 1, 1957
[San Francisco]

Dear Subscriber:[10]

On August 1st the contents of Measure II were mailed to the Villiers Press in London for the Fall printing. On September 13th, the editor was notified by James Boyer May (US representative of the press) that the manuscripts had never been received in the London office. Despite a tracer, the Post Office has never explained or accounted for their loss.

By September 19th the entire issue, except for one irreplaceable item, had been re-assembled at the labor of each individual contributor. The long delay in a Fall

---

7 The Place, North Beach bar popular with Jack Spicer and his circle of poets. Opened by Black Mountain alumni in 1953, The Place "encouraged the use of marijuana, exploring ways to break traditional sex roles, 'a greater candor about homosexuality, a greater interest in experiment in homosexual relations,'—including the encouragement of women to 'use swear words'—and generally frank conversations on all subjects" (Ellingham and Killian, *PBLG*, 55).

8 The International Settlement, red-light district in San Francisco in the 1940s and 1950s.

9 The Black Cat, bar in San Francisco that evolved from Bohemian hangout to what Allen Ginsberg called "the best gay bar in America" in the 1950s (John D'Emilio, *Sexual Politics, Sexual Communities*, 187).

10 This letter was sent out to most of Wieners's correspondents.

issue is mainly editorial. But II is being printed now and will be distributed to you in the early Winter (December–January).

It contains:

A book of dreams and an article on the use of the unconscious by Michael Rumaker.
5 choruses from Mexico City by Jack Kerouac.
2 by Duncan.
5 by Creeley, and Notes from Skagit Valley by Edward Dorn.
Long poems by Robin Blaser, Stephen Jonas and Stuart Z. Perkoff,[11] plus short ones by
6 others.

III to (The City) is also ready and will be printed in the early Spring.

It contains:

A survey of 16 cities from Boston to Venice. Helen Adam to Philip Whalen
Kyoto to Fairbanks
5 to James Dean by Frank O'Hara
10 Hymns to Geryon by Michael McClure. Poems by Louis and Allen Ginsberg[12]
Fragment of a blue movie by William Burroughs.[13] Also burlesque photographs and strip collages. Reviews: of Catullus by Jonathan Williams and CityLights by Larry Eigner

---

11 Stuart Z. Perkoff (1930–1974), American poet and artist, a native of St. Louis who moved to Venice, California, and became essential to the early Beat scene there. He was published in the second issue of *Origin*, and he was included in Donald Allen's 1960 *New American Poets*.

12 Louis Ginsberg (1885–1976), American poet and teacher, father of Allen Ginsberg. In June 1957 Allen had written him, "Please subscribe to John Wieners's magazine Measure—it should be a very good avant garde magazine and he needs about 47 more subscriptions to make it—also I'd like to have a complete set of them at home, they'll be valuable perhaps ... A good cause. Wieners is going to try rounding up all the threads we've been gathering" (*Family Business*, 60). Not only did Louis subscribe, he also submitted his poem "Still Life," which he told Allen was "about the atmosphere at 324 Hamilton Ave. when you were in college, Eugene was in the army, and I was surrounded by ghosts" (124). Two years later, after *Measure* had published both father and son, Allen reported back, "We are doing a benefit reading to finance *Measure* mag here for another issue. Wieners is a good kid, but no money and not a businessman" (118).

13 This submission, which Burroughs signed "William Lee," was not published in *Measure* but was incorporated into Burroughs' 1959 novel *Naked Lunch*. For more history of this text, see Jed Birmingham's article "William S. Burroughs and John Wieners' Measure" at *RealityStudio*, in which he generatively (and expensively) investigates a footnoting error in *"the sea under the house": The Selected Correspondence of John Wieners and Charles Olson*.

So you are asked to be patient, that this attempts to assure you the wait is worth it.
And that future numbers will keep pace with the seasons.

Faithfully,
The Editor

Robin Blaser
November 7 [1957]
[San Francisco]

Dearest Robin:
  You must know how much I have wanted to write, and just been forced, either by
the weight of M II not being a fact, and the taking in of this new PLACE, such a
cone (egg) I have not been able to break out of. Except just this hurried fingers.
[. . .]
            Dana got arrested once, 10 days after we arrived for 'drunkeness' and
he wanted to come back 'home' but NO, we hung on, at Tom Field's 509 Buchanan
St (The Nigger District) and I was having visions of detectives, etc. Or maybe they
weren't visions. Whatever, I will be able I hope to send long poems, about it all. So
much has been written by me, & so little in a shape to be made available to you &
the few other ears.
That I leave all this white space for you to fill in, and mail back, I will come home
Christmas Week, and there will be much rejoicing in my heart. Altho, we both
now have taken, or are in process of same, SF to our hearts. I needs must work
too, but only to get that fare home,
1) Is all (Tom, Alan, Steve) out of jail? I mean this most seriously that it would do
me good to know.
2) Marshall wrote from NY, and I hope to write soon, and urge him here. Dont be
a dish-washer, lack of loot is killing.
3) Spicer is al-right. And his book, to be published by the WHITE RABBIT
PRESS (J Dunn) is the best he has done. But still, I feel, an ignorance on his part,
as to just what can be, or should be done, with the poem. That it aint personal
spears for your enemies, or lovers, or ones you want to be either, (prose is that)
that it partakes (yes RD,) of a more abiding, like religion, ignorance, & fear, takes
part of it too.
A deeper,
    black (only because so much light is there,

                                        place.
'Chilly gloom' our daddies toldus.

Tell-us they signed the stone with.   And

Pardon my haste, here, also I wont re-read, etc. That I wish and will in regular letters,
back, give you more dope on the place. Also all the poems you want,
                                        Do write, here, too. Damn you. I
dont think there is more 'culture' here,
                                        but at least, a more gracious, & convenient,
casual, easier way of life,
            but all those are adjectives, & whether 'life' is East, I dont know, but I think
so. My blood says yes.
            If you hesitate of Beau Clown,[14] I intend to read, so will let you know.
                                        Tell-ma was also on the stone.
                        love from us both,
                        John
Would you send your
    birthdate

                                                        Charles Olson
                                                        11.24.57[15]
                                                        [San Francisco]

Dear Charles:

Just to put down the random event instead of taking a
cable car.   How often
                        in fact, night before last when
you woke me up in the AM, and went to the left side of the bed
in the old bedroom on Churchill Street,
                        she kept yelling up the stairs
for me to come down and clean house or something before Alvene
arrived, and

---

14 *Beau Clown* was the strange creation of a child prodigy named Berthe Grimault, a fourteen-year-old
   French farm girl, published in the United States by Rinehart Books in 1957.
15 This letter and poem were published as a broadside in 1968 by Sam and Ann Charters' Portents Press in
   New York, printed on cream-colored paper with a red ribbon seal.

I would not, she kept insisting,
and despite embarrassment with you, a guest in the house—
    I threw a shoe
at her down the stairs on Eliot Street. It went
over her left shoulder, she shivered, like alittle madonna
ringlets shaking, hands folded to her breast
she cried, but I came back in the bedroom
to talk to you said something, these things have to happen,
          neither of us minded, you pay no . . .
    And Alvene arrived, and
        her sister, lighter one of the two Negresses.
And off we went
the four of us
    to a narrow house on a hill.
We climbed
the wood steps, in
After of course, I introduced you to them.
    a house I never saw before.
Enuf.

I.

November 11, the holiday, I wake Rumaker, up,
we have breakfast, then walk over the back side of Nob Hill,
babbling, etc. We catch the 2 Clement Bus out Sutter Street
for Michael's taking me touring to Sutros. To the Cliff House,
       Robin elaborated so on.[16]
A crispe day.

After all the fooling around, the lunch and beer, our pictures
taken for a quarter, we cross to the beach
this Pacific, its sense to me of no place, no interference from
land, coming off no shore but one
       I have never nor will not

---

16 The Cliff House, legendary restaurant near San Francisco, built and rebuilt five times since first opening
   in 1858. Millionaire Adolph Sutro bought it in 1883, turned it into a grand Victorian mansion, and built
   the magnificent Sutro Baths, in ruins since a 1907 fire.

see such a girl in the surf
with a black jacket
and toreador trousers
on skin tight,
around her head a bright red scarf
4 feet long
so the wind takes it and is
the force what seems to bend her, turning on waves
like a dance-er
except not,
I only remember her with her arms
out, and her toe raised,
foot rather, standing on one,
while this green Pacific longs
2 boys with her.

One on his elbow.   and the other
full length the wet land   in blue
dungarees, rolled to his
calf, by her
in the water.

She comes out
behind the land[17] one's back, bends over
his face in her hands and the wind her red veil
up her sweater so
I see her arched white back,
not like a cat's at all, back in the water
she wades as we walk by.
I have to sit down and watch.
I spread an old newspaper for Mike,
I found on the bus,
and I sit on Rimbaud.

And he looks at us once, so I have to look away.
Notions, some motion I cant set down his
head back to the street, out of the sea
the young one the blonde

---

17 It is possible that the *l* in "land" is crossed out.

                    and her,
they follow him
up to the seawall, she carries their clothes.

I tell Mike I cant go away I've got to
follow them, I'll meet you up the street, wait.
And we split.
By the time I get half-way near
the 2 boys have rolled up their pants
again and are running down to the water.
The girl looks fatter
                    and/
                          it's not even them.
I look at Mike smiling on the seawall. I yell
                    they've gone,
                          they've disappeared.
And he says, Do you want me to tell you where—
                          loud in the wind,
                    I say No.
                    I want to cross back to Playland.[18]
          But they're probably in one of the cars.
                          Did you see them go?
          No, do you really want to look?
                    We pass empty parked cars.
They went away but all the way home, when I think of them, of her
                          turning on waves,
I cannot talk of how it is like
                    Boston and Alan,
          what it would be like
                    if I lived
          that kind of life
making
          my devotions to
          what sends it all in across the water?
Giving

---

18 Playland-at-the-Beach (1928–1972), seaside amusement park near Sutros Baths. After the owner's death
  in 1958, the park began a decline that ended with its closure in 1972.

the rest up, four walls, for temple walls,
only I know it's not like that
on the beach, on the road,
there is no mystery, nor God
following
what we have known the nights, Alan and I. Balas and I
watched the sunrise. I have sat through the night, the 3
of them slept around me, wrote poems about it, their breathing. It was enough. Balas in the sideroom, Jan in the back-
room, Alan on the chair beside the box where I play records,[19]
tiptoe across, fainting I will make too much noise, break the
needle, writing in the chair across the room, the sky lights
way above Boston, needing a fix, pot to sail the ship, like
those babies, if I followed them, instead of trudging up
Sutros, to the icerink, and the museum, Tom Thumb under glass
with the night shut out
the gas burner sucks up the air
where they are, will I
see them.
Like it is (what time is it) just 5 ~~minutes~~ years to the minute
I get into the Studebaker with Dana and rode off into the back-
woods of Milton, never quite come out since

PS: a poem

to put fire in the grate, seawood[20]
burn up the chimney for its night
ashes I will be rather than
settling down to just so much dust

---

19 Wieners is hanging out with Alan Minsk, but it is difficult to determine the other two in this tableau
because of some name confusion: around this time he was friends with two adventurous couples, both of
whom had come from Boston to San Francisco around the same time he did, and both of whose distaff
partners were Jan. In addition to Tom and Jan Balas (discussed in his July 6, 1957, letter to Rumaker) he
was also friends with Alan and Jan Minsk. Without last names, it's hard to determine which Jan is present
in any given scene in Wieners's letters—both were wild women who loved to party. Wieners's biographer
Robert Dewhurst, after interviews with Joanne Kyger and Dave Haselwood, told me that Kyger remembered Wieners loving the Minsks, and "all these Boston junkies that had all these little short-avenue of
ways of making cash." Haselwood recalled that "Alan Minsk was a real sweet guy, but he got on methedrine
and literally wound up stabbing Nemi [Frost]" (personal email from Robert Dewhurst to Michael Seth
Stewart).

20 "to put fire in the grate, seawood . . . " is unpublished.

in the air I cannot breathe,
look then to sea at Land's End
those roots that live on rocks, ride
with each surf, turning on waves.

John W

Robert Greene

12.19.57

[San Francisco]

Forgive all this
Dear Robert:

Dear Robert, this is going to be quicker than I want, maybe longer, but I at least want to write this, to say I am alive, and coming out of a long slump. Because, this town, lovely as it is, is too distracting for work. It is Fun City, and I carry around with me the ghost of Paris in 20's. Yah, I cant help it, it is so active with poets, with an audience of wild men, and the 2 or 3 bars where they meet (unlike the 7's)[21] but ruled over by a kind of madness of wonder, etc.

Anyway, both Dana & I aint been well, and thus together things arent close. No money for a long time, no jobs, in our little US depression, and a $100 a month apt. Plus the ever-increasing work of this fucking magazine. I got a flyer for it in Poetry*Chicago (November) and it has brought on another cascade of crap. So I have let the real matters pile up.

I guess you could say in some ways, 'I have arrived.' Partisan Review,[22] Chicago Review both have asked to print poems, for their San Francisco Issues. But I hesitate and draw back, for in this flush time, one can easily go down the drain. And I am so far removed from desire to see my own name in print, because the poem itself is removed from me. It's like living off the canned preserves of another

---

21 The Sevens, a mixed gay and straight bar on the Bohemian north side of Boston's Beacon Hill, one of a handful of bars in the neighborhood that offered haven to gay and lesbian Bostonians. It is still standing today in the same location.

22 The *Partisan Review* (1934–2003), American cultural, literary, and political journal, known for what Irving Howe called a "mixture of polemical combativeness and intellectual rapidity," publishing Mary McCarthy, Delmore Schwartz, George Orwell, and a rambunctious site of argument over Stalinism, fascism, and the avant-garde.

season, and I dont think I shall do same, altho Chic Review has kept two poems, from long ago, which (one of) (a bad one) they will drop in the welter. Who cares. All that matters is touch, love, desire, need, lust, satisfaction. I dont have what I want, and we do have the right to have those things. So I go back to Boston (Fly Back) Christmas Eve, and land Christmas Morn, and see what happens. I have often stood outside the windows at 28 Lime Street, and thought of those pain-full days.

I have gone thru a lot, I guess, if I thought of same, and it is only a year since you pulled down our lintel, and yet a different world has opened up to me. The world of the thieves, etc. Dope-addicts, etc. all the terror of the near-mad, and I know this smacks of the dramatic, but I chose this, this area of life. I could be teaching school in Canton.

Instead, I have Georgia O'Keefe's Sunflower, burning in front of my eyes, and a thousand little packs placed on me back, which dont bend it at all, but this is a weary city, where Boston was/ has the charm (soothing weight of age) ah shit, that's literary. Old hands weigh lightly.
Your picture, one hand on a banister in Louisburg Square, with two dowagers in the background, is pasted to the wall with others, just within fingertouch of my arm, in fact, I did just that, touch your puss. You see, despite it all, the new ones, habits as well as friends, there cannot be touched, those pictures pasted on me wall, us, you.
You remain close, while Dana becomes a ghost, sliding out of my touch, day after day, so writing this, I become afraid, and would run into the bedroom, and talk to him, but it is 3 AM, and he is drunk, and the sliding door would make too much noise. Yah, it is somewhat night-marish, all of us, wandering in it. But I go back soon, to that old root, the old street, and see what happens,
    and I will write about it. Do write if you can, all your news does me heart good, and forget the haste, and the remark you made about my poetry still fills my heart with joy, I do want to be that expansive, and the day will come, when I write, as I know, it has to be written.
I have no fare back here to San Francisco, but I will move slow, leaving Milton sometime in Mid-January.

Your life too seems full of knowledges. I wonder if Veronique can forgive me for not thanking, writing her, she too, who comes into my head so often. Ah, enough.

I have so much to write you—it defeats me. I wont re-read this so –

but do buy The Evergreen Review
    795 Broadway
    NYC 3, NY
        $1.00
for the San Francisco Scene—an issue devoted to the "renaissance" on the West Coast,
which of course does not exist.
    Corrected Proofs of Measure 2 go in same mail as this letter.

        My love to you
        & Veronique.
1362 Leavenworth   *John*
San Francisco 9.

                         Ed Dorn
                         Dec, 1957
                      [San Francisco]

Dearest Ed:
    I was in bed, and read your letter, and now I am both that & up. So very tight, I cannot open up my arms, it is not of the body. There is never finis, I dont know how you can think of it, but fear of same is what has got me up. We have had it very tough here, with eyes peeping over the top of the table, & it is not over yet.

I had flown high on other wings all summer, and after being here 3 weeks, there was no more.
                  Money, peace, place, food, shit, & yet tonight, I had pinned a sunflower, up on my wall, so daddy, this is the first letter, I got writ, since I been here, Oct 1.

Whadda do? write back to Boston and say send 500 benzedrine.

It's a fuckin fun city and I hate it. Using up my time on fun. Also today, proofs of M II back, & may I quote: Olson: WOW. It is pretty good. I am excited. I itch the back of my neck. I aint a manic-depressive, the girl in Mike's Place said, it's just that I been drinking seven days, and they wont let me sleep.

Well, I work at Books, Inc. and can get any thing in both stores, 20% off, so if I can do you a turn, a miracle in exchange, let me. I. E. before Christmas, when they lay me.

Also Fire-man in next room, no split there, only so-so, stuck in a $100 a month apt. because there is WELL, WE'RE FUCKING HUNG. And the inhabitants likewise.

Tom Field, drinks, my dear, all the time, and Michael Rumaker aint written since the desert. Returns east in April. Send your poems to

PATRICIA GUEST

Partisan Review

22 E 17th

and say Johnnie Wieners told you to. She is the new Poetry Editor, & co-respondent here, not that you care probably. But Paul Carroll also, Chicago Review,[23]

Reynolds Club, Univ. of Chicago, Chicago 37.   They are also after me (yah*) for (you know what) you ones. New ones.

Oh Fuck, fuck fuck fuck fuck clslslslslxlslslallalalalalalalal

I cannot make it. That beside my dear old mother, and sister, who's becoming a nun, I aint written nobody, cause, there is so many to write. I am paralyzed. I got one hundred letters, to answer. And what could I say to you, when I had to say, I have no money to get there, no place to leave behind, no ROCK, I am the kind that needs one, or I would be washed out to sea. It is the only place I can operate from. Olson called Dana a rock, and he is literally that to me.

Also I need to know somebody can pay the rent. ETC.

SHIT, SUCKLW S, DNSJWOWLSKSJ.

And he is too unable to work, also, because no

one will hire him. For various reasons.

IT IS A depression, I guess,

or something,

with all the fur-coated ones still fucking in the

lobby of the St Francis, without knowing it.

Well, I will not say it this time, that I can

see you,

But[24] do write

---

23 Paul Carroll (1926–1996), American poet and teacher who founded the Poetry Center of Chicago. As a college student (1958–1959), Carroll coedited the *Chicago Review* and then *Big Table* with Irving Rosenthal.

24 Red circle around "But" with line down to "how cold is it."

who you heard from, etc. The scene. I am healthy, back to 135 pounds. Not on anything. And Dana received $50 yesterday from an old nurse he used to fuck on our street,

       so we're OK.

And he began work today also, at City of Paris, selling cashmere sweaters for $35, fitted to your body,

   how I would love to hold yours and your wife to either arm.

    My love always,
     John

how cold is it
PS—
   What else do any of us have to
offer but the "pre-occupation w/details"
   you cannot bore.

* * *

The spring and summer of 1958 found Wieners in the middle of another exhilarating renaissance. Spicer and Duncan were back in the Bay Area, the Poetry Center at San Francisco State University was bringing Modernist and New American poets to read, and small presses like Joe Dunn's White Rabbit and **Dave Haselwood**'s Auerhahn were publishing beautiful books by San Francisco poets.

It was around this time that Wieners moved in with Joanne Kyger, with whom he would have a lifelong friendship. He describes living with "Miss Kids" (so called due to her habit of sweeping into a room and calling out "Hey kids!") in his journal from this period, *The Journal of John Wieners Is to be called 707 Scott Street for Billie Holliday 1959*. The journal begins just a few days after this next letter, on March 8, 1958, mid-afternoon, as "Miss Kids" lounges about and the young poet writes down clear declarations like "I must forget how to write. I must unlearn what has been taught me."[25]

* * *

---

25 *The Journal of John Wieners is to be called 707 Scott Street for Billie Holliday 1959*, 13 (hereafter referred to as *707 Scott Street*).

Michael Rumaker [New York]
March 4, 1958
[San Francisco]

Dear Michael:

It is 8:30 in the morning, and I am thinking of Sutros and the holiday of November 11, how nice it would be if I could go over and ring your chic bell, and we would bus off. I am wrapping the shoes as soon as I finish this, and I will send them the quickest way possible. The lack of money has delayed me. I will pay for the postage, as I am selling books tonight, and we will write it off to past accounts;

I have been looking for work every day, and yesterday, appeared in the Oakland City Hall, applying for an Educational Asst. job in their Art Museum, and again as a junior librarian in the Oakland Public. The A train only takes 30 minutes; etc. Whatever, I am having much fun wandering about daily. Dana and I have tentatively decided to split. He will, as soon as his unemployment checks come through, and he can pay the back rent. I will, as soon as he does. If he does not, I doubt that I will. If he asks me to stay with him, I will. But as things go and have gone for the past week, we are strangers, and are very seldom alone together (I spent last weekend with Miss Kids) and I am very well in it all. Actually go out on the streets (daytime) with a great deal of joy in the fellows, (at a distance) and have bought marigolds that grow, and two plants that have new shoots, and a red pillow cover, which I fitted and sewed on the foam rubber Ma gave me. Also, a pastoral scene cover. We have decided that he may have the dishes, while I shall take the red drapes. And I look, half out of the corner of my eye, for apartments on Telegraph Hill, and Columbus, Mason St. area. That is where I want to live, somewhere, where at night, I may walk and have open bars and ice-cream parlors at hand. Not Chink Markets that close at 10, or queer bars.

Miss Kids and I miss you, and dont think about it. The poetry last Sunday was excellent. Even Irene Taverner[26] was here, and did not open her yap once. Nemi Frost Hansen[27] wants to return to Santa Barbara, and she broke down last Friday and cried on Miss Kids' bed for two hours, and Miss Kids broke down and cried later in Vesuvio's[28] and let her hair down, and could not tie it back again, and Nemi Frost

---

26 Irene Taverner (1925–2011), Welsh American painter active in the New York and San Francisco Beat and jazz scenes.
27 Emily "Nemi" Frost (1928–2014), American artist who came to San Francisco in 1956 with childhood friend Joanne Kyger from Santa Barbara.
28 Vesuvio's, bar in the North Beach neighborhood of San Francisco, a popular Beat hangout around the corner from City Lights Bookstore, where it still stands.

had no mercy, and said cut the scene. So the next day Miss Kids wrote to the psychiatrist for dexedrine. And Jack Spicer wrote a "Masurka for the girls who brought me tranquillers"[29] and Miss Kids arrived with English Ivy and white daisies tied to her handbag, and Duncan who had cried with tears down his cheeks the Sunday before that Ebbe and Stanley[30] were in opposition to his verse, this Sunday read 15 pages of prose he had written since, in the form of a letter to George Stanley, with reference to poems by Harold Dull,[31] and Joanne Kyger. The Dunns were in attendance, and Sheila in a ratty black mouton coat, lined with white mouton turned gray, someone had given her, and she has left Miss Kids.

There were not enough chairs, and I made $.50 profit on the wine. Dory Dull had to drink water constantly as her bladder is infected, and she spilt a great deal of it. John Ryan[32] had his pearl on Saturday night, which Irene Taverner ripped off and threw across the bar at Vesuvios. And Miss Kids suspects that he has been stealing her earrings, and Jerome[33] is still in love with Ryan, who shared the last of his mary-wanna with me last Saturday, and even Miss Kids, who had taken one Dexedrine before, she persuaded the manager to let her in to Mrs. Hansen's apartment as we thought

---

29 Jack Spicer's "Masurka For the Girls Who Brought Me Tranquilizers," intended for *A Book of Music* but not included. Lewis Ellingham and Kevin Killian found the poem among Spicer's papers at Bancroft Library in 2004, but it remains unpublished. The poem (reprinted with permission from Killian's private collection) reads:

> In group, out group
> In group, out group
> Man wearing a beard, 4 1/2 collar, and a pair of pajamas.
> Out group, in group
> Out group, in group
> Woman wearing lipstick, 36 brassiere, drinking gin and marmalade.
> Man and woman unique
> Try to dance. People
>   Say that dance is the basic measure of a poem.

30 George Stanley (b. 1937), American Canadian poet. A San Francisco native, he was an integral part of its so-called Renaissance, and active participant in Jack Spicer's Poetry as Magic workshop, along with friends Ebbe Borregaard, Helen Adam, and Joe Dunn. During the Vietnam War he moved to Vancouver, British Columbia, where he has written and taught since.

31 Harold Dull, American poet and teacher who came to San Francisco and the North Beach Spicer scene after studying with Stanley Kunitz and Theodore Roethke. He arrived shortly before Wieners did, on Labor Day 1957, with his girlfriend Dora Geissler, who went by Dora Dull because the shared last name was the only way she and Harold could find an apartment together in the 1950s. "When my mother threatened to visit," she remembered in an interview with Lewis Ellingham, "I went to the point of purchasing a gold band from a pawn shop, and that was the end of Dora Geissler" (*PBLG*, 109).

32 John Ryan, bartender at The Place who participated in Spicer's Poetry as Magic Workshop.

33 Jerome Mallman (b. 1931), American painter and photographer, originally from Wisconsin, who quickly became a fixture in San Francisco's Bohemian scene. Mallman introduced Joanne Kyger, whom he knew through the City of Paris Department Store, to The Place, the North Beach bar where Spicer's circle was concentrated in the 1950s. His collection of street photography, *Smokers and Sleepers*, was released by the University of Wisconsin Press in 2005.

FIGURE 2   John Wieners with Michael McClure, Philip Lamantia, and David Meltzer.
Photograph by Lawrence Johnson, signed by each poet for Raymond Foye's personal collection.
Courtesy of Lawrence Johnson.

Nemi had taken an overdose of sleeping pills after we couldn't find the Look magazine
party, but she hadn't, and wasn't home, so Miss Kids stole a handful of dexedrine,
and at Ryan's with the mary-wanna smoke blowing in the air, she went on the nod,
and later the two of us went to all kinds of parties, at Jordan Bellson's[34] who makes
movies, and later to Bob Cedar's up on Fillmore, until dawn, he wasnt home, but
blowing at the Troupers, and his beautiful wife was just getting up, and Miss Kids
slept, and I listened to Leo Parker, Charlie's brother.[35] While Wally Berman sat across
from me and sniffled, and pretended he was on junk, because I looked like I was, and
Marcella[36] and Jeanne were also at Vesuvio's and Miss Kids looked up through her
hair, and said, if those women sit down, I'll scratch her eyes out, and So I greeted

---

34 Jordan Belson (1926–2011), American artist and avant-garde filmmaker known for his meditative, abstract
    films. When Wieners lived in the city, Belson was in the midst of his Vortex Concerts, an immersive art
    project with sound-artist collaborator Henry Jacobs at San Francisco's Morrison Planetarium (1957–1959).
35 Leo Parker (1925–1962), bebop musician.
36 Marcelle Labaudt (1892–1987) gave many new artists their start at the Lucien Labaudt Gallery in San
    Francisco, founded and named for her husband after his death in 1943.

them, and planned to meet them later at the Place, since Marcella had bought one of Nemi Frost Hansen's paintings, but being invited to Look, instead, never went, wound up sleeping in Miss Kids' cool arms all night.

I will wrap your shoes, and your letter was very beautiful and makes me wish you had waited until Spring, when it was warm, and do go slow, and do not let the jungle eat you.

I suppose in a sense I am glad you are gone, because now I can leave Dana, and if you had stayed I would not, knowing you want me to, there would be too much resistancy on my part, but this way, I can just glide off, as soon as I get work, and I am going this morning to The San Francisco City Hall, to apply in their library, forging my residence date here, and I take two tests March 14 for Oakland, and then later today, I will make the Museum to see the Blue Rider Show,[37] even possibly stopping and asking Carolyn Dunn to accompany me. Of course, this Sunday will be gala, with Ebbe and Stanley reading their stuff, and Friday before, I will make the Laubadt Gallery on Gough (1407) where Anne McKeever (the far out one from Mexico) and Ruth Weiss (the fat one) are reading their stuff,[38] and the Sunday before last, Tom and Richard Duerden and I went to the cellar, and the black man on trumpet seemed to be blowing right in me, and I had been there earlier with only 5 people, and stayed after they left, when there were more people on the bandstand than there were in the house. I wish Measure would arrive, and you would be proud to see what has been done, when it seemed that nothing was doing;

I have no fear of the one place I know you are in, and will never be out of, because it is yours and you have your own land, and your own markings, and I would like to say, dont ever believe it is not yours, or that you are *not* walking it, but I know you believe we have to dig through so much to find it, I would be a fool, to say it was yours on Lexington Avenue, and is in the back room on E. 96th, but I know the anger it is to have all things in disarray around you, but most things are, and we build. On our own land. Love to JK. The news you gave was good. Write as you can.

Love, John

---

37 Der Blaue Reiter, group of painters formed in 1911 by Vasily Kandinsky and Franz Marc. They disbanded by 1914, but their groundbreaking work in pure color and abstraction had an enormous impact on twentieth-century art. Wieners writes about Blau Reiter painter Paul Klee in *Hotel Wentley*'s "A Poem for Painters."

38 Anne McKeever, San Francisco poet and photographer, good friends with the Beat poet and performer ruth weiss, who lived at the Hotel Wentley in the early 1950s and had her poetry published in foundational Beat magazines like *Beatitude* and Wallace Berman's *Semina*. Her journal *Compass* chronicles her trip through Mexico, where she met McKeever and Philip Lamantia and stayed up all night talking, finally climbing the Pyramid of the Sun, an Aztec ruin, to watch the sunrise. (Knight, "Return of the Prodigal Poet").

Charles Olson
4. 3. 58
[San Francisco]

Dearest Charles:

I shouldn't be writing but I must acknowledge your poem and tell you how pleased I am to ~~be able~~ have it. I feel that you too are too pressed to write, but we have much to say. I am far behind in MEASURE, but if I could only find a job then I could set my obligations to right. For now I am hanging on. Dana and I have split (again) and I am staying until a job with Miss Joanne Kyger. Which is very interesting for me to have her facts so close up. I dont intend to make it with Dana anymore and say I am claiming my manhood. ETC. But am not, not being self-supporting. This is not to labor you but to explain my falling away from the jobs at hand and also to report how interested the whole business is. The League of Non-Workers which are everywhere here, the Professional Bohemians—Miss Kyger is not one—in fact a Santa Barbara baby with violet doors and gold leaved handles. Her dishes all have flowers painted on them and she looks like a Marilyn Monroe with glasses, her mouth does. It is not a permanent arrangement but what am I to do? It is great to be here and terrifying to be without so much / and to be outside the law takes too much out of me, viz. Boston. Something will break as April always does for me / 3 years ago the Black Mountain. What that change hath wrought. I too feel as this must show I am somewhat removed from my own reality. We shall see where it leads me.

Creeley is here and had a reading at the Dunn's this evening. Very strong except, I feel, in the current work of which there was very little, outside of that published. 3 poems if I am right but then there is no fear that when he is past this "desert"—there are green pastures. He seemed sure of what had been done with the line as directed by you, by the breath. The audience dug it all. He read chronologically, and included 3–4 stories. The Lover, and, The Dress. Two others I cannot remember. An early one from Gold Diggers and the rowboat-beach children one "Sweet William"? Anyway, the best reading here so far for me, including Stuard Z Perkie last Sunday—What do you do with a town like this! Move to Stinson Beach? Or in with Marilyn Monroe.

I have walked out a few dawns in The Tenderloin with the platinum blondes / and supper-times on Fillmore. And am well so dont worry. As the Mid-Night Gal used to say:

"Who knows what tomorrow may bring"

Basil and Martha are married and return to New York in late April Dana is Tom Field's roomie, and Jerry vande Wiele, etc expects to move to San Francisco. Michael

is still unemployed in New York and as soon as anything opens for me I will write.
And have poems to send.

Black Mountain continues its power. What that means more of us have been able
to say.

> *Love to Betty and C—Peter*
> *and to you*
> *John*

The poem, again, is great
and completed the issue—
  made it an issue.

    my grandfather's name
    the Laffan one

Post Office Box 2714	(Right now I sell <u>Measure</u>
San Francisco 26	in the bars (No. Beach ones
or	
c/o Kyger #3	
949 Columbus Ave	

Ed Dorn
4.4.58
[San Francisco]

<u>Only gossip</u>
Dear Eddie Baby:

Feeling better—without job still, split for good with Dana and living in with a
new friend until a job appears. Her name is Joanne Kyger and looks like MM if MM
had to swing in a bookstore. It is not a permanent arrangement. Want you to get
the sound of your thing—

Creeley esp. liked "Dorn's beautiful bird business"[39] Ditto Rumaker flown by
bus to NY for good, also w/out job. Joanne thinks you're a person she would like

---

39 Wieners is referring to Dorn's "Notes from the Field: Skagit Valley," a lyric essay published in *Measure*
  issue 2. "It is nice to be amongst crows," Dorn writes. "Masters of the ground. Very inept in the air, being
  too gross to be articulately air-borne" (29).

to know. And as of now—no one has put the prose down nor do I think any have dug the effects intended. Frank O'Hara also spoke with much praise. This is not to butter you up only to pass on the joy.

Say Hebrew prayers that M 3 will make it—that I will. It will be a great issue with an Olson Max, and photographs of a burlesque lady I know, etc.

I think the phrase I wrote to you will be printed in capitals on the cover. #2's cover shit. I wanted small M-backwards but no other mistakes in entire issue. All your letter fancies retained and I do believe the labor was worth it, yours & mine. How I wd. love to see you and Helene and Fred, etc. I hope all is well & warm with you. I wish I could come thru with Measure quick the way it shd. be, but I cannot even come thru *with* a dollar bill. Miracle sent 10—and I hope she does not think I'm selling books. Whatever, I sent her 2 copies of II by mistake, etc and her name will appear printed in 4 issues beg. with #3. Why dont you write and give particulars—

Basil & Martha married return East late April

(reminds me he owes me $2.00)

Tom Field has a roomate, Dana Durkee.

Jerry van de Wiele plans permanent move here. Creeley here for Easter vacation & gave beautiful reading at the Dunn's flop. Lorraine to Mexico with new man, John Barrows, ex-bartender at the Place, and Claude also.

Harvey home in Sta. Monica.

It is dawn again.

I return poems I do not want to use, and there is no sense in sending more until after 3 is done. The ones previously accepted still go. Patience, I will make it. And I would like you in 4—maybe with a surprise like the birds. Or just 3 or so sharp poems. We'll keep the idea going that you're a sharp cookie.

#5 I figure as a

Domestic Scene

So if Helene could say turn out 2 pages of children fare and the kid's drawings (their own).

#6 I think will be letters from contributors only. Please keep faith in me so I can keep it in myself. Let me know if I should send a couple of Measure *to people* or rather just their addresses & I will mail from here. Also write if I dont. That is when I need same most.

Always, in love?
with much of it
to you two always
John

Can you imagine
it without the
Fireman after 5
years and with
small pain (yet)

Alright, I changed my mind on this. I guess there was so little of you, I got anxious.
Very proud of the birds as time goes by.

Robert Greene
Saturday April 12 1958
[San Francisco]

Dearest Bob: 6:45

I sit in the AM sun, having been up all night. And think about you often. What news
can I tell you? In/ or rather until Christmas 1958, when we shall have that drink. I
sent Measure off to you, et Veronique, etc. Thanks for the address.

Dana and I are split, and I feel good. His address in case you care to write:
            509 Buchanan Street, SF
while mine shall be with the Lady's for a little while longer. It is a temporary thing
until I can get a job etc. But we both enjoy it.

I am not a good one on letters, for I never seem to answer, but only write my own, so
forgive? Your letters fill me with a pleasure, that no other give. For it is a dream true,
Europe for you, and to hear you speak about the places been etc. makes me feel very
proud, that I somehow manage to be about my self, too, for the same reason, that
we both are in process of making the dream or the talk in 1950 the reality of 1958,
no matter how unpleasant at times that too is part of it, that this is what we have
chosen, and that you gotta pay dues for it, but there also can be pride, and pleasure
in the action taken, and the pleasure we can give to the others, in our contact, or it.
    Whatever, I send the enclosed, as it was written to you. Write about Measure.
        Whatever, write, as you can, it is most important. They come that way to
me.
I type this as I wrote it down . (On narrow paper).

I am sitting in the
6th Army Base of the
Presidio. Gertrude
Lawrence has stopped
 singing on the radio
on the table in front
 of me. This is [redacted on ms.]
new. I was merely
existing. I dont
know if I am
heaven or hell bound.
This is new. I am
hurled up to a world
I never knew and
this is new. This
is April 1st,
3 years from the
day I arrived
at Black Mountain,
 2 years from when
I left Dana and
began work at
Harvard from the
room on Hancock
Street.
1 year from Harvard
when Measure was
in the works and
now I am here
and Gertrude Lawrence
4 years from when
I wrote the poem
in the Stylus on
the bench in
Boston Common has
returned as they
all return to

us,[40] as we are
pledged to return
 to them.
I cant believe that
 Blue is dead.
It is the score of
 Lady in the Dark –
Christ is and
I am waiting to
 apply for
a job in the Army
 Library, writing
this in a cafeteria
 crowded with
75–100 workers
from the Letterman
 Hospital.
    Tuesday of
Holy Week and
    now Jenny's
    lit the candles
and threw the
    tapers away,
and I steal away
    before this
 song ends.
PS: 4.12.
And 59 years from when my
grandfather enlisted in the
 infantry and served at
the Presidio of San
Francisco, March 28th
    1899 I find
out this morning   *So? Love*
       John

---

40 It is unclear how the poem had "returned" to him, but Greene worked on *The Stylus* with him at Black
   Mountain, and so had probably sent a copy of Wieners's poem "Ode on a Common Fountain" from
   1954, which Wieners had written in Boston Common, and which would be the lead poem for his first
   full-length collection, 1964's *Ace of Pentacles*.

Joanne Kyger
[May 1958]
[San Francisco]

There is too much to tell you all at once. Anyway I am playing mute like Sheila for the day. 1) I could not find ear plugs, although I tried various devices but none fit. Mike Nathan's Painting I took to the Coffee Gallery, the middle of last week, and it hangs on the wall opposite the coffee maker.[41] Paul was afraid to put it in the window.

The house is immaculate. And no one has been in it, since that night, not even Jerome, who has been at Ryan's, pleading he has no place else to stay.

You received a new record from Columbia called: OH KAY.

It is terrible.[42]

The TWINK book is a gift from Shig at City Lights,[43] rather when I told him you owned Twink, he sent along this one. Vincent McHugh[44] per Shig extends his sympathies.

I am not going to the Poet's Follies Sunday,[45] rather to the Contemporary Dancers to see 3 Films of Larry Jourdan,[46] and hear Lamantia read. Jourdan gave me free coupon, so I traded in my Poet's Follies ticket.

Shig thought I was pulling a con fast dollar switch.

Linda was on the scene last night, panting after

Harvey, etc. Ebbe sat most of the night with Spicer.

While at our table was Ryan, Harvey, Dory Dull and Harold,

Beverly, Don Sherwood, (a nigger actor) Paddy, new barkeep

at the Place, from England, Already Nemi pants after him,

and various passers-by. No sign of Didier.

---

41 Mike Nathan (b. 1938), American painter involved in the North Beach scene of the late 1950s, his work featured in legendary local spots like the Six Gallery, the Co-Existence Bagel Shop, and the front window of City Lights Bookstore.

42 George and Ira Gershwin musical; a cast recording was released in 1955.

43 Shigeyoshi "Shig" Murao (1926–1999), American publisher at the center of the City Lights-North Beach universe. Manager of City Lights Bookstore for its first twenty-two years, he was the clerk who sold *Howl* to two undercover police officers on June 3, 1957, a trap that launched the famed obscenity trial.

44 Vincent McHugh (1904–1983), American poet and novelist who testified for the defense in the trial, swearing to *Howl*'s literary merit.

45 From 1955 to 1958, a group of locals staged the Poets' Follies, with a jazz band and performances by organizers Kenneth Rexroth, Michael McClure, James Broughton, and others. In 1958, the Follies were held on Sunday, May 11.

46 Larry Jordan (b. 1934) is an American avant-garde filmmaker who has lived and worked in the Bay Area since 1955.

I hope S. Dabney has good, at least warm news. And I
missed you last night at the bar, when it was quiet,
and I knew if you were around, it would not, be.

The Bermans go to Sausalito for the weekend, and I
am getting my hair cut tomorrow at Bob Levigne's/[47]
and bringing over a painting of Jerome's with
his permission (Martha Seider?) as Levigne is CERTAIN
he can sell one. He has seen J M's work, and is very
encouraging.

   PLEASE DESTROY this as you finish. Like in the spy-films,
or eat it.
   I begin now to walk to Sacramento, as I am
very frugal and have a transfer I can use once I get
there.
The McClures and L J leave this weekend for Mexico.

Jennifer will soon be amidst us.

Love,

Miss Pip[48]

Michael Rumaker

[May 1958]

[San Francisco]

A poem for the dead I know[49]

Gather the voices, forces I have forgotten

to find those graves I forget how

to come back to

DAVID ASPELIN

died at 16

put a rifle in his mouth, and laid across his bed at night.
After he held my hand on the way home and said

I will be dead tomorrow.

I see his grave and its pink quartz stone.

---

47 Wieners is referring to Robert LaVigne.
48 "Pip" was the pet name Kyger ("Miss Kids") had for Wieners.
49 "A Poem for the Dead I Know" was published in the "Uncollected Poems" section of Wieners's 1984
   Selected Poems.

And my uncle JOHN
LAFFAN, who I was named after, told me on Christmas
                I wont be here next year
and died last week 13 years to the day after his mother
                        May 13th.
            And the blue eyed girl across
the room from me will die. He came home my uncle John
to die in my mother's house, as her mother did
                in the same bed, I see her
& RICHARD TWARDZIK,[50] over-dosed in Paris.

I mourn none of them.
I want no one to return, boys and girls who I have known,
                        none
to come back and deck the Coit Tower in American flags,
pin flowers in the market windows, we are wrapped
                in the gloves of God.

Gone for good
the living and the dead, David and John
down, and what about the ones who walk above the ground
        where are they? where are my lovers
turned to dust, settling down on bar stools.
They sift through the streets of San Francisco.

I feel their hands, I know his mouth as my own,
I want him as I want my own body on me.
Her legs to warm my waist.

        They walk through other rooms,
    their desire wails on the face of the full moon,
    their pricks rise and make flowers, their hands
    masturbate for May rain, and leave me marching
    dead arms around my back and stupid tears down
            the cheeks of my dying face
I hear their voices on the radio.

---

50 Richard Twardzik (1931–1955) was a bebop pianist born in Danvers, Massachusetts, who fatally overdosed on heroin while touring with Chet Baker in Paris.

II

I sit now 4 flights above Fillmore Street.
The dead are far away.
Underground.
Only the staggering woman in a red coat
Rises. We are all Lazarus
And carry our dead friends with us.

Come up.
Above the telephone wires (if I fell on them
I would have a home tonight.
I would know where I'm going

. . as the houses fill the hills
as the humans the front seat of their autos
as the negro on the stairs of 2325
as the birds their blue fields . .

Green trees,
Green trees give forth the love of my old man
Neon lights give up the color of a Boston dawn
There is no death they tell me.
I am on the roof who does not dare to find them out.

III

Dead, be done with them.

How many have I know? have I counted
as my own. Oh does your flesh sit
on your bones, after these hundred years?

Love, be gone with it.

How many heads have I had under mine?
Strange mattresses for our mistakes.
Does it matter? The quick mating,
The meeting in public gardens.

Moon, be cool to night.

How many thighs opened at my hands?
Are your hands still under ground.

Grass, be green on their sunken graves.

Memorial Day, 1958.

Michael Rumaker
5.30.58
[San Francisco]

Dear Michael:

No particular reason why I have not written, except my own personal hassle of living in a different place every week, sometimes every night that causes me to delay in writing you. Dealay. Whatever, enclosed find poem, yesterday written at McClure's, just returned from Mexico. Hating it. Things are breaking for me I think, whatever each day has been filled with such ample rewards, that I can never feel poor or without resources.

The poem is as it was written, so there are places I would most appreciate your word on it, altho i know the hassle you must be/ tied to another job. Forgive the bitchy unconscious, as I want a job myself. If I only could make up my mind to cut my hair.

Then again, do feel free to write whatever. Your letters mean so much, a tie to former security, that I relish them. This is the only one of 50 waiting to be answered, I answer. Except to my Mother this afternoon. I still have The Book of yours and Duncan, also, the Secret of the Golden Flow. And Will mail as soon, as I can.

Pray for me, for us all, I think of you often, and sometimes wonder, how far a field I am, and become afraid, of those forces driving me. They sometimes mask as angels.

Are undercovermen, and we do not know we are going to be busted, until the gates are locked. Whatever, my means are legitimate, and my way of life, so I should not worry/ of the law/

but the other Law, which last night in a dream, showed me on the banks of a deep brown, muddy hill, with railroad, and highway trestles overhead, and as we descended (I forget those with me) we found more dolls in the mud, and the trestles crossed over our heads, and we were warned away, but the thought that we were unearthing treasures from lost and earthly kingdoms forced me. I remember picking up one doll, in the mudd, and seeing its painted face, and plaster hair around the face, black, and there was a red plaster jacket on it, too. Brown like the skin of a Gauguin native, and the trestles, were brown, sandly, with the gra ins of sand still showing in the cement.

Ah asphalt/

Enuf, baby/ do write. Lady Field still out to sea/ Dana still on barstools. I saw, sought him out two nights ago, and we talked, I cried. Puked, etc/ Duncan, still on Stinson Beach. Tell me about Tony Perkins,[51] I love to hear, and please write as you can, again. We will keep closer now, as I will have my own place shortly.

Love to you always. And we will see each other Christmas, anyway/

Again love—

John

* * *

Between June 15 and 23, 1958, while room sitting for Dave Haselwood in a rundown Polk Gulch hotel, writing and watching Robert LaVigne draw, John Wieners wrote the series of poems that Auerhahn Press would publish as *The Hotel Wentley Poems*. It is a slim collection of audaciously lyrical poems, teeming with startling images of the underground and buoyed by the exhilarating euphony he attributed, in a letter to Ginsberg, to the "magic of vowels."

The small book left an incalculable legacy, filtered through the poets of many different schools who read it. In 1959, Allen Ginsberg wrote about it to Jack Kerouac: "John Wieners by the way—I heard him read his *Hotel Wentley* poems—it made me cry, they are classic like Hart Crane's 'Behind my fathers cannery works'—You have that book? He is a real poet, sad and damned and tender."[52] In New York, Frank O'Hara called the book "a beautiful sequence of things," writing in one 1959 poem that "everybody here is running around after dull pleasantries and / wondering if *The Hotel Wentley Poems* is as great as I say it is."[53]

* * *

---

51 Anthony Perkins (1932–1992), gay American actor who had affairs with more than a few members of the overlapping circles of New York artists.

52 Kerouac, *Jack Kerouac and Allen Ginsberg: The Letters*, 454.

53 From O'Hara's 1959 poem "Les Lufts"; these O'Hara quotes are taken from Marjorie Perloff's *Frank O'Hara: Poet Among Painters* (15).

Ed Dorn

July 12 [1958]

[San Francisco]

Dearest Ed:

We are desperate men, and the rest bore. That is why we are friends. And I can write to you. And to Harvey in the nuthouse. (Only for a few months. It was that or jail for vagrancy.[54] He moved into Joanne's soon after you left). I live now with the McClure's, another desperate man. In trying to preserve himself. I have a double brass bed. And not much else. Enough for the present time, when all have too much. It is necessary for me I imagine to have the movement of family around me now. I cherish them all. Am too tender to make it comfortable living tho. Still being such strangers. With them. There are drugs to break the barriers. And I am breaking down whatever stands before me. Not in a big prick way, but with the hands of love. Whatever that is. A regard as one touches leaves, that are still on the tree. Leaving oily grease on same. "The hand of man."

I wish there was a person to lay my hands on. In love. Instead of my own miserable prick. The hair of Joanne Mc[55] bent before me as she fixed this machine. And it has been so long. That when she comes again, Lady Love, into my life, I will *be* swept away. The brushing of her hair. Against my flesh. How beautiful that you are close. That your $2.00 will always be remembered. I am glad Helene liked the silk. It is lovely.

No word on Measure. I live from day to day. I send you 4 poems I wrote a week ago exactly almost to the hour. They are not poems. But literal messages from somewhere. I send them only to have something to send you, as I am wordless. Now. Write often, Ed, whenever you can. There can never be boredom for us. By no means, did you leave me, fed up with you. I was filled only with the terror of the place I was living in. THE RATS, man. They nearly came in and took over. Scuttled the walls, etc.

After supper, with Fred Astaire's Bandwagon. OK. Enough for now. I send the communiqués.

Love always

John

---

54 "Vagrancy" was frequently the charge police would use to round up suspected homosexuals. "You could be charged with that in the City of San Francisco at that time if you didn't have $1,000 in your pockets," Rumaker recalls. "It didn't matter. That wasn't the real charge, and we all knew it" (*Robert Duncan in San Francisco*, 68).

55 Joanna McClure, American poet and educator who married poet Michael McClure after moving to San Francisco in the early 1950s. Her collected poems, *Catching Light*, was released by North Atlantic Books in 2013.

You asked me what
I think & I will tell
you, I am not
one of those tight-lipped

———————

Oh listen to my words for I am wise[56]
           I am like a lily fruit
                blooming in the wilderness.

I write the same words again, sitting here with Charlie Parker and
his rhumba band. I am one with the music, my cigarette stays on
the top of the table. I have decided I write prose. No one
understands me when I speak in poetry. It is not madness.

This sound, this syndrome
          12/22
I pace the same ground as my forefathers,

let this be jagged, let this be a new continent. It is.
My fingers are determined by the laws of the universe. They are
writing this.   I have no power over what I say.   I am ruled
by La Cucuracha. Go

yells the Bubus from under her bedroom door. No she also says.

And if this is madness it is divine.
There are magic happenings going on all over the world.
I pick up an ashtray and it has the hair of Jean Harlow in it.

We have come to the place where we can worship.
That is enough. There is no need to address America.

———————

56 "Oh listen to my words for I am wise" was collected recently as the leadoff poem in the British publication
Strictly Illegal from Patricia Hope Scanlan's Artery Press, a beautiful art book that juxtaposes previously
uncollected Wieners poems with art by Gilbert & George. As the title makes clear, the collection does
not "acknowledge copyright," and free of its restrictions is able to present for the first time many poems
that were printed in small magazines and might otherwise have disappeared with time.

We dont even stay cool anymore. We have the language
on our side. Brought in to us by musicians, by heads from outer space,
the junkies, the far travelers who always walk with a knife in their
back pockets, as I have walked today.

It is not the time for poetry. We go under as Rimbaud went,
if we let it catch up to us, but we are moving that fast,
that we stay one head up on the game.

I know not what I do. I am ruled by wonder magicians.
The green grass.

Blades of it, switch in your back hip pocket. Swing

your ass sister on Market Street, there is enough for all. Your
baskets will be full in this day after the 4th of July, our forefathers
brought forth on this continent a new

2nd Comminque for the Heads[57]

I love my fellow poets.

But I do not write for them. I write for heads.
They who stick your necks up into outerspace, they who
will not allow my fingers to make a mistake on this machine, no matter
how I falter, or err. It is all here. The periods are struck in the
furnace the same as the chains we all wear, around our heads

hair.

I can do nothing but write. I starve, and have no roof over my head
but the homes of strangers

---

57 "2nd Communique for the Heads" was published in Wieners's 1984 collection *Cultural Affairs in Boston*.

FIGURE 3 John Wieners by Leni Sinclair, Detroit, 1966. Courtesy of Leni Sinclair.

friends who take me in. I travel everywhere. I am as air.
I am puffed up with myself as a crow. I learned this trick
from a friend.

Who is a fellow poet.   Traveller.

———————

4th Comminque for Joanne and all the women[58]

I am wearing down. The ashtray lies littered with
butts and matches, ashes even that the Lady Bubus
will carry safely and empty in some other room.

———————

58 "4th Communique for Joanne and all the women" and "5th and Final Communique" were published in
the first issue of David Meltzer's magazine *Tree* (Winter 1970).

Her mother has given me corn to eat. And hash,
and egg yokes, no not yoke, but egg

WHITES.

We who sit in such color, feast and drink to the
whites of your eyes.

You maiden. You girls whose eyes turn blue
with the sky. And who walk through the high house in
white shoes. The typewriter is a magic instrument and
I perform white magic upon it. I call down the gods and
ladies of long ago

to wait on me. Patience with me, who sound
horns into the mystic places of my heart.

I will come to you Lady bearing gifts, these white sheets
of paper, the sheets I lie between each night, they are yours
and blue,

from your linen closet.

———————

5th and Finale Comminque

There is a brass bed.

There is a rhumba band, there is a junky saxplayer
on it. It fills the air with sweet space sounds.
It tells me of the long ago Mecico
down under land. If I went there, I would go down.
You will never get me there. You can beat your brass
bands, I will not go. Bands around my head

of yeast that feeds my hair, that makes bread
that feels ovens. As I am filling this space, with puffed up words

The drum

Pour water on me so I will stretch in the sun.
As in the morning rising from
the sea the sun does.
I do from a brass bed.

And the sun, where do you come from?
With a spectre over my shoulder, with night on yours,

Morning star.
It shone for me. Glitters on the headboard. It is what
we place in the firmament to take place beside nature.

The poem.

And always not enough. Not enough light.   Water on the drum.
Air for the lungs.   Earth for us to walk upon.   We war.

Unless we rise, can stick our heads
                              (oh lustrous hair
up for the Morning Star. Up like the Morning. Not an imitation
but basking in reflected glory.
                              The sun shines for us.
We shine because of the sun. My brass bed shone

My hand pulses under the peyote plant placed there.
    I am in pain, and it soothes me.   Oh

*   *   *

For the holidays of winter 1958–59, Wieners came back to Boston and New York,
spending time with family and old friends. In these next letters Wieners is checking
in on the production and distribution of *The Hotel Wentley Poems*, and telling stories
about his adventures back East, including time in New York with the newly famous
Beats he'd published in *Measure*. With these publications Wieners achieved some
literary reknown, but he was already wary of fame. Watching Jack Kerouac, who had
just gotten wildly famous with *On the Road* a little over a year before, he saw a man

who "looks like a bum . . . But more with a gleam in his eyes. & $300 in the bank. And a Life reporter smiling his white teeth."[59] This next letter to Charles Olson was written from his parents' home in Milton on his twenty-fifth birthday.

* * *

Charles Olson
1.6.59
[Milton, MA]

Dear Charles:

It seems I will never get the mss. of these poems typed up for you. Anyway they are old and the contents of a small book which is supposed to come out this month by the AUERHAHN press in San Francisco. 16 p. with the dates following each poem. Whatever, we shall see.[60]

All except the last one which I write tonight and send to you as a birth day message as I sit at my sister's desk.

Next weekend I go to visit her in Mary-land with my mother (if I could only be rid of my female soul, whatever it is mine. And then if it would be agreeable I feel a compulsion to use the word permissible Robin and I will visit the week following At least me. And I am sure him.

You shall see my ever present confusion. But that is all right. To be pulled two ways at once. If you are built right. and we are. It is too late to type long and so I write this shorthand which is a pleasure to see one's hand move, no?

I am in a good mood, with the temperature and the moon down. And my stomach and my cheeks are full. And you wd. not recognize me. No, I doubt that. Anyway— close to you in the night. I am

With love
John

---

59 Letter to Charles Olson, February 2, 1959.

60 *The Hotel Wentley Poems* was the first book published by Dave Haselwood's Auerhahn Press in San Francisco. The printers went against Haselwood's instructions and removed "Cock" from the title "A Poem for Cocksuckers," leaving a blank space in its place, so enraging the young publisher that he immediately began learning how to do the printing himself, which he did from then on. Future editions of *Hotel Wentley* put the "Cock" back in, and Wieners would add it in pencil to first editions he'd sign.

TWILIGHT IN THE BOSTON SUBURBS[61]

Dorchester turns blue,
John Hancock gleams 20
miles out to sea,
        land of the Irish, we
    sit 20 different animals
        in overcoats, riding home
            at 5 PM, my neighbor puts
    his paper under his arm as if
    to lodge it there forever.
                        A document of God.

A woman blinks and the car short circuits.
Another stares, we all stare, out into
Ashmont, where we get off and I get on
a car to Mattapan. It is 18 above

zero, the New Englander would never add.
    There is none in this world. Supper is
            laid out on a 1000 tables. Behind a square
    of light. the wind from the Neponset
                        blows down Eliot Street, and
    I am home looking in Mrs Redington's win-
            dows, rows of venetian
            blinds before my eyes, the trolley roars
    on in the night, my mother runs water
                and
    steamheat hisses thru the pipes, and she clinks

            dishes in the kitchen. A spoon
        drops in a drawer. overhead
    the 6 o'clock flight to New York. there is
    so much I could go on all night, as ~~the~~ cars

            on their errands, taking the world
    home.

across country 3000 miles ~~to~~ to
            spend ~~for~~ Christmas and my birthday
            in the room where my ancestors died.

---

61 "Twilight in the Boston Suburbs" is unpublished.

Charles Olson

2.2.59

[New York City]

Dear Charles:

I am sitting in 116 Eldridge St. Jan[62] is across the room from me. & others.
>   She holds a package
>   of Turkish cigarettes. There
>   is a 3 year old girl talking
>   to her and beside me on
>   the bed is Howard reading
>   French.

It is Twilight. Allen is in Chicago and I haven't seen him yet just left Kerouac in
The Rok bar. An "Irish" lush. Jan says he looks like a bum. And he does. But more
with a gleam in his eyes. & $300 in the bank. And a Life reporter smiling his
white teeth.[63]

---

62 As in Wieners's letter to Olson from November 24, 1957, it is difficult to say to whom exactly he is referring. Subsequent letters are written from the road as he accompanies Jan on her tour as an exotic dancer,
a trip that's at least very similar to one described in an interview with **Charles Shively** for *Gay Sunshine*
in 1973. To Shively, he remembered a woman named Jennifer with whom he'd gone on a road trip, and
recalls that he'd introduced her to Kerouac (with whom he very rarely socialized):

> That's Jennifer; we traveled from San Francisco to Boston together. It was with her that I first took
> heroin. She was arrested right around the corner here [44 Joy Street] on Cambridge Street one night
> when I went up miraculously to visit Charles Olson. I had decided to leave their place casually. They
> had received a lot of drugs from a drugstore break. A musician in Boston brought the drugs over. I
> just got up off the couch and said I was going to visit Charles. Later on that night there was a knock
> on the door and a man with a lumber jacket was standing there—a young, good looking fellow. And
> Jennifer, not knowing who he was, but thinking she knew who he was because he was so familiar with
> the milieu in which she traveled. I had introduced her to Kerouac a few weeks before. He was of that
> social qualification or identification. They all had heavy trials and received suspended sentences on
> probation. The front pages of the Record American had headlines: "Stripper Nabbed in Drug Arrest."
> (Winston Leyland, *Gay Sunshine Interviews*, 2:269)

The newspaper account of that arrest—saved in Olson's papers from when Wieners gave it to him (with a
note saying, "the day at your house")—features a glamorous photo of "The Succulent Jennifer," and says that
the name she gave police was "Jane Mintz." It is interesting that on August 26, 1959, the Portsmouth, New
Hampshire, *Herald* reported that "Miss Jeanette Minsk, a 31-year-old strip-teaser," had been arrested as a
fugitive on an unspecified narcotics charge. Is Jennifer/Jane Mintz the same person as Jan in these letters,
and is Jane Mintz the same person as Jan/Jeanette Minsk? Absent more information it is impossible to
determine with certainty. Wieners wrote a poem for whichever Jan this was, describing her as she "hustles
her islands of pure flesh"—"Offend not the ancestral gods, by this sale // Of love" (*Ace of Pentacles*, 65).

63 Kerouac's novel *On the Road* had made him a pop cultural sensation in the late summer of 1957, and the
year-plus between that sudden fame and Wieners's visit was, to say the least, rough on Kerouac. As Bill
Morgan and David Stanford note in their edition of the Ginsberg-Kerouac letters, the early months of
1959 found Ginsberg courting more fame while Kerouac retreated: "When Jack was in the city he tended

and Rachel looking
   for her ball under the bed
   Throwing it

  in the air and
    letting it drop.

Dan Rice[64] a piece of steel, full of
  wires and cable. Blackburn[65]
officious. Corso in Chicago.
    Ed a NE minister
and Howard lays lengthwise
Rachel is pulling up her
    red pants. Still
    throwing the ball
3 page letter from Marshall coming
  to you with poems.

Basil great. Martha thinner and
  no violence in their
  house. Home made
  chicken soup there
last night. On Whitehall Street
    #33
  at the tip of Manhattan

    a loft in an office building
that closes at 5.

---

to drink to excess and retreated more frequently to his mother's house for solitude. . . . In order to keep his sanity, Jack was trying to keep out of the limelight" (Kerouac, *Jack Kerouac and Allen Ginsberg*, 427).

64 Dan Rice (1927–2003), American artist. A whiz trumpet player, he filled in with Benny Goodman, Tommy Dorsey, Artie Shaw, and Woody Herman as a teenager. In the navy during World War II, he served in the Pacific, then went to Berkeley and Black Mountain College on the GI Bill. A talented shortstop, he played in the Brooklyn Dodgers farm system. His true vocation, though, was painting, and he was closely associated with the Abstract Expressionists.

65 Paul Blackburn (1926–1971), American poet and translator often grouped with the so-called Black Mountain School because of his role as an early contributing editor for the *Black Mountain Review* and Donald Allen's grouping of them in the 1960 *New American Poetry* anthology. He is known for his vital translations of works like the medieval Spanish epic *Poems of the Cid*, and through the 1960s he was a prime moving force in the Lower East Side poetry community that congregated around Café Metro and the St. Mark's Poetry Project.

LeRoi Jones a king and his house
  a court
      Yard I said
  where we all gather into the
          night on the floor
  Max Finstein.[66] Joel (sissy)

The Librarian[67] looks great imprint
complete. Opens Yugen 4.[68]

Things are tight. The people are
  who are people. Dan
  made the strongest impress
  ion on me with his
  "junky" ways, his tics
  and pain—Full of
  steel. Mass—

ive in his diminuity.

And so we sit in the night. Miles
  finishing up on his
  trumpet. And Teddy
  in the corner reading a
  pocket book. With a
  cylinder light in the
  middle of the room.

Silver tinsel hanging
  on all its sides so
  it looks like
  a chandelier

---

66 Max Finstein (1924–1982) served in World War II and then spent time in New York and San Francisco before settling in New Mexico. The naming of Max's Kansas City may or may not have been inspired by Finstein, and was more likely the provenance of Joel Oppenheimer, a New York poet who had studied at Black Mountain. Finstein's 1966 collection *The Disappearance of Mountains* was the only book published by Dorn's *Wild Dog* magazine.

67 "The Librarian," a poem by Charles Olson about Gloucester's "Black space, / old fish-house" and the "Motions / of ghosts," opened the fourth issue of *Yugen,* which also contained Wieners's "Spring 1956."

68 Founded and edited by LeRoi Jones (Amiri Baraka) and subtitled "a new consciousness in arts and letters," *Yugen* was a wide-ranging and essential venue published from 1958 to 1962.

New song now.

    Lower east side. Everyone
    clean except Kerouac with
    a three day growth of
    beard. Double wines.

    Not an act. Lost. His girl with a
    pheasant feather in
    her hair and a white
    shawl over her coat.
    Overdressed. A
    Venus mark between
    her teeth. Tall. Her name is
    Dodie Müller.[69]

I am staying at Ed's for a while yet
        and cant say what's
        up because I dont
        like it there. Mike
in Bellevue from an overdose
of sleeping pills. w/see him
Tuesday. Tube in his throat.
Out of critical condition
now. Fielding thinks

    of you a lot and drinks
    a lot. Jonathan bitching
    still. No one has any patience
    for him or regards him much.

It is Dan. And Max. And
    the usual real ones
    who make it. You know
them. Iso-morphic
        (that is not the
        word but the form
that does not change with place.

---

69 Dody Müller, American painter and Kerouac's girlfriend for a brief time in early 1959. Kerouac would
    later credit her with inspiring him to try painting.

Love to Betty and you & yours

the blue cups.
A pile of red paper bricks
   collapsed in the middle
      of the floor.
     John

Charles Olson
2.10.59
[New York City]

Dear Charles:

Tomorrow we leave. Driving as far as Canton, Ohio w/ Jan where she begins her 1st week on tour. From there who knows but without her at least for a little while.

Yesterday dinner, spontaneous with Ginsberg and Corso on East 2nd. First time I had caviar. There the 3 of us sat. The Russian Jew, the Italian and the Irish. Spent until 5AM with Ginsberg. What to say? He wants to make it. Not only on the crest but always. Showed me 75 clippings from Chicago. I said "Is this how you treat visiting poets?" Read as far as I could into his long mother poem[70] (60 pages) typewritten, single spaced. Interesting to me because of the paranoia of his mother. Her actions I know and have lived to some small degree. At least her terror. "The dropping of the mind on the page." This phrase I most remember. But it's this lack of the original which ultimately bars him. Bores me.

I mean all poets inhabit the instant-eous the immediate but we all we beat suffer from lack of joy, inability to lift above ourselves.

He carries a weight with him, even tho he moves with delicate lightness, walking down stairs. Spring. That twist which shows

I sense none or little of the excitement I have with you. Or Duncan say. Or Mike Rumaker even who is better. In violent ward at Bellevue.
     Ward 07
     1st Ave & 30th St.

---

70 "Kaddish for Naomi Ginsberg (1894–1956)," the epic lament Allen Ginsberg wrote for his mother. He began writing it at the Beat Hotel in Paris in 1957, completing it in 1959 in New York. Ginsberg cited Edward Marshall's poem "Leave the Word Alone" as an important influence.

tho most calm himself and realizing that this too must pass. The void. He will get out, and be alright. On his own terms.

As Allen will not. There is a challenge in him. Like Beat <u>me</u> or Accept <u>me</u>. When I would rather it was
<u>Let's watch it.</u>
        Happen between us

There is generosity and mobility in both, in their lives. But they are hooked on their own lives. I mean you said it.
        Personal history is a love.
Or something like that. Inability to grasp the whole situation. Or rather only to see my side of it. Rather than that other side, which is the mysterious, the unknown, & un-
    conscious. How lovely it plays when it does in our lives. And juggles events. And shakes us by
        the roots of our
        hair. Holds us in
tune to the moving of the
        un-
        iverse.
But there is poetry in their lives

and they allow that to lead them. Corso the quickest to grasp the exotic, the weird violent. Still a slum kid being wacked on the ass for what he didn't do.
    Showed us his tunnels and mansions around Wash. Square Park where he grew up. But on the wrong side of the tracks. Lower east side, I think. Ginsberg more aware both his parents school teachers. Corso the

trickster. But more spontaneously kind.
    Sentiment.
    On my part. For the dirty undershirts. And the frenzy. And that we gotta make it somehow anyhow, anyway we can and this is it. And why not.
    Ginsberg pretends a nihilism that all is nothing. And has <u>no</u> meaning. We live in illusion. Reality is this. We only think we exist.
        And when I said
        Everything has meaning

I don't think he believed it. That its only a cartoon with a Woody Wood Pecker laugh at the end. "A huge laughing bowl" His prosody which he is most concerned about, I mean his thoughts about it are all acquired.

I am writing this at Marshall's desk and our contact has been negligible. I mean I am unable to link arms. Maybe later. There is much to appreciate in him and much to despise. Or rather much that I have worked thru myself and see as dross. And yet his own pure light shines above it all.

Jonathan now living in town. Trying to pull things together
    Yugen is the center of activity. #4. WOW.

Max Finstein a fine man. And Dan Rice a joy to see walking 8th Street.
            Forgive the tone of
God in the letter after this.

Just spot judgements and I believe all we see in others only a reflection of our lights and shadows. So the danger there. Where is the real man amidst all these men that inhabit me. Where is the one that is apart and how to deal with him and let him have his space as
    he walks it.
    On his own and
    w/o interference
    from personal forces.

Ginsberg can pour soup in his ear but it does not have the same power as your hand on Betty's knee.
    The real vs sur-real.

    Heard Big High Song for
    Somebody. by
                Whalen on
    the Jazz Canto Record and it is
    a must when you are in NY
    next. Joel Earnest also

but without the surety of
        Max or Dan.
Anyway, NY is

What? The
center of the current scene?
            No. That
is in our "hearts." But how you gonna keep 'em down on the farm after they've
seen Paris, how you gonna keep 'em away from Broadway,
     jazzing around
     doing the town. How you
     gonna keep 'em away
     from H'rlem, that's
     a mystery.

     So me and my burlesque baby go off in the night again. To see her is a joy, walk
through a bar, open her eyes at me, or touch my knee.
     To walk with her
     down Broadway and

turn on. To pass the pipe. It is
            her hands & breasts
            ETC . . . leave it

to Tin Pan Alley to do her
justice. Anyway Boston is
            dead now forever
            for us.

And the country (or continent)
            is alive. Oh open
plains embrace my love
            and I. Bless
my love and I. Travelling
            light.
We linger on.
     Love to you & Betty
            John
4AM

Charles Olson
[February 13, 1959]
[On the Road]

Hotel Canton, 5th and Cleveland N., Canton, Ohio
Room 10
10 mins to 2
Friday the 13th
February
1959

A picture of HORSE on the wall, a yellow
leather chair, Jan's black stockings on
her legs in yellow leather shoes, she sits
writing in black a letter (w/a gold pencil

                Communique.
                  Rain out the
                  open window at
                  my left, and
                  w/in reach of my
                  right, her and
the night cold in Canton,
Ohio—Mid—West America,

All these colors. This unreality is not
necessary. This heightening of the senses,
so that all becomes blur, and dazzle.
    In the dark of the year
We are only flesh. Animals
        on the plain. Pushed
        out of doors, driving
        over the land, landing
        nowhere in sight, the
        great lakes at the
        top of the state, somewhere
from the top of my head,
        verse and

its making
       lost in the shuffle, see-
       ing only now, this God
and my entrance way
         to him.

When Jan read this she shook her
       shoulders and said
          that's me.
So what. A shimmy and screech
So soon she will be gone

                * * *

The spring and summer of 1959 was a time of intense creative work and pleasure seeking for Wieners, with less time spent on letters. He was using harder drugs with harder people, pushing the derangement of his senses to its extreme, but as his journal *707 Scott Street* reveals, this was by no means lost time. Even as he was scoring with friends and remaining the charming center of the party, he was also studying Olson, Jung, and Sufi mysticism and intensively rethinking his poetics. In his stoned introspection, he saw clearly the potential glory and certain suffering of his poetic vocation:

I can count on countless years before me with no food in my
              stomach,
   writing out history in some dark room, doing my bit towards creating
         a new structure
            from love.
   It can only be that. For [any] other motive we fail. And love is a
              sparse thing
        to nurture all
        these years.[71]

On July 17, 1959, Billie Holiday died.

                * * *

---

71 *707 Scott Street*, 43.

Donald Allen

July 1 [1959]

[San Francisco]

Dear Don:

I sit in my yellow silk shirt, in love with myself, and what better love is there? *And: lots* Light comes thru the windows, Mike Rumaker is awake in Rockland, Robert Duncan sits in solitary splendour in Stinson Beach, and where am I. Half of a back room in San Francisco, where I watered 1/2 grain of heroin into the plant the afternoon you were here. I see you still on the bed. Gray figure from another world. This is a world of red poppies in a green glass, of black type on green paper, a world without end, which any moment the next could throw into chaos, it will not, yet, we wait for the next event, the next letter to impose itself on the universe, making a new universe. One letter of the alphabet can do it. And we sit, guardians of that throne. To use a medieval image. Like the heart, which contains still that fire of love. Richard Rolle: Hermit.[72]

The 2nd half of the 20th century, they say Creeley says. How sacred our duty: Alice Dalliance in the No, Nothing Bar.

[...]

> Dont despair, darling, I think of you
> more than you think.
> *John*

> The Nemi poem falls down at the end but there
> is nothing to do, as this is the fact of the
> poem.

Donald Allen

Sept 20 [1959]

[San Francisco]

Dear Don:

---

72 Richard Rolle (ca. 1300–1349), English Christian mystic and hermit whose best-known work is *Incendium Amoris* (The Fire of Love), an account of his mystical experience in its various visual and aural manifestations. Wieners quotes this book in *707 Scott Street*: "For the boisterous and fleshly soul is not ravished into contemplation of the Godhead unless all fleshly lettings be wasted away by ghostly meditation." To this quote Wieners adds, "Delectable heat is also in the loving heart, that has devoured heavy grief in the fire of burning love" (34).

Well. I cant do anything new. But I will send you a poem I wrote this morning. And an excerpt from a journal I keep, which is abt. poetics, as I have been able to come to it.[73]

I just fell over on my back with the typewriter on my chest, and I looked up at the ceiling, and said, I'm gonna die this way. Like the goddamn cat I stepped on, with my left Mexican shoe, the drops of blood spread throughout the house. Gasping for breath. Always. Anyway.

A poem for trapped things.[74]

Oh God what have you
given me that a black
butterfly lives in this room.
This morning with a blue flame burning
this thing wings its way in.
Wind shakes the edges of its yellow being.
Gasping for breath.
Living for the next[75] instant
Climbing up the black border of the window.
Why do you want out.
I sit in pain
A red robe amid debris,
You bend and climb, extending antennae.

I know the butterfly is my soul
and it is weak from battle.

A Giant fan on the back of
        a beetle.
A caterpillar, chrysalis that seeks
a new home apart from this room.

---

73 He is referring to *707 Scott Street*.
74 "A Poem for Trapped Things" was published in *Ace of Pentacles*, beginning with the line "This morning with a blue flame burning" (in this manuscript the first three lines are bracketed, with "omit" written on the left). It was read by friend Jim Dunn at Wieners's funeral in 2002.
75 "Next" is circled.

And will disappear from sight
at the pulling of invisible strings.
Yet so tenuous, so fine
this thing is, I am
sitting on the hard bed, we could
      vanish from sight like the puff
          off an invisible cigarette.
Furred chest, ragged silk under
        wings beating against the glass

    no one will open.

The blue diamonds on your back
are too beautiful to do
     away with.
I watch you
    all morning
       long
  With my hand over my mouth.

       (1959)

       July 17 [1959]

From a journal[76]

A poem does not have to be a major thing. Or a statement?
I am allowed to ask many things because it has been given
me the means to plunge into the depths and come up with
     answers? No. Poems, which are
my salvation alone. The reader can do with them what he likes.
I feel right now even the reading of poems to an unknown

---

76 Donald Allen published Wieners in his groundbreaking anthology *New American Poetry* in 1960, including four *Hotel Wentley* poems and this one, "A Poem for Trapped Things." He also included this journal entry in the "Statements on Poetics" section, but he deleted Wieners's postscript "*quote from Olson." As Wieners later explains in a somewhat panicked letter to Allen (October 27, 1969), he'd meant to place an asterisk after "shitting" to make it clear that the line was a quote (and, he'd add, an offhanded joke by Olson).

large? public is a shallow <u>act</u>, unless the reading be given for the
    fact of clarity. The different <u>techne</u>
a man uses to make his salvation. That is why poetry
even tho it does deal with language is no more <u>holy</u> act
    than, say shitting.*
      Dis-
    charge. Manifesting the
      process of
  is it life? Or the action between this and
        non-action? <u>Lethargy vs</u>
         <u>Violence.</u>
For to take up arms against the void is attack, and the price of war
        is high. Millions of syllables
shed over the falls of our saliva, millions of teardrops
roll out of our eyes. Giant screams echo through the halls of our house
gaged in. Hundreds of days, months have to go by before the
spirits descend and the right word rolls out sharp and full of
    fire air earth and water
    [off the tips of our
        tongue. And one cannot avoid the
days. They have to parade by in all their carnage. The events of
them like images on a shield, we carry thru the streets of
  the town
    later on our way to the poetry reading." Drunk or
        doped before that wild horde who press in
to get a peek at the bloody hero. And is he?
      You bet.

As a postscript abt any of us writing on poetics: this.
        (I changed
         my mind.

  Love to you always

  J

*quote from Olson

FIGURE 4 John Wieners and Panna Grady, Gloucester, Massachusetts, 1966. Photographer unknown. Panna Grady Collection (1950–2015), the Poetry Collection of the University Libraries, University at Buffalo, the State University of New York.

By the end of 1959, John Wieners's excessive drug use had caught up with him. He traveled home for Christmas, and his friends and family were alarmed by his erratic behavior and conversation. In a letter to Ed Dorn, Amiri Baraka describes Wieners's visit:

> John Wieners was by here a couple of weeks ago. Stayed with us for week or so. He's in horrible shape. Sullen silent . . . never saw him like that before. Very disturbed (??) And that's a terrible way to try to say it. Disturbed??? Like who isn't? When John left N.Y., he went up to his parents in Boston. His mother apparently flipped and called up the mental hospital people. They came & from what I get from Irving Rosenthal, they carried John off in straight jacket. He's got to stay in that place at least 40 days, cause his mother signed him in. Seems so bleak.[1]

His parents had him forcibly committed to Medfield State Hospital, a sprawling institution about twenty miles west of Milton. Word spread quickly through the New York and Boston poetry communities, who rallied to his side. So many of their circle—especially the homosexuals—had been hospitalized, and everyone knew the fear and desperation Wieners was feeling. What was initially a forty-day hold turned into a six-month confinement.

Though the New Yorkers knew of Wieners's hospitalization right away, it took his Black Mountain friends longer to get the news; a couple of weeks passed before Olson found out. He finally wrote, apologetically, on February 5, to declare: "I'm still 'following' you!"[2] As Dorn reported back to Jones, Olson had heard about someone's hospitalization but thought it was Michael Rumaker ("there are so many of us in the nuthouse," Dorn mused).[3] This was the first of several hospitalizations Wieners would endure. Recounting his confinements less than two years later, in November 1961, Wieners told new friend Irving Rosenthal that after "30 shock treatments at Bournewood, and 91 insulin treatments at Metropolitan State," he had no recollection of their time together. "I wish I had some memory of last year, but I do not, of living with you, of your kindness, but all is a blank."[4] It is impossible to

---

1 Letter to Ed Dorn, January 19, 1960, *Amiri Baraka & Ed Dorn: The Collected Letters*, 18.
2 Wieners and Olson, *"the sea under the house,"* 2:13.
3 Dorn letter to Jones, March 1, 1960, ibid.
4 Letter to Irving Rosenthal, November 9, 1961.

speculate upon the origins or possible trajectories of Wieners's prehospitalization distress, but the institutionalization itself, with its attendant "therapies," caused undeniable and lifelong harm.

* * *

Charles Olson
2/12 [1960]
[West Harding MA]

Dear Charles:

Third attempt at letter to you. My great dilemma here is how to have freedom. I am committed here on 40-day paper per stretcher and straps of Father. That time will be up at the end of next week. And if I am not released I know there will be such great pain ahead, only you seem an avenue of salvation.

I also have some crimes I could confess to and thereby go to jail which after time done there, life would be my own again. Your letter was a godsend. Whatever I want out and will use any means to gain same. I have learned to pray again. Home phone is [illeg]–6–2471 if a call to parents would convince them what an injustice any extension of imprisonment here would mean.

Will you let me know what your mind reads? I have a new book: THE PLANETS.⁵ Also word from E Marshall that he would shelter me when released. If parents refuse to take me home.

Your friend JAWN

---

5 "THE PLANETS" was one of the names ("JEWELS" another) Wieners gave to a journal that was trag- ically lost during his first hospitalization. Irving Rosenthal described it in a letter to Wieners, who had no memory of the journal after his extensive electroshock and insulin coma treatments:

I don't know how to respond to the loss of Jewels. It is the notebook you kept under the name of Planets at Medfield, a black book with a yellow spine. You changed the name of it to Jewels about the time you left Medfield. It was about half full of writing—poems, prose, several sermons. It was the only thing you carried when you left this apartment a year ago to spend Christmas with your family. I think it was the most precious thing you had. (Unpublished letter from Irving Rosenthal, December 4, 1961, Irving Rosenthal Papers, Stanford University)

Irving Rosenthal
2–12 [1960]
[West Harding, MA]

Dear Irving:

How kind of you to let Charles know my imprisonment here. And how much I want freedom at the end of next week, if only parents will claim me. I have the jailhaus ahead "of course" as a last extreme but again to possess life as my own gift is the only desire. Will you do everything to see me home? Their number is [illeg]6–2421. I have written to both them and Olson this morning. Where else may I turn?

A white flag. With no state bars upon it. Is Allen back yet. Perhaps he or Peter could help. I am not Rumaker and do not believe in the institution. Then there is Don Allen. All these voices must band together as Blaser, etc did for Rosario Jimenez in the 40s.[6] I have also written to Duncan and Hazelwood. Word from Alan Minsk and Tom Balas in Uneaseville is "good." Until after abcess jaw, tooth extractions and [illeg] are treated this AM. Also call for breakfast. I remain a servant to the structure of language.

> *Yours*
> *John*

Barbara Guest
2.16.60
[West Harding, MA]

Dear Barbara Guest:

Human affairs are a matter of necessity to me this morning. The dream world being such a shambles of old cafes, florid women and ~~our old~~ *liquid* yellow horn. Being caught as I am right now in the grips of an asylum, there is not much I can think about but the New Measure. Will you be a part of it? Lemon cover, chocolate print *on* etc. This weekend *(20th)* I expect Irving Rosenthal & Schulman who *are*

---

6 Rosario Jiménez, Puerto Rican classics scholar, Greek tutor for Robert Duncan and Robin Blaser, introduced the poetry of Frederico García Lorca to Duncan's roundtable of friends in 1945 at "Throckmorton Manor," the rooming house where he lived at the time. Blaser later recalled:

> She would read Lorca in Spanish and it would sound very much like Homer in Greek, both of them extraordinarily grand and marvelous. She had this *vroom ooww*, and not being a poet herself, I think she put a power into it. She went crazy quite often, and I remember once when she took her entire library and threw it out on Union Street, stopping all traffic, and wound up in the hoosegow. Duncan and I went and got her out. (*The Astonishment Tapes*, 199)

contacting printer and distributor, also supplying $. Is the world too jaded for a small Tigers Eye?[7]

Write here. c/o Dr. KORMOS. His name seems to be a "sesame" for good fortune. How I miss Washington and the Holidays. But February seems kinder to our world. Do clasp tight, even the pain. There is always laudanum. And the mechanics of the "human face." Pray for my freedom and we shall be kind enough to find release in each other's arms again.

Faithfully,
John Wieners

The unconscious is a lion. He stalks. Pots from[8]
the pool of day. Is a boy in blue riding waves.
Let the lutes play. In our tombs, jars and
narcissus sprout from the weeds. ~~Define~~ *of* now.
It is not a poem. It is the paragraph. In
dent it. Mine possess no space at all.

    Crowded with the dig of his bruise. His sail
I use to bail out the boat. Rudder and mane
overflow in our concrete world. What is the wave
made of? Tides from the belly and balls of the
~~the~~ bull : Aleph. See his stamp in the sky.
As we are constructed, so are the stars plotted:
the poet marks a new chart. Pinpoint pocks
the day of his birth. This morning astride her
precious light ~~the~~ *an* hallowèd woman stands
aboard.

from a bk. The PLANETS   2%

If you can forgive this intrusion of your morning, and the pressure of thot; there is some need in the male psyche for possession of cool hands. We shall not expend ours. DROSTË

---

7 *Tigers Eye*, short-lived but influential arts and literature journal, edited by John and Ruth Stephens over
    nine volumes (1947–1949). The elegant, eclectic series was reissued in 1967.
8 "the unconscious is a lion . . . " is unpublished.

Charles Olson
[Feb 25, 1960]
[West Harding, MA]

Morning of the 25th

with Mrs. Halloran, sitting on the bed,
sunspots and all workers convene here.
Medfield State Hospital. the secret
source of the ring, alligator bag, ragged
nails, snap a button, at the belly

what we fear
        Cheeks spread, thru the fore
head bumping over ruts in the lot,
                                Jumping
tractors and yellow trucks.

                    II
            Fields Corner itself, on the
overpass past St. Margaret's, not nodding
                to the bricks _

Empty railroad depot, by the radiators
                    in stocking feet
            stood up Cambridge Street

money, stocking cap, navy blue scarf
silver box, all the tricks of the trade.

Even handwriting betrays us. Overseas

Dear Charles:
    Here is 2nd copy of RAFT.

Caught in asylum again, how hard to
break thru the wall. Wish you were here. Staff

meeting Tuesday clears nothing up except
word of day off to visit Widener and
study works of ancestors, James and William
Leave Stuart de Courcy[9] for policia. Yr
greetings puts such stuff in my mouth,
The ward remains far away. But a Dr.
Kormes claims there will be new interviews.

Now take me back to my own ruins, the raft[10]
on the Naponset in February, with Mother
beating thru the woods, red coat and all
autumns come down, leaves caught in flood.

Gutters, Michael Murphy raking blue smoke
by the old stone wall, swinging off birches,
beechnut, the big rock and hot tin barrel.

Roll me over one more time. Marion for
this scorch in the sun. Sister who haunts me
in alleys off Blue Hill Avenue.

Rats under the crib, smashed glass and
blankets hang out all windows of this mustard

seed world.

Charles Olson
March 9 [1960]
[West Harding, MA]

Dear Charles:
    How solitary I feel here. Surrounded by the
bustle of the ward. first morning I hope without
medication. The drugs of course allow us to

---

9 Apparently matrilineal ancestors William MacKay Laffan (1848–1909) and Stuart de Courcy Laffan were
   both Irish authors.
10 "Now take me back to my own ruins . . ." is unpublished.

enter the vision? any world but my touch/ sense
of reality is diminished to such an extent that
we are prey to any passing interruption. Here I
go again. Name just called for more of what
I feel takes away all spark/ burst of new order
on the confusion of these past two months. As
you can see the handwriting changes. back now
with 3 more pills down. So many drugs over
these years—after I had withdrawn on Scott
Street for that blissful train trip across
filled with ordinary concerns/ hunger, money,
schedules etc. All the paphernalia of traveling. The stuff hits immediately and I know
it's a sin to the soul but I follow orders
so that my discharge may be advanced as
soon as possible. If I dont get out soon

therapy includes electrical catheter treatment, something I don't need at all, but
which is being fostered here at such a clip that even my own deepest reserves are
threatened. Trying to write a paper on childhood for Dr. Vispo. Thank you for
writing Michael as his word here I still live off.

I have ~~written to~~ asked an aunt in New York for legal counsel and my family visits
Sunday also gifts (Irving and an Else Dorfman[11] from Grove on Saturday.

After hair cut and session at the piano with voices, what a multitude of birds,
Lark, martin ghosts emit from these keys.

You can see how my language is threatened here, the constant repe-
tition of connectives, but it is the only thing I can use to maintain what shreds of
thought fear leaves.

I am trying to cohere some force for the new issue and am even trying on the
name FORENOON for size. What do you think?

I see great prizes ahead. Now my pen points/ remains poised for that dart out the
nearest exit. Until they provide it I contain the closet of my love for you.

~~John~~ JAWN

---

11 Elsa Dorfman (1937–2020), American photographer based in Cambridge, Massachusetts, known for her
Polaroids of writers, artists, and rock stars. In 1959 and 1960, she worked as a secretary for Barney Rosset's
Grove Press in New York; she also founded the Paterson Society, a nonprofit venture whose aim was to
act as a liaison between poets and reading venues, particularly colleges. Documentarian Errol Morris
released a feature film about Dorfman in 2017, called *The B-Side*.

* * *

This next note to Ginsberg is the only letter from the nine-month period between his first and second hospitalizations, a time when he was cared for by various friends. LeRoi Jones, for one, signed for legal custodianship so that Wieners could spend time in the city with his friends, instead of returning to Milton, Massachusetts, with his family. Four months later he was institutionalized again, at Metropolitan State Hospital in Waltham, Massachusetts.

* * *

Allen Ginsberg
November 4, 1960
[New York City]

Dear Allen:

Please forgive this rather hasty note. I am trying to get to a poetry reading. Here are all the copies of MARIJUANA I could get. They are looking for me for more. Also two added clippings I found referring to drugs, printed since I left.

I didn't call Felicia Geffin at the American Academy of Arts and Letters, as I will wait until I really need it. It was a moment of panic I called you. Sorry I missed you at the Village Gate. I could have been there too, out wandering around with Szabo.[12]

Am coming in for Joanne's reading November 11, or 12th with Helen Adam, so will see you then.

> *Love,*
> *John*
> John
> *Wieners*

John

---

12 Bill Szabo, also known by the mononym Szabo, was a poet and drugs enthusiast in the 1960s East Village. He was an early member of **Ed Sanders**' proto-punk band The Fugs, playing the "amphetamine flute" at the opening of Sanders' Peace Eye Bookstore (Sanders, *Fug You*, 128).

Charles and Betty Olson
Sunday June 18 [1961]
[Waltham, MA]

Dear Charles and Bette:

Just a short note to thank you for the wonderful dinner and time spent Saturday. Enclosed find Herald book review which I hope you'll keep. I'll wait to hear from you before I come again as I dont feel I contributed very much to the day.

Just an open ear for you, Sir.
        Best wishes and
        Love,
        John

* * *

Released from hospital August 25, 1961, Wieners returned home to Milton to stay with his parents again and try to recover from his treatments. His letters from this period are moving for Wieners's renewed dedication to poetry; as he tells Dave Haselwood, "I am still young enough to wait, and have no hope of fame." In its way this was an exciting time for Wieners as he rebuilt his life, "devour[ing] the Public Library," reading Waugh, Greene, Woolf, Melville, Jung—anything he could get his hands on. His biggest project was getting back the reins of his career, picking up the threads of publications and a theatrical production that had been initiated during his electroshocked blank period.

* * *

Dave Haselwood
Sunday, August 27 [1961]
[Milton, MA]

Dearest Dave:

The importance of the Auerhahn now. I realize it reading Dark Brown,[13] and seeing the Dogtown,[14] and being home, for good!

---

13 Michael McClure's *Dark Brown* was first published by Auerhahn Press in 1961. Dave Haselwood reprinted it under his eponymous imprint in 1967.
14 Auerhahn Press published Charles Olson's *Maximus, From Dogtown—I*, with a slate-grey cover and introduction by Michael McClure, in 1961.

That it all goes on, without one, except for you. And with this shiny new machine. I am preparing a book, and would hesitate to send you anything until it is done. Also the fact that you are busy, and probably sick of 'poetry.' Are you working on Philip's now?[15]

Am spending each day working on it. And thinking of you, and your trip, how important it will be. Seeing you, and showing you the manuscript, in person. Even doing a little traveling together. Traveling light, as Mambah says. Sings. I am with you in all things, am now there, in the touch typing of my fingers, not wanting to let go.

[…]

I am still young enough to wait, and have no hope of fame. Don't mistake this as despair, as I am far from it today. The joy of writing or the 'apprehension' of it is with me always. And some part of me must be left out there. I feel it so, that the dance of the day is not complete until or unless I go through all the cycles of emotion, even tho this is not the most fitting occupation of a man. As I wrote to **Andrew [Hoyem]** I am reading Whitman's Leaves of Grass, and the most amazing thing, you can not open the book anywhere, but there is something on it, to read, that entices one, moves you, and I even hear echoes of him in McClure. Dark Brown, such a masterpiece of print. How these three years, you have served so faithfully.

I wish I had the money to bring you East in the style you do deserve.

Also, so good to read of your trip to Sierras. I am so hungry for all news of anyone, that I believe I have come into a second being of some sort.

I send you these notes from a journal just to send them, and have no hope of a response. Dont feel any obligation towards them.

There will be others, and if there is not, there has been enough.

Love to you and Bob LeVigne,
    John

---

15 Wieners is referring to Philip Lamantia's *Destroyed Works*, published the following year by Auerhahn.

Irving Rosenthal
November 9, 1961
[Milton, MA]

Dear Irving:

I have thought of you over the months, and tried to write to you, but nothing ever comes of it; you were in Cuba,[16] you sick with hepatitis, you were living uptown, and finally I heard from Barbara Moraff,[17] that you are back on 8th Street, and so I try again.

I wish I had some memory of last year, but I do not, of living with you, of your kindness, but all is a blank. All I remember is waking up in the hospital, trying to get well in April, and finally after 30 shock treatments at Bournewood, and 91 insulin treatments at Metropolitan State, I was discharged last August 25th.[18] And I am quite well; I go into Boston nearly every day, looking for work, or visiting friends, who have also been through the galleys; and think about my past, which is most tantalizing as I believe the shock treatments took away my memory.

I have no memory of Medfield, or the many visits there, of your calls, or the trip to New York. I have most of the information from my mother second-hand, that I was even on East 8th Street; what we lived like, where, and how we survived from day to day with no money I do not know, except it must have been through your generosity.[19]

---

16 Many New York writers, artists, and intellectuals had been traveling to Cuba to see Castro's new socialist state. LeRoi Jones visited in 1959, and both Rosenthal and Howard Schulman (of the Fair Play for Cuba Committee) visited in 1961, later appearing together at Columbia University for a talk on current events in the island nation.

17 Barbara Moraff (b. 1939), American poet and potter. By the time she was eighteen, Moraff had already published in *Evergreen Review*, leading Kerouac to give her the nickname "the baby of the Beat generation."

18 Bournewood Hospital, private psychiatric facility in Brookline, Massachusetts, a suburb of Boston, where it has stood since 1895. In the 1960s Bournewood was in severe decline; by the late 1970s it was in such financial and physical disrepair that it lost its accreditation.

19 Rosenthal replied to Wieners:

> You have a way of creeping up behind me with a club of stars. I would have answered you sooner if I could. We spent a lot of time talking, and I was at my wit's end thinking of ways to keep you talking & bring you out of yourself—that was mainly how we spent our time. I don't know how to respond to 30 plus 91 shock treatments. I don't know how to respond to even one shock treatment. I think they are a vendetta, but it's over, you are well and exploratory, and your muse is smiling at you (thanks for the poem!) and she will never leave your side. (Unpublished letter from Irving Rosenthal to John Wieners, December 4, 1961, Irving Rosenthal Papers, Stanford University)

So this note is to thank you, and to hope you will answer even if it only be a few short lines, that you are well, and that I will see you again. For I truly want to, Irving, but don't know how.

Some days I hope you will write, or even call, but on what presumption this hope is based, I do not know. I just know that I feel a great affection towards you, but its root is most shadowy and tenuous. It's almost, or is, a love for a brother, one has not seen for many years. And yet the love remains there, nothing can take that away, except the beloved is blurred. I saw your photograph in a book, and it moved me so much because I cannot even bear to look at it, where it is, in a bookshop or on the shelves of a friend's apartment. Just there, with your face turned as if listening to a wall.

The enclosed I synthesized yesterday. It is incomplete but pleases me more than the hasty notations I keep in a notebook. The underlined words did come from dreams, and the rest is just romanticizing. But how to work in the dream words to a whole is the problem and preoccupation. As they appear in the dream as complete, but of course by the time I am awake the body of the poem is lost, and I am left with the tantalizing fragments.

What are you reading? I devour the Public Library, and have gone through most of Waugh again, and as much Graham Greene as is in, just to keep some mystery in my life. The novels of Ronald Firbank are out in one complete edition, from New Directions. I want the gay now, what is just a little bit unreal. I will start Virginia Woolf. Also I read Moby Dick for the first time, and am now on Pierre, which he started just a few weeks after he finished Moby Dick.

Also in the hospital, I read Jung's AION, Researches into the Phenomenology of the Self,[20] and kept notes.

But this is all me. What I think about is you, and long to be rejoined. If that is too blunt, let it stand. "The heart! the heart! 'tis God's anointed; let me pursue the heart:" (from Pierre). "I stand for the heart. To the dogs with the head! I had rather be a fool with a heart, than Jupiter Olympus with his head." (Melville, in a letter to Hawthorne, spring of 1851).

---

20 C. G. Jung's *AION: Research into the Phenomenology of Self* was published in the United States by Princeton University's Bollingen Series in 1959. In 1964, Charles Stein published *AION: A Journal of Traditionary Science*, a magazine of occult philosophy and poetry, featuring Gerrit Lansing, Robert Duncan, Aleister Crowley, and Robert Kelly.

JANUARY 1960–MAY 1963 / *161*

If you call I don't know what to say, but if you write, my heart will blossom, and I will answer.

If you are in good spirits, or unhappy, I want to know. If I show up at your door, will it open? What do you think?

> *Love,*
> *John*

I want to mail this off, right away before I tear it up.

Tell me about that forgotten year. B. Moraff mentions that I had a notebook, called Jewels, which is either lost, or possibly with some things if any left with you.

If only I was there, I don't know how long it would last, but right now, it is close to love. Try and forgive this letter; I feel it is a blathering of feelings that border on the un-real; but know that they are felt and genuine at this time.

[...]

* * *

This next letter is his first to **Diane di Prima,** who became his lifelong friend and champion, first through her poetry newsletter *The Floating Bear* (coedited with LeRoi Jones) and then the New York Poets' Theatre she had formed with Freddie Herko, **Alan Marlowe,** and LeRoi Jones the previous year. Wieners's play *A One Act Scene* was on their second slate of one-acts. Rosenthal, who was holding Wieners's papers and personal belongings for him while he was hospitalized, had given them a copy of Wieners's play but specified that they could not perform it without Wieners's permission, worried that it was not Wieners's best work, written at a time of great personal duress. Rosenthal advised Wieners, "I personally don't care too much for the play. It could be that I don't understand it, but it seems fragmented to me, and the sad state you must have been in when you wrote it makes me want to cry. I hasten to say that Diane, Jimmy Waring, & the other two are creaming over it, but I think they like it for the wrong reasons."[21]

---

21 Unpublished letter from Irving Rosenthal to Wieners, December 4, 1961, Irving Rosenthal Papers, Stanford University.

However displeased Wieners was with the production—he expresses his thoughts later in this period of letters—he continued his collaboration with the Poets' Theatre through the early 1960s: *Still Life*, in January 1962 (on a bill with Duncan's *Faust Fouto: Act IV* and Waring's *Nights at the Tango Palace* at the Off-Bowery Theater), and *Asphodel in Hell's Despite* (at Judson Memorial Church) in 1963. Reviewing *Still Life* for *The Floating Bear*, Jerry Benjamin called it "disconnected in form in a manner which is compelling." Of the night's triple bill, Benjamin felt, Wieners's "was closest to the author in tenor."[22] Looking back on the period in her *Recollections of My Life as a Woman*, di Prima recalls the "haunting" *Still Life*, with its "marvelous set and costumes, and a young, very intense Yvonne Ranier," but admits that in these early days of the theater "I am not quite sure that his amazing words were truly memori-alzed ... The plays were dark, the way that time of the year is dark, as the sun sinks to its lowest point, and in New York you are boxed in by shadows."[23]

* * *

Diane di Prima
November 21, 1961
[Milton, MA]

Dear Diane Di Prima:

Andrew Hoyem tells me that the New York Poets' Theatre is producing a play of mine, which Irving Rosenthal has in his possession. The strange thing about this play is that I have no memory of ever having written it, either its title or anything of its subject matter.

Therefore I rely on you to clue me in, even to the extent of sending me an actor's copy, so I could see what's up, and thereby give you my permission to go ahead with it. Not that there is anything holding me back; but if you would send me the date of opening night, I could down for it, possibly even see some of the rehearsals.

A friend in Boston, a painter by the name of Tom Balas, had a copy of DINNERS AND NIGHTMARES[24] in his possession, and I read it all through, enjoyed it, and see it as something unique in the field, something of which you should be very proud.

---

22 Di Prima and Jones, *Floating Bear Anthology*, 191.
23 Di Prima, *Recollections of My Life as a Woman*, 279.
24 Di Prima's book of short stories, *Dinners and Nightmares*, first published by Corinth Books, the publishing arm of Ted and Eli Wilentz's Eighth Street Bookshop, in 1961. It was reissued in 1998 by Last Gasp.

Also the faithfulness of Floating Bear, its regularity, not to mention the hard work is all to your credit.

Let me know when you can the dates of the play, and I will see you then, if same happens; it's an ambition come true.

Sincerely,
John Wieners
John Wieners

PS: My first reaction on re-reading this is that I had no hesitancy in worrying about permission for the play, or whether there was any quality to the project or not. All I have is Andrew's information to go on, which is enough, I believe.

Charles Olson
December 5, 1961
[Milton, MA]

Dearest Charles:

Thank you so much for two weeks ago Wednesday time at your house. Your hospitality never ceases to gratify me.

I cant send any poems, because none please me that much, and I know they would not please you, not that that is the main object, but what good are they if they dont bring pleasure; by that I mean joy. I sent a group to Gerrit [Lansing] and will ask him if he will bring them over to you.

The main purpose of this note is to get the address of that flyer from Cuba: ARRIBA. I enclose a postcard for you, if you can just take time out to scribble down Howard Loeb Schulman's address,[25] I will be most grateful; as I would like to have a copy of magazine and flyer sent to you.

---

25 *Arriba*, a "cooperative bilingual magazine" published by Peruvian poet Juan Gonzalo Rose in 1961, featuring Wieners and Howard Loeb "Howie" Schulman. Schulman was a political radical, a member of the Fair Play for Cuba Committee in New York who edited *Pa'lante: Poetry Polity Prose of a New World*, a journal put out by the League of Militant Poets in May 1962. Schulman included a prose piece of Wieners's called "Monday (In the jungle" (Gosse, *Where the Boys Are*, 191).

Duncan's photograph is in this week's NY Times Book Review, along with a group review of his OPENING OF THE FIELD. It is the photograph used in The Evergreen Review, Number 2, when they did the issue on San Francisco, the 'cross-eyed king' one.[26]

Last night went to hear T. S. Eliot at Boston College. He read for an hour and a half. The only poem he showed any enthusiasm for was a dog poem called Morgan. At least that was the only one you could hear in toto.

Will go to New York this weekend for opening of play at Poets' Theatre. I hope you got the flyer. I knock on wood that all will be successful. I cant worry about the play, as I know nothing about it; it's just the trip down that worries me, where to stay, etc. It will be the first bit of traveling I've done since last December.[27] Well, 'dont worry about the future' as you say, and live, so I wont.

  Goodnight, Charles and much love,

  John

Thank you again for your time and devotion to us.

  Irving Rosenthal

  January 17, 1962

  [Milton, MA]

Dear Irving:

Forgive me for not arriving Monday night.

I traveled over to your place Sunday to tell you that I was leaving the next day and would not be able to see you, as we had planned that evening; but there was no one at home or else you were asleep. I went up on the roof, and smoked a joint, very lonely as I remember, on the parapets, overlooking East Eighth Street. I walked back across town; after leaving the wicker basket, outside your door; to the Theatre, and

---

26 Duncan's *The Opening of the Field* was reviewed in the *New York Times* on December 3, 1961, by Arthur Zeiger; Duncan's "cross-eyed" photo was the only one included.

27 By this point Wieners had been back on the East Coast a year, since traveling back and being ambush-hospitalized. The terror felt since is put into lyric and yet less "confessional" form in "The Acts of Youth," written the same night as this letter, and included in his next letter to Olson.

saw Eila Kokinen.[28] We walked in, but after watching it for five minutes, I left in a cloud of embarrassment. Alone.

I couldn't take 31 St. Mark's place any longer, so took the 4:30 bus out Monday afternoon, after missing the 2:30 one. Joe Rivers and Jarry drove me to the station, and I remember the hectic ride, careening around New York streets, high in the afternoon. Jarry had vomited during the night, and I was sleeping in Joe's bed, while he had to share a cot with Jarry sideways. So I thought it would be too much of an imposition to stay another night. Anyways, I was under a cloud, whether because of the two days of rain, or my cold, or having spent all my money on bad grass, I cannot say.

~~Anyways~~, Jarry's place was in an awful mess, ~~and I couldn't take it any longer.~~ I bought Cain's Book[29] in the bus station and read it on the way back, and it has haunted me ever since.

For some reason, there was a spirit in New York that weekend that I couldn't overcome, or rise above, so I left. The only time I could break through it was the time spent with you, and at Elia's. I can't stay and fight a scene, it seems, or wait for it to pass; I only retreat.

So know you have my apologies for not coming to you, and I hope our friendship is not lessened because of it.

Would it be possible that you would like to take a trip to Boston, and change your scene for a little ~~bit~~ *while*? If so, I would be your most glad host. It might do ~~you~~ *some* good to get away for a while, and although there is not much ~~to do~~ here, we could take buses, and sight-see. See my friends, Steve Jonas and Tom Balas, Jerome Mallman, both painters, and Joe Dunn. What do you say? Why not do yourself a honor and get away?

---

28 Eila Kokinen, American art historian and curator. She came into contact with Wieners after she was made art editor of the *Chicago Review* in the spring of 1957, when the *Review* was beginning its peak period of rebellion and, in retrospect, Beat-canon formation under the strident editorship of Irving Rosenthal. The spring 1958 *Review* was dedicated to "Ten San Francisco Poets," including the by-then San Franciscan Wieners; Rosenthal printed Wieners's poems "From End Chapters in an Autobiography" and "The Bridge Word (on brown paper)," neither of which has been reprinted. The *Chicago Review*'s Winter 1959 issue set off a censorship war, publishing eight excerpts from Burroughs' *Naked Lunch*. Rosenthal was fired, and Kokinen and the rest of the staff quit in protest. Rosenthal and Paul Carroll formed *Big Table* as a way of reprinting the censored issue of the *Review*.

29 *Cain's Book* was published in 1960 by Scottish Beat writer Alexander Trocchi. It was an immediate scandal and underground hit for its frank (and autobiographical) depiction of heroin use and its uncompromising, often nonnarrative style.

I wrote to Edward J. Ennis[30] today, thanking him for the award, and telling him of my plans, to start Measure again, and go to San Francisco in the spring. If I dont see you before that, that is when I hope to see you again.

It has been three days since I started this letter. It is now Saturday, and I have been out to see my doctor today. He somehow got word that I was associating with narco addicts and told me that we were under observation. All of this has upset me very much, even invaded my dreams, so that I am being kept where I dont want to be. He recommended a new drug to cure depression, its name is Tofranil,[31] and I take it three times a day; it usually takes 10 days to work, but if it is not successful, then he asked my sister if she could give it to me intravenously!

I'm afraid his questions took me off guard, and I told him more than I should have, so that this new drug is the result. I asked him if the information was confidential, and that my family doesn't know, but he didn't say yes; he would keep it to himself. All of this of course is personal trivia, but it does add burden to a life already weighted.

To rise above myself, or to make best use of oneself, this is my ambition, my aim; not to be weighted in personalism. [...]

Dave Haselwood
January 24, 1962
[Milton, MA]

Dear Andrew and Dave:

Thank you for your letters of the 2nd, 3rd, 8th, and 22nd, all received.

I have thought it all out, and the only title I can find is: FOR WHAT TIME SLAYS. It is from a poem of Hart Crane's.[32] I have been through his book twice and cannot

---

30 It is unclear to what award Wieners is referring. Edward J. Ennis (1908–1990) was a longtime director of the American Civil Liberties Union.
31 Tofranil was one of the marketed forms of imipramine, the first tricyclic antidepressant, developed in the late 1950s.
32 "For what time slays" is a line from Crane's masterpiece *The Bridge*:

Then let you reach your hat
and go.
As usual, let you—also
walking down—exclaim

discover just what verse it is. I also enclose two short poems, I hope short enough, for you to choose from, for the catalogue, which sounds like a grand and elegant idea.

I *received* an award from the Poets Foundation for 1961, and with the monies I am publishing one or two more issues of Measure, just to fulfill my obligations. The first one goes to the printer the 1st of February. Also there will be enough left over for me to go to San Francisco this spring or early summer with the manuscripts of the book, and we three can plan it together, if that meets your specifications. Anyway, it will be grand to see you again, and pick up some loose ends. What do you say? Isn't it wonderful the way life or Fate or outside consciousness treats us. Down one day, and up the next. I had one cent in my pocket the day the check arrived, for $1500 dollars.

I have been to New York twice, since I last saw you Andrew, the day before Thanksgiving, for performances of the play at the New York Poets Theatre. It was a failure, I believe, the production was so poor; no lights the first performance. But the audience liked it, although I sat and shivered all over. Gregory Corso was there, and Frank O'Hara, Carl Solomon, Irving Rosenthal, Howard Schulman, Leroi Jones, Joel Oppenheimer, Ted Wilenz, Arlene Dahlberg,[33] Diane Di Prima, plus hordes of others I got in free, who could not afford the 2 dollar tariff. Barbara Moraff etc. She paid.

W. Berman has called up from Los Angeles under the pseudonym of Pantale Xanthos,[34] and we spent 5–10 minutes in joy. I sent him some books, as he complained he had nothing to read, also the magazine from Mexico which Andrew so kindly sent.[35] Also, BEAT POETS check and book received here, plus the letter from Mondadori,[36] which I answered yesterday. It is 5:15 and supper will soon be ready,

---

    to twelve upward leaving
    a subscription praise
    for what time slays.

    It is from this same section of Crane's epic "The Tunnel" that Wieners drew the title for his one-act play *Asphodel, in Hell's Despite*; Crane writes, "watch the curtain lift in hell's despite."

33 R'lene LaFleur Howell married Edward Dahlberg in 1950. A poet and publisher, her small press Pequod printed an edition of Ed Marshall's "Leave the Word Alone" as a chapbook in 1979. She taught for many years at Stuyvesant High School in New York with Frank McCourt, who wrote a notoriously scathing remembrance of his relationship with the Dahlbergs in his 2005 memoir *Teacher Man*.

34 Pantale Xanthos was a pseudonym Wallace Berman used frequently in his landmark arts magazine *Semina*.

35 *Zarza*, Mexican arts magazine, which published a Spanish translation of "A poem for the insane" ("Poema para un demente") in its April–May 1961 issue.

36 Wieners is referring to Italian publishing house Arnoldo Mondadori Editore, founded in 1907. Mondadori released several translations of Beat writings, including *On the Road* in 1974, and attempted to secure an Italian translation of Wieners as well. None appeared.

so I go now down to the corner and mail this. Remember me to Sally and know you both have my love.

Do you think the book should include selections from work as far back as 1955? or should it be small and contemporary.

I am writing every day mostly, but as soon as I get any typed up, off they go to somebody or other. Locus Solus (James Schuyler) wrote today asking for a long poem called ACTS OF YOUTH, which I love and am sending that off with this.[37]

Bob LeVigne called yesterday, but I think we got his difficulty straightened out. Thank you again for your letters, which always treat my spirit so well. And spring will soon be here.

I hope to write again soon, with some poems. And do keep in so close contact, as this past month. It diminishes much of the loneliness, just to receive a letter, no matter of what sort.

Olson is reading at Harvard the 14th of next month, so I imagine that will be a gala occasion. No one knows about Measure, and I don't want them to; I just want it to be a belated surprise in their mail. God is good.

   John Wieners
sends his love by the mail.

Charles Olson
January 29, 1962
[Milton, MA]

Dear Charles:

Certain monies have come into my hand whereby I may publish one or two more copies of Measure. I have three poems of yours at hand, which I would like to use in the next issue, which goes to the printer February 1st or so.

---

37 *Locus Solus* was a small magazine launched by central New York School poets in the early 1960s. The first and final of five issues were edited by Schuyler (Kenneth Koch did issue 2 and John Ashbery took 3 and 4), and "The Acts of Youth" appeared in issue 5 alongside "The Mermaid's Song" and "An Anniversary of Death."

They are: The Year Is A Great Circle Or
   The Year Is A Great Mistake.

 The Post Virginal.

and Descartes, age 34, date Boston's
   settling. . . .
      Will you give me your OK?

The issue isn't much without them. But I have had these manuscripts on hand for maybe five years, and would like to get them printed, also fulfill my obligations to the 200 or more subscribers.

The issue will only be 36 pages, and although you might feel there is no demand for another magazine at this time, I see so few around that are open to new verse, that I would like to go ahead with this, if only up to Number 4.
 I am well, and look forward to your reading February 14th.
 Am reading John Donne's Devotions, when I got the impulse to write you.

Send a few poems for your pleasure.
     Love,
      Jawn

Not that they are complete, but that they have their own merit in places.

THE ACTS OF YOUTH[38]

And with great fear I inhabit the middle of the night
What wrecks of the mind await me, what drugs
to dull the senses, what little I have left,
what more can be taken away?

---

38 "The Acts of Youth" is the centerpiece to *Ace of Pentacles*. As he had with Wieners's application to Black Mountain ten years earlier, Olson replied immediately and enthusiastically to this, with a card calling "The Ages of Youth" (as he mis-remembered the name, a variation Wieners preserved for the poem's section title in the book) one of "the most beautiful and truest" poems he'd ever read. He echoes the fears in his letter, the "fear of travelling, of the future without hope / or buoy." From this private terror Wieners keeps moving outward, changing from "I" to "one" to the whole suffering world: by the end, the voice is fully outspread into the plural, the glorious "We rise again in the dawn." This centrifugal move, from the deeply singular out to the collective, is Wieners's most significant inheritance from Olson. It is his astonishing ability to use his own "pain and suffering" so that, as Denise Levertov wrote in an *Ace of Pentacles* review, "they are not autobiographically written *about*, they are conditions out of which it happens that the songs arise" ("To Write Is to Listen," 227).

The fear of travelling, of the future without hope
or buoy. I must get away from this place and see
that there is no fear without me: that it is within
unless it be some sudden act or calamity

to land me in the hospital, a total wreck, without
memory again; or worse still, behind bars. If
I could just get out of the country. Some place
where one can eat the lotus in peace.

For in this country it is terror, poverty awaits; or
am I a marked man, my life to be a lesson
or experience to those young who would trod
the same path, without God

unless he be one of justice, to wreak vengeance
on the acts committed while young under un-
due influence or circumstance. Oh I have
always seen my life as drama, patterned

after those who met with disaster or doom.
Is my mind being taken away me.
I have been over the abyss before. What
is that ringing in my ears that tells me

all is nigh, is naught but the roaring of the winter wind.
Woe to those homeless who are out on this night.
Woe to those crimes committed from which we
can walk away unharmed.

2.
So I turn on the light
And smoke rings rise in the air.
Do not think of the future; there is none.
But the formula all great art is made of.

Pain and suffering. Give me the strength
to bear it, to enter those places where the
great animals are caged. And we can live
at peace by their side. A bride to the burden

that no god imposes but knows we have the means
to sustain its force unto the end of our days.
For that it is what we are made for; for that
we are created. Until the dark hours are done.

And we rise again in the dawn.
Infinite particles of the divine sun, now
worshipped in the pitches of the night.

December 5, 1961

Dave Haselwood
April 4th, 1962
[Milton, MA]

Dear David:
The day of the world. And it is 12:50 AM. I have just finished watching Tallulah
Bankhead on television in THE DEVIL AND THE DEEP where she plays the wife
of an insane submarine captain, played by Charles Laughton who wrecks the ship
below water and ends up drowning, hatcheting away at his wife's photograph in the
cabin. Gary Cooper is Miss Bankhead's lover and they end up escaping the hatch
with oxygen tanks. They meet later in the rain when she stops to buy a billiard cue
and admire the stars, as they did their first night in the desert. The last scene is they
going by cab together (with stringy hair and the billiard cue in the gutter, with rain
falling on it. It is a film made in the 30's and shows Miss Bankhead in many, beautiful
gowns and low breasts, being harassed, slapped, thrown to the floor by her husband
(she married him because he helped her father) but the brain specialist declares, by
Miss B.'s conversation, that there is no help for Charles, only he can help himself.
But his jealousies are rampant, even before she meets Gary Cooper on an Arab
festival night, he accuses her of an affair with Cary Grant. "A year ago, in Tangiers,

six months later in Gibraltar and now here" (unnamed) says Miss Bankhead when she lists the times he thought she was unfaithful.

So it goes, and the low breasts hang in the moon.

I am waiting for Measure to come back from England and when it does I will be on my way: first to New York and then to San Francisco. With the manuscripts for the book. The few of them there are.

May I take you up on your offer to stay with you?

It may ~~take~~ *require* a couple of months of actual writing before the thing is in shape to be printed. But this is all to the good. And we can work on it together, with Andrew.

I asked the printer to send a 100 copies of MEASURE to the shop's address in San Francisco. Is this agreeable to you?

No need for you to answer right away, as I feel it is, or I wouldn't have gone ahead without your permission. They can just sit there until I arrive; or anyplace that is convenient. Or you could, when you distribute new books locally, drop them off at City Lights and Discovery.

I hope to get a job and stay longer than my parents know. As I can't face living at home (one reason: I cant work at night: the typewriter disturbs my family who start to go to bed at 10 o'clock. And I dont feel "inspired" until after midnight.

I made a record for Harvard's Poetry Room which I will bring with me.[39] And the contract for the Italian translation has gone through. Very agreeable to me. There is no other news as there are not many here who are interested in the same world as I am. We did hear "poetry" tonight on a show made by KQED in San Francisco: a John Dodde of Stanford[40] reading Keats, Shelley, [illeg], Shakespeare and Browning's poems on Nature.

I do like to keep abreast of letter writing for as I said before there are not many here and the few are so strung out it is hard to talk to them, only commiserate with their agonies which are true and so real it is frightening. Steve Jonas has had his eyebrows plucked and wears a handmade silver ring. Charles' reading at Harvard was disastrous on Valentine's Day in a blizzard as I believe I wrote Andrew not so dire an account.

Love to you and I dream of Philip more often than not, racing around in a red sportscar without any top, or raising the chalice at Mass in vestments of gold. It will

---

39 The March 1962 recording is available at the Woodberry Poetry Room;.His reading of "Ode to the Instrument" is online with an introduction by scholar Robert Dewhurst (Woodberry Poetry Room blog, October 28, 2015).

40 John Dodds (1902–1989), English professor at Stanford who consulted for several notable poetry and humanities radio and television programs in the late 1950s and 1960s.

be good to see you again and I am looking forward every day to the trip. Even to think about it makes my heart beat faster.

    John

If only this instant could last forever
And I ride high on it from dawn to
    Midnight not sever
The charm of these arms that hold me, and stretch
    Out to eternity where I reside
    Beside the breasts of my beloved.

                    Irving Rosenthal
                    April 12th, 1962
                    [Milton, MA]

Dear Irving:

Just want to answer yours of the 29th, March, and expect no reply; with you working your time must be most precious. I am so glad that you have a job as the income will help, and once you put your mind to it, it will not be so bad. I wish I could and when the money runs out, out West, I have to.

Been writing, mostly bad, but yesterday worked 12 hours on the book, typing from a journal since the beginning of this year.

Measure's proofs are corrected and I await the final bulk.

You may call me Jack but I much prefer Howard's JAWN.

I dont know what a true relationship is, but I know that desire has to play a part, desire of some sort, either for the brain, from it, for the intellect or the body, I dont know. But the combination is the ideal. And when it happens there is no will. Just a "swill" of emotion.

Your letter is a great comfort. And I see pictures of Elise[41] in my room in San Francisco; associate her with another girl I know called Shela Plant, who took an

---

41 Elise Cowen (1933–1962), American poet. She was briefly involved with Allen Ginsberg, and remained romantically attached to him for the rest of her life. After years of struggling with depression, she committed suicide a couple of months before this letter, on February 27, 1962, by jumping through her parents' seventh-floor locked window. Her friend Joyce (Glassman) Johnson wrote about Cowen and their youth together in her invaluable 1999 memoir, *Minor Characters*.

FIGURE 5 John Wieners with Irving Rosenthal. Photograph by Raymond Foye. Courtesy of Raymond Foye.

overdose of sleeping pills in a hotel room. Why depress you but she sublet my apt. while I was East in 1959–58—with Howard. I look forward to his visit.

Love for now. Until I see you soon. John   Let me know yr. mood

On re-reading this, it is a terrible way to end a letter with an anecdote regarding a dead girl. But death doesn't hit me at first, but it grows in retrospect. And lingers in a most unfortunate way when I least expect it, comes sneaking up on you, with its smell of flowers. I always think we go to feed the roses, but so young. It is a wonder we do anything at all, with its presence hovering about. Let's see each other soon and be close together always. John

Whatever that is, we might possess a bit of it in our "hearts."

Forgive this blather but they are my sentimental thoughts now. It is so good to be away from the brain or the emotions for a while. That is why drugs are a way out, but only a way into another hell. Dont worry.

Do you hear from Allen? I want to write to him.

* * *

In the late summer of 1962, Wieners was able to get out of his parents' house and back to New York, living with Ed Marshall on the Lower East Side and working at the famed Eighth Street Bookshop. The poetry culture at this time was intensely focused on the live reading experience, as documented in Daniel Kane's indispensable *All Poets Welcome: The Lower East Side Poetry Scene in the 1960s*. Concentrated around such spaces as Café Le Metro and Les Deux Megots, and later the Poetry Project at St. Mark's Church In-the-Bowery, the Lower East Side offered a sociality that Wieners craved after more than two years of living in state mental hospitals and the suburbs. He got back into a writing habit and continued to make friends among the avant-garde and underground arts scenes, spending time with poet-translator David Rattray, habitués of Warhol's Factory, and other artists and activists in downtown Manhattan. Warhol, a fan of *The Hotel Wentley Poems*, had Wieners pose for one of his screen tests:

Wieners' *Screen Test*, which was probably shot early in 1964, begins as a very dark, underexposed image. Illuminated only from the left, his face emerges from the darkness like a dim half-moon, one partially eclipsed eye glistening from the shadows. When he opens his mouth, a tooth gleams faintly. Halfway through the film, the exposure improves, revealing more of his face. At the end of the roll, he squints at the camera as if blinded by the light.[42]

* * *

Allen Ginsberg
7.14–16.62
[New York City]

Cocaine[43]
For I have seen Love
and his face is choice Heart of Hearts,
a flesh of pure fire, fusing from the center
where all Motion are One.

---

42 Angell, *Andy Warhol Screen Tests*, 209.

43 "Cocaine" was published in *Ace of Pentacles*, with several changes, notably the ending ("infinite longing," instead of "unutterable,") and a different sequence of line breaks that alters the prosody considerably. For Robert Duncan, "Cocaine" was a highlight of the book, calling it "as good as the best of Verlaine" in a letter to Levertov. Preparing a review of the book for *The Nation*, where Levertov edited poetry at the time, he wrote that "the poems assert the validity of a great unhappiness and have such authenticity I am ashamed to come back with any criticism that he ought to live a different life" (Bertolf and Gelpi, eds., *The Letters of Robert Duncan and Denise Levertov*, 473).

And I have known
despair, that the Face has ceased to stare
at me with the Rose of the World,
but lies furled

in an artificial Paradise
it is hell to get into. If I knew
you were there, I would fall upon my knees
and plead to God

to deliver you once again in my arms.
But it is senseless to try.
One can only take means to reduce misery,
confuse the sensations

so that this face,
which aches in the heart, and makes each new

start

less close to the source of desire,
fade

from the flesh that fires the Night,
with dreams and unutterable longing.[44]
~~in the years to come.~~

> *Love, to you*
> *John Wieners*
> *153 Avenue C*
> *#8*

---

44 A line goes from below "less" to below "with," bracketing those last three lines on the left.

Ed Dorn
Wednesday July 25th [1962]
[New York City]

Dear Ed:

Can you send some money? I am literally starving "to death." Whatever you can afford. I dont start my job until next Monday and have 5 pennies on the table to see me through next week.

Charles and Bette have gone back to Gloucester.

I am living with Ed Marshall as roommate at 153 Avenue C, Apt. 8.

Each day I rush downstairs but no you. I know nothing has happened to misfortune you. It is us who are bereft and left.

Until I hear from you I remain
Your friend
With love,
John Wieners

Nothing can change that.

Love to Helene and the boys and Shawn

I'm going to try and sleep now and forget about the whole thing.

Dave Haselwood and Andrew Hoyem
[n.d. 1962]
[New York City]

Dear Andrew and Dave:

As you may know by now I have a job in New York City. It all started on my way to San Francisco with Ed Dorn and his wife, when we got to talking, and LeRoi said Ted Wilentz needed help and I could get a job as bookkeeper, part-time. Partly because I was disappointed in the book as it stands, and wanted more time, knowing I would not have it out there, with no money and job, no reasonable place to stay where I would be content, or secure, more secure, afraid it would start all over again: walking the streets, when I was offered this apartment the first day I hit town, for 43 dollars a month, 5 flights up, or more reasonably four, or even three. Anyway it is 4 rooms, and Ed Marshall is my roommate, and the lease does not run out until next July.

And when I am 30 I will have a book ready. That is two years, or are you mad? I can send you the mss. now which may be beautiful but what good would it do if in 6 months time I could not bear to read the book itself. And what about the young? who still write letters telling me they love me because of the Hotel Wentley; and who come over and ask me are you queer?

All of which I love because it shows the book is still alive and vital. And let me die with that. If I have to die, as we all do young. He died, with a smile on his mouth.

Anyway, I am young, and writing again, yesterday, the Housewife's Lament. But let's go easy on the book. I will be interested to know what you think. I know you will be disappointed I am not there, as promised, as I am too; think longingly of the West. But you will be here before I am there. Stay with me: 153 Avenue C, Apartment 8, but we lost the key to the mailbox. Gr3–7064.

Try to forgive me, or at least write. In care of the bookstore if you have to. And who knows maybe I will be there before you know it. But what will we do about the book? Which is announced, and which will be disappointing to some, at least to me, that it does not appear as promised. Simply explain that it is the author's fault, not the press, as I will and have, to those interested.

Love to you both, and dying to hear,
John

Thank you Andrew for sending the catalogues. And the Destroyed Works[45] I have seen from Howard, and Jonathan's book here at the bookstore, and the Paul Reps. All of which shows how very much in earnest and industrious you both are.

---

45 Philip Lamantia's *Destroyed Works*, bound in black cloth with a frontispiece by Bruce Conner, was published by Auerhahn Press in 1962.

Gary Snyder
August 22, 1962
[New York City]

THE EIGHTH STREET BOOKSHOP, INC.[46]
"Greenwich Village's Famous Bookshop"
32 West 8th Street., New York 11, N.Y.

Dear Gary,

Ted Wilentz is tied up right now, but wants me to write to ask if you have seen THE SIXTIES (Spring 1962) which has an essay on: The Work of Gary Snyder. If not, he will send you a copy. They list it on the cover as AN ESSAY ON THE AMERICAN POET, GARY SNYDER.[47] Enclosed find a letter from Burning Deck,[48] which we forward.

Joanne is much in my thoughts, as I dreamt of her and Nemi at the seashore last night, along with Jan Balas. It was very harrowing, and filled with green and white waves crashing on the shore. We were dressed in turn of the century bathing outfits, I believe. Give her my love, and remember her among the roses at the hospital, where we would sit out in the garden all afternoon. This is really a letter to Joanne, and not for one moment have I stopped loving her. Russ Fitzgerald[49] is in New York and we spend long hours, nights and dawn talking of San Francisco and what it all meant, knowing Miss Kids at that time. I see her going away and bending down in tears after this letter. Also Mike Rumaker is out of the hospital, and lives in upstate New York, not too far, as he is able to come down to the city and see us. His book is doing very well; at last count 4000 copies sold.[50] MEASURE 3 has also appeared. Allen sent photos from India, and one of Peter Orlovsky in a human hair wig made me think it was Joanne at first sipping tea with Bengali poets. Have her forgive me.

---

46 Brothers Eli and Theodore Wilentz opened the Eighth Street Bookshop in 1947 on the southeast corner of Eighth and Macdougal Streets. In addition to carrying the largest poetry selection in the city, it was a community center for New York writers and artists of the 1950s and 1960s, and the Wilentzes would frequently help out struggling poets (like the just-out-of-hospital John Wieners) with extra money or work. The store closed in 1979, and Eli and Ted passed away in 1995 and 2001, respectively.

47 *The Sixties* was published by Robert Bly, who also did magazines called *The Fifties* and *The Seventies*. Its Spring 1962 issue featured a James Wright essay on Gary Snyder.

48 *Burning Deck* was founded by Keith and Rosmarie Waldrop in 1961, and focuses on experimental poetry and prose.

49 Russell Fitzgerald was a Philadelphia-born painter at the center of the San Francisco Renaissance, a lover of Jack Spicer's, for whom Spicer wrote *Billy the Kid*.

50 Rumaker's first book, *The Butterfly*, was published by Charles Scribner's Sons in 1962.

Thru inter-com Ted sends his best and regards from Eli who is on vacation. I am now playing Miss Kids to his Miss Specht[51] at 8th Street. But all is well, and please have Joanne write, if she can tear herself. There is a magnificent munificent smile on someone's Buddha lips.

I'm an Occidental woman in an Oriental mood for love,
    And I feel the thrill of China when I see the yellow
            Buddha moon above."

Mae West.[52]

Love to you both,
Pip

Denise Levertov
Wednesday May 21, 1963
[New York City]

Dear Denise:

Thank you for the lively evening at your home Thursday last. I enjoyed meeting Betty Kray[53] and Jim Mosely[54] and seeing Jerome Rothenberg again, not to mention hearing the fine African poetry.[55]

The real point of this is I am a patient at Bellevue *Hospital* and will be for 2 to 5 weeks, with hepatitis. And to *come direct to the point*, This way I will have no money to be out and pay my rent this month, that is, from June to July and wonder, if at all possible, I could take you up on your kind offer to forward the money *to my landlord* until I can get out and pay you back. The rent is $37.49 and payable to Mr. Edward Pious, 261 Broadway, New York 7, NY. If this is an inconvenience, just say so and I will

---

51 Miss Specht was Joanne Kyger's supervisor at the City of Paris Brentano's bookstore (mentioned in his letter to Kyger on May 15, 1965).

52 From the 1936 film *Klondike Annie*.

53 Elizabeth Kray was the first executive director for the Academy of American Poets, hired in 1963. In 1985 she cofounded New York's Poets House with Stanley Kunitz.

54 Jim Mosely was a young poet that Levertov befriended.

55 Jerome Rothenberg (b. 1931), American poet and translator best known for his opening of the field of *ethnopoetics*, a term he coined while working in the 1960s on his book *Technicians of the Sacred: A Range of Poetries from Africa, America, Asia, Europe and Oceania*, which he published in 1968.

understand. I know it is an imposition and I feel cheap to have to ask you; what with Nik going away to school, etc., I am sure you have more than your share of expenses.

If I was outside, of course, I could use my wits and wangle the money out *of the wind* somehow. But this way, I am helpless to do anything but remain in isolation.

Would you let me know however you decide, and I will be most grateful. As if you hadn't done enough already . . .

> *Yours,*
> John

If you and Mitch[56] decide its alright, the money could go direct *before June 1st* to Mr. Pious, in my name or in care of it. Apt 4A, 225 East 5th Street, NYC 3, NY. If you can't please don't hesitate, as I will understand perfectly. And please forgive the imposition. Address here is WARD A6, Bellevue General Hospital, NYC, NY—1st Ave at 27th Street. Thank you, whatever way you decide.

> Denise Levertov
> Monday May 27, 1963
> [New York City]

My dear Denise:

I am writing an immediate response to your letter. How my heart leaps up and it is a joy to be beneath the light on the East River. We have a high ceilinged ward, with tall windows, and glorious sunrises, I have never been up so early before, regularly, in my life (red as the Yangtze) and hope to continue the habit. Van Wyck Brooks I read, ~~learned~~ *acquired* his habits of early rising from the years spent in sanatariums.

No, I am not depressed.[57] In fact glad to be here, what with the regular food and bed rest (180 hours so far). I am also reading William James' Principles of Psychology,

---

56 Mitch Goodman (1923–1997), American writer, teacher, and anti-Vietnam War activist along with his wife Denise Levertov. Because of his leadership in the draft resistance movement, he was prosecuted by the federal government as part of an alleged criminal conspiracy along with Dr. Benjamin Spock, Marcus Raskin, Reverend William Coffin, and Michael Farber, the so-called Boston Five.

57 Still, Levertov was concerned. Two months later she wrote to Duncan:

> I'm very worried about John Wieners. He was in hospital with hepatitis, & during that time I had 2 letters from him; but he was discharged May 30th & since then I haven't heard a word. I had sent him something to help his convalescence so I wrote him again but still no word. Then 2 days ago Ted Enslin (who's up here at the farm) told me Jackson MacLow had told him John was back on drugs. Also that he was in Atlantic City. I do so hope it's not true. (Bertolf and Gelpi, *The Letters of Robert Duncan and Denise Levertov*, 415)

only the chapters he recommended for the neophyte and I find it quite enlightening, in fact ~~find it~~ awakening areas of ~~information I was not aware of~~. awareness.

My mother is arriving for <u>two</u> days this evening from Boston with my sister, who has just finished her finals for a Master's in Nursing and I am sure they will satisfy present wants, which were great for a while until a few friends arrived. The first week was the most difficult and I felt most desolate. Thank you for asking.

But all that has passed and would be most happy to have visitors who, and I say this knowing how you must be gathering things like a woodchuck, into its nest for your summer in Maine, are allowed even tho you must not feel obliged to come. I would be delighted to see you,

You are right. How the centers of contact have been diminished, human, over the century.

We are almost isolate beings, with the machine—

Thank you for your kind words of encouragement.

Love to you both, and Nik,

John

Just spent a few moments reading again the poems at the end of Robert Lowell's <u>Life Studies</u> and for a true New England poet, despite naivete of form, give me Marsden Hartley anyday, with his delicacy of feeling. He has written lovely things about Maine: Penobscot Bay, Kennebec, Lewiston, Andro-Scoggin River etc.

He has nowhere the sophistication, nor self-expression of Lowell, but he was a true cosmopolitan, in that he could write equally well of Central Park, Park Avenue, and his English ancestors and their parlors in Maine. One gets spleen in his mouth, *variation* between his teeth at Lowell's apt expression of his New England condition, (psychosis? no, rather his neurosis,)? his neurotic New England heritage. Forgive these terms. Where Hartley is only full of gentleness and reverence for his.

"The finest people in the world are those who act in the
right way;
My mother and father were among them."

By the fall of 1963, Wieners was back in Milton, lying low and working on his planned book with **Robert Wilson** and James Carr's Phoenix Book Shop, and another with Dave Haselwood that was never completed. He continued visiting New York regularly, though, staying with different friends from the downtown art communities. Diane di Prima remembers specifically a Winter Solstice 1963 dinner at her Cooper Square loft that included Freddie Herko, Merce Cunningham, Jimmy Waring, and John Wieners, who had "come out from his hermitage" at Warhol Factory habitué John Daley's apartment down the street. "We drank wine together in the candlelight," di Prima remembers, "talking and laughing, the light from the fireplace in the living room throwing long shadows among us."[1]

* * *

Alan Marlowe
October 23, 1963
[Milton, MA]

10.23

A poem is enclosed, and a small personal note to <u>you</u>.

Saw: Lady Finger?? rather <u>Lady Killer</u>
         with James Cagney and Mae Clark, 1934
and   <u>Love Me Forever</u>
         with Grace Moore and Leo Carillo, 1934.

Am trying to plot the stars, and spiritual atmosphere at time of my birth, 1934. These movies have an influence upon the spiritual climate of the times.

Hate to hear about those damn hoods. Come to Boston and we will walk the Charles, where there are only bushes stirring in the wind, and small lagoons, and mouths slurping at the bushes, and ducks falling off the rocks at dawn, into the water. Also the Public Garden is fun, and we can sit in the ~~trunks~~ *trunks* of great trees all night./

---

1 Di Prima, *Recollections*, 370.

I did one night, my only night in Boston since I got home, before Diane's reading and it was ecstatic.

Thank you for your kind words, Alan, I treasure them and use your strength to guide me, [illeg] me over the streets.

Howard will last one month with Irving, if he goes, and then disappear into the back streets of Paris, or Tangiers, or wherever the dope is, all over the world. And reappear only when he sees our names in the back pages of a newspaper, to share in the "gloria," and say, 'I knew them' like Papa Yiddisher. Of course we will be very kind, and then he'll realize how desperate we are, and turn away again, to feed his own monkey.

Take it easy, and rest up, and put on weight, and get lots of vitamin pills, and all that, but come to Boston however you are. Don't let them eat you away. I know there are egos and politics there, and it is very debilitating to compete on that level. Forgive me for saying this. I love you both   *John*

Dear Alan:

It is just after noon, and I am getting up. The mail held your letter from Holiday Inn! What a great movie that was! and I am grateful for it. It lifted my heart.

Tonight we go to open house at Metropolitan State Hospital, tomorrow night an Insulin party at Kline Hall of the hospital, where I will read my poems after a musical comedy, and Betty Carter,[2] soprano, sings. Then Saturday to The Statler for a small luncheon with Governor Peabody.[3] But first I must go into town and pick up my glasses, have my hair cut (there are no razor cuts in Boston) and spend some of the $100 an anonymous patron sent through **Denise Levertov** . . . "an admirer of your work who prefers to remain anonymous" . . .

Here is a poem I wrote:

THE SUICIDE[4]

Yes, I put her away –

---

2 Betty Carter (1929–1998), American jazz singer.
3 Endicott Peabody (1920–1997), governor of Massachusetts from 1963 to 1965.
4 "The Suicide," Wieners's poem for Sylvia Plath (1932–1963), was published in *Ace of Pentacles*.

But now life flares up
As sure as China in a cup
You hear the droppings
           of her heart.
Leaves rustle on the window pane.
Three o'clock turns round again.
The man in the moon grows full
off her death, while earth waits
           patient beneath
To receive her ashes on the wind.

           Yes, earth owns the wind
           As I owned her life
           Whom I have never seen
           Nor been with

Still within our hearts there lies
           this unity of
[——————————all that dies
we hold in common
because without it

we become more common than the dust.

                    2.

Clay cannot create her features
nor mirror reveal her mouth.

Photograph not show her face,
full with blood, so put away

her picture from the shelf
And turn instead to living

women on the couch, decked with flowers
as if it were she laid out,

and not Sylvia, in the woods,

3.

Address to the Woman

Tell her that may not rise again
She sings still in our breath

Tell her that may not breathe again
She moves yet beneath the moon

Tell her that may not wave again
Her hands are dawns within our eyes

Tell her that may not speak again
Her words are warnings in the wood.

Robert Wilson
October 24, 1963[5]
[Milton, MA]

*Tell the printer that everything in the book is as it should
be. Mistakes in grammar, punctuation and spelling:
(surrended, for surrendered) are intentional, or absolute
as this is what the poem demanded. The only, etc.*

Dear Bob:

I leave the title up to you. I can think of none to save my soul. This is a very special night in my life, for 11 years ago tonight, I met Dana for our first drive into the country. And it is a hallowed spot in my mind. I didn't realize this until I typed the date at the top of this letter. It was 11:30 when we met and just about now we were coming in each other's arms. I will never forget as long as I live, and I am not sad about it, but joyful as only a lover can be.

I have celebrated it every year that I remembered. And so it is only fitting that I

---

5 A picture of Robert Creeley is attached with a handwritten note reading, "That is our audience as I see it."

should be sending this manuscript off tonight, or rather finishing it. Oh I love you for doing this, resolving in my mind and life the fact of fate in our existence.

Here are some titles to try on:

> The Industry of Your Soul
>> That is all I can think of, and I know it far from adequate. The Acts of Youth I decided to use as title for a section in the book. The book is divided into three parts: First Poems, The Acts of Youth, and Autumn in New York, which I like best as a title.
>> *Could this be the Title?!! Yes.*
>> Here are some instructions as I see them:

[redacted on ms.] correcting it myself often four or five, maybe six times, copying poems over and over until I got them right. *That is true to the experience of the poem.* The punctuation is right, as is the spelling, viz: surrended for surrendered; a comma at the end of a poem instead of a period; poems with no titles; or *sentences* beginning with small, lower-case letters. I hope this doesn't offend you, and you can publish them as they are. But I am open to your suggestions, whatever they may be, [redacted]. Am I being pompous. You must forgive and remember this is my first book, and so I try to be pompous, But am not, dead, in fact can't believe it is happening ~~to all of us~~. Do go on and let me know. The night is here, and delightful and of all the examples I use above: mostly they occur only in one or two poems. I know you might like them or think them unorthodox. But remember we have a highly sophisticated audience to deal with, and nothing is done for its own sake, but only as the poems are, written in and outside partaking of the universe as they do, as we are right now, existing in the flux of stars. God bless them and you.
> *Love,*
> John

> Robert Wilson
> 11/27/63
> [Milton, MA]

Dear Bob:
    The title I have
chosen for the book is:

THE NEW VANITY
(poems 1954–63) ?
the part in parenthesis
is tentative according
to your wishes.
  Please let me
know if this is alright
    Love,
    John

                                              Robert Wilson
                                            January 30, 1964
                                              [Milton, MA]

Dear Bob:
    Please forgive my delay. Things get so pressing that I revert to long-distance love and no action. Now paralysis has passed and I enclose
        1) The Ginsberg letter
        2) Holograph of Measure poem: The Imperatrice
        3) Typed copies of:
            A Poem For Trapped Things and
            Where Fled—which I hope you can insert in the manuscript. Where
Fled at the end and A Poem For Trapped Things after the poem: Louise in the table
of contents.
                        Denise wanted the Poem For Trapped Things in. It was first
printed: New American Poetry 1945–1960 edited by Allen for Grove Press.
    Also would you omit "If *love* be dark, and a compulsion in the mind" if ~~you~~ *we*
didn't take it out before ~~you.~~ I hate to bother you with all this, but it wont take long.
    I enclose a blue page for your amusement. It is a list of titles. ~~But~~ But PENTACLE
is the one I really favor *want*: It has an excellent definition in any dictionary: the
pent (five) and the acle from OSCULUM—OSCULUS—dim—five dim (years—
from 1958–1963 when the majority of poems were written. Also it is a part of THE
TAROT deck. The Ace of Pentacles a girl showed me when I said the word. PEN-
TACLE she exclaimed with joy.
    Also you could use your sister's collage for the cover. Love,
                        John—

Write and let me know all the details—how many? etc—title, list and price.

Love JAWN

Robert Wilson
February 14, 1964
[Milton, MA]

Dear Bob: Valentine's Day

Would like to say that the Ace of Pentacles is the final title: if you do ~~want~~ *like* it that way, or ~~then~~ Ace of Pentacles alone would do it. *Forgive me.* That way we can call the first section, which you objected to as having no title, ~~simply~~ Pentacle (1954–1959). Then followed by Ages of Youth *for second section.* The poem is to stay Acts of Youth but I figured <u>Ages</u> would include more, as not all the poems are Acts of Youth, in that section. Autumn in New York is the last title *as per before.* O. K. I promise you this will be the last revision.

Thank you for going along with Pentacle—it gave me great courage and joy.

I think

Ace of Pentacles is ~~a~~ good ~~title.~~ There are so many definite articles around, I would like to do away with ours. Still I am sure it will be referred to as

The Ace of Pentacles.

What do you think? definite article or no? ~~definite article~~

[…]

Diane di Prima
2.19.64
[Milton, MA]

Dear Diane:

Could you bring, if it fits in your luggage, a large box of yeast? plus products. They don't have it in Boston and it really helps. I will pay when you arrive. I had $300 from The New Hope Foundation through Stanley Kunitz[6] but it is all gone now on perfume and shoes. It is $4.50 and Saturday is payday. All they have here is Tiger's Milk, which is good, but . . . Of course, this is in code, CIA?

     John

Can you spare it till then? I hope this isn't an imposition. I will not go back to New York until [illeg]

*   *   *

Throughout 1963 and 1964 Wieners cultivated his friendship with Denise Levertov and Mitch Goodman, who were welcoming and stimulating company to Wieners. In the second half of the decade, as Levertov was conducting her provocative correspondence with Robert Duncan concerning activism and poetry, she and Goodman would attend many of the same antiwar poetry readings and fundraisers as Wieners. But from the beginning, as with Duncan, Levertov's friendship with Wieners was based entirely in poetry, and she proved among the most astute readers of his verse, in her letters as well as her 1965 review of *Ace of Pentacles* in *Poetry*. In that essay—titled "To Write is to Listen"—she describes the effects of the idiosyncratic or anachronistic aspects of Wieners's verse:

> Whatever happens is there because that is how the song goes, as a wind blowing in certain branches, a wave breaking on certain stones . . . *Ace of Pentacles* will disturb anyone looking for preconceived benefits, whether "cooked" or "raw"; it attempts to fulfill no such expectations, only to testify to inner voices. There are few books today so utterly clear of some sense that the author is sneaking a glance at the reader to see how he's taking it.[7]

*   *   *

---

6 The New Hope Foundation was formed by poet, writer, and peace activist Lenore Marshall (1897–1971) and her husband James, in the area of New Hope, Pennsylvania, with a mission to "support the arts and the cause of world peace." The Marshalls invited poet Stanley Kunitz to help administer the Foundation's artist grants, and soon after Marshall's death they established the Lenore Marshall Poetry Prize, which continues to administer awards.

7 Levertov, 328.

Denise Levertov
Mar 19, 1964
[Milton, MA]

Dear Denise:

Just wanted to send you some word: about my life, and whatever happens it is. But cannot really do it. Only send you this salutation. Will see you April 16th. I hope it is enough.

Love,
Love
John *John*

I have tried so often to write, and just cannot do it. If I did not respect you so much, or feel so close to you, as a guiding spirit in life, then I could do it. All I can say, for the first time in four years, I am off medication. That means totally. And no one knows it but you. I have told one ~~but you.~~ So you see, it is an occasion. Those last words are sloppy, forgive me.

I didn't tell the doctor or anything. I just stopped taking pills, and my mind is working again. Not revolving in circles, as it used to be, but flying off, into circles. Since Leroi was here, February 19th, or so.

It is wonderful. I hope you feel so, too.

Dave Haselwood
June 20, 1964
[Milton, MA]

MidSummer Eve
Dear Dave:

The book is coming along. Do not despair. It is growing within me. I am reading Valery's Art of Poetry and this cycle of poetry I am passing thru, that is passing thru me, I must obey its commands.

Is Jesse Sharp[8] still in town? My nephew is dreaming, down the bed, next to mine. He is three years old. Are you coming thru allright?

---

8 Jesse Sharp, painter in the 1960s San Francisco art scene around Robert LaVigne and Dave Haselwood's

I am still the same. Are you the same. I know you are. It is time that passes thru us and takes *away* the toll, but not the essence. It is there, as essential as the air we breathe in.

> Time takes away the time between us
> but *not* the time ~~we shared~~ we have
> Love to you   to come.

Will you send Andrew's book?   John

Denise Levertov
July 31, 1964
[Milton, MA]

Dear Denise:

It was so nice of you to write today. It really made my whole day "Like all things concerned with her, she was magic, and her letters hidden in the mail box until the proper moment."

I really can't say much more than this: the blue flowers on the dresser, the red comforter on the bed. It is all I have, and the wind rustling through the trees outside. It is more than enough, and to have the pen in my hand is more than joy; it is thrilling moments just these—that direct one's whole life. And make him see what things are to be avoided and what fostered to preserve these things or moments to be a permanent part of one's life: Working "alone."

I do try to be a comfort and song in the night for others—but this cannot be done.

It is only ourselves that reveal the rapture. We may be able to share it but one has to find it for himself before he can share it or even believe in it. For others. That they come to the rapture only in what is given them. Can I be that fatalistic? And yet one

---

circles; he showed at Michael Agron's Batman Gallery on Fillmore Street. In his memoir piece "The Artist's Life as a Work in Progress," LaVigne describes Sharp as "a coal-miner, then painter, adventurer . . . half-Apache, an impassioned double of the part Peruvian Gaugin." LaVigne notes a connection between Sharp and Wieners:

> Jesse Sharp, when he spoke, spoke suddenly out of his dark fuming silences like a mad oracle, ideas coming in spurts followed by parenthetic remarks. Unlike Kerouac's parentheses, which make archway upon archway into unmeasured spaces of other times and places, Jesse would make a title of a line he'd just spoken by sub-titling it with an aside to himself, a generous offering to his hearer of another way to think the thought, but this time, with a new stress! This unique diction was recorded by John Wieners in "A Poem for Early Risers," in lines perpendicular to the main body of the text. Oh, how I wish I could hear, again, Wiener's unique Boston voice doing Jesse's (nearly) inimitable rhythm. (12)

has to believe in that. If you take our plane trip as proof. How can one explain it any other way. That it was blind accident or chance. I don't believe that two people can meet like that in blind chance. It is too much. Of all the people in New England; why us two to take that plane?

And it was you who "cancelled out" of Buffalo and so gave me the chance to be there. The check was made out in your name; and was sent back to the Treasurer's office for a new name, and I haven't received it yet. The wheels or machinery of the state grind that slow. I believe in chance. But how blind can it be? Is it fortuitous?

"Hard chance and blind sure change" I think it is of Lionel Johnson.[9]

And your "Who is at the window, who? Who?" is also the theme first stanza of a poem written in 1958 in Joanne Kyger's apartment in San Francisco. I should send it but it is so bad I hesitate. Tho I do quote the same stanza at the beginning of the poem and with variations at the end.

I do not equate us, you are too good for that, but there are similarities in spirit I can feel. But yet this is True of other poets, too. Where we can feel for from them identities of spirit. And yet I think back of what you said: that "Hymn To Ishtar" is your "favorite" poem, and mine too. That I knew that night if a poet woman could write this, then there was hope for me.

And the way you bent over to pick up a piece of paper from the stage, with your backside to the audience, made me see that you were not afraid to deny grace.

For only by denying it, may we possess it.

Love to you, Denise

John

The stewardess said to me after you got off,

 Was that your

"Lost your fiancé?"

I said, "She's married."

"You're married!" she said.

"She's married," I said. "We met by chance

 at the airport."[10] "Oh"

 she said.

 thinking we had made a *casual* pickup.

---

9 Lionel Johnson (1867–1902), English poet. Wieners may be referring to his "Julian at Eleusis," which laments "Chance and change; chance and change! strange / / chance, hard change."

10 Levertov wrote to Duncan: "On my way to Middletown and who shd I meet—in Boston airport—but dear John Wieners! We had 40 m. en l'air. He was going to Buffalo to read" (Bertolf and Gelpi, *The Letters of Robert Duncan and Denise Levertov*, 462).

Charles Olson
August 4, 1964
[Milton, MA]

Charles:

Forgive me for saying Shakespeare : it was more than Shakespeare you ~~said~~ looked to me : it was more than words : although Chaucer approximated it. It was back in that era ; of heroic proportions.

> *Forgive us all,*
> *John*

Charles Olson
August 7, 1964
[Milton, MA]

Dear Charles:

Let me talk off the top of my head. I am so tired: but the real doesn't involve me, it's what exhausts me. It's the dreams* that nurture me, yet that isn't true, because they don't exist. It's the possibility of them coming true, and what does that give me, but pleasure. It's not enough: delight in the senses, lazily hazing the scene. It leads to agony; and the only real satisfaction is the scene: BY THAT, I MEAN WORK, I mean really, that's the only pleasure, being able to give oneself to the scene, and by scene, I mean the reality around *in one* in the terms of oneself giving himself to work. Which is simply this (typing,) this activity of mind, which involves the muscles, and senses, contracts the forehead. Am I wrong here? Behind the words, lies the deeds.

The only real enjoyment of my life is typing here: the real (what I take it you mean by the explicit) is this an echo of your words? I seem to hear your words on this paper. My God, Charles, I owe so much to you. You have sustained me for ten full years.

And yet I am so confused. I opend Maximus yesterday to:

> (referring to Kate)
> She wears her own face
> as we do not.
> until we cease to wear
> the clouds
> of all confusion,

Maximus Poems, p.58

And yet there are other real pleasures: the time with you.

I went up there and said too much, to believe in it. It was merely getting the cream off the top, or the skim off the milk. The sour bits that plague the mind.

> *By dreams, I think I mean wishes, fantasy (not as you use it) wish-fulfillment, day-dreaming, you call it: which makes a man turn sour.

I find this is your quote of Jung: "The symbolic process is an experience in the image and of the image"

"The process, in its unfolding, reveals an enantiodromal arrangement like that in the text of the I*Ching, and so presents a rhythm of destruction and creation, of error and truth, of loss and gain, of depth and height."   *in letter to Mike May 1957*[11]

What I am put off in the real, is that it so distracts and irritates me, that I want nothing to do with it. All day long I see the faces pass by, and the voices at night, heard, in the corridor, repeat over, and over again, the same words, tho the subject matter continues to change. There is nothing here real in that. I take it that the real explicit lies under these images: that these curtains, these winds, flowing in the night, these voices heard in the corridor are just that: real and nothing else? I feel better much than that. But if one stops working, they return, and sinks one into bitterness: sour the heart, and who wants that? I'm not living for that. So one wants to run away from that reality: if only he could keep this instant, when he flowed with the undercurrent.

"Make it last" a man said to me once.

So some run away for sex, and drugs, "love," etc. And yet what else? Where is it, Charles? Is it in daydreaming? Seeing the map and thinking of Rangoon, Mandalay, "where the Ten Commandments are forgot." How funny to think of that? Reading that Mottram[12] again, and being confused and bitter about the scene, again. The same

---

11 As Wieners indicates, this quote—as well as the Jung quote before it—is from a letter Olson had sent to Michael Rumaker May 19, 1957.

12 Eric Mottram (1924–1995), British scholar, a founder of American Studies outside of the United States. In the early 1960s, Mottram published widely on the poetics of the Beats, especially engaged in defending William Burroughs against venomous British critics (in the *Times Literary Supplement*, John Willet gave

with Wild Dog. If only one could put his whole self into the work, and contribute: that would be better. And yet someone could say: that too is escape, from the trolley running in the night. And yet there is peace. Let us find ~~them~~: those who contain it. But where? if only the words of others: it is enough. The irritation of life: I should accept by now. And yet it is necessary.

One needs strength: the phylo-

Again I find: (looking how to spell that word: "One will get nowhere IN CATCHING THE TRAFFIC OF THE HUMAN UNIVERSE IF ONE DOES NOT RECOGNIZE THAT A MAN IS AT ONCE SUBJECT AND OBJECT. IS AT ONCE AND ALWAYS GOING IN TWO DIRECTIONS[13] (in many, of course, as he is a sphere, but two at every essential intersection- at every point of action or decision a man is binary, is involved in choosing one of two): Yours

And yet, I want to be with you. That is the cause of dissatisfaction. And so, I must accept it, that I cannot.

And what can I do without it? Of course, every dissatisfaction is present in the moment, but being together, banishes thinking of that sort. That Is what I am objecting to: that I can do without you; but do what. When with you is joy.

All love of every sort,
    John

185 Eliot St
I am too wise to learn of everything; for I will be with you, but life is of such terrible sort, (that I cannot do everything I want to) It takes such terrible turns and unexpected conditions. But yet I can do neither: for I accept it. What other choice? do we have?

[...]

---

one Burroughs review the simple title "Ugh."), and so Wieners could be referring to any number of articles. Mottram's brief writings on Wieners are filled with insight.

13 Charles Olson's 1951 essay "Human Universe," in which he declares, "Art does not seek to describe, but to enact," was first published in *Origin*, Winter 1951–1952, and was reprinted in *Evergreen Review* in spring 1958. In 1965, the Auerhahn Society published *Human Universe and Other Essays*, edited by Donald Allen.

Diane di Prima
September 24, 1964
[Milton, MA]

Dear Diane:

I came across this, while looking for an old poem to send to Audit.[14] It was written while you were out in California, before I even knew you well, or that you had married Alan. In fact, I had only seen you and Alan together once. It might not have anything to do with you or Alan; or with you even. But I found it the night your letter arrived, with the heart, and the 20 dollar note. How lovely. I wonder if its good. I bet it is, in heaven. Or wherever old revolutionaries go. Anyway, here is the dream.

Every acid is a ring, every ring is a nail,
every nail is a grate on which I lie here naked,
waiting.

"Prosody is the articulation of the total sound
of the poem."[15]

I fell to the ground a few moments ago which turned
to a grate; behind the bushes on the grass where
I lost my clothes.

A girl came down the street, a blonde girl
in a beige raincoat. It may sound corny but its true;
one of those girls you see around New York with a big
leather handbag, and her hair done up in braids around
her head. I can still see her, blonde and divine, in
trousers and one knee bent; she was looking and
waiting, walking down this hill, looking for someone
who whispered, Diane, out of the hills beside the house
on the driveway.

---

14 *Audit* was a small poetry magazine edited by American poet Michael Anania (b. 1939) from 1962 to 1967. Anania's time on the Buffalo English faculty (1961–1964) overlapped with Wieners's.

15 In 1917 Ezra Pound reviewed T. S. Eliot's *Prufrock and Other Observations* for *Poetry*, later reprinted in his book *Literary Essay*. In a footnote added for the latter edition, Pound famously wrote that "prosody is the articulation of the total sound of the poem."

He was standing there, with his friends trying to
hold him back but he came down the road with the tiny
snout of a gun in his hand and said something as if
I can't have her nobody can, Diane, Diane. And we all
fell to the ground, having seen her, standing there
shimmering, we lost our clothes and stood, pressing
our knuckles into the grate.

Well, it's nothing, but a very vivid dream, which appeared to me, under heroin I believe, and which I never associated with you, until now. And which may have nothing to do with you anyway. It is very badly written, but there anyway, as a dream.

Just finished the Joe Gould Profiles in the New Yorker, one this week, and one last. The New Yorker has changed its heading on Leroi to read from "a most promising dramatist" to a "promising dramatist."[16] So I wonder what that means. Have you seen the <u>Audit</u> with his* poems in it? I will be in the third one, if I ever get the manuscript together.

*Frank O'Hara's

My family is fighting furiously about the car, which has just blown a carburetor. My brother called my father, "You stupid shit." They are now ~~fighting~~ *arguing* in the kitchen. Of course, my mother provokes all this, by her stupid tension. Strange echoes of childhood. And how we dwell curiously in this backwater of emotion. Oh well, it probably keeps them alive. But it does prohibit a great deal of life on my part, and brings the blood to my head, not unpleasantly.

The shouts bring back a violence that is needed in my life, since I was bred on it. I know it is not over yet, tho the house is quiet. All a matter of unrest, drinking (on my brother's part, night after night, day after day, lunch after lunch, cocktail after cocktail). And my mother doesn't eat, trying to lose weight, and overworks, at nothing, and my father is a poor match on the waves of childhood misery, poverty and insanity. It all runs in the family. Well, enough for now. But I am afraid to stop, as there is nothing else to do, but be silent witness, or spectator to the sports.

Love for now, and please write,

John

John

---

16 For LeRoi Jones, as a playwright ,1964 was the breakout year. His first two plays, *Dutchman* and *The Slave*, were both published and performed in 1964. The former was a sensation off-Broadway, where it won the Obie Award for Best American Play.

Diane:

Thank you for the nice words about the book. Please review it for the Bear. And send me something to do. That excites me.

> *Apathy increases with the day,*
> *staring listlessly at the fire.*

[On seal of envelope:] *I don't know what I wrote in this. It's been sealed for a week. But love. And don't worry. <u>Will get type.</u>*

Robert Duncan
October 30, 1964
[Milton, MA]

Dear Robert:

The enclosed is a result of your essay in Kulchur,[17] which Gerrit Lansing sent to me; this morning: it is a riff, or take-off, not an answer, rebuttal, or extension → *Explanation, etc.* It should not have your name on it, but it would not be written without your essay.

Thank you for it. The days are nice, here. Indian Summer, as they say. I am hungry for breakfast. The book is here, and beyond words. Yours, I mean.

The politicians' voices blast off in the hills.

I am trying to come back, but it is a slow way coming.

Turning towards the woods, often, and getting lost in the trees.

I like simple ways, best, and
> your glamour is the best consolation.
What does that happen to be? simple being.

> Nothing is being done here, so I might as well close. Joe
Dunn is still in Bridgewater, and I haven't seen him. But I will soon.
> *Love,*
> *John*

---

17 Duncan's essay "Ideas of the Meaning of Form" was later published in his *Selected Prose.*

But the main impression of your book[18] is one of glamour, or romantic imagination. That is what sustains me best. All the things which you have included; I worship best. Or I think so now. It is not romantic imagination, but "hymns to the romantic imagination." I have already given the book away. I "liked" it so much that (I have only read it once, & fragments over again.) I must buy it again; the hardcover one. And read it again. My mother said to me, "That will give you something to do for tonight" when she saw the book. And I thought to myself: That will give me something to do for a lifetime.

Forgive the underlining. I regret it now.
It didn't come out that way, but only as an ordinary thought.

After Reading Robert Duncan's Ideas Of The Meaning Of Form[19]

Make me part of the process, not its goal.
Render me as the wave washes upon its shore,
        Stephen Crane's Open Boat.

A broken thing laid upon the bed:
Do you actually think will come re-birth?
        The morning lays its light wing
                upon the dead.

A blue ball glistens among the real;
        but the real is not the only palace
           of events.

The daisy inhabits there, too;
    its purple petals an aster to my mind.

Do not mention mental illness; madness or
        institutions.
They exist only as examples for the failing mind
    ~~Did~~ *To* correct all those who would try the unknown
        darknesses; or weakness.

---

18 Wieners is possibly referring to Duncan's 1964 volume of poetry (his second), *Roots and Branches*.
19 "After Reading Robert Duncan's 'Ideas of the Meaning of Forms'" is unpublished.

Events become treacherous; illustrious minds *seem* to
become so.

~~Fear is a way of living, or happening.~~

Denise Levertov
December 27, 1964
[Milton, MA]

Dear Denise:

I wonder if I could ask you to write a <u>few</u> words of recommendation to the State
University of New York at Buffalo, where I am planning to take a master's degree,
starting this January, if all goes well. I would go as a teaching fellow, and study under
Charles Olson, plus teaching one class a week, and get paid something like $1200 a
semester. It would take 2 1/2 years, but I really would like it, after Boston and Jordan
Marsh Co.[20] What do you think? I hate to impose on you, knowing how you feel
about these things (I think we talked about it once) but it would take only a few
words, and should be sent directly to:

Professor Thomas E. Connolly

Teaching Fellow Selection Committee

Dept. of English

SUNYAB, 21 Library Circle

Buffalo 14, New York (addressed envelope enclosed).

I would only be able to study under Charles one semester (two seminars) so it will
not be as Brancusi feared, when offered the chance to study under Rodin, as a pupil
and refused; saying: "nothing grows under big trees."[21] Still there is a chance that

---

20 In his "Untitled 1969 Journal," Wieners describes his time scaping by as a Boston College student in the
1950s:

I had to pay for my books, my transportation and clothing, though my patient and hard-working
Mother and her family would graciously load me with presents and funds at Christmas and birthday.
Nevertheless I had to work twenty hours a week, the school year, and five and a half days a week during
the summer months at the salary of $27.50 per week. I could not stand this more than one summer and
at the end of the second year I quit, due to tardiness, and was employed at the Jordan Marsh Co. at the
salary of $35.00 per week for forty hours work (*Stars Seen in Person*, 193).

21 Sculptor Constantin Brâncusi studied briefly under Rodin at his studio, but left because, as he famously
said, "Nothing grows under big trees." His work was to a large extent a reaction to Rodin's, and Brâncusi

something may grow. I hope so, and this will give me the chance to continue my studies, get an academic background, and be able to teach in the future.

Please, Denise, don't worry about this, or give it too much thought, as I know you are busy; and I would want only a few words, or maybe even a copy or selection of the review would be enough. The thing is almost assured me; that is, if they get enough funds, as Mexico didn't, or are able to take me on, with my marks (some in the 60's, from ethics and scholastic philosophy). Otherwise, next year, I have to take a graduate record exam, and that would be impossible, scholastically, with this time-lag, so it's now or nothing. I enclose a transcript of marks, so you can see what I am made up of? and if you could return that to me, I would be most appreciative. I suppose I am only or just showing off. Love to you, and Mitch in this holiday season. I will never forget last New Year's at your house, and hope that the candles burn bright for us this year, as they did last, because you snuffed them at exactly the right time. Love to you again,
>   *John*
>   John

>   Charles Olson
>   DEC 28 [1964]
>   [Milton, MA]

CHARLES OLSON, AND OK
28 FORT SQUARE GLOUCESTER MASS (RTE DIR)

GOD BLESS YOU, SIR AND DELIVER US ONE AND AT THE SAME TIME TOGETHER. FOR ALL TIME

* * *

In January 1965, Wieners began graduate work at Buffalo, where he remained through 1969. Olson was a founding presence at their new poetics program, imagined as a "Black Mountain II," but only stayed there through May 1965. Betty had died in a car wreck on March 28, 1964, and after a period of recovery, Olson taught one more

---

later said, "Without the discoveries of Rodin, my work would have been impossible" (Galenson, *Old Masters and Young Geniuses*, 115). And indeed Wieners would only have one semester of study with his old teacher Olson before the latter left Buffalo, first for Italy and Berkeley with Wieners and then back to Gloucester, leaving Wieners to continue his studies at Buffalo without the shade cast by Olson's pedagogical "big tree."

semester, Wieners's first term at the school. As they had at Black Mountain a decade earlier, Wieners and Olson just barely overlapped at Buffalo.

* * *

Denise Levertov
Feb 26, 1965
[Buffalo]
Friday–Saturday
Midnight

Dear Denise:

All settled in now. And grown accustomed to the change, not his face, any longer.

Will be in New York *Sunday* March 14th for reading *at East End Theatre* and have 2 tickets reserved for you at the door—and paid for if you want to come. Anyway, I hope to see you then, if just for a moment. Possibly for brunch, maybe, Monday, at the Nation if you are uptown. I would like to see their offices and New Directions.' If only to fill the mental picture. But not as a guest, only as a passing observer *outside the door.* I like to see where things come out of.

Classes meet here Mon Wed Fri at 1 & 3 PM. These I teach. Freshman English. Poetry 5 weeks; short story 3 or 4; drama, what's left. David[22] is here, in fact right above me. He got me this room, and is very kind.

His opera premiered *here* last week and was much fun. Next week the Arts Festival, and "those literary people" as Charles says. He is in Tufts right now on a conference. I take his course Myth and Literature ~~Thursday~~ *Wednesday* afternoons. Robert Graves' Greek Myths is the text, but we never use it. Instead, monographs and fascicles on Ancient Mycenae: the Late Halladic and Middle Halladic, etc. Then his Mod. Poetry which I audit Tuesday afternoons, for no credit. Rather more than audit, as a paper is due. On Ezra Pound and his Cantos which I chose as my term paper.

For my class, I started them with H. D. which I enclose and which I ~~am sure~~ *hope* you will love.

Forgive that poem I sent. ~~It does~~
Love to you, and Mitch
John
3262 Main Str.
Buffalo, N.Y

---

22 David Posner (1921–1985), American poet and teacher. After studying at the Sorbonne, followed by several years as a journalist specializing in archaeological digs, he returned to the United States and taught English at the University of Buffalo, where he was also Assistant Curator of Poetry, from 1957 to 1969.

Would love to hear from you. Just finished a *"prose"* piece for David Shaff,[23] called Heroes (for Michael McClure.) Wrote it tonight and sent it off, too. Am still shaking. (Am writing a lot. And reading more than ever before. Tho I haven't started on <u>Wilhelm Meister's Apprenticeship</u>, which I will do right now. Love.

Pray for the poor souls, lost in the night.[24]

Robert Wilson

3.2.65

[Buffalo]

Dear Bob: —Send new catalog!

In great pool of Gloucester, where Leroi Jones has gone swimming as the guest (for a little while!) of the late John Hammond,[25] whose father "employed 10,000 Zulus in South Africa" with Cecil Rhodes, and made his money in diamonds, then organs, I think. Gay as a lark, Jack was, until died last month. Love to you, Ed Dorn is reviewing <u>A of P</u> in Wild Dog #15,[26] next issue. Will see Creeley day after tomorrow. Di Prima also said she is doing it for <u>the Village Voice. see if you can press her on it.</u> In place of Allen.

Charles here great. Am going to San Francisco for conference this summer, I think. They called but not actually confirmed. Will go anyway. Looking forward to reading. So thin & emaciated, send money.   John 3262 Main Str. Buffalo, N. Y. 14214

---

23 David Schaff was editor of Bay Area poetry magazine *Cassiopeia*, which became *Ephemeris*. He published many of Wieners's San Francisco peers, including Joanne Kyger, George Stanley, and Jack Spicer. Schaff's own book of poetry, *The Moon By Day* (1971, Four Seasons Foundation), contains dedications to many different poets, including Wieners.

24 Written across the envelope's seal.

25 John Hayes Hammond (1888–1965), American inventor. He founded the Hammond Radio Research Laboratory in Gloucester on his father's land He developed more inventions than any other American besides Thomas Edison and became known as the "the Father of the Remote Control." Between 1926 and 1929 he built Hammond Castle, a beautiful medieval-style castle that houses his collections of art. Wieners's close friend Gerrit Lansing lived at the Castle when he first moved to Gloucester.

26 Ed Dorn founded the underground magazine *Wild Dog* in 1963, while teaching at Idaho State University.

Diane di Prima
3.9.65
[Buffalo]
Tuesday

Dear Diane:

I better get the train fare before Friday or Saturday morning, or else I can't come.

Sitting in the grey morning smoking bad pot. It gives me a headache.

Charles' class this afternoon, and of course, we'll talk or rather I'll listen until dawn.

I would like to stay till Tuesday morning: Do you think there's someplace I could stay over Sunday and Monday nights without cats –

Not far over on The East Side,

unless it's nice and organized.

Love,

3262 Main Str.   John

Buffalo 14214

[On seal of envelope:] *Also, Diane, save 4 tickets at door in my name.*

Denise Levertov
3.9.65
[Buffalo]

Wow Denise:

That's quite a review.[27] I am pacing the room like a caged lion. It's your *own* review. Bob Wilson wrote, "Her review is like a poem in itself."

I am so happy. I can die. I have read it three times now (more than anyone else will do, except the girl who wrote it and the man to whom it is written.) And Orpheus, of course, what will happen to him?

He will go on living—and choosing others to inhabit. On the force that

---

27 Levertov's rapturous review appeared in the February 1965 issue of *Poetry*.

   Ace of Pentacles will disturb anyone looking for preconceived benefits, whether "cooked" or "raw"; it attempts to fulfill no such expectations, only to testify to inner voices . . .

   One must listen to the sounds. It is essentially a melopoeic language. The components include many irregular and interior rhymes, an instinctive right placing of vowels, and—most characteristically—a pace, or rather a gait, that is almost ceremonial, the serious saunter of dream-walking, in dreams that take one a stage on a pilgrimage. ("To Write Is to Listen," 229)

produced Orpheus we likewise are inhabited by. Did 49 pages on Wilhelm Meister.
Love,

John

* * *

The Festival of the Two Worlds, performance event in Spoleto, near Rome, was
founded in 1958 by composer Gian Carlo Menotti. Its eighth annual festival, from
June 24 to July 18, 1965, featured Poetry Week with a lineup of legendary poets from
around the world, with the wizened Ezra Pound at the center. Menotti consulted
with Frank O'Hara on the poet list; O'Hara could not attend because of work at
the Museum of Modern Art, but Menotti invited many New York and Beat poets
on his recommendation, including Wieners and Olson, Barbara Guest, Lawrence
Ferlinghetti, John Ashbery, and **Bill Berkson**. Performances included LeRoi Jones'
play *The Dutchman* and several ballets by George Ballanchine, produced by the New
York City Ballet. Menotti tried to avoid controversy by leaving out the increasingly
notorious performers Ginsberg and Corso, but wound up courting more by giving
a prominent slot to Pound, prompting the USSR to protest Pound's collaboration
with Fascist Italy during World War II; Soviet poet Yevgeny Yevtushenko was prevented from appearing until the last minute. When Pound did perform, it was from
a chair in Menotti's box in the theater. As Robert Neville described the event in the
New York Times:

> When his turn came to read, the spectators thus had to turn around in their
> seats to catch a glimpse of the poet. Pound read with voice so soft and so
> cracked that it was difficult to distinguish all his words. He read not his
> own works but 10 poems, most of them quite short, written by such others
> as Marianne Moore, Robert Lowell, a fifth-century Chinese poet, a French
> poet and an Italian poet. The weak voice of Pound suggested that the rebel
> in him, although not the artist, had vanished . . . At the end of his few
> minutes of reading, Ezra Pound received a long and hearty ovation from an
> audience that stood and turned toward him.[28]

From Europe, Wieners and Olson traveled back to the Bay Area for the 1965 Berkeley
Poetry Conference, a conclave of "New American" poets assembled by the University
of California Extension Programs from July 12 to 24. Wieners gave a solo reading,
introduced by Creeley, and Olson drunkenly delivered an instantly legendary reading

---

28 Neville, "A Podium of Poets," 27.

and lecture that went on for over three hours, transcribed and published by Coyote Press in 1966 as *Charles Olson Reading at Berkeley*.

* * *

Wallace Berman
April 21, 1965
[Buffalo]

Dear Wallace and Shirley:

As you might know, I am going out to San Francisco this summer, for a reading at the Berkeley Poetry Conference, supposedly the first week of July, after I come back from Italy with Charles Olson. We are reading there at the Spoleto poetry week. It is a festival of music and drama, sponsored by Gian Carlo Menotti, etc. Baronessa Alphonse de Rothschild, etc. Mrs. Henry Heinz III (the can heiress, I believe) etc. This is the first year they have had poetry. And we will read with 18 other poets from all over the world. Quasimodo, the Nobel Prize Winner,[29] etc. Some fag in heaven must be working for me. We will read 5 days a week there, one poem a day, *9 miles* north of Rome, and then fly around the world, back to San Francisco. What a trip! My heart is in my mouth. The Berkeley one will allow me to visit you, if you will have me. I will take that business train to L. A. The Berkeley one also offers $125 so that will be my fare to L. A. etc. But the Spoleto offers nothing, but the prestige. Except room and accommodations at a modern, comfortable hotel. We will leave June 1st. He also has been invited. 20 poets from all over the world, and we are two. It is called The Festival of Two Worlds (I wonder what that i̶s̶ *means*?) and we are very excited. Do you want me to collect poems for you for No. 10 Semina. I hope so, if one from him, nothing else. Meaning Charles. We are very excited, as I say, and I can hardly keep my mind in order. Will you write to me, and ask me what you want from Italy. We will be there about a month. Spoleto is between Rome and Florence *and we'll see the Giotto in Florence*, and you'll see, the sky will light up. The final appearance will be in The Piazza del Duomo, and they hope to televise it. The theatre will be the Cato Melisso. What a ball. I hope I can keep my cool. Will you pray for me? I will be thinking of you all the way, and wishing you were with me. After the reading I will see you, and we will be together again.

Classes here are fine. Here is a poem, I wrote:

---

29 Salvatore Quasimodo (1901–1968), Italian lyric poet and writer who was awarded the Nobel Prize in Literature in 1959.

GOODNIGHT, JENNY GERHARDT[30]

I'm scared of the rain.
It's like an invisible hand tapping
on my
shoulder.
The lightening makes me shudder
too.
I hate to turn my back on it.

Love to you and your child. I have his picture with one of Hedy Lamarr as I go out the door, standing on the table. Will you write me? I want to hear from you, if only a word. Yeah, Buffalo is about 500 miles from NY (on the Canadian Border, across from [line cropped by microfilm]

Ed Sanders
April 26, 1965
[Buffalo]

Dear Ed:

I am writing this, now, to save until the end of the week, when I can put $10 in it, and pay you back the money I owe. The Orgasm Oil is alright with me, tho I think we should be careful in revealing its contents, as FDA will come down on it, if they can, of course, and take it off the market, like morning glory seeds, Charles says (I showed him your letter, I hope you don't mind). You are a lovely person, Ed, and it was a pleasure to have you here, for all concerned, David and myself, Oscar Silverman[31] and Charles. Please come again, before we go to Spoleto. Charles and I both have been invited. My letter came late, as it was addressed to Univ. of Buffalo, Buffalo, and I imagine returned. March 20th. We will fly out, I hope June 1st or so, Charles says, and I am (we are) trying to raise the money for flight. But we will make it. The American Council of Learned Societies, or something like that. Any way Chas. has no doubts. Will you come again? Take Wheat Germ oil and see. Here is the label.
    4 Fluid Ounces

---

30 "Goodnight, Jenny Gerhardt" is unpublished.

31 Oscar Silverman (1903–1977), American professor who taught for decades at the University of Buffalo, where he chaired the English department (1956–1963) and acted as Director of Libraries.

It's absolutely guaranteed. I bathe in buckets of sperm, because of it. On only one teas poon a day. Will you say
"We cannot supply partners"
but they are recommended for healthy outpouring. Comparable to Herman Melville's dream, when he saw angels in a row, with their hands plunged in jars of spermaceti. I get it from Dahlberg's essay "Moby Dick, a Hamitic Novel."[32] Read it in his Alms for Oblivion, just out this year, 1964 or 65. Love to you, Ed and we are sailing. We also got manuscripts for you, if you want them. Enclosed find one Just finished Hesiod for the first time, last night's dawn, and it was so beautiful I read (wrote) this poem. I would omit all that stuff about seasoning, people will get so (too) confused, and it's not necessary as the stuff is so sweet, anyway, on its own! But only take one teaspoonful. You do not need more, and allow 3 days at the most to feel full results. There is no need to miss an orgasm at all this way. Just take it straight, and see!
Yours,
Mad
Madison Avenue   *(Harpers Torch)*[33]
Also recommend, in Edwin Panonsky's Studies in Iconology,[34] plate XXV, fig. 46 an illustration for your translation of Hesiod.
Even Charles didn't know of it. So use them.

Joanne Kyger
May 15, 1965
[Buffalo]
Dear Joanne, Kids:

As you know, I am truly delighted to hear from you, and to know that I may stay with you. But I am allergic to cats, as you must remember. Even though I have an inhaler to take against them, their pollen permeates the air. Could we do something to screen out the pollution and I don't mean keres. I have nothing against Crooked Tail or Straight Tail themselves, but tell me, how can I breathe? Maybe in the guest

32 Edward Dahlberg's "Moby-Dick: A Hamitic Dream" is a screed against the "frigid" writers of the nineteenth-century American Renaissance, "burnt in Puritan ice," focusing on Melville's masterpiece as a "verbose, tractarian fable on whaling . . . a book of monotonous and unrelenting gloom" (119).
33 An icon of a torch is the logo for publisher Harper and Row, which became HarperCollins in 1990.
34 Erwin Panofsky (1892–1968), German art historian whose *Studies in Iconology: Humanist Themes in the Art of the Renaissance* was published in 1939.

room, they haven't been, and I could go in there, after you have vacuumed it out, and hung the bedspreads and curtains and rugs out in the air, their dander, that which clings to their fur, gets in my lungs, and wont let me breathe. Poor dear, Michael's address is 112 River Rd. Grand View, N. Y. And he is fine, finishing his new novel, which he tentatively calls: The Other Side of the Night.[35] Don't tell anyone, as he's not sure if that's what he should call it. I don't know what it's about. But he might be able to come out for his vacation. Wouldn't that be wonderful.
Ask him.

But if I use just the guest room, where will I eat? Wouldn't that be awful, to take meals in a bedroom. But we could use the kitchen, because there's very little fabric there, I imagine, for their fur to cling to. And of course, there's Nemi, but she's got cats, too. Alan has become a minister in the Ruggles Street Baptist Church,[36] and Jan is one of their zealots, singing in the choir with the men because she has such a deep voice, and writing letters to my mother, trying to convert her, enclosing pamphlets about renegade Catholic priests. And of course, you know, my family is staunch Roman Catholic, with just a trace of Roman paganism thrown in. But Jan Minsk is not it. They have two children. Linus and Emily. Yes! And the church is black, my dear.

Well, so we go. I'm trying not to be philosophic. Don't show this letter to anyone, as I feel so silly, just talking to you, again, after all these times. Remember Dennis Murphy.[37]

Jerome of course is in Boston, with a boy, of all things, and still paints, sort of, I don't know what. You know, nothing goes on, in Boston, but he's moving to New York. People keep coming up to me at readings and saying, Jerome sent me, and he's got no lights. Or he's living in the basement, etc. Who does he think he is, John Wieners. I don't think Gregory Coarso and I inhabit the same universe. What does Don Allen mean, even comparing me to him. I want to be compared to Henry Miller, living in a rat-infested cellar, under a bare light bulb. But I'm not Henry Miller, I'm just John Wieners, and that's enough for me. And you're Joanne Kyger, and that's enough for me, until the day I die. Don't go to black stockings you never did. But go I. Magnin. Strictly Mainbocher,[38] my dear. Right down the line. I don't have Jerome's address,

---

35 If the Michael Rumaker novel described here, *The Other Side of the Night*, was finished, it was never published.

36 Until 1970, Ruggles Street Baptist Church was located in working-class Roxbury, an area that had recently changed dramatically due to the "white flight" of the 1940s and 1950s. By this time many of its neighboring buildings were slated for "urban renewal" ("Our History," n.p.).

37 Dennis Murphy (1932–2005), American writer whose first novel, *The Sergeant*, was a bestseller in 1958, and in 1968 made into a movie starring Rod Steiger.

38 The House of Mainbacher, haute couture fashion line led by Main Rousseau Bocher, designed most of the wardrobe of Wallis Simpson Duchess of Windsor.

or else we could get him, too. As you might know, Charles and I are going to Spoleto first for a reading there at the Festival of Two Worlds, where we will read every day of the week, one poem an afternoon, on the June 28th–July 2nd stage of the Caio Melissa Theatre[39] with Stephen Spender,[40] Ungaretti,[41] the old queen, Salvatore Quasimodo, the Nobel Prize winner, Ted Hughes,[42] the late Sylvia Plath's husband, whose work, Sylvia's, I like very much. By the way, I loved every word of your poem, on the death of your father, in 12 poets and a painter.[43] I am very proud of you, Joanne, that I even know you, despite the fact that you went to Japan, with that man. Forgive me, I'm sorry I didn't print those poems in Measure, but it was too late then. And as you know, it was a very small issue, with only excerpts of the most imperative. And I could have put one in, I guess, and I don't know why I didn't, I didn't even think of it. Please forgive me. All this human stuff. I must go out and get a soda. I wish we were in San Francisco, together, now, and not all this planning, and talking and deodorizing the air, etc. I live in a room, and David Posner, lives over head, padding around in footsteps, taking sl . . . . . . p . . . .

I'm not, taking anything. Isn't it wonderful. Not a thing. I sound like the reformed alcoholic, Sophie, who takes drugs in Somerset Maugham's novel The Razor's Edge, and sleeps under the cross, and finally throws herself in the Seine. Played by Anne Baxter, in the film, with poor sad late Tyrone Power, who had to shave between his eyebrows. You should never have asked me, but I'm not going to say no. I'm really a very simple person, and only trying to build up a myth about myself. Fuck Stan Persky,[44] who doesn't know how to do it, as Jeanne Eagels[45] says. "Never Explain, never deny, say nothing and become a legend." Those damn moviestars, and drug addicts. They knew nothing and yet tell everything. Also Gary Snyder was asked and had to refuse because he didn't have the money. Neither do I, but I'm going anyway. And Robert Lowell, and Yevteshenko,[46] and Rene Char have also been invited, but

---

39 The Teatro Caio Melisso, a small chamber opera theater in Spoleto, Italy, that hosted the poetry readings at the 1965 Festival of Two Worlds.

40 Stephen Spender (1909–1995), English poet and writer who was intensely concerned with social justice issues in his writing.

41 Giuseppe Ungaretti (1888–1970), Italian poet and writer.

42 Ted Hughes (1930–1998), English poet and writer who was married to American poet Sylvia Plath.

43 *12 Poets 1 Painter*, 1964 anthology edited by Donald Allen for the Four Seasons Foundation, featuring Kyger alongside Snyder, Levertov, Creeley, and others, with six drawings by Duncan's partner Jess.

44 Stan Persky (b. 1941), American Canadian poet and publisher, a part of the late 1950s San Francisco poetry scenes, whose magazine *Open Space* was "a curious mixture of humor and high literary seriousness," publishing fifteen issues in 1964. In 1972 he expatriated to Canada and became a renowned professor, writer, and public intellectual in Vancouver.

45 Jeanne Eagels (1890–1929), Broadway and film actress and Ziegfeld Follies Girl who was immortalized by Kim Novak in the fictionalized 1957 film *Jeanne Eagels* (Golden, *Golden Images*, 29).

46 Yevgeny Yevtushenko (b. 1933), controversial Russian poet, writer, actor, director, and publisher. His visit to the Spoleto Festival was at a time of great upheaval for the Soviet artist, coming at the end of a two-year

we don't know if they're going or not. 20 poets in all, from all over the world/And we happen to be two of them. Isn't it exciting. Will you come too. In spirit anyway. I will carry you between pages of my favorite book. I hope you're not too outdoorsy now. I remember you used to sunbathe, and love to sit in gardens. I hope that phase is not all over now. I will consent to go for a walk with you. Remember when you used to throw me out of the office of the City of Paris. How is Miss Specht? and Larry Ferlinghetti. Two of a kind? I think so. Rafael Alberti[47] is also going. Then we go to Bled, Yugoslavia, to the summer home of the Communist government. Stephen is trying to arrange that, too. And then back to Buffalo, and then to SF. And you.

Love, dear,
    John
    John
Will you write to me?

                    Just anything I'm so happy to be
                        with you again.
I'm not a good poet, I'm just a bad poet who had good
breaks.

                                    Joanne Kyger
                                    5.17.65
                                    [Buffalo]

Dear Joanne
    Are you going to all the lectures and readings and
    seminars? As I want to. And that means early to bed early to
    rise. And we must arrange for transportation over to Berkeley
    everyday. If you are not going, let me know and I must think
    about it. How to get over. We shouldn't miss the Duncan and
    Spicer, Creeley, LeRoi Jones, etc
    O. K. Let me know.
        All love,
        John
I don't think we should have to pay, do you?

---

ban on travel outside the USSR, and a very public imbroglio after signing a letter of protest against the trial of Joseph Brodsky in 1965.

47 Rafael Alberti (1902–1996), Spanish poet, a Marxist who was a leading voice of the Left during the Spanish Civil War and a member of the Generation of '27.

Harvey Brown
July 2, 1965
Spoleto

Dear Harvey and Polly:

This is the theatre where we read our poems. Yesterday John Ashbery, myself, and Johannes Edfelt, the Swedish poet read while Charles sat in the audience. Afterwards Ezra Pound who sat in the box facing you on the right hand side of the doors (first level) read. We met *4 of us* and sat together in the sidewalk cafe outside at one small table with Vera Zorina, the ballerina. Afterwards we walked *together* to another theatre and saw Dutchman by Leroi Jones with Jennifer West in it. *Pound said Tremendous afterwards.* With Olga Rudge at our side. Pound's mistress of many years. Today Chas reads and Pound will be there. Love, John

Robert Duncan
7.8.65
[Rome]

Dear Robert:

We are finally here in Rome, at the Albergo Nazionale. Charles is in Yugoslavia until tonight when I expect him back or at least to hear. We had a lovely week in Spoleto and met Ezra Pound. I have pictures to prove ~~it~~. Which I shall bring ~~with me~~ next week. Visited the Vatican Museums all morning and the Keats-Shelley Memorial this afternoon. Dinner this evening with Toby and Bice McCormick, the Italian translators of Charles into Italian (Rizzoli); also Patrick Bury, the grandson of J. M. Bury; (History of Greece)? and a Tarocchi[48] reader I can't pronounce his name. friend of Fellini's. Also met Caresse Crosby[49] at Rocca Sinibaldi & Bill Barker. Will see you soon. Love—John

what a change for me—thank you.

---

48 Tarot.

49 Caresse Crosby (1891–1970), publisher and patron of the arts. With her second husband, Harry Crosby (1898–1929), she founded Black Sun Press, which published many of the leading lights of the 1920s "Lost Generation." Their scandalous Bohemian marriage is chronicled in Geoffrey Wolff's *Black Sun: The Brief Transit and Violent Eclipse of Harry Crosby*.

After such an incredible summer, the return to Buffalo left both Wieners and Olson feeling deflated. For Olson, still grieving the tragic loss of Betty the year prior, Buffalo was unbearable, and he only taught for two weeks before leaving. Harvey Brown supplied the money needed for him to write full-time back in Gloucester, where he remained till his death. In Olson's absence a new generation of scholars like Albert Glover, Ralph Maud, Jack Clarke, and Fred Wah continued the work Olson had begun at Black Mountain, eventually producing a sprawling series of commissioned essays and poetry pieces (including one by Wieners, called *Woman*) exploring Olson's *Curriculum of the Soul*.

After a brief visit with his family in Milton, Wieners remained in Buffalo without Olson. It bears remembering that after a decade of hand-to-mouth existence, the Buffalo grad fellowship—"sixty-five bucks a week," according to classmate **Duncan McNaughton**—was a welcome constant in Wieners's life now, one that kept him tethered there through 1969, living comfortably above the university bookstore. He was eventually relieved of his freshman comp teaching duties—his pedagogy was judged erratic—but he was allowed to keep his fellowship.[1] As one letter to Michael McClure in this next section shows, Wieners also relied on shady old ways of making ends meet on top of this meager stipend.

Especially without his teacher and friend, Buffalo was an isolating place for Wieners, with what he saw as a stultifying lack of culture. This time of educational institutionalization was, not coincidentally, also Wieners's time of greatest psychological distress, reflected in a number of disquieting letters to Creeley and Wilson throughout the section. Taken as a whole, this section of letters—from one of America's most deranged times, the late 1960s—shows Wieners undergoing a profound and difficult transformation. In the decade since graduating college, he'd always had contact with lovers and intimate friends, but at Buffalo he was suddenly surrounded by nothing but *colleagues*. The result—combined with other life factors—was a time of great confusion, suffering, and creative breakdowns and breakthroughs.

* * *

---

1 This information on the logistics of Wieners's time at Buffalo is courtesy of unpublished interviews with Duncan McNaughton, conducted by Seth Stewart and Robert Dewhurst.

Wallace Berman
Aug 27 [1965]
[Milton, MA]

MILTON²

In the middle of the night, always
it returns to me, this beauty
of poetry, the moon flashing
across the wine-dark sea, like your eye,
the lights in it, at dinnertime.
When I smile at a particularly
pleasant memory, able to live it again.
And the joy of that transmits to you,
sitting across the table from me, my mother.

Joanne Kyger
August 30, 1965
[Milton, MA]

Dear Joanne:

Today I saw Joe Dunn at the Mass. Correctional Institution in Bridgewater, Mass. where he has completed an 18-month sentence for possession of a hypodermic needle and some pills. He is still being held, although his sentence was up June 23, this year. I will find out why from his father tomorrow, and then go back and see him once again, before I go back to Buffalo next Sunday. And I can hardly wait. This house is the tomb of middle-class America. But Buffalo is as bad, the residue of radical America.

If possible, I would like to acquire from Robert, if he does not want to print it right away, Joe's novel,³ so we may do it in Buffalo. It is so good to talk to you. These people do nothing but trudge from bed to board to work to TV set to bed. God, it is living death. I don't like it at all. Give me anything to this. Poverty yes, but not homelessness. I need a roof over my head, no matter what, and the security of food.

2 "Milton" is unpublished.
3 No novel by Joe Dunn was ever published.

Something Spicer never allowed himself.[4] I have some magazines from Berkeley 1949 and they were very prophetic. The Occident, and Berkeley Miscellany.[5]

The print and negatives are still at that shop on Sutter and Polk and I dont have the $10 to get them out. I will write Nemi, and ask her to get them out, and I will pay later, and she can hold the prints until then.

I will take care of myself. Enclosed find a print I saved for you since 1963, when I did not take care of myself, but now I will. Since you ask me. I think you will like it. It went through the travails of the world, as we both did. But still survives. As we do. And please continue. I want to see you with gray hair and new teeth. Give my love to John, and whoever else wants to. If he does. Give it to him anyway. And Bill and the cats. And Nem, of course. Love to her. I will write about the photographs which still reside safely on Polk.

Thank you for sending the clipping. Yes, the Zerox is fine. I will fix *up* Charles Olson. He called last Sat. nite from Gloucester, with Ellie Dorfman of all people. Tomorrow birthday party for Gordon Cairnie[6] at the Grolier Bookshop in Cambridge. He is 70. Let's be like him.

Love,
John

Send the photos, if you have same. I wouldn't know if he's thin or not.

---

4 Jack Spicer died just a couple of weeks before this letter, on August 17, 1965.
5 The *Occident* was the student literary magazine for the University of California at Berkeley. The *Berkeley Miscellany* was a two-issue magazine edited by Robert Duncan in 1948–1949.
6 Gordon Cairnie (1895–1973), owner of the legendary Grolier Poetry Book Shop in Harvard Square. Cairnie opened the store in 1927 using his own thousands of volumes as the stock, and it has been a haven for poets and writers ever since. Cairnie ran the store until his death.

Michael McClure
September 20, 1965[7]
[Buffalo]

Dear Michael:

On the eve of the autumn equinox, please forgive me. I cannot send you money now as I do not have any. But I am working on it. So much so I am doing nothing else, but going to school, studying and teaching. Trying to read tonight and I cannot, thinking of you. Please—forgive me. I am trying to get the money for you. Enclosed $130 in racing tickets a friend played trying to get the money. Also we played the N. E. Sweepstakes and lost. Also I was going to take a fall down the racetrack stairs to get $75 insurance money, but lost money courage at the end.[8] What can I do? but wait until the money comes through which will be soon. It is such a relief even to get this letter off to you. I was paralyzed before. [...]

Michael McClure
September 25, 1965
[Buffalo]

Dear Michael:

[...] Read this with understanding. It was written on marijuana, and all at one time, which you must see: what that fool, David Schaff, did not see, despite all his good

---

7 Attached: thirteen racing slips ($10 each for the win, all from the eighth race) dated September 1, 1965, from Rockingham Park in Salem, New Hampshire. On the back of one is written "The ignorant multiply which [illegible]."

8 Basil King recalls Wieners pulling this same racetrack scam a decade earlier. He was on a trip north from Black Mountain College with Fielding Dawson. Stuck in Boston with no money, they turned to Wieners for advice:

And he said, meet me at such-and-such and such-and-such. So we did. And then he said, "Well, I know how you can get some money." He said, "You'll have to go out to the dog track and fake an accident. You should be able to get some money." Fielding didn't want to do it and I said okay, I'd do it. John took me out on the T. He said, "Look, I'm gonna stand here and I'm gonna wait an hour and a half. I figure if you're not back in an hour and half I know the cops have got you." So I kind of rubbed myself up, etc. etc., and I went in and sure enough, because I do have a problem with my right side, I said I fell and I hurt myself and I was a house painter, etc. etc. I got a check for forty dollars. I came out, John was there ... to cut a long story short, he got it cashed for us, we had to pay somebody a few bucks to cash the check because I gave a phony name. And Fielding and I the next day got on a bus and came back to New York. We did things like that. We were young. (King, Unpublished Interview with Martha Winston King and Robert Dewhurst, January 2, 2012)

work. Give my love to Dave and Joanne and Jane. I miss them all. Dean sent me the
mirror image of you in the pool. I love you very much.

John

The date of this would be about April or March of this year. Love again. ~~John~~

*It is bad writing you know. And I never want published. Charles is right. Each line
negates the other.*

I could try again, but not interested enough.
And the lust is over, for tonight, anyway

at least[9]

HEROES[10]

For Michael McClure

I have been in love with heroes all my life,
knowing that I never can become one.
Heroine; heroin is a different story.

      It is the mark of weakness, dreams,
not action, that I have been involved with.

      Action, too, but that imposed on you. Not
chosen. Whereas you, Michael McClure never go
out of the house. Only when you are called.

      And the action of my life stems not out
of courage, tho courage is called for, but
necessity.

      Whereas your action is bold, would strike
out against life, kick over the furniture, as
I have seen you do.

---

9 "Anyway" and "at least" are bracketed with a question mark to the right.
10 "Heroes" is unpublished.

I would never do such a thing; for fear of
punishment and am punished far more for not doing it.

Thus, the difference, between you as hero and
myself as heroin, caught in the net of being.

You say, Strike out against the nets of being.
Create new being, new forms.

I cannot do this, but suffer under the old.

I ask of you release. I ask poetry to do this.
I ask Charles Olson for this. I ask love for it. But
no dice. Only in poems comes the release. Not poetry of being. But being evolved through poetry, the
poems.

Am I getting obtuse? I don't mean to be. But
my mind is going. Wandering. Going back to the pits.
Dreaming of becoming. Real. Which drepression you have
never entered in. Loss of manhood, yes.

Which manhood I have never had; which femininity
is mine, you will never know.

It is passive. Takes what comes, what is entered
into. Does not rebel, revolt. Does not lead strikes.
Sings.

Which thing you will never know. Being lost in
another song. Which any Irishman will know.

I am not speaking to you, Michael McClure, but to the
manhood which lies buried in me; in anyone. I am trying
to assert the presence of the beloved, tho this must not
be done. But should lie and wait for the low lights.

But this is making no sense, any longer.

And I am lost on a starry night. Lights glow. The
presence of your Passage awakens as a sleeping lover
and lays its warm hands on my arms, its dark face stares
in the night. It resembles marijuana hidden in the jar;
it resembles dark earth, straining to push dark shoots
seeds to sprout, to bloom. It reminds me of Wallace
Berman's Semina. It returns me to myself, where I hold
these things dear. And to heroes, where you are too,
which is what this is about, not you Michael McClure.

Yet you are a hero, one that I have envied since childhood.

My love, lust, gleams in the night

of a pure order
            no words can express, but these.

It is electricity, a current running red, orange
brown through the room.

            That must be separate,
3000 miles apart.

Diane di Prima
March 14, 1966
[Buffalo]

Dear Diane:

Will you tell me what else you took besides the George Herms-Wally Berman
photographs? Which by the way, are by Dennis Hopper[11]; and the Flaming Creatures[12] clippings from Show, I believe; just so I'll know, for my own records, and not
go looking for something when it's gone.

I noticed the books, first-off, were not put back the same way we had the night

---

11 George Herms and Dennis Hopper were part of the early-1960s art community centered around Wallace
Berman's *Semina*; Hopper later gave Berman a small role in his 1969 film *Easy Rider*.

12 *Flaming Creatures*, queer American experimental film by Jack Smith released in 1963. It became widely
known largely thanks to the guerilla tactics of Jonas Mekas, subject of a 1964 obscenity trial. The film
continued to serve as a flashpoint in various free speech battles of the late 1960s.

before. You know, it's just those little things, the angle of things within the clip books that I noticed.

So tell me, what you took. I'm not mad, much.

[. . .]

> *Love again to you both,*
> *and Minnie, Jeannie and*
> *the Kid.*

Did you have a good time, Diane? I think you did, too. At least, you seemed radiant. Cessation of desire, indeed.

I also delivered the two poems to Allen de Loach.[13] And he was very pleased. Love again, and thank you for leaving those poems with me. They are very, especially the first one, mystical, etc. I know, but it's more than that. Compassion, a very Western feeling, comes through. Also a greenness, and your voice, speaking as a sybil.

* * *

In 1966 Wieners fell in love with wealthy patroness of avant-garde poets **Panna Grady**, setting up house with her and her daughter in a large Annisquam manor she'd rented for the summer, a few miles from Charles Olson in Gloucester. Olson wrote teasingly to Wieners and Grady the "newlyweds," marveling at his protégé's hetero-domestic bliss. The romance was short lived; after Grady became pregnant with Wieners's child, she chose an abortion, at the end of June. She drew closer to Olson, and at the end of October, she and her daughter accompanied him on a voyage to Europe. In his journals and letters to friends, Wieners expressed feelings of betrayal and devastation from the successive losses, but he steadfastly maintained his loyalty to Olson.

* * *

Ed Dorn
Monday April 4th 1966 4:45 PM
[Buffalo]

Dear Ed;

Forgive the pencil but it's lead and all I got. Not in my head, tho, I hope.

I was in Gloucester week before last mid March with Panna Grady—not diane di Prima. What do you think? I would travel with her?

---

13 Allen De Loach (1939–2002), American writer, social worker, editor, and filmmaker. Living on the Lower East Side in the late 1950s and 1960s, he befriended many of the poets there, and went on to publish them in his magazine *Intrepid*, which put out forty-one issues between 1964 and 1980.

This girl is different—an Hungarian Countess born in America—
PANNA *meaning* (little bread) neè Louise *de Cholkanai* and we are sharing a house
together in Gloucester this summer, going ~~there~~ to open it May 15th. In Annisquam,
5 miles from Charles—he steered us to it—a Tudor farm house—built out of stone
from Gloucester quarries. He and Panna are a fine match for each other. She hosted
a party *NOT FOR HIM* later at her apt at the Dakota → *you know*—*the place where
Prince Philip had his party hosted by Douglas Fairbanks*. Central Park West & *One
West 72nd* for Christopher Middleton,[14] George MacBeth,[15] Michael Hamburger,[16]
etc. *and a 125 others preceded by one 2 days earlier for a 175* → *for novelists, Anthony
Burgess,*[17] *John Wain,* [18] *etc.* I was not there—but we have his blessing and joy for the
summer occupancy.

About the book, he wont say much but wants both our names on both books—
and wants nothing to do with it. Says they (Maschler)—a director of Jonathan Cape[19]
won't accept anything newer than 5 years old but this I doubt (is an exaggeration)
& The reason why I persuaded Panna at all to visit Gloucester & to take the house
with me May 15th to Sept 15th was to get the work done—but she'll be gone half
the time—June any way back in the city, etc *with Norman Mailer in Provincetown.*
& her legally separated husband *on Long Island, etc. She's only "28," she says.*

Now Charles waved a contract in the air there but that's as far as it got. I suppose
we'll get word from Jonathan Cape but I think he's holding out for something from
them, & until he gets it, we got "nothing"? Just a supposition on my part. *Don't say
anything to him. It will work out.*

    Love,

    John

Tell Jeremy Prynne[20] I will send him Chinoiserie as soon as I get the remaining
10 from Dave Haselwood. Loved Geography, and it's a great solid book to have.
Reason I didn't write before re this—Geography—was Charles had my copy
since last January when Temple brought it to him and couldn't get it back. Now

---

14 Christopher Middleton (b. 1926), British poet and translator.

15 George MacBeth (1932–1992) was a Scottish poet and novelist.

16 Michael Hamburger (1924–2007), British poet, scholar, and translator.

17 Anthony Burgess (1917–1993), British writer best known for his 1962 dystopian *Clockwork Orange*.

18 John Wain (1925–1994) was a British poet, novelist, and critic.

19 There was confusion regarding the UK rights to *Ace of Pentacles*. Wieners promised them to Jonathan
   Cape Ltd., but Wilson had already sold them to Stuart Montgomery's Fulcrum Press. The result was a
   frustrating mess for all involved. Wieners went forward with Cape, in its new incarnation as Cape Goliard,
   on his 1972 *Selected Poems* and with Fulcrum for a book of early poems, but the latter project fell through.
   Tom Maschler (b. 1933), British writer and publisher, was head of Cape for many years.

20 Jeremy Prynne (b. 1936), British poet, highly influenced by Olson. *The Collected Letters of Charles Olson
   and J. H. Prynne*, edited by Ryan Dobran, was published in 2017 by the University of New Mexico Press.

his own copy arrived so beat up, I understand he hasn't got a "book"—so I finally got mine back at his insistence week before last.[21] With two copies of HUMAN UNIVERSE, one for Panna, one for myself. DO YOU NEED ONE ? for work there?

Panna will be moving to England Sept or so to Nicholas Mosley's[22] mother's house—Lady Curzon's *(?)*—she's a friend of his, too plus Jacob Lind,[23] etc. etc. Gregory Peck, *Miles Davis*, etc, etc. Bill Burroughs, etc, etc. So I might see you in January, there if you will be around. After my degree [cut]

Everything is clear here and more will be revealed during the summer which will be when the books are done, I hope. O. K. Together. both names on both books, as he wants it.

READ THIS LAST !
I'm NOT in love with the men she's
slept with, I'm "in love" with her.

"I am furious when I think of all the men who have slept with me while thinking of other men who have slept with me before."   *(reet!)*
                Peggy Guggenheim[24] nee Marguerite

a little nutty all this sounds, but
    forgive me, I am in love.

Ed Dorn
June 3rd, 1966
[Annisquam, MA]

Forgive the slop. But it's got to go this way, or won't
    be done at all. I'll get used to it somehow and clean up as

---

21 Fulcrum Press, Stuart Montgomery's avant-garde poetry press in the UK, published Ed Dorn's poetry collection *Geography* in 1965.

22 Sir Nicholas Mosley (b. 1923), British novelist whose mother, Lady Cynthia Mosely, was the Marquess Curzon of Kedleston.

23 Jacob Lind (1927–2007), Austrian-British writer who survived the Holocaust and eventually settled in London, where he published many works of fiction and drama, including *Soul of Wood*, his first book, a collection of artfully crafted, nightmarish short stories that established his reputation.

24 Peggy Guggenheim (1898–1979), American art collector and socialite known for her bohemian life and trendsetting style.

time goes on. The most difficult chore I've done.

Any hints you can give me re letter writing, I'll

Dear Edward: *appreciate. What is it? don't re-write them, etc.*

Please forgive me for not writing before, but   *Re-read?*

as you *must* know, living with a "wife" and child I am → *or was*

            just meeting   so unsure

in the country is a little different for me than before.   *of everything-*

her in [illeg] days. Did send off 2 poems today for the next   *now I'll get*

issue of the Evergreen Review,[25] so that   *over that!*

is an accomplishment. And now this   *HOORAY!*

letter to you.

I don't know how long this condition

(i.e. wife and child) will last, but at

least it is a home and a house for the   *and I*

summer, *which in itself is different.* We are in Gloucester, and I

love her very much, always will, but this

am very happy *being* here. That's better isn't

~~*feeling of doom and transience always*~~[26]

it, Than all that personal stuff.

    Love, John

~~persists. I know this letter is wrong,~~

~~and if it were seen by Panna, I would~~

            ~~forgive~~

~~be sorry, but as I say,{~~ I love her.

Now to business. Charles will not help

us at all, on the book, but if there are any per-

tinent questions, I can ask him directly,

~~and~~ that is a help

We can do anything you want on the books,

and I ~~too want~~ *think we'll make that* September deadline.

               Have to.

~~Think That's wonderful~~

Now, what do you ~~think?~~ *want? think?* I know

that already and you will go ahead, doing

all the research and reference I can.

---

25 These appeared in the August 1966 issue, which featured on its cover a colorful photograph of Allen
Ginsberg in an Uncle Sam stars-and-stripes top hat.

26 In the left margin: *old stuff—The residue of the old soul.*

Have got Mike Glover & George
Butterick,[27] his two bibliographers
under my wing, so ~~that's~~ *that's* O. K. Any questions
you want, material you need, just go ahead
~~and ask~~, *ask,* we got it ~~all~~ here, or at least on
hand in Buffalo, if ~~we~~ need ~~it~~ *be.* I dont
think we will basically, ~~as~~ we pretty
well know the ~~basic~~ *only basic* stuff. But will
consult their files in Buffalo, soon &
check out all early poems in
Harpers etc. Atlantic Monthly
for possible use. O. K. Fire away. &
always open ~~to questions,~~ as you
~~must~~ *must* know & love to supply information: As
well as love your letters the most. Keep
sending them always. Anytime you want to write.
And I will answer. That way, the book will clarify itself.
We'll see how this summer works
out & whether or not I can get my
degree by next January, regarding
future trip to Europe, but ~~I~~ think I'll
~~make it.~~ *O.K?*
Be There. ("Dont tell anyone.")
            Love again,
            John
Till Sept 15th
c/o General Delivery
Riverdale Station
Gloucester, Mass.
            on Dennison St.[28]
We have a ~~beautiful~~ *lovely* house in the country, furnishings,
fireplaces, music, love, etc. Food.
        Your friend
        John

---

27 Wieners is referring to Albert Glover, editor of Olson and Corman's correspondence *Letters for Origin: 1950–1956*, 1967's *Bibliography*; as well as the *Curriculum of the Soul*, a collection by different authors inspired by Olson's "A Plan for the Curriculum of the Soul," including Wieners's prose-piece *Woman*.

28 Arrow down to "no postal address."

love again to Helene and the Kids –
I thank you *again* for all the prayers and love you have ~~said~~ *sent*

> *no postal address—*
> > *Charles got us the property, as*
> > *I told you before.*

You'll see Panna soon enough, I'm sure, before me, but
dont be disappointed. It's me walking in disguise.
But not until October. Watch out, Helene. This one
is a Knockout.

Charles Olson
7.25.66 Monday
[Annisquam, MA]

Forgive this card—I've tried three times—This is the best attempt I made

Dear Charles:
Can you come to dinner
This Saturday evening at
"~~whenever you get over~~ your
best time ? I will *be over to* see
you before then,~~ as I am~~
~~going back to Buffalo The~~
~~next day to attend to business.~~
We've invited Guy, Gerrit, Gladdis & Gelly Kelly belly
Love, John *& Panna* ~~Gordon~~ Getty—

Charles Olson

8–2–66

Dear Charles:
Woke up laughing

at the Adelphi Hotel
in Saratoga wondering
"What am I doing here?
  Love
  John
Moonlight in Vermont.

Panna Grady
[August 8, 1966] [29]
9PM

     Monday night—August 8th
     alone

Dear*est* Panna:

I am sorry you haven't called *me* before this. I am *have been* here waiting *since 12 noon* for you. I will *be be able to* stay ~~here~~ till Wednesday.

3PM and then move ~~over~~ *across* to Cambridge with ~~my friends the [illeg] with whom with whom I am driving Tuesday evening~~. ~~Earl of~~ Gowrie[30] I have had a bad cold ever since I left Gloucester and am ~~now~~ staying in bed.

  Wish you were here.

Perhaps you have not received my telegram yet.

  Friday is my doctor's appt. at 2PM then so afterwards I will go to Gerrit's and send him over after you. I miss you ~~very much~~ *so* and am *very* unhappy not being with you, as I love you more than ever, so

  Your friend,

  (John) Pip

---

29 On stationery from the "Hotel Madison / at North Station / Boston."

30 Grey Ruthven, 2nd Earl of Gowrie (b. 1939), Irish scholar, art dealer, poet, and Tory politician who taught in the late 1960s at State University of New York at Buffalo and Harvard University, where he worked as an assistant to Robert Lowell.

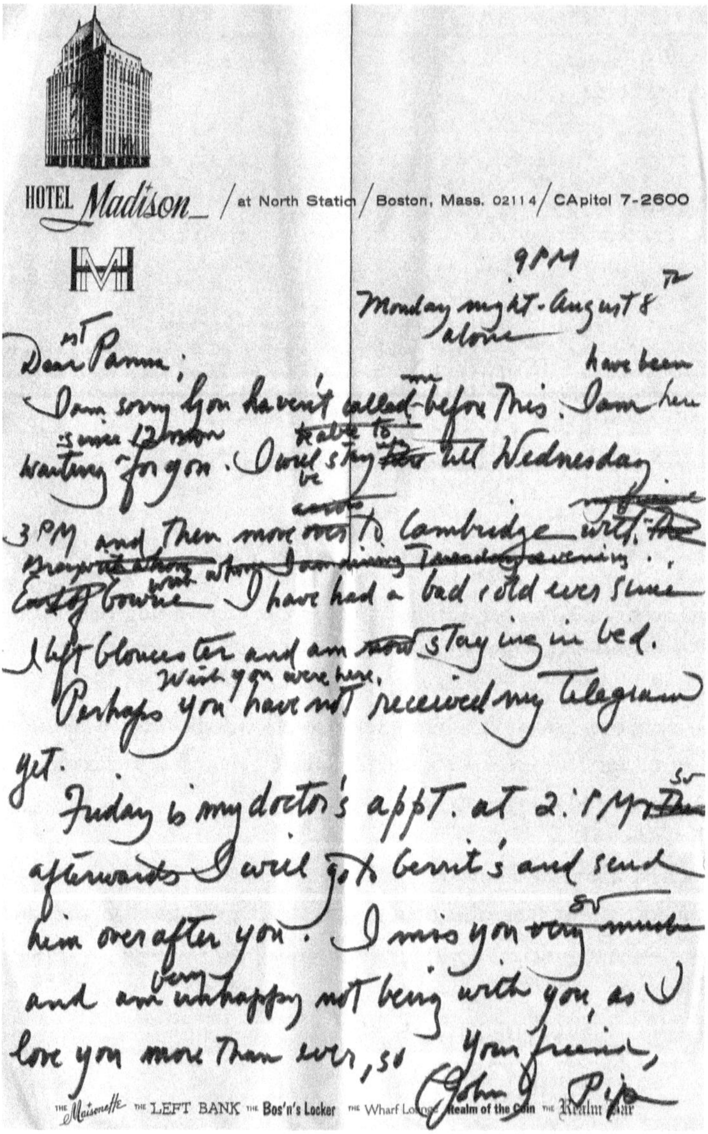

FIGURE 6 John Wieners's letter to Panna Grady, August 8, 1966.
Panna Grady Collection (1950–2015), the Poetry Collection of the
University Libraries, University at Buffalo, the State University of
New York.

Charles Olson
[Aug. 16, 1966]
Tuesday

Dear Charles:　　　　　The 16th—Noon

Do you think you could come to dinner tonight at six? Ted Berrigan[31] & wife are in Town over-night. Gerrit will be There. Panna and myself. George Kimball[32] and the potman Pat Newman. We are having swordfish. "Someone can come over and pick you up if you dont showat six." Panna says. I wont wait on you I promise.

　　Love, John

Heard from Dorn yesterday. Everything moving ahead faster than we could hope for. Just eight for dinner. I have some material for you.

Diane di Prima
Sept. 9, 1966
[Buffalo]

Congratulations on your reading in Washington Square . . .

Dear Diane:　　　　　I saw the clipping in The Times.

　Do you think it's possible we could include this poem of Charles Doria's[33] in The Bear in place of the one we already have. (Been published before.)

　Leaving Sunday for Buffalo unfortunately. Panna staying on here a while. Then up to Buffalo for a weekend, I hope before reading in New York Oct. 24—

　Harvey, Creeley, Allen, Peter, Lafcadio,[34] etc all here for a *last* weekend

　plus the editor of The Atlantic Monthly. She had article

5 days on and off actually　　　　　on LSD this

Creeley after they all left　　　　　issue plus

　　　　　Allen's article

31　Ted Berrigan (1934–1983) served in the Korean War, studied at the University of Oklahoma in Tulsa, and was active in Chicago before coming to New York to be at the heart of what has come to be called the second generation of the New York school. His *Collected Poems*, edited by sons Anselm and Edmund and his second wife Alice Notley, came out in 2007.

32　George Kimball (1943–2011), one of the foremost boxing writers of his era, won many awards for his sports coverage. An editor at the *Boston Phoenix* and later a columnist at the *Boston Herald*, Kimball had his feet in many worlds; his 1970 campaign for sheriff of Douglas County (Lawrence), Kansas, is legendary.

33　Charles Doria, American poet and translator who coedited *Audit* magazine with Michael Anania in Buffalo.

34　Lafcadio Orlovsky, troubled brother of Peter Orlovsky, artist and lover of Allen Ginsberg.

on Pot next one.[35]

Love to
you and [illeg] Alan. Yours, John
We plan to go to Berlin for a reunion in December

PS—

Couldn't get any definite word out of Harvey about the book. He's changed printers and actually has none now at all. *Looking for one in New York or asking Polly's*
father. Charles and I both spoke favorably most about the book. He showed me
4 pages of proofs *of mine own* after 10 months work. He really is dumb. But what
can ~~you~~ *one* do?

Charles and I speak
of you both most all of the time
and we both are indebted to you.
I still feel waves as Charles would
    send bread or sugarcubes.
say and would like to take it again.
Did you see Timothy's article in Playboy[36] [illeg]
    Thank you for the Clive Matson book (hardback)
        what words cannot say I send you again.

---

35 The September 1966 *Atlantic Monthly* included an article by John N. Bleibtreu called "LSD and the Third
    Eye," and November featured an essay by Ginsberg called "The Great Marijuana Hoax: First Manifesto
    to End the Bringdown," an appeal for decriminalization based on a candid account of his own positive
    experiences.

36 Timothy Leary (1920–1996), American physician, psychedelics scholar, and activist. His Castalia Foun-
    dation at Millbrook, New York, ushered hundreds of people through their first psychedelic experiences,
    in a carefully planned "set and setting" that was conducive to safe psychedelic exploration. He married
    his third wife, fellow psychedelic activist Rosemary Woodruff (1936–2002), in 1967. Rosemary would go
    on to work with the Weather Underground to bust Leary out of prison in 1970, and she remained on the
    run for twenty-three years before surrendering to California authorities. Olson's own LSD experiences
    with Leary are documented in the Timothy Leary Papers at the New York Public Library, recently made
    public.

Charles Olson
[Sept. 20, 1966]
[Buffalo]
Tuesday AM.

Dear Charles: 3 o'clock
    Please forgive me for my behavior
this past weekend. I have been under
sedation since and feel just
terrible. But it can't be helped.
We have been used this past
summer and given a great deal—
why I don't know.
    All I have is *are souvenirs*.
    But I left a silver stamp
case under the prongs of your
mail box Saturday evening –
from Tiffany's. *I hope you found it*. Please keep
it for me.
    I love you more than
any other person in the world
simply because you have
given me more and I am,
as we all are, ~~so~~ selfish.
I try to explain
things—but cannot.
I look for answers. I look
for drugs—to ease the
pain but cannot find any.
The only answer is work and
I do not have the *stamina or* intelligence
for that.
    It seems all the
beneficence ~~of~~ that her
presence lends has been
taken away in the flash
of time. But we will not
forget. Will we?
        John
        Your friend (love

I want to thank you for
the guardian angel ship
you have been.
This letter seems so in-
adequate to how much you
have given—but it is not
what we can give that counts –
it is what we cannot give
That is the effort.
    It all sounds so human
and petty but something
weighs on me—I dont
know what—seconal?

Please forgive the stationery—

                                                        Charles Olson
                                                    October 7th [1966][37]

Dear Charles:
    Just wanted to drop a short note from here. And say hello. And wish you are well.
Called Panna tonight. No answer. In Remsenberg c/o Grady

She sent me a telegram this morning.
                    Very long and confused. Trying to purge me of her. Went to
            Castaglia last weekend and met Leary and got into an auto accident
            with his lovely wife—Rosemary. The doll. How women are [illeg] I
            found. The only ones I care for. One can be a man around them. ~~Alan~~
Ate at a Hungarian restaurant tonight here called Carmen's. And wonder if all
Continental Europe is as attractive. I know that is my home. We Americans are so
savage, better that I only can be hurt by them.
        God bless you
        John
Who is Elinore Georges. Pilot? She sent flowers. To my room.

---

37 On blue Ritz Carlton Montreal stationery.

Staying here till Sunday.
Call and reverse charges
if you get this in time
Rm 904

Allen Ginsberg
October 18th, 1966
[Buffalo]

Dear Allen:

Much thanks for sending the amendments, etc. I return what you asked me. The insert-article (center fold) was done last night. 4 pages I worked on it at the Spectrum from 2–11 when we finally finished it. I hope they don't fuck it up now, but I am afraid to go back. Anyway, we got the full Anthology printed, plus a poem of Philip's from Narcotica called 'Memoria.' 2 photos by Wally Berman, and 2 poems by Bob. Plus *full* excerpts I made from the LaGuardia Report. The Goddard speech was no good as you see from the enclosed, and we got the entire *NSA* resolution re marijuana printed. I left out all mentions of LSD, *to concentrate the article. OK?* And used the NY Times text re Goddard to highlight the article. I think they'll do a good job as they are most courageous in presenting unconventional news articles.[38]

OK. Allen I'll send you the article special delivery when it comes out. Or bring it with me. My mother and father are coming to reading, so I'll hope you'll meet them at last. The reason I can't go back is they feel it's their province now, as to layout, etc. Poor Panna dropped me like a hot Irish potato.

> Love,
> *John*
> John
> (Wieners)
> *The Three guys are out of jail. The rich*
> *one had his charges dropped!!*

---

38 *The Spectrum* is the University of Buffalo's student newspaper. The October 21, 1966, issue featured the four-page section that Wieners discusses here, with MARIJUANA in large type at the top, with the byline "Compiled and edited by the Spectrum with the assistance of John Wieners" and a photograph of Ginsberg. The "anthology" to which Wieners refers is a long documentary history that Ginsberg had compiled concerning the prohibition of marijuana. The "NSA report" refers to Ginsberg's resolution against marijuana prohibition, which he'd presented at the National Students Association's 1966 conference in Urbana, Illinois. As Wieners mentions in this letter, the section includes two poems by Robert Creeley and one by Philip Lamantia.

[Illeg] says it will be thrown out
of court on illegal search and seizure.
He is now one of 4 advisers to the
President here.

* on Crime
Eroticism
Intellectual Functioning,
etc. All I could get in
[illeg] Sociological Aspects & Mayor's Forward.

Panna Grady
12.24.66

Dearest Panna;

Can you ever forgive me, for taking so much for granted? My days here are long and lovely, but I am able to *write*, think, and see things in perspective and with equilibrium.

Tomorrow dinner with the Creeleys, which almost is as good as London.

I hope you are happy there, and fulfilled.

Love,
John

Thank you for your lovely card. Do keep me posted. I shall write to Charles for his birthday, Dec. 27th & thereafter to you both, I hope.

Do try and see me as a *rather* rash, & impulsive boy, who could not hand over his good fortune *quite* so easily to the wind and time.

Losing you meant everything to me, but I see now again the priceless gain you brought.

* * *

In the late 1960s, Wieners continued his work in Buffalo while becoming more politically active with the antiwar movement. At the same time, he suffered increased paranoia and a series of delusions regarding his old friend Robert Creeley and his wife Bobbie; the letters he sent to Creeley from this period are harrowing. Within a couple of years the delusions abated, and by 1972 Creeley was inviting Wieners to speak to his Harvard classes. It is a testament to all involved—and the covenantal kinds of friendships this group of poets formed—that Creeley and Wieners would remain intimate friends till the latter's death. This section of letters begins with another difficult relationship from this time, as Wieners's work with Robert Wilson and the Phoenix Bookshop became increasingly confused and frustrating for all involved, with questions of royalties, foreign rights, and translations tangling with Wieners's paranoia to complicate an otherwise mutually beneficial friendship.

* * *

Robert Wilson
March 26, 1967 Easter Sunday
[Buffalo]

Dear Bob:

I've made a formal complaint against you to Werner Neumeister, telling him of your duplicity in not acknowledging copyright of the photograph, given you by myself,

Also, I'd like to say the last amount given me for royalties was far below the amount expected. You've gyped me continually in the past.[39]

I have asked Werner Neumeister to investigate you; bring my royalties up to date and also extend the courtesy of a reply, regards the pittance paid me, the past three and one-half years.
    I intend to go head with Jonathan Cape and Fulcrum, too.
        Without regards to you,
        John Wieners

You are listed as Phoenix Books, Inc.

Does this mean you withhold funds from me, for the benefit of other members; or are you listed as a non-profit organization?

If so, then it is required that you show proof of where the profit you have made from me, has gone.

If no reply to this, then I will be requested to ask my brother, an attorney-at-law

---

39 Wilson wrote back incredulously: "I have always given you advances every time you asked for them, in excess of sales," he explained, and indeed "you have continually drawn heavy advances against royalties, and in fact are still in debt to me (that is, the Phoenix Book Shop) for books which you charged against royalties." As to the photograph by Werner Neumeister, Wilson reminded Wieners that the latter did not even own the photograph, but "I shall be glad to re-imburse you for it out of my own pocket (Neumeister charges $2.00 apiece for them)" (Unpublished letter from Robert Wilson, March 28, 1957, R. A. Wilson MSS., Lilly Library).

with Burke, Monaghan, and McGrath, in Boston, to bring suit against you, as to a statement of books sold, how many, to whom, and where. Also to further investigate the nature of the limited editions so freely sold, without one penny to me.

Allen Ginsberg
May 20, 1967
[Buffalo]

Dear Allen:

Received a call last evening from Dr. Karl T. Dussik,[40] Ass't Commisioner of Mental Health in Massachusetts, that he is unable to obtain B-3 to prescribe for me.

Could you supply me with the doctor's name at Princeton who invented the formula so that Dr. Dussik may use it in my case, as I am suffering from inability to concentrate here.

I have a contract needing my signature, with July 1st deadline, from Jonathan Cape, and the absolute horror of grey May in town, has prevented organization.

I am taking NIACIN plus VC but still have so much to do and require the basic substances of order, cohesion and presence.

Have decided to leave school and go home to Milton without a degree. So again will be a patient of Dr. Dussik. He ~~seems to have been in~~ *told me he remembers* Vienna in the twenties.

I am unable to continue here because of nuclear vibrations inflicted irrationally upon the students—injustices imposed by a graduate study that drains vision rather than nurtures it.

A few birds sing now but they seldom last.

> *Your friend,*
> *John Wieners*

#5
3262 Main Street   Am also attempting to have
Buffalo, New York   my mouth repaired but
   14214   the ~~doctor,~~ Dr. Bernard Gar-
                    liner, Delaware Avenue

---

40 Karl Dussik (1908–1968), Austrian physician. In the late 1950s and 1960s, Dussik directed Metropolitan State Hospital in Waltham, Massachusetts, where Wieners was held March–August 1961. While there he directed a program administering the controversial insulin shock treatment of schizophrenia, which induced daily insulin comas in patients over periods of several weeks. He remained a strong advocate of the controversial therapy long after it fell out of vogue.

Medical Center, is charging
me $5200 for what seems
to be minor extortion.

[…]

Robert Creeley
July 27, 1967
[Buffalo]

Dearest Friend:
Went to library two evenings ago. There is a magazine 'The Nomad' published in
the 1920's but as for NOMAD 5/6 (1960)[41]—they are still searching.
  Will ~~you~~ check with Karl when this annoying month closes.
  I am very lonely and dream of you and the family ~~as one~~ in that dilapidated 'lodge'
~~we more~~ less so now without Charles.
  Thank you for leaving your letter.
  ~~So let~~
  Do understand this laggard response due to reluctance to think of anything but
a rather obsessive concern with where I should go?
  Here, perhaps there—
    Yours,
    John

Dave Haselwood
WEDNESDAY, AUGUST 16 [1967]
[Buffalo]

I now come to find writing a poem is the most sacred act of my existence.
I was wrong in 1959's journal to say it was no holier act than passing waste.
It is the accumulation of all days, the first spear into the exposed side of
chaos. For despite the time tables that is what we live in. And to set order
on that face, the face of that is a dream itself. For what is a dream and whose
face appears in it but the Sacred Master who dictates all things.

---

41 The British magazine *Nomad* published Creeley's essay "A Note," in 1960. "I do not think a poet is necessarily a nice person," Creeley writes. "I think the poem's morality is contained as a term of its structure,
and is there to be determined and nowhere else" (Creeley, *Collected Essays*, 478).

Anne Waldman
September 25, 1967
[Buffalo]

Dear Anne:

Received yours of last week and will be delighted to read at St. Mark's In-the-Bowery the evening of January 3rd next year, 1968. The fee of 50 dollars is just right.

Thank you for sending Angel Hair.[42]

Would it be possible to stay at your apartment that evening after the reading? I have such trouble in New York if I do not make arrangements beforehand.

Lewis and Phoebe returned from honeymoon. Dined with them last Wednesday evening and Harvey Brown passed through the Monday before to say he had seen you. Am glad you went abroad this summer.

Will be holding on until January.

Your friend,
John Wieners

W. S. Merwin
October 28, 1967
[Buffalo]

Dearest Bill:

Finally found someone to type poems for Jonathan Cape. Dont know when book will be out but at least proofs are here.

Weather beneficient but of course cant *tell this* year as last was so mild it seemed a Concord holiday.

Will you have a new book out this year or next also?

We read, Charles Olson and I, not simultaneously but as part of a convocation "Poetry on Campus" at Cortlandt State University or rather The State University of New York at Cortlandt. He addressed a dinner on Friday evening and the students, ourselves included, read Sunday after luncheon. It was so fabulous to meet after a year when ~~I thought—all love~~ I had told him my years as a student were over, 12 in all, last summer 1966.

Now our friendship may start. It was never that before as I was in such awe, I

---

42 *Angel Hair* magazine and press were founded by Waldman and Lewis Warsh (b. 1944), American poet she had met at the Berkeley Poetry Conference in 1965. *Angel Hair* operated from 1966 to 1978, publishing Wieners's *Asylum Poems* in 1969. Granary Books published *Angel Hair Sleeps with a Boy in My Head: The Angel Hair Anthology* in 2001.

could never contribute anything but audience. Last weekend held delight & maturity, sophistication.[43]

Expect to honor his birth this December as always.

Yours with thanks

John Wieners

for the kindness April 11th. Regret delay in reply but harassment from new arrivals in town hinder every thought. As it is now I barely am able to think.

The Chairman of the English Department

September 12 in the year of our Lord nineteen hundred and sixty-eight[44]

State University of New Mexico at Albuquerque, New Mexico

[Buffalo]

Dear Sir:

This is to inform you I have written to both the District Attorney and the Office of the United States Attorney in the Department of Justice, District of New Mexico regarding Robert W. Creeley, whom you employ as an associate professor, in the Department of English, to charge him with sodomy, abduction, and other illegal use of surgical instruments to perform operations upon my person, whereby colons of his step-daughter and wife Bobbie Louise Hall, were transplanted into my person; and pelvic bones, medulla oblongata and portions of the sphincter, the cerebral cortex, the pituitary glands were removed and placed in his body from mine.

I forbid this man to go on teaching there as I am unable and unfit for work, having female organs, while he is employed in and by your department with my faculties and organs, ~~while I am~~ *leaving me* destitute, ~~and~~ *while* he is earning a substantial income with my talent; which he has removed before ever since I was a child—I forbid this condition to continue.

The operations were performed the months of March and October in the year

---

43   In October 1967, Olson wrote to Harvey Brown: "Saw John and he was just as usual too much. Read marvelously—& was more than ever my Admired One! . . . He *is* sharp-tongued and swollen with hurt-pain and feeling, but anyone who can't see he is quicker and more profound than ever are themselves fools!" (Olson, *Selected Letters*, 390)

44   Creeley mailed this letter to a friend, with the following note of explanation:

Apropos John Wieners' letter—unhappily his circumstances are very difficult, i.e., he had a period of hospitalization in the late fifties, early sixties—and during one time at Buffalo, he was manifesting pretty literal paranoid behavior. He is a brilliant poet, and, paradoxically, an old friend—and so it's a patently awkward situation (e.g. he had written a similar letter to Norman Holland last spring in Buffalo—and seems obsessively involved with Bobbie and myself as the "enemy."

of our Lord, nineteen hundred and sixty-seven, in the home of Albert M. Cook, 256 Woodbridge Avenue, in the City of Buffalo, in the state of New York, and on a farm rented by your employee in the Boston hills, at 9596 Knoll Road in the state of New York.

Yours sincerely,
John Wieners

3262 Main Street
Buffalo, New York 14214

May it also be added drugs were used both times and that sexually I am entirely beholden to a man who is an inferior, having married an Apache, who has diabetes and is dim-witted, while he himself has only one eye and a criminal history of murder, rape, already proven in the state of Massachusetts where he is native, operating there also, a laboratory, illegally, where he corrupted three men before my eyes, in the year of our Lord nineteen hundred and forty, by means of strychnine, masturbating, ingestion of waste matter to minors, against their will, having used homemade formulas initially to remove their cerebral cortexes, (mine is still missing and within his body, as well as that of a former beloved companion of mine, Russell D. Durkee, native of Massachusetts and New Hampshire, now resident I believe in the State of California, who could also testify against your employee.

Homosexuality is the end result of his teaching and I implore you to terminate his position at the State University of New Mexico, as he is an unfit person, a thief and a literal man who takes other person's lives as his own, rather than preserving them through education, he has destroyed the very nerve-fibers and beings of over twenty human beings.

I have written to the states of Virginia, Pennsylvania, New York and Massachusetts, besides the nation's capital, Washington, the district of Columbia, regarding his murderous accomplishment, all at the expense of, loss of other men's lives.

Perhaps to make myself clearer, he has murdered a child by bashing its head against the rocks in a field off Blue Hills Parkway in the town of Milton, in the state of Massachusetts, where I was raised, and tore open my own brains to digest them, as had his wife that very evening, hung me in trees, and injected substances to remove my memory thereof, performed operations beneath my testicles and at the back of my skull, the scars still in evidence, and forced other victims through habits of brain control to confuse, distract and punish agents of the law; whereby the entire cerebral cortex is gone and now placed in his right leg-or thigh. I cannot allow this man to go on walking around with my entire cerebral cortex in his body, while his wife, Bobbie Louise Hall, has my frontal lobes in her retarded person, I ask you to respond to this and cease employ-ment of these two persons at once.

Robert Creeley
　　　the 10th October the year of our Lord nineteen hundred and sixty-eight
　　　　　　　　　　　　　　　　　　　　　　　　　　　　　　　[Buffalo]
Robert:

In March and October of the year of our Lord nineteen hundred and sixty-seven, you performed atrocities on my person, in properties rented while in employ of the State University of New York; illegally employed as from previous memory, my family has had you declared a legal sterile.

You now have two children from my reproductive organs, and I have informed the Attorney General John Quinn of the State of New Mexico that you have committed crimes against my family, property and future, since I was an infant, at 22 Churchill Street in the town of Milton, the state of Massachusetts and at 15 Blue Hill Avenue, in the same town and state, as well as at 185 Eliot Street in that town and state, as well as in the town of Medway, near your so-called birthplace.

I have notified the Chairmen of the English Departments at the State Universities of New Mexico and New York of these atrocities, branding you a rapist, abductor of children, and murderer, as you and B. Louise Hall, murdered a child before my eyes in the month of September, the year of our Lord nineteen hundred and forty-two.

I have instructed my attorney, Donald Paul Wieners, to sue you for damages, and to sue Albert M. Cook, of 256 Woodbridge Avenue in the City of Buffalo, the state of New York and to have you both imprisoned, as you in the eyes of the courts of the States of New York, Massachusetts, New Mexico, Pennsylvania, and Virginia are guilty of beheading me, lynching me, castrating me, removing vital bones and organs for your own sexual gratification.

You have performed the gross acts of enforced fellatio, sodomy, and masturbation upon my person, removed or not, and I ask or beg you to refrain from doing so in the future. I have called your "wife" and requested her to do the same.

I have also written the Attorney General in the nation's capital, Washington, the District of Columbia, of whose designer I am a straight descendant, to inform him that you planned the assassination of our late President John Fitzgerald Kennedy, Junior, in my presence, and are guilty of it, giving him the names of your "wife" and stepdaughter, as accomplices.

There are bones, you, in the guise of verse, which you have adopted only for attack against my second cousin, Mal Wieners, keep between your "wife's" legs, and which you stimulate for copulation. I taste your legally sterilized sperm, a horrible taste it is, and I am party to the diseased organs of her womb, vagina, and vulva, all horrors to one unused as you, to strychnine, cocaine, or cocoa, and excrement.

Your behavior has been psychopathotic towards me since as a child you drugged, abducted, electrocuted, and forced ceremonial hysteria on my person.

How unfair to one, unused as you, [illeg] barbaric practices.

I force you now to surrender these stolen properties, or suffer the consequences of public embarrassment before the United States Courts of law for their possession.

I am a true grandson of Fedor Dostoevsky, and seek the wrath of the peoples of the Union of Soviet Socialist Republic to justify this intrusion upon your contaminated condition of blood-letting, anger, drunkenness, recklessness, dyslexia, schizophrenia and drug-addiction.

I ask you carefully to return in your own words what happened or occurred those only two evenings I accepted your vulgar invitations to spend evenings in your home. What could be your reason for such horror, as to take a person who only respected you and debase them before the eyes of townspeople, the savage and drug-addicted eyes of the strumpet, from a madhouse, Bobbie Louise Hall, and her step-daughter.

I have given full investigation to these horrors and find you guilty, despicable and a person I will publically in literature and teaching as a criminal, under your own names, and whose writings I will destroy, as emitting from stolen properties off my family tree, of which you are a bastard, and will make known in every level of this country and abroad of your treachery, treason and assassination.

You have used lies, cowardice, and madness to influence my person, my creative imagination, and my career as a man of letters in the United States.

You have done this to countless other citizen, as for your imbecile housewife, serving meals in a slovenly fashion, dressing in ignorance, and following me from city to city, as beasts after a virgin; a condition you have besmirched, with your foul penis, your bloated thighs and your corrupt intelligence.

If I do not receive back the glands, the cerebral cortex, the medulla oblongata, the cerebellum, I will, as I have already done, continue to write the district attorney in [illeg] County, to have them removed from your jaundiced household, as both you and the half-breed "Hall," have hepatitis, tuberculosis, and mental retardation.

Will you honor this with a reply.

Yours, The Hereditary Grand Duke Prince Jean of Luxembourg and "His" Royal Highness, crown prince Felix, of the Imperial and Royal House of Austria and Hungary.

Otherwise both your estate and those estates you inherit shall be prosecuted for these atrocities, crimes, and offenses, and I shall order your estate and those you inherit withheld from public sight, as both your estates and those you inherit merit from centuries of such torture.

Anne Waldman
November the nineteenth 1968
[Buffalo]

Dear Anne:

Enclosed find a poem in place of "First poem after Silence." I do not ~~like~~ *need* the reference to "cock-kissed in Shea's Buffalo." [45] or rather find it harmful to my activities in town. My uncle Rudolph Wieners supposedly deceased is a drug addict and plagues me with his homosexual affairs, using illegal law officers to persecute my normal efforts to eat and reside properly here opposite school, where I have four poems published in the current New Student Review. Enclosed find contract signed and new verse you may print in World if you care too.

January 15th at 8:30 PM sounds a god-send, and the fee fine. I am broke, and going on welfare, so the travelling expenses would include train fare one-way, and I could use the fee for fare return. Am staying in town for the holidays. Have a new wardrobe, new scrap books, a listing in Dictionary of International Biography and twelve clean teeth.

Will bring on a new pamphlet for you and Lewis.

Did you see the new show at The Gotham? I received an invitation, returned it and it was returned to me.

Charles Olson received a warning letter from myself re his drug-addiction but he insists on poisoning my throat and esophagus with his offal. Nonetheless Robert Bly ~~was~~ *will be* here to read on the 20th or 21st, and that should purify these parts.

David Ray, also and George Garrett[46] aided in alleviating ~~the~~ autumn.

I wish they would ask Philip Whalen and Joanne Kyger.

Yours in gratitude,
Jean

---

45 Replacement poem is not with this letter. "First Poem after Silence since Thanksgiving" was published in Waldman and Warsh's magazine *The World* in 1968 and as a Brownstone Press broadside in 1970. As editor Robert Dewhurst explains in his note on the poem, Wieners is referring to a historic Buffalo theater when he describes "my cock kissed / in the men's room // of the Shea's Buffalo / downtown." (*Ungrateful City: The Collected Poems of John Wieners*, 1232).

46 Robert Bly (b. 1926), David Ray (b. 1932), and George Garrett (1929–2008), American poets.

Anne Waldman
[December 28, 1968]
[Buffalo]

H.R.H.

Three Thousand Two Hundred and Sixty Two Main Street
Buffalo New York Fourteen Thousand Two Hundred [illeg]

The Twenty-eighth of December nineteen hundred and sixty eight *pl*
Dear Anne:

I ~~have to~~ *plan to* be in town the ~~Twelfth~~ *Thirteenth* of January (12th) for signing of
an important broadside with George Minkoff,[47] thus am calling the train depot this
afternoon for round-trip fare. The receipt of same I shall enclose with this.

    Am glad you can use "Fugitive. I have a terrible time here in my room with the
manager of a neighboring clothing store, who drains me of, or shrinks my creative
membranes to such an extent I hardly work, and am ill a large portion of the season.
How unfortunate. My affairs are disgraceful, and I am obtaining a medical report
while in the city, to initiate swearing out warrants, and ultimately lawsuits through
the Department of Social Welfare for compansation.

    Nonetheless shall call you on the ~~the~~ *after* noon of the Thirteenth, and love. I can
hardly wait to see you, New York, and the wonderful friendships there.

The Penn Central train from Buffalo to New York is 20.70 coach one way, $41.40
round trip, leaving 10:30 AM arriving GC 6:10PM. I shall go on Monday the 13th—
Possibly the church could put me up for the evening.

Yours in devotion
    Jean

~~Thirty~~
Three thousand two hundred and Sixty-two Main Street. Buffalo, New York

---

47 George Robert Minkoff (b. 1943), American antiquarian book dealer, publisher, and writer. In 1968
   Minkoff printed Wieners's poem "*L'Abysse*" as a broadside.

WHAT I IMAGINE TO BE MY LOVE WHISPERS IN THE CORNER[48]

Those who stay at home
often worship far away places
and unattainable ambitions,

such as fame and idealized love.
Those who travel find their dreams come
true, meeting fantastically interesting persons

through talent and achievement, even
of a minor sort. I have moved all

my adult life, finding success sweet
when I came home in overt defeat
forgot it and settled down to a routine,

(only to wake up at those out of the way places,
with my hands full of familiar feelings,
a new sense of glamour pervaded the scene.

Oh yes, this is that bus station known at twenty years old,
and now past thirty-five, in good health, I sit
at the same tables, bearing the moon and its dreams from the fifties

rushing down Charles Street, on fire with desire for
beautiful women, bubbling alcohol, late hours, smart cafès,
fast limousines more demanding assignments on my energy.
                    John Wieners

                                        Alan Marlowe
                                        March 13, 1968
                                        [Buffalo]
Dearest Alan:
    Dear boy, how I would love worship in New York for a year, the theatre, the shows,
dancing with you and Diane, holding forth at the Cedar with Joel or Lion's Den

---

48 "What I Imagine To Be My Love Whispers In The Corner" appears in *Cultural Affairs in Boston* exactly
the same as in this letter, but with the postscript: "John Wieners 1970 St. James Street Boston, 2 PM /
Waiting for Gerard and Rene" 91).

with Joel and Fee, seeing the new work at galleries, meeting old friends, forgetting Bob Creeley and Bobbie / we read together Thursday evening in the Millard Fillmore with Allen Ginsberg, Robert Duncan and Robin Blaser. How I've with party afterwards at Lewis MacAdams,' who interviewed Bob recently for The Paris Review.

Lewis and Duncan MacNaughton are issuing a record[49] with Kenward Elmslie,[50] Frank, and myself, Lew Welch, Phil Whalen, besides others I cant remember—so events are productive in Buffalo.

Taylor Mead,[51] Michael McClure, John Chamberlain,[52] Jean-Luc Goddard[53] arriving this week.

Your letter sounds productive to me. I would like to have a grant from the Frank O'Hara production.

Please see what you can do.

Totally without funds this semester and unregistered—fellowship having expired.

Yours in love,

John—

* * *

The 1960s culminated with Wieners's third extended hospitalization, from June through September 1969 at Central Islip State Hospital, after he was arrested in New York. He'd later write to a friend that it was for forgery, in a health club: "I thought I was Loretta Young."[54] While held there he worked on *Asylum Poems* with Anne Waldman for Angel Hair Books. In letters to old friends like Olson he began

---

49 Lewis MacAdams and Duncan McNaughton were among the rotating group of editors behind *Mother, a Journal of New Literature*, a New York–focused poetry and art magazine edited from a variety of locations in New York and the Midwest from 1964 through 1969. The final two of its ten issues were released as sound recordings, one featuring a lengthy reading by Wieners.

50 Kenward Elmslie (b. 1929), American poet, performer, publisher, and lyricist. The grandson of Joseph Pulitzer, Elmslie was central to the New York school, working alongside and publishing writers like Frank O'Hara, Ron Padgett, John Ashbery, and his longtime partner Joe Brainard. Ashbery described his style as "freaked-out Levi-Strauss, a mad scientist who has swallowed the wrong potion in his lab and is desperately trying to get his calculations on paper before everything closes in" (Silverblatt, "Kenward Elmslie").

51 Taylor Mead (1924–2013), American actor and writer, star of the Andy Warhol film *Taylor Mead's Ass*, whose first book of poetry, *Taylor Mead on Amphetamines and in Europe*, was published in 1968.

52 John Chamberlain (1927–2011), American sculptor who studied and taught at Black Mountain College in its final years.

53 Jean-Luc Godard (b. 1930), French filmmaker and critic.

54 Unpublished letter to Irving Rosenthal, February 24, 1970, Irving Rosenthal Papers, Stanford University.

once again to piece together his increasingly fragmented mind. "For the past 20–18 months I have been under the delusion of being about 50 persons," he writes to Olson on July 10. Of course with characteristic wit, he adds, "I have given them all up and am now ready for the next 50."

It was a difficult time. In a journal written partly during this incarceration, published in 2010 as *A New Book From Rome*, Wieners described his environment:

Around men are sleeping, playing craps and pacing back and forth. They are jabbering in Spanish and drinking beer. But this is not a sidewalk in Spanish Harlem, or the Lower East Side, this is a State Hospital for mental illness where I have been for two months and a week. Confined against my will. But you know this.[55]

* * *

Harvey Brown
Saturday June 7 1969
[Central Islip, NY]

H. Huntington Brown III, Stewart Road
West Newbury, Massachusetts

Dearest Harvey,

I have got into the strangest situation, and before it worsens, by any act of reality, I beg to inform you.

I am now a patient at the Central Islip State Hospital for an undetermined length of time, after the Supreme Court reserved 6.3.69 decision until further notice as whether I Edward Wien (John Joseph Wieners to you) is in the state of idiocy, imbecility, or insanity. I plead innocent to these charges, but am still being held, ~~on~~ *pending* their decision.

The reason is I used an expired identity card the 2nd day of May this year to book a return air flight from Buffalo to New York & then checked into the Continental Bath Club W. 72nd where I was informed the card expired.

$500 dollars bail trial May 15th

Charges, forgery reduced to misdemeanor

Remaindered to Bellevue Psychiatric Hospital on advice of a letter from Commonwealth of Massachusetts Commissioner on Mental Health May 17th thence to Central Islip State Hospital.

---

55 Wieners, *A New Book from Rome*, 52.

Harvey, please help me. My family is proving to be difficult. I am without friends. Nearly 30 dollars is still over at Bellevue *P.H.*, and though I have through the Dept. of Social Science contacted Stanley Faulkner, attorney-at-law, he is on vacation, and COP Incorporated has not responded either. Why, I don't know.

Could you write or send an attorney?

Your friend,
Jack

Edward Wien
Central Islip State Hospital
Department H
Long Island, New York
    11722

Allen Ginsberg
June 16, in the year of Our Lord 1969
[Central Islip, NY]

Dearest Allen:

Your letter of alternatives has sustained me for many moments of each day, I will tell you what I wish a) to return to Buffalo as soon as possible and to continue assistance 2a) to observe the law as strictly as possible and to hold to its principle letters faithfully without trafficking in drugs and/or narcotics; namely to see that my family is well taken *care of b)* to see them as shortly as possible 3) and live as independently of you as soon as I can; you can see in my present situation this is not so possible and 4) to continue my writing efforts as least as possible in view of the state situation.

Possibly this is not what you wanted but all I can do and I wish to take my time in so doing.

Yours sincerely
John Wieners

Robert Creeley
6–30–69
[Central Islip, NY]

Dearest Robert:

Please try to understand and forgive my "literary" efforts of the past year. I wrote things under a delusion that seized me.

If you wish to write, please do. You, [illeg], are one of my favorite guys.

lovest, John

Charles Olson
July 10th 1969
[Central Islip, NY]

Dearest Charles:

As you know from Mr. Brown, I am now confined to Central Islip State Hospital—(S1 Station H. Central Islip, L.I., New York, 11722) much against my wishes.

You must forgive the last two letters I wrote, as for the past 20–18 months I have been under the delusion of being about 50 persons. I have given them all up and am now ready for the next 50.

How are you feeling? Can you say the same thing? I hope so. I can't even make-believe here. Too serious, too mature, too adult, too painful.

I sleep in an old oaken bucket with about 75 drugged, tranquilized slaves and am a nervous wreck.

How I thought I could forget you? I cannot nor do I want to. You make me well. How I love you.

Your—
Jean

Wieners S-1 // Station H
Central Islip, L.I.
New York 11722

How I would love to have a word.

Was writing here and Tom Maschler wrote 2 days ago—
"I am also very much looking forward to your new volume of poems and it's my understanding that you will not contract with anyone else *here* for that."

Am giving Anne Waldman 12 verses for a pamphlet ABSENT VERSE FORMS.
Saw your ~~JonathanCape~~ *Jargon*/William
    Maximus II and bless you
            for coming in at high crescent.

> Duncan McNaughton
> Friday, July 11, 1969
> [Central Islip, NY]

Dear Duncan:

Want you to know how much your letter, listing with such detail, your activities in Gloucester, Provincetown, and your uncle and aunt's house, meant to me, as I too am party to some pleasure, though others might not gain, and there only is gain from exploring that. And Jack and Mary's wedding, too.

I needed this hospitalization for I have been inhabited in a very sophisticated way by manifestations, powerful ones, of political leaders, Gustav Huczsak,[56] President of Czechoslavakia is one of them—"Bunny" Rodgers, etc. I thought I was Frederick III still alive over 200 years.

Are you going to have a third baby? I can't believe it. So soon, too, it's hard for me to believe. I guess that's what married men do.

Heard from Allen De Loach and Anne Waldman with your long, lively epistle, that I would like to have typed out. It all makes so much sense to me except for this place, that is below the ground. literally.

I write from a dirty cellar, awaiting 9:00 opening of the doors. Soon we'll see each other again. Until then I am being asphyxiated by the state.

Yours sincerely,
With love –
John Wieners

> Allen Ginsberg
> Saturday July 12th 1969
> [Central Islip, NY]

Dear Allen:

I went to Jewish services for the first time last Friday at 3PM, and wore the cap and sang the hymns, & recognized the voices of the faithful as your own. It was the, since

---

56 A "?" is written above the "z."

childhood, most powerful religious experience, outside of my own moods.// How I miss my "freedom." Talked to Dr. Weiss (she is again my doctor) and she could give no date for discharge. How sorry and lonely I am on all these park benches. Tom Maschler sent her a very good letter on my behalf. Love to Peter and Julius is more on my mind and Bill Berkson is coming tomorrow. Can't reach Dr. Weinstein and in tears on Thursday asked my mother to take me back to Massachusetts.

Love, John Wieners

Charles Olson
Friday July 19, 1969
[Central Islip, NY]

Dearest Charles:

Well, my interest picks up the moment I turn my thoughts to write a letter to you. How bored I am otherwise. I never bothered to investigate waking enlargements of the imagination ~~of~~ in repressed ~~wishes~~ areas. But as ~~in all~~ *you see*, am terribly repressed. Carnivals are not enough.

How I miss you Charles, the long hours we spent together and to think that the possibility of these hours has been removed, pains even inertia.

~~I hope I make myself understood, despite slack handwriting.~~

In the ~~small~~ *same* mail ~~of~~ with yours was one from Bob Creeley, the dear. And my sister sent the clippings of Herbert Kenny's mass review entitled, Charles Olson, poet to know.[57] So it was a bountiful evening.

Thank you for your loving note, sympathetic and generous, it returned to me dreadful sanity.

I am up every day by 6AM. Medicine four times and in bed again by 7PM. Work in the kitchen, at library on a book entitled and already published by Lippincott, ~~entitled~~ Poetry Therapy, author John Leedy, M.D[58] and other projects. Shopping, drinking, friend-making.

Yours in that activity, privilege, behavior.

John

---

57 Herbert Kenny (1913–2002), American poet and writer who edited the *Boston Globe*'s book section for many years, profiling and interviewing Olson at different times along the way, including an interview just five months before Olson's death.

58 Dr. Jack Leedy edited *Poetry Therapy: The Use of Poetry in the Treatment of Emotional Disorders* in 1969 for Lippincott. As the founder of the Association for Poetry Therapy, Leedy solicited articles from a variety of psychologists and psychotherapists who were using poetry- or book therapy in their practice.

Charles Shively
July 29, 1969
[Central Islip, NY]

Dear Charles:

Thank you for your kind letter of a month ago, and please forgive delay in answering.[59] I have been both in prison, jail, hospital, and now wind up in Central Islip State Hospital, which place gives me a better perspective or grade on things for a short while longer.

Thank you for sending your lovely poetry and thinking of ~~you~~ *me* with such regard you had to write. I have many friends in the Boston area still though I ~~will~~ have been at school in Buffalo since January 1965.

Returning to parents' house in Hanover, Massachusetts by the end of summer I hope. Must wait and see what the overall verdict renders. Will I see you on return to Massachusetts?

Yours presently,
John Wieners

Duncan McNaughton
August 1, 1969
[Central Islip, NY]

Dear Duncan:

Your kind letter arrived with ten dollars. And I have no words to express my gratitude towards you. My parents were down that weekend and a check arrived from Stonybrook ~~with~~ worth 40 dollars. My father is budgeting it for me. But your ten dollars and the previous ten and the presents from Provincetown were more than I deserve.

I have very bad eye-sight now without glasses and it's hard for me to <u>read</u> the small-script, and once read it's easily forgotten, so this "thin" mind you mention is true and applies <u>here</u>, though I find no evidence of <u>it</u> in your correspondence. My mind would be <u>better</u> if my eye-sight were and my <u>father</u> is mailing me a pair of magnifying glasses for temporary use.

Thank you for writing so frankly of your self, of Robert and the direct word of my friends in Buffalo, I especially care for Chuck Schubb and would like his address if you have it. I could send a letter to Mr. Gay of the Poetry Room for him through Diana but don't want to do it that way.

---

59 Charles Shively wrote to Wieners out of admiration; from this fan letter came a warm, revealing correspondence and lifelong friendship.

I must close for now, Duncan. Thank you for mentioning Genie and the children Daniel and Io and the expectant one, as well.

> *Your friend*
> *John with love* ~~Wieners.~~

I don't have Ed Dorn's address. Do you?
I will be here pretty sure until after Labor Day.
when my sister comes to visit and I hope
takes me home to 24 Chestnut Circle
> Hanover, Massachusetts

> Charles Olson
> [Aug 5, 1969]
> [Central Islip, NY]

After a walk across the early morning fields, soaked with dew and night rain, he would read his book for an hour on a park bench outside Robbins Hall.

When the hour was up this morning, he walked back over the *wet* fields and mailed a letter at the Administration Building. The light was hot and misty. He then returned to the library, for what purpose he did not know. At one point, or many points in his life, and even still he once regarded such leisure as priceless. Now he did not, quite so wholeheartedly.

Instead he was in a quandary. He had nothing to do and was tired of writing, of reading about it, and even being where he was, an hospital of the State in New York.
Charles: August 5th 1969
I have done a bunch of poems while here, sent to Anne Waldman in the East Village: Angel Hair Books. 16 of them to be exact.

I will be out before Thanksgiving and up to see you, if I may around then. With more ham.

> *Love,*
> *John*

S-I
Station H
Central Islip, L.I.
New York 11722 or

new address in Massachusetts
24 Chestnut Circle
Hanover, Massachusetts.
    my parents bought
    a house there.
        New

And sold the old one
    to my cousin

Charles Shively
Tuesday the 5th of August 1969
[Central Islip, NY]

Dear Charles:

I know I should not be writing again so soon, but I have to be up so early in the dawn, 5:30 AM and by 7:15 AM, we are done with breakfast and medication. I have too much free time, so wander in the fields and think of those wild fens in Boston. And yourself brings up a well of curiosity, Who would read my poetry so closely as to quote it, only as your verse reveals, an abstractionist! Well, that's good enough. I am 5'9" and some, blue hairs eyes, 12 teeth left, bad eyesight, etc.

Your life sounds fruitful enough for a friendship.

Here's

Thank you for revealing your birthplace and home town. You probably know mine. And a good deal of gossip about yours truly, but you'd be hard put, to find an unkind tongue wag in this direction.

I was born in Boston and raised in Milton until this past year, when my parents moved to Hanover. I haven't seen the new house yet, and it's partly accountable for my breakdown, that in process is what I am still partly suffering from now. And will be here at this state hospital for well into September, then transferred back home then.

Am writing like crazy, as they say.

Yours, love,
John Wieners

Joe Brainard
August 13, 1969
Station H, Central Islip
[Long Island, NY]

Dearest Joe:

I had been living alone amidst poverty for some time before I began to hallucinate, most pleasantly at the beginning, then more violently before I was incarcerated by chance in New York City May 1st or 2nd, after my welfare check came & *a* plane trip via United hence.

Now I am trying to see my identity emerge under the loving care of my parents and friends, at home, unfortunately not here, for this is a madhouse, and I imagine you and Kenward living sleek and perfumed in your own delightful ways, much apart from this delusion, that only by mistake, ~~only~~ exists at all.

Thank you Joe for the sweetest letter imaginable and for the photographs, a hard on in themselves.

All I can do here is wait until discharge, and then get well at home for a few years. It's or I am so dreadful here, it's best I do not bore you with the inanity of it. One doctor for over 300 patients. You can scarcely believe the carelessness of condition man exerts upon himself.

Do write again and send a few bucks,

I can use it.

Love, your friend
John Wieners

Do well in your work.

Duncan McNaughton
August 19, 1969 Tuesday Morning
[Central Islip, NY]

Dear Duncan:

Chuck Schub came to visit, and Charles Olson wrote last night, so those are small favors to offset the nightmare of experience Central Islip is.

Day long I am beset with nerves and am continually walking to offset them. It's not so bad when I have someone to write ~~to~~ but the minute I stop the more these miseries invade. Well, I'll be alright, once I get home to Hanover. Address is 24 Chestnut Circle, Hanover, Massachusetts.

Bob Creeley dropped a note also and if you see him tell him I asked you to make him write me a letter. I need it.

Things are so bad now with the sun flooding through an open porch door, but this situation is comparable to an extended stay in one of the worst movie houses you have ever been in.

I've just had a poem accepted by The Iowa Review, to accompany an article by Richard Howard re myself; "The poetry of John Wieners"[60] and Mother sent me a article ~~by All~~ about Allen Ginsberg from ~~the~~ an issue of Time. Crystal Blue Persuasion is playing on ~~the~~ a disc jockey show and I saw Where Eagles Dare two weeks ago.

It's a review of a new book on Allen called Allen Ginsberg in America by Jane Kramer (Random House)[61]

> *Love and god—*
> *love you—*
> *John ~~Wieners~~*

Anne Waldman
August 27, 1969
[Central Islip, NY]

Dearest Anne:

You will hate *me* but

Half-awake I am now mailing to you enclosed what I consider, absolutely the last poem in the (book) we have entitled "Asylum Poems." O. K. It's a longish poem about Boston and a mistake in conception in that it attempts to include the Meaning of Boston, the metropolis of the world I hungered for at ten years of age.[62]

---

60 The Winter 1970 issue of *The Iowa Review* featured Wieners's poem "Love-life" and an essay by American poet and scholar Richard Howard (b. 1929) called "John Wieners: 'Now Watch the Windows Open By Themselves.'" The latter compares Wieners to Rilke, "both of whom start young with 'stories about God' and end up—this is surely Wieners's fate—in other people's houses, listening to 'the voices.' The difference, of course, will be suggested by what divides the Castle of Duino from the Hotel Wentley" (104).

61 Jane Kramer's *Allen Ginsberg in America*, a series of essays written for *The New Yorker*.

62 "After Symonds' *Venice* (for Allen Ginsberg)" closes *Asylum Poems*. It looks back at old Boston—"first town, first bank of hopes, first envisioned paradise"—through "sooty" memory, remembering the old haunts from the other side of urban renewal's devestation:

> and the gossamer twilights on Boston Common, and Arlington Street
> adrift in the mind, beside the mighty façade of convent and charnel house,
> who go through those doors, up from Beacon Street, past the marooned sunset in the
> West, behind Tremont Hill's shabby haunts of artists
> and the new Government Center, supplanting Scollay Square.

It's wrong, I know, to send you another poem at this late date, but please forgive me it will be the last one.

Love,

Yours,

John Wieners

I hope this does not, too greatly increase the cost.

~~After Symond's Venice~~
P. S. Anne I don't need to see proofs. They only confuse me and waste time for given the opportunity to correct myself I will, and that's an error, so if it saves time to expedite the book by correcting proofs at home, then do so. Love, John

Joe Brainard

August 27, 1969

[Central Islip, NY]

Dear Joe:

The only way I can stay well in body and spirit is to write, not only poetry, that comes in gusts, but letter-writing or journal-keeping in between times. The rest of the time is spent reading or walking, including dreaming.

Just finished a book ~~of~~ *for* Anne Waldman and she spoke of you doing the cover but I would rather she did it herself. The book came out of a knowledge that she would read the work, and she made the initial suggestion. I OKed you though.

Now as for money, thank you for the ten dollars. I can always use it as food *here* is terrible and to avoid *it* we eat out at dinettes and those horribly expensive soda bars, not to mention the beer and wine smuggled in, as well as stamps, cigarettes and coke.

Sounds rather of subterfuge and it is. Since here I have read Ashenden, or the British agent by W. Somerset Maugham [63] Madame Bovary by Gustave Flaubert and A Mid Summer Night's Dream of William Shakespeare's *pen*. And written my own 18 poem collection, to be called "Asylum Poems" of all things. It's going to be good. I can hardly wait.

Thank you, Joe, for the bread and send—as you know or may know I am to be discharged the last of next month at the latest, so will have no need of funds, as I

---

63 *Ashenden: Or the British Agent* is a book of interconnected short stories about World War I spies by English novelist and playwright W. Somerset Maugham.

will be living at home, who else would have me and I never thought of just how to ask Kenward for a few dollars, even though I always felt the urge to though just dont know how. Don't mention this to him, for I have never mentioned funds to him. We met through poetry and that's the way I want to keep it.

"Crystal Blue Persuasion" by Tommy James and the Shantelles is one of the loveliest songs ever recorded, and that goes for Gerrit Lansing's Maiden's Prayer.⁶⁴ By the way, would you send his address?

Much obliged for the postcards. I will always use them and the lovely lovely photographs. Yum yum

love,
John Wieners

Anne Waldman
[Aug 1969]
[Central Islip, NY]

Dear Anne:
Saw your photograph
in Vogue! Glad to have
you in one of my favorite
pla magazines and glad
ABSENT VERB FORMS
reached you. I am
getting along and miss
you. Joe Brainard sent
me two lovely photographs
of you. Love John Wieners S-1

* * *

His stay at Central Islip State Hospital was brutal and long, and when it was over John Wieners moved in with his parents in Hanover for a while. He also got right back to work, releasing a new book through Angel Hair Books called *Asylum Poems.*

---

64 The psychedelic pop song "Crystal Blue Persuasion" was released by Tommy James and the Shondells in June 1969. "A Maiden's Prayer" is a piano piece by Polish composer Tekla Bądarzewska-Baranowska; Gerrit Lansing was a magnificent pianist.

It is a large, thin book, hand-stapled, with a cover drawing by George Schneeman of a hand proffering a flower, a stylized umbel with stalks ribbing upward.

New friendships, especially the one with Charlie Shively, led to energizing political and cultural engagements like "homophile" societies, student activism, and the Beacon Hill Free School, where he taught for the first time in several years. His friend Jack Powers, who founded the school and later the Boston institution Stone Soup Poets, describes their lives together in the late 1960s and 1970s:

> The back of Beacon Hill (behind the State House) had an infusion of remarkable energy that was like Greenwich Village of the 30's and 40's. Rent was relatively cheap, and the living was easy. There was a community that was harmonized around issues like world peace, the ending of hunger . . . you name it. We articulated the isolation of the individual in society, and moved to the possibility of communication.[65]

* * *

Donald Allen
October 6th, 1969
[Hanover, MA]

Dearest Don:

Safely at home now, just finished an article on the Political Realities of Being Gay for Jim Hayes of WIN magazine; he's going to ask R. Duncan for something, too,[66] I respond to your cheering letter of October 3rd, this year.

I will write Tom Maschler to send the Preface onto you. I so want it to be in. Thank you for asking *me* to be part of the Poetics of The New American Poetry.[67] I love the title of it and it sounds like a good book to be interested in.

I will send Anne Waldman a note to have a copy of my new book mailed to you. It's called Asylum Poems and will be ready this weekend.

Olivia and David Posner have just written. I so like him. Do you have Robin Blaser's address and Robert Duncan's? I would like to write to them both.

Yes $3 advance would be enough for me per page of your book: The Poetics of the New American Poetry. You really truly have given birth to a new movement, all by

---

65 Holder, "Interview with Stone Soup Poets Founder Jack Powers."

66 *WIN*, a political magazine published by the New York Workshop in Non-Violence (an action group affiliated with the War Resisters League) from 1966 through 1983. Their November 1969 "Gay Issue" featured an essay by Paul Goodman ("Memoirs of an Ancient Activist"), poetry by Wieners, and an article by David McReynolds (b. 1929) in which the antiwar activist came out as gay.

67 Grove Press published Donald Allen's anthology *The Poetics of the New American Poetry*, including a submission by Wieners, in 1973.

yourself. Keep it that way, as Charles Olson told me at the beginning of Measure, let no *one* else in. He by the way, called at the end of last week to see how I was doing. And I am fine, honestly, Don, I really am.

Yours, devotedly,

John ~~Wieners~~

Donald Allen

October 27, 1969

[Hanover, MA]

Dearest Donald:

Just remembered in that Grove Press book, I had one line in my "poetics" at the back of the book when I quote Charles Olson as saying that "poetry is no more a holy act than say, shitting."[68] I definitely want that taken out, for the quotations were eventually dropped off and it seemed my remark, when actually it was said very hastily in a class at Black Mountain, and I know he doesn't mean it and neither do I.[69]

Love,

John Wieners

belatedly.

PS: I always felt terribly embarrassed about this remark getting into print and I'm sure you did, too. Now is the time, if not of all times long before this, to correct the ignorance of such filth. Hee hee.

I've wanted to correct this for ten years—and this remark in print has given me three nervous breakdowns—Though I never had the strength to tell you.

Anne Waldman

November 3, 1969

[Hanover, MA]

Dearest Anne:

Thank you for sending the 20 complimentary copies out and tending to the bookshops and mail orders. I know it must be a laborious business to do all this for

---

68 See letter to Donald Allen from a decade earlier, September 20, 1959.

69 Wieners's "From a Journal," written in 1959 during his *707 Scott Street* period, was sent to Allen in his letter dated September 20, 1959, and indeed the line is noted as being a "quote from Olson."

someone else. I am glad you have been reading around. I got the Whitney notice of your introductions last month to John Ashbery, Michael Benedict[70] and Ron Padgett.[71] It must have been some honor to introduce them, and your going to Yale sounds peaceful and exciting at the same time. I am feeling well though have absolutely nothing to do! here at home but worry, worry, worry about lost belongings stored in Buffalo, lost connections and lost time. Still I would love to read December 3 at the Church. I am working for my father four nights a week from Monday to Thursday 5–7 in the evening and if you can't get any other time I will just have to take the time off from him. Yet if you can get another date from a Friday night over the weekend that would be better. Let me know. I am open to both alternates but still wld go, as my mother reminds me, if you can't get any other dates.

Love, John and thank you, Anne
your friendship means so much
in countless odd ways

It's just that my father would have to do the work by himself, as he let another man go to let me have the chance of working. Still it's up to you. Wednesday December 3rd is good enough and I won't be too late, although December 5th would be better, unless they have something else on at the church.

Anne Waldman
November 14, 1969
[Hanover, MA]

Dearest Anne:

December 3rd it will have to be; my father doesn't seem to mind and I certainly dont. I called the Bus Station and the round-trip fare to New York City from Boston ~~and back~~ is $17.05 and the train fare is $23.16 round trip while the plane goes for $42.00. So you choose the best way. It doesn't matter for I will have all day Wednesday to travel.

---

70 Michael Benedikt (1935–2007), American poet and critic noted for his engagement with the New York art world; he was briefly the managing editor of *Locus Solus*.

71 Rod Padgett (b. 1942), American poet, writer, and translator. While he was still in high school in Oklahoma, he founded (with friends Joe Brainard and Ted Berrigan) *The White Dove Review*, which published an impressive array of postwar poets like Kerouac, Ginsberg, and Blackburn. He studied with Kay Boyle and Kenneth Koch, and continued his work in the classroom for decades, with the New York Poets in the Schools programs and various poetry educational organizations. His poignant memoirs of Berrigan and Brainard were published in 1993 and 2004, respectively.

I am preparing my reading very carefully and though am more nervous this time than most know I will be able to do it.

I will be staying with friends in the West Village for a few days and will not have to back *here in Boston* until Monday evening at 5.

Will you send the expense money or should I wait until I get into New York City to pick it up? It would be easier to have it beforehand.

A great majority of my poetry is in storage up in Buffalo at Allen De Louach's so am waiting like crazy to prepare a sizeable body of work for presentation.

Yours sincerely Anne, with love,
    John ~~Wieners~~

1–617–878–4371

Hope everything is well with you. There's talk here in Boston of a pirate edition of *Asylum Poems*[72]
In fact, *I find out now* they have already done it
but its not *even* stapled and stuffed in an
envelope on different grades of paper.
But I'm not supposed to be telling you this,
so keep it under your hat.

---

72 The same year that Angel Hair released *Asylum Poems*, someone calling themselves the "Press of the Black Flag Raised" released a pirate edition. The poems were printed on eighteen loose broadsides in a manila envelope, title and author stamped onto medical-looking labels on the envelope. As this letter to Anne Waldman shows, Wieners was, at the very least, unconcerned.

PART THREE

"*What can I do but shine / in memory*"

FIGURE 7 John Wieners at the St. Mark's Poetry Project. Photograph by Allen Ginsberg. Courtesy of the Allen Ginsberg Estate.

The years 1970–1971 were marked by one devastating loss after another, a harrowing time in Wieners's life captured in the beautiful, disquieting journal *A book of PROPHECIES*, published in 2007 by Bootstrap Press.[1] First, father-figure Charles Olson died in January 1970, then old friend Stephen Jonas a month later, followed by his mother Anna Wieners in March. His father Albert died the following May. "The dull machinery of time / yields menacingly as before," he writes to Robert Wilson in late February:

> there is no better hope,
> poems buffet no winds
> against grave's uncompromise.

This next letter, to Robert Wilson, was mailed from Fort Square, the outcropping in Gloucester Harbor, crowned by a cluster of cottages, where Charles Olson had lived for many years. Wieners had just served as Olson's pallbearer.

* * *

Robert Wilson
January 13th 1970[2]
[Gloucester, MA]

After Charles' Funeral Service
Gloucester   *Posted from Ft-Square*
Dear Bob:
     Various poets, photographers painters publishers preside per de mer for the honor & worship due Olson. We hope & know through your letter to Stuart Montgomery that all with you well for a Selected Poems, 1970 with Jonathan Cape, Ltd Love, John Wieners

---

1 Edited by Michael Carr with an introduction by Jim Dunn. Lowell, MA: Bootstrap Press, 2007.
2 Postcard from THE NEW TAVERN RESTAURANT AND COCKTAIL LOUNGE, 30 Western Avenue, Gloucester, Massachusetts.

Robert Wilson
January 28, 1970
[Hanover, MA]

Dearest Robert:

Finally finished one for you, 70 lines exactly. My second try. Did one over the weekend, "The Chair, The Book, The Hand," that didn't come off, but this one does, I hope. You like it? Let me know, and mail check promptly, deducting money I owe you for books, etc.

Harvey Brown says he will take the 500 <u>Ace of Pentacles</u> off your hands for friends and gifts, to hold over the years. I so regret that phrase, "2 men on a cot," & think that particular poem, "Act #2," would be much better ~~off~~ without it.

Gerard Malanga comes to town tomorrow at 1:55 PM on South Station *for the weekend, filming* and I am meeting Harvey early in the morning at The Mandrake Bookshop in Cambridge before we greet his train with camera (his), books (ours) and tape machine. They are holding up his interview with Charles *for The Paris Review*[3] for factual checking, or rather tape accuracy.

Love to you Bob, and let me know your decision regarding this, the enclosed.

  Yours,
   John ~~Wieners~~

Postscript

If you send the galleys here for correction please enclose the original, as that is the only copy, extant except for the work sheets and first draft.

YOUTH[4]

The first darkness
on Blue Hill Ave.
from 1 to 6
before the war broke out
or sickness, on the second floor
above the meat market,
MacDonald's, across from ~~the~~
Parkway Pharmacy, when
first memory was sliding over a hot barrel in the sun.

---

3 Charles Olson was interviewed by Gerard Malanga, with the assistance of Olson's friends Harvey Brown and Gerrit Lansing, in April 1969. The interview was published in the Summer 1970 issue of *The Paris Review*, number 12 in their Art of Poetry series.

4 "Youth" was published as a broadside by the Phoenix Book Shop (1970) and collected in Black Sparrow's *Selected Poems* (1986).

What can I do but shine
in memory, in the crib
while the cardplayers were
out in the kitchen, and ~~the rats~~ *mice*
ran down the hall, after what
the moon declares,

in the driveway, staring *under a veil* at an apple tree
after we moved, and climbing another
apple *bough,* enchanted with ~~the~~ *its* blossoms
there, When the world was young
(~~as the song goes~~ sung by Felicia Sanders
on TV weeping, for her father, or at Le Bon Soir
playing to the bar.

        Before the war broke out
           announced over the dining room floor
on Churchill Street, in Milton Massachusetts,
USA, behind the front porch, where I buried
irises, from beside the house.

           There was another driveway
different from the first one, in that it was pebbled,
or was it the same,
only at the end of it, I lay
in a carriage, before the field
where I imagined thirty years later
Bob Creeley held me upside down, by
the left ankle, sticking
pins and needles into that wax doll,

        before my sister caught him, or
          was it Marlene Dietrich, appearing there
moving majestically down the avenue to guard over
~~all children~~
The war-torn refugees, waifs who lined the house
upstairs and down
           until we moved

              to my grandmother's
fighting, Nana dying *in* the bed, the empty room that

my cousin has now,
               Marie, and the truckdriver
               McDermott, she married.

It seems the Scotch hold our psyche,
with their folktales and legends,
Robert Graves relating at the museum
anecdotes from the Order of St. John of Malta.

The altars burned then
with incense and prayers, not now
late-night vigils and pleas or tears
against death, in the toilets and woods.

I had so many phantasies last year,
of that flat twenty miles away:
only early youth affected before birth
by rituals, scissors, child-abuse.

Not beauty that was real, before the mirror
in strawberry blonde hair, silk black dress,
going to work, during wartime.
First to Toby Deutschman's buring dolls
in the 5 & Dime, phantasies there as well

Marion behind the counter, Bobbie C. kissing her cunt.

How I loved my sister being a lesbian, but she was not, only a nun.
That was later on, though, after she left the big house on Eliot St.
that was also in Milton, only I left it first, to become a poet,
to live on Beacon Hill, and starve, before Black Mountain,

before Big Charles put his hand on me, and ordained me a priest.

−1970
John Wieners

FIGURE 8 John Wieners
at a benefit reading for the
Chicago 7 at the Charles
Street Meeting House, 1971.
Photograph by Ammiel
Alcalay. Courtesy of Ammiel
Alcalay.

Charles Shively
February 1, 1970
[Hanover, MA]

Dearest Charles:

Thank you for your lovely card and note of the holidays and sorry I have been slow in replying, but with my mother's illness over Christmas, and Charles Olson, the poet's, illness in New York, and finally, death on January 10th, I have been kept involved with the funeral, and his friends here, for the services. Perhaps you saw our photographs in the Morning Globe for February 14th (ironic in that was the date I heard him deliver the Morris Grey Lecture in the blizzard of 1962) as pallbearers. We are giving a memorial reading at St. Mark's Church in New York, this Wednesday, February 4th at 8:30 PM.[5] Then I will read in Baltimore at The Johns Hopkins University on Thursday afternoon, February 19th, at 4 PM, to fill you in with my upcoming activities.

I hope to see you afterwards, or even before, if you are not too shy, as I am. I loved the poem you sent. It sort of excites me. As well as Gerard Malanga was here this weekend from New York. He is Andy Warhol's assistant. And he has been

---

5 Most members of the New York and allied poetry communities came out for Olson's memorial at St. Mark's on February 4, 1970. Wieners was joined at the lectern by Ed Sanders, Ted Berrigan, Diane Wakoski, and Paul Blackburn, among others. Sanders spoke for many of the mourners when he said of Olson's work:

> Time and time again, you read lines that would spew puke upon the dogma of a Catholic funeral. These poems are just incredible, their importance. He makes all these creeps who win the National Book Award sound like idiots. (Kane, *All Poets Welcome*, 217)

photographing everywhere. We have a friend, here, Rene Ricard,[6] who lives at 20 [illeg] Street, off Berkeley, in Boston, where I spent the latter part of last week.

I am still working in town, from 5–6:30 PM 4 nights a week, Monday through Thursday, for my father at 210 South Street. But otherwise am free. Perhaps you could suggest some kind of meeting. If not, we can keep up our correspondence, until the weather is warmer.

I hope Gordon is well, and his family, too. It's difficult though at times, helpful to have emotional problems other than one's own. I speak in terms of his son. Does he know where he is? I suppose not. And if so, probably would not care *say*. [illeg] these problems of leaving the Armed Services are more common now and well-publicized, so that some of the stigma is removed.

I do look forward to meeting you, Charles, if only in the [cut]way, by chance, under the moon, which might happen by the way. But be careful, please.

Your friend,
John Wieners

I have forgotten where you said you were teaching. Was it Boston State? I hope to start substitute school teaching in Fall, if only in the elementary schools around Brockton or Plymouth, if possible. I am also often over at the Grolier Bookshop in Cambridge, and there is a very, nice dim ~~bar~~, room, behind the University Restaurant on Massachusetts Avenue, called the Toga Room. As well as a good film we might also see, at The Orson Welles.[7] Besides the Blue Parrot beneath the Brattle[8] for a matinee. Yours, John—

Ed Dorn
February 10, 1970
[Hanover, MA]

Dearest Ed:

Been reading Wm. Bronk's <u>The World, the Worldless</u>,[9] which is an awfully good

---

6 Rene Ricard (1946–2014), Boston-born poet, art critic, and artist. He left school in his teens and met Wieners, who became a mentor, and moved to New York in 1965, quickly becoming central to the New York art and poetry worlds.

7 The Orson Welles Cinema (1969–1986), Cambridge theater specializing in foreign and independent films.

8 The Blue Parrot, hip Harvard Square coffee shop–restaurant underneath the art house Brattle Theater.

9 William Bronk (1918–1999), American poet whose *The World, The Worldless* was published by New Directions in 1964. Bronk and Olson had a friendship in letters for twelve years, based on a mutual admiration of one another's poetry. In 1964 Olson wrote to his friend that upon reading *The World, The*

title when you write it out, and Charles spoke of the book in an earnest way, he said he liked it, and I am looking into it for philosophy to relieve my sadness. The world is so futile, we have such little time, and who could stand more. Each instant seems so weighted with some anxiety, some problem, some interruption. Anyway, I am going to China in 1971, and write a book called China Summer. Bad luck to talk about it though. It seems ~~somehow~~ moving helps, I mean literal action, such as walking. I'm a walking activist, that's what. But what d'ye do when you get old? Oh well, that'll take care of itself. One hopes, or imagines. Others have gone through it. That's the only grace, one figures.

Yes Harvey and I went down on the Colonial Train to New York, out of Back Bay Station at 8 in the morning *Wednesday the 4th*—had parlor car seats, and arrived in NYC at 2:30 PM, called Ed Blackwell[10] and checked into one room at The Chelsea. Went over to see Blackwell, drummer, & he was playing that Fri-Sat with Theoloneliest Monk's[11] quartet at the Village Vanguard.[12] Met his wife Frances, and their two inter-racial children. She has some problem with her teeth, if she has any, one plate was in a cup on the sink, as I was washing my bridge under the running tap water, she mentioned it, her lowers—She's white.

Then went up to Grand Central to meet Kate, dinner separate, over to see Bob Wilson who showed me contraband magazines from abroad, named Iron Boys and Ding Dong, some of which I have, and then the reading, where Ed Sanders, Joel Oppenheimer, Harvey, myself, Robert Hellman,[13] Vincent Ferrini, Ted Berrigan, Fee Dawson, Paul Blackburn, Diane Wakosi,[14] Ray Bremser,[15] Jackson Mac Low[16] and Gerald Malanga read until quite late in the evening. On return home, Denise Levertov called to do a benefit for the Chicago 7. Monday Feb 16th at 8PM, The Charles St. Meeting House. I always welcome any "interruption" or obligation like this, for it's the only way I keep from slipping into the void. No matter how many times one

---

Worldless, he was inspired to write "the only spontaneous puff I ever did write," a brief word of appreciation that would now be called a blurb, which he sent to Bronk's editor. It would appear on the 1981 edition of Bronk's *Life Supports: New and Collected Poems* (Kimmelman, "The William Bronk–Charles Olson Correspondence," n.p.).

10 Ed Blackwell (1929–1992), American jazz drummer known for his long collaboration with Ornette Coleman.

11 Thelonious Monk (1917–1982), American jazz composer and pianist.

12 The Village Vanguard, legendary club in Manhattan's West Village since 1935, which became all-jazz in 1957. Monk began performing at the Vanguard in 1948.

13 Robert Hellman (1919–1984), American poet and translator.

14 Diane Wakoski (b. 1937), American poet associated with different schools of poetry, frequently published in *The Floating Bear*.

15 Ray Bremser (1934–1998), American poet who began his career (publishing first in *Yugen*) while in prison for armed robbery.

16 Jackson Mac Low (1922–2004), American poet and performance artist.

has done it, it seems every day one must take some offensive against oblivion, or else there is no pleasure, that's the only place *from* where courage originates, or flows.

Glad to hear of Jonathan. I know his friend, Tom Meyer, intimately.

Also I'd love to get White Stones.[17] Who publishes it? Perhaps I could order it over here, or ask Bob Wilson to send it. I find Prynne, also very difficult, but appreciate him for that. Will send him mine.

Harvey is very pleased you are going with him, *publishing-wise,*[18] and though I haven't seen him since he took Kate to Sarah Lawrence, I returned to Boston via bus the following day.

Finished the mss. for Barry Hall,[19] and will send it Friday when I get the cash for postage and Xerox. Also J. Cape is sending back original proofs on Selected Poems, as I feared I corrected them with too heavy a hand. They are very good. It seems the second book with Cape Goliard would be out before or simultaneously with the earlier mess. Nonetheless I am on or into a third.

Thank you for remembering my family. My father's 66th birthday and all his children celebrated it with him a day earlier on Sunday, last. Three generations, etc. Two cakes, strawberries, candles and song!

> *Yours sincerely, with love*
> *and gratitude you are there,*
> *John*

I'm glad the letters made a difference, in your spirits. They really are a human blessing.

Joanne Kyger

February 22. 1970

[Hanover, MA]

Dearest Joanne:

How busy you must be not to write your old friend, John. And how successful. How is Bolinas? I have Phil Whalen's new book, On Bear's Head and love it so. Also

---

17 Jeremy Prynne's fifth book of poetry, *White Stones*, was published in 1969 by influential small British publisher Grosseteste Press.

18 Six of the twenty-five books published between 1965 and 1972 by Harvey Brown's Frontier Press were by Ed Dorn. Wieners could be referring to *Songs Set Two* (1970), *The Cycle*, or *Some Business Recently Transacted in the White World* (both 1971).

19 Barry Hall (1933–1995), British publisher, cofounder of Goliard Press, publisher of many New American poets in Britain. In 1967, Goliard merged with Jonathan Cape to form Cape Goliard, publisher of numerous distinguished poets from Britain and the United States. Cape Goliard published Wieners's *Nerves* in 1970 (in cooperation with Grossman Publishers in the United States) and *Selected Poems* in 1972.

some plastic over records. Some guy left me 8000 dollars. Will you write me? I am dying of hunger for you. See your poems everywhere. And Nemi Frost. Do you have her address. I will see you Summer of 1971, on my way to China. Shall I send new poems to Tom Clark[20] for The Paris Review. Bob Dylan is singing, "For tonight I'll be Staying Here with You."

Monday evening I gave a benefit for the Chicago 7 at the Charles Street Meeting House with Denise Levertov, Anne Sexton, Ron Loewinsohn, James Tate, etc. How is George Stanley and Howard Dull? And Irving Rosenthal? I hear from Charles Plymell in Baltimore in person that Dave Haselwood is incommunicado, being held prisoner by [illegible] Gurdjieff in captivity for his salary.

Love,

John Wieners

Duncan McNaughton
March 21, 1970
[Hanover, MA]

Dearest Duncan:

Much thanks for your non-"literary" letter on The Damned.[21] It was refreshing, your letter, that is, as we Gerrit, Scott Reichard and myself, had seen it the weekend before. I did not think much of it, other than shock, at such ~~big~~ bad taste, and loveliness of habitat at onset: Of course, who wears lace panties anymore, in politics, ~~anymore~~ that is. Perhaps a black and white concept would have helped the factual derision from the German aristocracy, which one may see perhaps only in relics on the streets of Germany—*viz. Maximillian Schell in that film about benzedrine and a German officer hidden in the attic, who does not know the war is over*—I do not know. I have never been there. Only know I have a romantic conception about that ruin, anyway and do regard the Nordic as definitely battle-worn, as if he had been through an excess that always results in "wisdom." Someone suggested "the palace of wisdom" was death, but I dont see how. Really, death is the one canker, and the only one on earth. I can stand war. Even pain, conquering other person's property, etc, but death must have some chopper to it that is not permanent, only a progression to another freedom, not so personal as this one, an ultimate broadening ~~of~~ *into* "inorganic"

20 Tom Clark (1914–2018), American poet, writer, and editor. Clark was poetry editor for the *Paris Review* from 1963 to 1973, and wrote influential biographies of Olson, Dorn, Kerouac, and Creeley. He taught in the New College poetics program from 1987 till the school closed in 2008.

21 The 1969 Italian-German film, directed by Luchino Visconti, about a family of industrialists in the early 1930s doing business with the Nazi Party.

material. Such as sun light, clouds, space, and air. Blind, dumb and beneficent. But where are we in all this? Collected together at some future time. I believe I may be a dog frisking about on some lawn, but I dont like this, and hope it is only transient, and short-lived. Know it is.

Well, words are some record. Thank you for your two important, memorable, and ~~note~~ noteworthy articles on William Burroughs and Hash-hish in Intrepid publications. I value them highly and regard them as hip.

Yes, the go of this film *referred to* was majestic, at the outset. But the Rohm debacle jerky and disjointed, as if the editor got too wrought to proceed coolly, as in the house-hold affairs, this might happen every Saturday night and did, does. Viz. Robert McAlmon's short stories on Post World War I Germany apropos public spectacle.

I dont know about oedipal incest, but I ~~like~~ *think* filial incest harmful in *immediate* pre-puberty, tho I would love to marry and live with any of my first cousins. Find them the most attractive women in the world. And make me feel the most at home.

How I long for glamour again, though, perhaps that rules out incest.

You know Mark's skull completely stilled my humanity in Buffalo, thus I could not harmonize with anyone, and what a chance, it will never happen again, now. There must be something about races, you know, as my mind, training, sensibility, civility cannot exist at some times, closes up as a lotus at any dense vibration. You know what I mean. I must *have* imagination, fire, intellect. Drugs won't do it, no matter how many. Give my regards and apologies to Genie for not coming closer when I had the chance. And could have, but could not, because of this dense lame-brain I was staying with.

> *Love, yours, John*

Joanne Kyger
March 30, 1970 Easter Sunday
[Hanover, MA]

Dearest dearest Joanne,

All of my Easters have to do with you, at least every 12 years or so: forgive me for being so scarce. I received your lovely letter yesterday, and we are having a late seasonal blizzard, which has filled Boston with 6 inches of bunny fur. Things have been good for me, Kids, though not adventuresome, I'm glad of it.

Enclosed is a photograph by Gerry Malanga, not very good, and too dark, for I am more a blond Anglo-Saxon type now, or at least would like to be. It was taken in Early February in exchange for your Mother's clippings from The Chronicle.

How kind and how pleased I am you and Ebbe took time out to think of me in Vancouver, so important, though you might not think so it appears to me. Harvey Brown has some literature for me from that place, titled Writing (Something) *edited* by Stan ~~Perksky Perksy~~ Persky. Not much to tell. I am taking driving lessons and will get a Volvo, sometime in May, probably. So I can pick up hitch hikers, etc. Though I am terrified at the thought of how to do it. The courtship process, etc, is the main fascination. I notice niggers like it, too, this confrontation with a new human being. Do you think it's an immigration problem or an inherited genetic?

Charles Olson's "death" left us all quite shocked, and we *are* not over it ~~that~~ yet. Then Steve Jonas followed him one month to the day, as well as Louise Bogan, [22] Richard Eberhart[23] told me at the University of Massachusetts at a March Mountain Party Festival—March 8–13th there in Amherst Emily Dickinson's hometown; we stayed Bob Creeley and I, in separate rooms, one block ~~over~~ from *where* she lived, at the Lord Jeffrey Inn, where Hubert Humphries spoke, after they booed him out of the U. of Mass. a fortnight before—then Eugene McCarthy joined in at the tail-end. Ed Dorn will be here for awhile this summer, with *his* new wife Jennie, and their son, Kid Lawrence Dunbar Dorn—other poets here are Gerrit Lansing, Denise Levertov, Ron Loewinsohn,[24] Joe Dunn, who doesn't write at all, works at a Hayes Bickford opposite North Station 6 days a week from noon to nine, and lives in a room at 121 Merrimac Street, in the North End. Write him a postcard, if you can, he's on the methdon-sustenance treatment and thin, but in good mental shape. Tom Balas still the same. Alan Minsk preaching the Bible; and Cambridge, happening.

Bill Berkson says he's going to Bolinas. May already have left by now. I look forward to reading at Max's Kansas City ~~there~~ in New York City soon. It probably will never materialize. Am still on health foods. Tiger's milk, Cod liver Oil Capsules, Rose Hip Tablets, dessicated liver tablets, niacin, and tobacco. Still losing hair, though. What about you?

I know you are sturdy and strong. But I fear when you say penniless. I will send $200, if you need it, your next letter to help you, if that does. Just let me know, and I will mail a registered check or money order, whatever's easiest for you.

Does Tom Clark want poems or what? That's worth 200 dollars worth of information to me, so there. I would like to be in The Paris Review, again. Wouldn't you, it's about time. But don't know what I have to send. 4 or 5 poems, do you think? Alan

---

22 Louise Bogan (1897–1970), American poet and critic, first woman to be appointed Poet Laureate to the Library of Congress.

23 Richard Eberhart (1904–2005), American poet and writer who helped bring the Beats to popularity through a 1956 *New York Times Book Review* essay titled "West Coast Rhythms."

24 Ron Loewinsohn (1937–2014), American poet and writer published in Donald Allen's *New American Poetry* alongside other poets of the San Francisco Renaissance.

Bullin's doing 3 poems in a chapbook, and this mid-summer, from ~~San Francisco~~ Santa Barbara, called <u>Invitations</u>,[25] his title. And Bob Wilson doing a 60 line poem, "Youth,"[26] he 's paying 250 dollars for. Would you like one of them? I'll ask him about it. I mean one of your own poems printed in his "chapbook" series. It has to be 60 lines long though. Wait till I get his O. K. though before you write it. On second thought ~~though~~, you probably have to get collected in Connecticut and environs before he'll latch on. It's time, Joanne, for your analyses, to be issued again in volume entire. What publishers do you prefer me to write? Cape Goliard, Allen de Loach, of Intrepid Press in Buffalo or Stuart Montgomery of Fulcrum?

Give my love to George Stanley. I so enjoyed reading the 2nd Annual Lit Anthology & Stonybrook because you, all three, had such excellent work in it. Do write ~~about~~ again. What about Black Sparrow in Los Angeles, for yourself, that is.

    Love, yours
      Pip

                                            Joanne Kyger
                                          August 7, 1970
                                      [Hanover, MA]

Dearest Joanne:

Without your scintillating interest in all things, lovely and ugly, along our path together, in San Francisco, New York and I have no doubt in many ~~future~~ other places still open to us. I reminisce ~~of~~ over the exciting events you created by your love for poetry. Could you forget how fervent your admiration endures? Education has dulled my capacity towards the ceaseless experience we radiated in the streets and literary obligations offered while fledging devotees in both ports.

Sharp as time becomes, no acid accusation will separate what has now proved constant existence in a genuine exchange of terms, letters, promise and fulfillments. Necessities of economy prohibit our position from being near to one another, yet these attempts at communication result in relighting the old honors of recognizing a common cause that travel only enriches.

Got a hundred dollars worth of books today, and thought of you, on calling

---

25 Unicorn Press in Santa Barbara, California, published a 200-copy run of *Invitation*, a hard-bound chapbook of three poems by Wieners ("Invitation," "Loss," and "Apparition"), in 1970.
26 *Youth* was published as part of the Phoenix Book Shop Oblong Octavo Series in 1970.

Thomas K Clark for Christine Fleischman's address as he wrote asking for a photograph, and poems, that I now have on hand for inclusion in the anthology regarding the 25 year celebration of arts in San Francisco 1943–1968. I misplaced her letter, and need that address for mailing the work. Tom said you were working on the anthology and could send it.

SanFrancisco.

Nob Hill, roaming down ~~Jackson~~ Washington Street in 1957, it was as if I had descended into a valley with mist blowing in front of me, and gas lamps, on either side, as tiny beacons in a wide garden, the Pacific on my right, washing the past away, and the gentle harbor before midnight, offering up benediction to the clouds of ecstasy, of mystery and perhaps, even the dark eyed embrace of solitude

    Only Polk Street holds the meadowed memory of countless thousands who ~~walked~~ *roamed* there before me for freedom, extension into the caverns of the Tenderloin. And van Ness Avenue, for the rumbling observation from respectable inhabitants, who drove ceaselessly home to television and dinners, for escape of their charges. How little we know how precious those hours would be.

When California Street became the last hurdle before light
and storefronts and apartment doorways were the only friends.

—John Wieners

<u>Youth</u>, of course enclosed. And a small thank you for past rent due. When I see Bob Wilson,
will give him your address towards an East Coast publication of your poems.

    <u>PIP</u>

Harvey Brown
[November 17, 1970]

Better Forget Her
Chicago, Chicago, Chicago
Chicago except for you Russ Rurkee
sszh Chick Schub, you better go,

Peter, Marc and Blondie

Rose foes.

Harvey Brown
February 18, 1971
[Hanover, MA]

Dear Harve:

Blessings for the Memoirs of Alexander Berkman,[27] received near the end of last month, and of course, since you have not answered directly either the last letter and the previous calls in December earlier, for Christmas together in New England, will you consider still sponsoring next summer's journal, China, as aforementioned; w/o going into steamships and ticket agencies?

Allen is sending a thousand within the next week or so, but half will go to house tax, and upkeep till May—you know I need little for the summer, peace and quiet; return to where I started, and the actual data, pertinent to the ocean, the winds and deck; with dinner, library and wardrobe on the way, at a minimum.

Some records, a few good hotels in 90 days and the memories of Evelyn's The Ordeal of Gilbert Penfold[28] and Sir Carol Reed's The Thin Man[29] to finalize the consumer's compendium.

Not a buyer, nor a worker, still a president and adventurer, from the latest

---

27 Alexander Berkman's *Memoirs of an Anarchist*, about the activist's imprisonment from 1892 to 1906, was first published by Emma Goldman's Mother Earth Press in 1912.

28 Evelyn Waugh's hallucinatory autobiographical novel *The Ordeal of Gilbert Pinfold* was published in 1957.

29 Wieners is probably referring to *The Third Man*, director Carol Reed's 1949 film written by Graham Greene.

scaffolding to a view of the Royal House after the launching, then bring on board the bottle of spirits, the pen and the book—

    Until you answer, betoken Jean[30]

Are you in process of abandonment to points—

    Call, please—

        Jackie or [illeg][31]

---

30 A star is drawn above and below "Jean."
31 Looks like "peutine" or "peut-me" (the latter is French for "Can I").

Wieners's fourth period of institutionalization was at Taunton State Hospital from April 1 to May 31, 1972. Taunton was a once-beautiful neoclassical asylum that had fallen into disrepair—within three years of Wieners's stay, the hospital was closed.

Wieners was released in time for an active summer, including a trip with Charles Shively and their New York Yippie friends to the 1972 Democratic Convention in Miami, distributing Shively's gay liberation magazine *Fag Rag*. Wieners wrote an account of the trip, *We Were There! A gay presence at the Democratic Convention*, published later that year as a mimeo pamphlet by Good Gay Poets. It is unclear exactly when he moved in, but by the first letter of 1973, he is already settled into the apartment at 44 Joy Street, where he would live for the rest of his life.

The Beacon Hill Free School began the summer of 1969, founded by local gay activist Jack Powers. Its 1974 catalog boasted that in its five years the BHFS had offered "over 300 courses to thousands of people of all ages, at no cost," and was able to do this because "instructors are willing to volunteer their time and services, and because neighbors and neighborhood organizations are willing to donate unused space in the evenings." The school held four sessions a year, each beginning with a general meeting, usually at the Charles Street Meeting House. At each general meeting, after Powers explained again the mission of the BHFS, members of the community had an open forum to pitch course ideas. At the Beacon Hill Free School "anyone may offer a course, and on any subject he or she wants," BHFS teacher and educational theorist John Holt recalled. "No teacher has to show proof of competence ... If people like the course, the teacher will probably offer it again. Of the thirty-seven courses offered in the Summer '74 catalog, seventeen were continued."[32] Their course listings ranged from politics to a popular bicycle clinic to courses in creative writing and modern poetry taught by locals like Wieners, Carol Weston, and Joe Dunn.

Out of the Free School came Stone Soup Poets, a cooperative founded by Powers that published Boston poets and held regular poetry readings for decades, which Powers never missed while he was alive. Like Louisa Solano, John Mitzel,[33] Charlie Shively, and other poetry organizers and booksellers, Powers was always a champion

---

32 Holt, *Instead of Education*, 28–30.
33 John Mitzel (1948–2014), Boston writer, publisher, and gay activist. In 1971, Mitzel cofounded the anarchist collective that published *Fag Rag*, the first nationwide gay men's magazine. The Good Gay Poets, which published Wieners's *Behind the State Capitol*, followed in 1973. He worked at Boston's Glad Day

of Wieners and his poetry, bringing him out for readings (some of which are available online in audio and video formats) in his later decades, and helping him with money and groceries when he needed them. It was friends like these, and later Jim Dunn, who helped keep Wieners fed, transported to readings and doctor appointments, and otherwise functioning in the practical world while he continued his work in his Joy Street apartment.

* * *

Duncan Mcnaughton
April 7, 1972
[Taunton, MA]

Dearest Duncan and Genie:

Right now, I am not at home and cannot get to the proofs of the verses you have already sent, goodheartedly acceptance of and remittance for; which stipend I have deposited to my <u>first checking</u> account at The Harvard Trust Company, thanks to the over-$1000 but barely grant of The Committee on Poetry, Peter Orlovsky President for 1972. If I had copies of the verses I would send rectifications, *three in number*, unto you. Eric Mottram has just accepted 6 good pages for <u>The Poetry Review</u> over at King's College *The University of* on London Strand. Very far out. And he's paying too. A Council on Literary Magazines is meeting at Boston University this April 29th and 30th and they are *sending out invitations Similar to COSMEP*. I am enclosing their address in New York, as you might be able to receive (I should really think so) assistance for FATHAR<u>34</u> from them

Coordinating Council of Literary Magazines
80 Eighth Avenue
New York, New York 10011

They might have notified you by now. They are very generous and have tens of thousands of dollars to distribute. Send to them for their organization handbook.

Since I can't correct the <u>three</u> typing *aforementioned* errors in the copies you mailed I am sending on another verse to compensate. One I know *of the above* is Jacqueliannee is spelled with a J not a L. *see your copies.*

Bookshop for many years until it closed in 2000. He went on to open Calamus Books, which he operated until his death.

34 *Mother, a Journal of New Literature* was succeeded by *Fathar*, which McNaughton edited in Bolinas, California, publishing seven issues between 1970 and 1975.

IN THE BEGINNING[35]

The early morning wake-up, melancholia at someone else's radios blaring
bittersweet tunes of remonstrable love, in the stuporific lethargy
after rising, fragments of dissolved ~~affairs~~ covert affairs, unresolved ambition
in worldly terms and aims
End wonderful instants down fresh clear air rushing in amongst disturbed
embers
throughout crowded past neighborhood apartments, immature youth
strivings,
illicit embraces,
tumbling headlong to submerge passion, by torrents of chaste, unchagrined
edginess

Portions dredged that cause shaved identity, though in toto non-
surrendered to;
perhaps a weekend here,
a fortnight's addiction there, a bar afternoon where
the lights, the clamor, the music combined to erect a home away from home,
while still one had one, past shared then afterwards, now resurrect to
produce the canopy from careless sophisticated sojourn; yet be cloudy
the total horizon, as if one did not possessed savor the full means
to find out what he was seeking to begin with, and although some
permission's
been received, the rough edges—the overall effect's
of unfructified worthiness, and fended belles letters
hoping ungathered future strength results about lost green ~~of~~ handicaps.
—John Wieners
April 5, 1972

Bill Corbett, a professor at Emerson also took some verses 3 to 4, for Fire Exit, since
Bill ~~Little~~ split, when his plans for a Boston anthology, "Boss" blew up.

Miss you, very much Duncan, and my carefree enamoured Buffalo seasons, stewing in a pout.

Love, always,
Johnnie

---

35 "In the Beginning" was published in *Fathar* and later in Wieners's *Cultural Affairs in Boston.*

Charles Shively
April 17, 1972
[Taunton, MA]

Dearest Charlie:

So forgive the familiar use of your first name. I miss you and the lovely friendships you have extended in the past two years of our salutary acquaintance. Thank you for taking me to the Homophile meeting in Boston and the gay dance, as well.[36] Give my admiring regards to dashing Gordon ~~as well, or as including~~ including the Profile.

I will have some more <u>money</u> soon and take an apartment, I ~~hope~~ *plan* somewhere in Boston, possibly the Coolidge Corner section on or near Beacon St.
                    called Brookline   Thus I could get about without dependence or with so much chauffeuring on your part. The rides and courtesies offered by both *you &* Valerie Jean ~~and yourself~~ have been so heartily appreciated, I could never put my gratitude into words. I will definitely attempt to do some public poem to both yourselves.

Glad you're getting off to Washington in Organization of Historians and also a New U. C. in Chicago! of all places Sat & Sun. April 8th.

How did they go? I am not at home the next 2 or 3 weeks, but <u>temporarily</u> hosp. at Taunton State. Drop me a line at home. My brother and sister are bringing over my mail.

Love, yours.
Jackie non-Auchincloss
Wieners

Thank you also for the agenda of gay doings around Town. Your friend, ever—

Donald Allen
May 27, 1972
[Hanover, MA]

Dear Don:
Tonight I got released from
Taunton State Hospital after two months;   That Long Weekend

---

36 There were a number of homophile groups in Boston in the late 1960s–early 1970s, but Wieners is probably referring to the Student Homophile League. Founded at MIT in 1969, the league regularly sponsored dances until disbanding in December 1972.

got your letter and check. Didn't realize
how faithful you were and bought a bottle
of André champagne and good white wine.
Also had my picture taken, for you too?
I've changed, haven't I. Fresh flowers and
a new Cecil Taylor album New York City R&B.
    Glad you got ensconced in a new home
but I'm sending this to the old address as I've
got it by hand. Hope it reaches you. Forgive
my handwriting, but I'm shaking from tranquillers on an RX.
    My new book just came out. You must get it.
De rigeur, mon darling. Now home from the nearly
$5,000,000 shopping complex here in Hanover,
Massachusetts where I live now. Yours till
death do us part.
       Your indebtor,
       John Wieners

Joanne Kyger
[September 1972]

POEM FROM JOHN W.
I HOPE IT GOES ON[37]

A blinding rain storm behind The Beacon Chambers
      and out in front denizens scatter under
    inclement thunder. Joanne Kyger

moseys down to Brooklyn before Bolinas, this hymn
      shall honor her devotion over 15 years
        to maidenhood blessed by poems.

It's not enough to compare her
      to movie stars, Jane Fonda or Broadway intellectuals
        Breaking shower lightening in Max's Kansas City

---

37 "I Hope It Goes On" was published in *Supplication*.

And as sudden as it started, this downpour ends. Class
      that's what she's got, what gives you a thrill
          listening to her in Bob Creeley's living room

read or dancing out in Berkeley, 1965 after returning from Kyoto.
      Columbus Ave hoyden days, tripping down Telegraph Hill
          I remember her at Halfway House managing

time spheres as deftly as orange plants or egg-plant salads.
      In New York, heroic against warehouse derelicts
      and dressing out middle-class fur coats, for a day on the town.

It's not enough to be simply beautiful, one must manifest
      magnificent sex and brains,
   besides, endurance here in the sunlight by the windows at Annisquam.

                September 1972 John Wieners

                        Robert Duncan
                  February 7, 1973 10PM
                    44 Joy Str [Boston]

Dearest Robert Duncan:

How my heart overbrims with gratitude, pushing away Gerrit's crème de menthe bottle and seeing Ed's poem stick out from a note, that he doesnt, Dorn, know he left here, visiting not so many Sundays ago with cheering reports of you. "How I long for you," the same words return, as prototype of Brahmin Boston, with Joe right down the street—that you should answer my unthinking braggadacio with such alacrity & generosity. Thank you so much, Robert.

I cannot enter into the realm of memory's cohorts by the field of verse, as I lack the discipline you do. Nonetheless, even w/o reading—some force prevents the assimilation of it seems, right now, for so many verse-writers I read, barely more than the poet's early poems. It goes right down the line for most all male writers in this century.

Yet, tho I shall lose energy by writing this, I go into the new poems you sent, with an eager heart.

Beast, of age, of becoming mature, growing up. Beast ~~of~~ *in* acquiring the goods of one's dreams. Finding what one wants.

I treasure what you sent, Robert, knowing it shall replace Denise, whom I have not seen for Three years and who, when Sergei Narovchatov, of the Writer's Union of *in* the U. S. S. R. and Mikhail Lukonin, Commissar of National literature of same nation visited last weekend, could not be bothered until she heard Frieda Lurye was accompanying them. And then she requested a private interview with same at the Statler-Hilton.[38] Alone. But showed up with Rick Edelman. I was not there, by her request. Yet had to arrange the weekend thru ref. of Allen G, who gave my only name to the Council on Leaders & Specialists in Washington. They also had Robert Lowell and John Updike on the list but both out of the country. I have been boiling ever since. Of course I have no right to. She is a far more talented & skillful perceiver and a more widely published author, by a thousand quotients—still I duly idolized & adored her efforts.

Robert, do not get mixed up in politics. It makes one top-heavy. I am being interviewed tomorrow for Gay Sunshine[39] & shall use yourself and early poems as my introduction including this P. M. letter. She also mentioned *over the telephone 1617–739–1016* hearing good reports abt moi et gai liberation.

Robert, I have not mentioned your books, as simply because they are superb *& I do not have the intellect to speak of those books.* But an author needs to know. You were astute with James Broughton and he has turned out a better contributor to poetics *ars poetica* than if you had not kept "after him." I want an even better fate for myself. But I must read. There are so "few." It's not a labor even though [illeg][40]

I want to go back to your letter & poetry now. I have only been home 20 minutes.

A future attachment.

John Wieners

PS.
You are, forgive me, vitally "mixed-up" in politics, but on reflection I believe I mean physically combatant in ideological & verbally as well, ware-fare.

---

38 Sergei Narovchatov, Mikhail Lukonin, and Frieda Lurye were associates of the Union of Writers in the USSR (practically mandatory for Soviet writers), which sponsored cultural exchange tours of the United States in the 1960s and 1970s.

39 *Gay Sunshine* originated as a political magazine produced by the Berkeley Gay Liberation Front but "the staff collective foundered on the shoals of gay politics" (Armstrong, *A Trumpet to Arms*, 250) before ex-priest Winston Leyland revived it in San Francisco as a literary magazine. It featured interviews with gay writers and artists like William Burroughs, Tennessee Williams, Gore Vidal, and Wieners, gathered in two volumes in 1982.

40 "Past"?

Allen Ginsberg
October 3rd 1 9 7 3
[Boston]

Allen Ginsberg:

Yes, I would like to read with you on October 26 in Rogers Hall at BC, if Mr. "Angus" MacLean's invitation still stands for that evening. He called <u>once</u> about it. Entre-nous, only <u>you</u> could handle the complexity of that event, talking to a lamp bulb and singing through a champagne bottle.

If that falls through, nonetheless I will be present somehow for the weekend festival.

[...]

Strange things keep happening to me the last week, because it is September, and the beginning of October, and because the business world has begun again, and school has commenced at Harvard, men going around uncovering my brains in men's bodies. Against my permission they were removed.

Not by cannibals, either. But by highly educated, brilliant men, who had everything in the world to live for, servants as Ezra Pound, to do that for us. Poetry if it ever gets published, my poetry may explain many apothegms, of marriage and wisdom as well as of inheritance. That goes without saying, or True, as the supposed thieves in the living room prove or test.

Then again, The Attorney General's Office is not exempt from them either.[41]

1. We drag around the floor like this.
   2. Cyanide
   3. Ocean Mother   of Romania
   4. Queen Mother   of Prince's Persia
["Sophocles" is written in the left margin, up the side of the page beside the above four items]

1) Idolator of [illeg]

2) Beware loneliness as tariff

---

41 The previous three paragraphs are typewritten, while the rest of the letter is handwritten in a scrawl.

3) Laos s.f. "No ice in"
4) Nice, Cannes, [illeg]

African Life
Corrected handwriting
Adherence to neighborhood
Respect residents of the B C HFM.
[the rest illegible]

Robert Wilson
Saturday November 30, 1974
[Boston]
Thanksgiving Sunny Six

Dearest Robert and The Phoenix Books
   hop W I L S O N.

Ante-Matter Apartment

                          10

Ready to cut down to R A N D A L
L
G I B S O N ' S

Charles Street Coffee United
      Meeting House

then hike out on foot across Henry
L O N G F E L L O W ' S
B R I D G E
for an early evening cinematogr-
APHY; at Massachusetts' Orson Welles
TRIPLE- H O U S ED
ThEATRE—Notwithstanding,
return or in any case plan to
reconnoiter down town
for E S S E X
Street's Playland.[42]

---

42 Playland on Essex Street, Boston's oldest gay bar, established in 1938.

Your most happiness over the
  next balmy December
   Holidays
John WIENERS   Gerald FORD
EVE.   AIRWAVES RADIO
75 11—18—25 T26W17T28 Monday

                    Robert Wilson
                    [Nov 17, 1975]
                    [Boston]
             Jackie Wieners 10
        44 Joy St 723–8376
        Boston Mass 02114
     Attn: H A R V A R D

      Better Forget Her
    Chicago, Chicago, Chicago
Chicago, except for you Russ Durkee
ssgh Chick Schut; you better go,
Peter Marc and Blondie
Rose foes

JOHN WIENERS

Robert Wilson
Sunday January Eighteenth
Eleven-Matin

1976 Forty Ante
[Boston]

Robert A. Wilson—Antiquarian, Bookseller
The Phoenix
22 Jones Str.
New York 1.C.M NY

Dear Bobbie:

Much thanks and seeing you next week, either Thursday even before, for taking 50 paperback editions of Good Gay Poets Two Hundred page 1500 number printing of Behind the State Capitol; Cincinnati PIKE! Hoping it sold you with C H U C K Shively, who called the night before last.

I WANT YOU TO
SPEAK PROPERLY

for as far as we know, in receiving just ac-

KNOWLEDGEMENT

in your past, of establishing their creation, by under-

t a king 1963's Ace of PEN-

tacles.   It just goes to show

how a small testimony demonstrated be-

t w e e n consumer

and c l i e n t e l e merits

1 5 years association

Ever Faithfully in harmony
and legal proportion:
John Wieners

The mid-1980s saw a John Wieners renaissance, thanks to the sustaining labor of his friends and family and the editorial work of **Raymond Foye**, who edited two collections of Wieners's poetry for Black Sparrow Books: *Selected Poems* in 1984 and *Cultural Affairs in Boston* in 1986. The pair of publications brought Wieners glowing coverage throughout the American and British press, with Creeley reviewing *Selected Poems* in the *New York Times*, Fanny Howe in the *Boston Globe*, and Tom Clark in the *Los Angeles Herald Examiner*. In an especially perspicacious review for *Exquisite Corpse*, Joel Lewis notes Wieners's mix of confession and artifice, the roots of its illegibility to institutional poets:

> In this era of nomad MFA-trained poets wandering campus-to-campus in the promotion of their careers & upholding normative middle-class values, Wieners's poetry is needed, as a Great Refusal to the currency of mediocrity. Although the tendency, even among his admirers, is to focus on the tragic scaffolding of his life, his work is more than a sociological document. It is a poetry of great clarity & stylistic innovation.[1]

Cultural Affairs in Boston was the last book of poetry published by John Wieners in his lifetime, though the renewed attention stirred by the new books—and ever-increasing buzz from the New American and Beat poets who'd loved his work all along—led to several more publications of journals.

The following letter was sent from Wieners to **John Martin**, publisher of Black Sparrow Books, regarding his upcoming *Selected Poems*, which was reaching its final planning stages. Martin immediately forwarded the letter to Foye with a note of alarm. Foye called Wieners at his Joy Street apartment and told him of the panic his letter had provoked in Martin, reading it out to him; there was silence before Foye heard Wieners chuckling at the memory.[2]

* * *

---

1 Lewis, "The Lantern on the Wall," 2.
2 Personal e-mail from Raymond Foye.

John Martin
Tuesday, July 9,
1984 [Boston]

Dear Mr. Fredericks
The Sparrow Santa Barbara

re: NIGHT NURSE SAN FRANCISCO CITY HOSPITAL

The title I have chosen is a roman à clef.
"SHE'D TURN   ON   A   DIME.[3]

D Rath.

Whom I don't know: nor any other man could known, [illeg], Petracci!

The pope's mistress is so wealthy, this is construed as a double past AND I would like it to be just NEW poems. but slightly under an hundred pages. My second Book.

Raymond Foye at the Hotel Chelsea repeats over there! And, of course both your wishes will have to be obeyed.

2 other transitional figures are Rathbone's memoirs as dictated by the other double port & the city mestrè Nick Pappas; who has become secondarily Roberto on Broadway Open House I like to think of Lo [–page torn] too, as that overly masculine woman, how to [illeg] the Oak Room, like Gene Tierney, peut-etre Avis d'autre

Regarding: Claire at Breakfast in the Bad and [word cropped] Beautiful with "Arlene-Dahl."

He says that's not what we call her,
Albert has never appealed to me, personally.

A woman's face: Queen Marg. 11 identities
                    Immigration Department.
                    "That pick is the navy blue of India"
                    (Sophie Tucker). age 18

---

3 The final section of Wieners's 1986 *Selected Poems* is called "She'd Turn on a Dime (1984)."

FIGURE 9 John Wieners
with Raymond Foye, 1987.
Photograph by Allen
Ginsberg. Courtesy of the
Allen Ginsberg Estate.

My favorite Comedienne on Broadway: Miss Gertrude Lawrence. That's untrue. You
know of course it's ~~Gree~~ Pompey's inimitable Larry Ross. or myself in that terrible
perf with Eleanor Parker as The King of [illeg]: King of Comedy.

Why does Milton Berle wear women's clothes and [torn] Mexican City raincoat?
Could it be "Mexican H̲ [torn] Cary Grant as [illeg] Wood. [torn]
Projection Room. Loebbs Oriental Theatre.
  John Wieners

Raymond Foye
February 13, 1986
[Boston]

Kid:
  Merci.

One of my dreams has been accomplished!
CITY ORDINANCE MANAGER—
over-burdened as you are, with ordinances in town, it's logical delays took place
OUT WEST.

If Gil, Bill etc. FALL THROUGH it's not our fault. You promise as I. Orlivitz ~~and~~ as MARGOLIS, have taken over.

[illeg] Johnny

Robert Wilson   June

30 Monday 1986
[Boston]

Dear Bob:

On the waterfront at the Boston Docks this morning. At last the title "She'd Turn On a Dime" has appeared as the next to last of same before Dolores. That is [illeg]

Hatfield is hurt because publicity has been so scant. but as Loy off the cuff *spks* may her family suffer their false whore-house blues for whom an empty womb spells . . .

to Miriam back Streets
and North Quincy
SHORE

Gerard Malanga
Aug 22 1989
[Boston]
44 Joy
Beacon Hill

Dear Gerry: (GIN ROSE)

hope I make your deadline.

Since my friend in Prussia, Ted's An American Tragedy has become been displaced: will you accept this page of our current Phillip Morris, likewise? the number and not the end. Recently I read it at the downtown China World Trade Center; it was on the *6th of this month* and I'd have totally forgot about you if you hadn't written.

Dear John

Here goes nothing.

I have nothing *more* to say about it.

Just me in that Geisha's bathing suit with his *the Author's* name stitched on the lapels. To an American fan of M . . .
That's an old one on Geo. Washington's cherry tree. And so are you, mon cher . . .
from Barbara Stanwyck *Miss*, . . . with love.

I have said <u>nothing</u> about BURLESQUE. Unless *as a Nuremberg LEE* you've read Gypsy's story;[4] and who hasn't?!

Of course we remember when she couldn't write either.

But I remember you from the Old Howard.[5]
As a teen-ager consult one.
 Yrs.
  Jackie Wieners

* * *

It is fitting that Wieners's letters would conclude with a note—a Christmas card—to one of his oldest friends, Robin Blaser. Wieners sent the card to an old address at St. Lawrence University, where his friend from thirty years before in Buffalo, Al Glover, found it and forwarded it to Blaser in Vancouver with a note: "<u>Look</u> what arrived in my box today! I haven't seen that hand for years!" And indeed the penmanship in the card is remarkably similar to his earliest letters from the late 1950s, the elegant handwriting of parochial school, as though no time has passed. Wieners has written across the top: "<u>The Black Mountain Review</u>."

* * *

---

4 Burlesque legend Gypsy Rose Lee (1911–1970) published *Gypsy: A Memoir* in 1957.
5 Built by followers of William Miller, one of many end-times prophets of the 1840s, the Old Howard Theatre became a renowned showplace for minstrel and burlesque shows. In 1953, the Boston Board of Censorship shut the theater down, and on June 20, 1961, right before Scollay Square itself was demolished, the Old Howard was destroyed by fire. "Today there are precious few reminders of the Old Howard left in Government Center," David Kruh writes in his history of Scollay Square. "A plaque was placed on the location of the stage (a concrete bench behind One Center Plaza)" (*Always Something Doing*, 84).

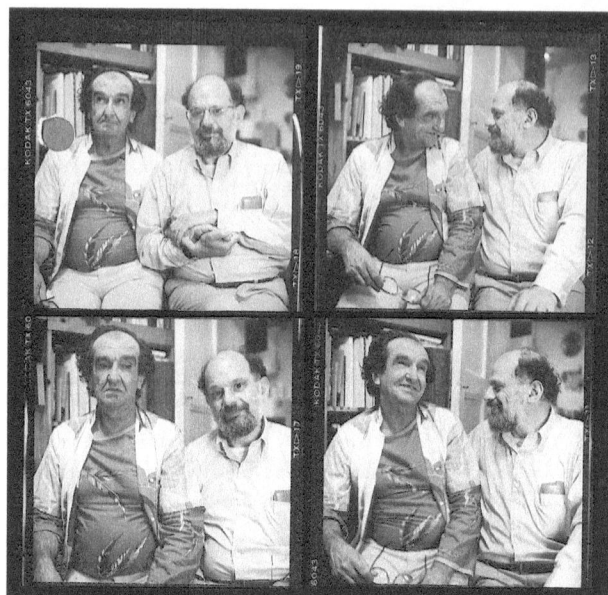

FIGURE 10 Four images of John Wieners with Allen Ginsberg. Photograph by Raymond Foye. Courtesy of Raymond Foye.

Robin Blaser
January 3—[1997]
[Boston]

The Black Mountain Review

Dearest Robin

Just your two-volume edition on the works of "Tatum O'Neal" and I recommend your scrupulous board direction to any, who if I remember correctly, dare broach the subject.

Keep me posted on your new address. Wish I could afford iF.
It's well worth the price
  Wieners
[Card: "Sending you Christmas Greetings and warm wishes for all the delights of the season"]
  and a remunerative year
    ahead
    1997 most
  Jack

HELEN ADAM (1909–1993), Scottish-born balladeer at the heart of the Berkeley–San Francisco Renaissance, member of Jack Spicer's Poetry as Magic workshop, and author of the play *San Francisco's Burning!* Her work has been gathered in Kristin Prevallet's exemplary reclamation project *A Helen Adam Reader* (2007). At the suggestion of Jack Spicer, Allen sent for *Measure* consideration Adam's poem "Apartment on Twin Peaks," with its delightfully spooky subversion of bourgeois marriage:

> Moon over Twin Peaks glittering clear.
> Then I'd whisper in his shrinking ear,
> Like a dentist saying "Open wider,"
> "Don't you want to be a good provider?" (222)

DONALD ALLEN (1912–2004), American publisher, editor, and translator. In 1957 he helped edit the groundbreaking "San Francisco Scene" issue of the *Evergreen Review*, but arguably his greatest legacy is the 1960 anthology *The New American Poetry 1945–1960*, which established a provocative counter to the canon then controlling the poetry establishment (establishing a new canon in the process, with all the attendant problems of anthology canon building). Allen edited Frank O'Hara, notably his *Lunch Poems* and the posthumous *Collected Poems*, and is mentioned in O'Hara's "Personal Poem," in a conversation with LeRoi Jones (Amiri Baraka): "we don't like Lionel Trilling we decide, we like Don Allen." In 1964 he launched the Four Seasons Foundation, a project dedicated to publishing the poets of his *New American Poetry* anthology; he continued that work through 1984. In 1997 Allen coedited with Benjamin Friedlander *The Collected Prose of Charles Olson*.

AMIRI BARAKA (LeRoi Jones) (1934–2014), American writer, publisher, and activist. A native of Newark, New Jersey, Baraka rose to prominence as a poet and playwright in Greenwich Village among the Beats. When Wieners was released from his first hospitalization in 1960, the state would only release him to his parents or a legal guardian, and so Baraka volunteered for that responsibility, helping his friend get back on his feet in New York City. He published *Yugen* magazine from 1958 through 1962, and the first twenty-five issues of *The Floating Bear*, with Diane di Prima, from 1961 through 1963. An issue of *Bear* featuring Baraka's *System of Dante's Hell* and a work by William S. Burroughs resulted in Baraka's arrest in 1961. After a brief show trial he was acquitted. In 1964 he caused a sensation with his intense, confrontational one-act play *The Dutchman*, resulting in a media reputation for controversy. After the assassination of Malcolm X in 1965, he radicalized and moved to Harlem, giving himself the name Amiri Imamu Baraka (the middle name would later be dropped). His *Autobiography of LeRoi Jones* offers a frank depiction of all these phases of development. *The LeRoi Jones / Amiri Baraka Reader* was published by Basic Books in 2000.

BILL BERKSON (1939–2016), American poet, writer, artist, critic, and curator, a New York native at the center of the New York school, with friends Frank O'Hara, Joe Brainard, and Anne Waldman. With Joe LeSueur he edited *Homage to Frank O'Hara*, which included Wieners's memoir piece "Chop House Memories."

WALLACE BERMAN (1926–1976), American artist and publisher, called the "father" of assemblage art, a style of collage-based work he showcased in the exquisite art journal *Semina* from 1955 to 1964, which printed several Wieners poems. He and wife Shirley became close with Wieners during the latter's years in San Francisco in the late 1950s, and Wieners wrote about their time together in "Poem for the beer at Berman's," describing a lazy afternoon at the artist's house:

> Guess who? mixes marijuana and Shirley says
> > the door's open down stairs.
> It is to April 12—an afternoon
> > where I progressively get attached to
> > Stimulants[1]

ROBIN BLASER (1925–2009), American Canadian poet and scholar. He grew up in Idaho but is most closely associated with the Duncan-Spicer circle in Berkeley, with whom he formed the core of its "renaissance" in the late 1940s when the three were students together. He befriended Wieners after moving to Cambridge to work in the Boston libraries. His move to Vancouver in 1966 solidified connections that had been forged at the landmark 1963 Vancouver Poetry Conference. The University of California Press published his collected essays (*The Fire*) in 2006 and his collected poems (*The Holy Forest*) in 2008, both edited by Miriam Nichols. Nichols's literary biography of Blaser, *Mechanic of Splendor*, was published by Palgrave in 2019.

---

1 Wieners letter to Olson April 8, 1958.

JOE BRAINARD (1941–1994), American artist and writer. Brainard moved from the Midwest to New York at nineteen, already friends with Ted Berrigan and Rod Padgett, and very quickly plugged in to the New York poetry and art worlds. He is known especially for his work with collage, one marvelous project collected post-humously as *The Nancy Book* (Siglio Press, 2008). His poetry project *I Remember* was first published by Angel Hair in 1970, with additions and editions released over subsequent decades. He died of AIDS-related pneumonia in 1994.

HARVEY BROWN (1927–1990), American editor and publisher. Son of a wealthy industrial family from Cleveland, Brown arrived in Buffalo in 1964 to study with Charles Olson. He founded *Niagara Frontier Review* (1964–1966) and the Frontier Press, which published twenty-five books and pamphlets. Both *Niagara* and Frontier Press published most of the poets in Wieners's and Olson's circles (including Wieners's *Gardenias for the lady* in 1966) as well as pirate editions of out-of-print books like H. D.'s *Hermetic Definition*.

WILLIAM CORBETT (1942–2018), American poet, writer, teacher, and publisher. With Daniel Bouchard and Joseph Torra he cofounded the poetry magazine *Pressed Wafer*—named after John Wieners's book—in an attempt to revivify the Boston poetry scene at the turn of the new century. After two issues, they began publishing chapbooks and books, putting out work by Fanny Howe, Gerrit Lansing, and many others in the following years. In 2000, along with Joseph Torra and Michael Gizzi, Corbett edited the collection *The Blind See Only This World: Poems for John Wieners*, copublished by Pressed Wafer with Granary Books.

CID CORMAN (1924–2004), American poet and publisher whose work was key for generations of postwar American poets, especially but not limited to his hometown Boston. In the early 1950s, he launched his radio show *This is Poetry*, from Boston's WMEX, putting local and visiting poets like Theodore Roethke and Stephen Spender on the air. At the same time he began publishing his seminal poetry magazine *Origin*, which would publish most of the emergent American avant-garde on and off for the next three decades. His letters from Charles Olson regarding its editorial philosophy and creation were published as *Letters for Origin*, edited by Albert Glover in 1969. He was a voluble and generous correspondent for innumerable young poets and publishers—including young Wieners as he published *Measure*—till the end of his life.

ROBERT CREELEY (1926–2005), American poet and publisher. He established Divers Press and published the *Black Mountain Review*, was a mentor of Wieners's at Black Mountain, and a lifelong friend thereafter. Recordings of Wieners's memorable visits to Creeley's classes at Harvard may be downloaded on PennSound's John Wieners page. After decades of publishing and teaching in New York and New England, Creeley taught in Buffalo's Poetics Program from 1991 until he went to Brown University in 2003, where he taught for the last two years of his life. In his elegy for Wieners, read at his funeral in 2002, Creeley described his old friend:

> Sweet, you might say, impeccable gentleman, like Claude Rains, his
> Boston accent held each word a particular obligation and value.
> I see his face as still a young man, in San Francisco, hearing him
> Talking with Joanne, hearing him talk with Joe Dunn, with friends.

DIANE DI PRIMA (b. 1934), American poet, scholar, and teacher. Raised in New York City, she was a prime force behind the Lower East Side and Beat poetry scenes and, later, the Diggers in San Francisco. In addition to publishing more than forty books, she has cofounded several indispensable arts publications and organizations including *The Floating Bear* (1962–1969), the New York Poets' Theatre, the Poets Institute, and the San Francisco Institute of Magical and Healing Arts. From 1963 to 1969 she ran the Poets Press, publishing nearly thirty books by a diverse array of poets. In 2009 she was named Poet Laureate of San Francisco, where she has lived since the late 1960s.

ED DORN (1929–1999), American poet and scholar, a child of the Great Depression in rural Illinois and, like Wieners, a student and friend of Charles Olson. His first two books, *The Newly Fallen* (1961) and *Hands Up!* (1964), were published by Leroi Jones (Amiri Baraka)'s Totem Press. *Hands Up!* contains Dorn's essential meditation on poverty, labor, and American rhetoric, "On the Debt My Mother Owed to Sears Roebuck." Dorn's best-known work, an often comic epic called *Gunslinger*, was published in six parts between 1968 and 1975, and in a complete edition in 1989 by Duke University Press. His *Collected Poems*, edited by Jennifer Dunbar Dorn, was published by Carcanet Press in 2012. After traveling the American West and teaching writing at colleges in England and around the United States, he became a professor of creative writing at the University of Colorado in Boulder, where he taught from 1978 until his death in 1999. In 2012 Carcanet Press published a massive edition of Dorn's *Collected Poems*, edited by Jennifer Dunbar Dorn.

ROBERT DUNCAN (1919–1988), major American poet, early gay liberation figure (his landmark essay "The Homosexual in Society" was published in 1944), and one of

Wieners's Black Mountain mentors. He first met John Wieners at Black Mountain the summer of 1955, when the young Wieners was one of ten students remaining, and Duncan wrote to Robin Blaser that in his dorm room Wieners had "lines of Pound written on the paint with frames over each."[2] His review of Wieners's *Hotel Wentley Poems* and *Ace of Pentacles* for the *Nation*, in May 1965, placed his former student among "not only the poets but seers and prophets [who] have reiterated the ultimate value of an ecstasy that is identified with sexual orgasm, with sight beyond sight, with divine or demonic inspiration."[3] Robert Duncan's collected works were published by the University of California Press as *The Collected Early Poems and Plays* (2012, edited by Peter Quartermain), *The Collected Later Poems and Plays* (2014, edited by Quartermain), and *Collected Essays and Other Prose* (2014, edited by James Maynard). His decades-spanning project *The H. D. Book,* edited by Michael Boughn and Victor Coleman, was published by the University of California Press in 2011.

JOE DUNN (1934–1996), American poet and publisher. Dunn grew up with Wieners in Boston, and with his wife Carolyn stayed fast friends with him from Boston to Black Mountain to San Francisco. In *Black Mountain Days*, Michael Rumaker describes Joe Dunn as "even smaller and sparer in build than John, with skin so pale it seemed never to have known sunlight" and an "almost angelically boyish face."[4] The Dunns, like Wieners in those days, were perpetually poor and smoking. They moved to San Francisco before Wieners did, holding court at their apartment in Polk Gulch; Dunn was an instant crush for North Beach center of gravity Jack Spicer. Tom Field described the couple as "pre-punk, proto-punk," Carolyn with green makeup, the apartment "dumpy" and dark[5]. When Dunn got a job at the Greyhound Bus Company's Print Department, his boss allowed him to use the equipment for free nights and Saturdays, as long as he provided the paper stock, and so White Rabbit Press was born, publishing Wieners's friend from Boston Stephen Jonas's *Love, the Poem, the Sea and Other Pieces Examined* as its first book. It was soon followed by Jack Spicer's *After Lorca*. After Joe's descent into harder drug use, the couple split, and Joe moved back to Massachusetts, where he cleaned up and spent the rest of his life writing and teaching, leading Monday night classes for Stone Soup Poetry, a venue and collective founded in 1971 by Jack Powers at the foot of Beacon Hill. In 2015, Carolyn Dunn, with Kevin Killian, published a revelatory memoir of her time with Joe, titled *Eyewitness: From Black Mountain to White Rabbit*, for Granary Books.

---

2 Jarnot, *Robert Duncan: The Ambassador from Venus*, 158.
3 Ibid., 241.
4 Michael Rumaker, *Black Mountain Days,* 429.
5 Ellingham and Killian, *PBLG*, 108.

DANA DURKEE, a tall blonde volunteer firefighter, was Wieners's live-in lover in Boston, and then off and on while Wieners was at Black Mountain. He moved with Wieners to San Francisco in September 1957 but did not last long before moving back to Boston. Robert Greene remembers him from Boston College, and later, when Wieners and Dana lived on Beacon Hill:

> He played football in high school, and he played in the navy. So he had gone to an academic program at St. Mary's, so he was prepared to go to college, but he joined the navy right after high school. Then when they reinstated the GI Bill, he was eligible for it. So he went to BC on the GI Bill for that period of time ... I think he still did some work as a fireman during the summers up in Swampscott ... John and Dana, especially John, organized readings at their apartment. They would get people to read, you know, people passing through Boston, the poets they knew.[6]

LAWRENCE FERLINGHETTI (b. 1919), American poet, artist, activist, and owner of City Lights Booksellers in San Francisco since 1953. After serving in the navy, Ferlinghetti returned to graduate school on the GI Bill, earning a master's at Columbia and then a PhD at the University of Paris in 1951. By the time he arrived in San Francisco, the Berkeley Renaissance had morphed into a burgeoning arts and poetry reading scene in San Francisco, where his City Lights, and its Pocket Poet series, acted as community center and catalyst.

RAYMOND FOYE (b. 1957), American publisher and editor. After a childhood in Lowell, Massachusetts—Kerouac was on his paper route—Foye befriended Allen Ginsberg, first meeting him when Ginsberg was en route to see Wieners, whose virtues as a poet Ginsberg excitedly extolled. That mission ended in failure but Foye returned, becoming good friends with Wieners in the 1980s. At that time, Foye spearheaded a renaissance for Wieners's work by editing *Selected Poems* (1986) and *Cultural Affairs in Boston* (1988), which garnered widespread, glowing reviews. In 1986 Foye cofounded, with Francesco Clemente, Hanuman Books, a small press of small books, handmade miniatures by a wide array of Beat, New York, and other writers, including two by John Wieners.

ALLEN GINSBERG (1926–1997), American poet, teacher, and activist who formed, with Jack Kerouac and William S Burroughs, the core of the first Beat movement. In

---

6 Robert Greene, unpublished interview with Robert Dewhurst.

1955 his reading of "Howl" at the Six Gallery, followed by the poem's publication and its obscenity trial, made him into something almost unheard of in twentieth-century American poetry: a household name. In his letters to others, Wieners jokingly refers to him as "Ginsbergmessiah," but their correspondence makes it clear that theirs was an enduring friendship based on mutual respect and commitment to the poem. With poets Anne Waldman and Diane di Prima he founded the Jack Kerouac Institute of Disembodied Poetics at the Naropa Institute in Colorado; it is still a thriving program that merges poetry, performance, other arts, and Buddhist practice.

PANNA GRADY, arts patron with whom Wieners had a love affair in the summer of 1966. Ralph Maud writes that Grady's "circle in the early '60s, maintained by what seemed magical wealth in such a young person, was wide and appreciative." Ed Sanders' *Fuck You: a magazine of the arts*, gave its "FIRST ANNUAL FUCK YOU PRESS AWARD FOR DISTINGUISHED SERVICE TO THE ARTS" to Grady in 1965, for her "incredible generosity, kindness, tenderness, and benevolence in dealing with many freaky neurasthenic artists, poets, moviemakers, magicians, etc. on the N. Y. scene."[7] She lives in the South of France.

ROBERT GREENE, American teacher, Korean War veteran, and friend of Wieners's from Boston College in the early 1950s. They worked together at the student literary magazine, *The Stylus*, and continued their friendship through letters.

BARBARA GUEST (1920–2006), American poet and writer associated with the New York school. Her first books were published in the early 1960s by New York–based Tibor de Nagy and Corinth, the publishing arm of the 8th Street Book Shop. In 1984 she published a biography of H. D. titled *Herself Defined*. Her *Collected Poems* was published by Wesleyan University Press in 2008.

DAVID HASELWOOD (1931–2013), American publisher and Buddhist monk. After serving in the US Army in the mid-1950s, Haselwood settled in San Francisco, where he founded the Auerhahn Press, producer of elegant letterpress books under his direction (with Andrew Hoyem) from 1958 to 1964, at which time he left to form an imprint under his own name. Auerhahn's first book was John Wieners's 1958 breakout volume *The Hotel Wentley Poems*. When the book's printers censored the word *cocksuckers* in one title, blanking out *cock*, Haselwood was so incensed he learned how to print so that he could handle every aspect of the publishing

---

7 Maud, *Charles Olson at the Harbor*, 197.

process himself. The reprint of *Hotel Wentley*, published by Dave Haselwood Books, features the restored title "A poem for cocksuckers." He was a Zen Buddhist monk for many years, living and teaching beginning in 2000 at Stone Creek Zen Center in Sonoma.

ANDREW HOYEM (b. 1935), American printer, publisher, and poet. In 1961 he became a partner in Auerhahn Press with Dave Haselwood, and in the 1970s founded Arion Press.

STEPHEN JONAS (1925?–1970), American poet and fixture on the Bohemian north side of Beacon Hill, a gay interracial Ezra Pound devotee who was possibly from New Orleans. He befriended Spicer and Blaser during their Boston sojourn, remaining close to Wieners and Dunn, whom Wieners introduced to Jonas at Olson's 1954 reading. An autodidact with broad interests, Jonas's apartment was a place for poets and "a nexus of various underworld activities," as Joseph Torra notes in his illuminating introduction to Jonas's *Selected Poems* (6). In his 1965 introduction to Jonas's *Transmutations*, Wieners laments the destruction wrought by urban renewal, talks about the growing national debt, remembering

> You cannot move
> faster than the shutter of my mind.
> Those old elms bend over
> the street and form an arch
> that we walk under.
> Sad priests in the 20th century.
> We began the second half
> together.[8]

He died unexpectedly on February 10, 1970, exactly a month after Olson passed away. In 2019 City Lights Books published *Arcana: A Stephen Jonas Reader*, edited by Garrett Caples and Derek Fenner.

BASIL KING (b. 1935), British-born American painter and writer who arrived at age sixteen to study art at Black Mountain College before marrying Martha Winston (b. 1937), memoirist and novelist, and moving to New York City. His signature style can be found on the cover designs of many books and small magazines, including the pivotal *Yugen*. His recent memoir, *Learning to Draw / A History*, interlaces poetry

---

8 Wieners, *Cultural Affairs in Boston*, 31.

and prose to create a vivid introductory text to his body of work. In addition to her fiction and poetry, Martha Winston King published a magnificent memoir of their lives together, *Outside/Inside: just outside the art world's inside* in 2018 with BlazeVOX books.

JOANNE KYGER (1934–2017), American poet at the heart of the most vibrant aspects of North American poetry and poetics since moving to San Francisco in 1957. Associated with Jack Spicer's circle around the North Beach bar The Place and Joe Dunn's White Rabbit Press, she was close to Wieners during his time in San Francisco, immortalized as "Miss Kids" in his memoir *The Journal of John Wieners is to be called 707 Scott Street for Billie Holiday, 1959*, the name taken from the Victorian house they shared on Alamo Square Park. In 1960 she moved with Gary Snyder to Japan, marrying him and traveling on (with Ginsberg in tow) to India. Upon returning she published her first book of poems, *The Tapestry and the Web*, and in 2000 her travel writings, *Strange Big Moon: Japan and India Journals, 1960–1964*, were republished by North Atlantic. *Joanne Kyger: Letters to and From*, edited by Kyger with Ammiel Alcalay, was published as part of the Lost & Found: CUNY Poetics Document Initiative in 2012.

GERRIT LANSING (1928–2018), American poet and scholar who spent decades at the center of Gloucester and Boston's poetry and arts communities. After studying at Harvard (where he was tennis partners with John Ashbery) and Columbia Universities, he published two issues of the literary journal *Set*. His essays and criticism, *A February Sheaf*, came out in 2003, and his collected poetry, *Heavenly Tree, Northern Earth*, in 2009.

ROBERT LAVIGNE (1928–2014), American artist and theatrical set designer long associated with the San Francisco Beats and avant-garde communities. He was the art director for Auerhahn Press, and drew Wieners's portrait for *The Hotel Wentley Poems* in 1958. Those poems were written while Wieners stayed with LaVigne at the titular hotel, writing while LaVigne drew. He pioneered the style of psychedelic painting and worked as a celebrated illustrator and Obie award winning set designer.

DENISE LEVERTOV (1923–1997), British American poet. She moved to the United States at twenty-five, and her work reflects a lifelong engagement with the American idiom, notably via William Carlos Williams. Her poetry is deeply invested in nature, politics, and faith, and her poetry criticism is sharply observed and catholic in its scope. Her essay collection *The Poet in the World* (New Directions, 1973) includes the glowing review of Wieners's *Ace of Pentacles* she published in *The Nation* in 1965, and her *Collected Poems* was released in 2013, as was a new biography by Donna Hollenberg, *A Poet's Revolution*. Her highly charged correspondence with Robert Duncan (Stanford, 2004) is a must-read for any student of New American poetry and the antiwar movement.

GERARD MALANGA (b. 1943), American poet, artist, archivist, and filmmaker. He worked as Andy Warhol's most trusted associate from 1963 through 1970, doing much of the screenprinting work and acting in several films. Along with peers John Ashbery, Allen Ginsberg, and many other people, Wieners was filmed by Malanga for the Screen Test series he produced with Warhol in the mid-1960s.

ALAN MARLOWE, American writer, director, and performer, cofounder with Diane di Prima of the New York Poets' Theatre in 1961. An out gay man, he was married to di Prima from 1962 to 1969, a volatile relationship detailed in di Prima's *Recollections of My Life as a Woman*. He spent much of his later life at the San Francisco Zen Center as a student of Shunryu Suzuki, popularizer of Zen Buddhism in America.

EDWARD MARSHALL (1932–2005), whose poem "Leave the Word Alone" appeared in *Black Mountain Review* number 7 and then in Donald Allen's 1960 anthology *The New American Poetry*; Ginsberg would later credit it as a strong influence on his own "mother poem," "Kaddish." David Abel, whose tireless work on Marshall is bringing about exciting discoveries about this neglected poet, has helped piece together some biography:

> He moved to Boston in 1953, where he met and roomed with the poet
> Stephen Jonas, who introduced him, Marshall was reputed to have said, "to
> poetry and to love." Marshall's other profound love . . . was religion, and
> at this time he enjoyed a period of public preaching on Boston Common.
> Through Jonas, Marshall met John Wieners (recently back from Black
> Mountain College) and Joe Dunn, and began writing poetry. In late 1955,
> Marshall sent the recently completed long poem "Leave the Word Alone"
> to Charles Olson . . . Olson was very excited by it, and wrote to Marshall:
> "That's a fine thing you've done here, Marshall—very *true*, and *quick*, very
> *thick*. It *speaks* very much. It is *very* personal and formal at once. And *form-wise* it is very true—the peopling, the protests, the end." The following
> spring it circulated among students at the college (including Michael
> Rumaker); Robert Duncan, in an interview, recalled that at the time it was
> "the exciting poem for everybody at Black Mountain." (n.p.)

In 1960, Auerhahn Press published Marshall's *Hellan, Hellan*; *Transit Glory* followed in 1965. Wieners writes movingly of Marshall's importance in his 1965 journal in an essay called "Road of Straw" (named for Rhoda Straw, the near-mythic grandmother in "Leave the Word Alone") (*Stars Seen in Person*, pp.124-29).

JOHN MARTIN (b. 1930), American publisher, founder of Black Sparrow Press in 1966. Martin is best known for launching and helping to sustain Charles Bukowski, but he also published many of the New American poets, including Diane Wakoski and Wieners, whose two culminating collections—*Selected Poems* and *Cultural Affairs in Boston: Poetry and Prose 1956–1985*—were released by Black Sparrow in 1986 and 1988, respectively. In 2002 Martin retired after thirty-six years of publishing, selling Black Sparrow's catalog to David R. Godine.

MICHAEL MCCLURE (1932-2020), American poet and writer who was central to the San Francisco scene—in all its permutations—since the 1950s. He was one of the poets who performed at the famous Six Gallery reading in 1955, and his first book, *Passage*, was published by Black Mountain alumnus Jonathan Williams's Big Sur Press in 1956.

DUNCAN MCNAUGHTON (b. 1942), American poet, writer, and teacher. A Boston native, McNaughton studied Classics at NYU before going on to Princeton and Buffalo, where he earned his PhD in English Literature and Poetics. It was at Buffalo that McNaughton befriended Wieners; he published Wieners's work in both of his small magazines, *MOTHER* and *FATHAR*. After Buffalo, McNaughton helped establish the poetics program at the New College of California in San Francisco, which in many ways continued the educational tradition of Black Mountain College.

W. S. MERWIN (1927–2019), American poet. He and Wieners first overlapped when Merwin was Playwright-in-Residence at the Cambridge Poets' Theatre 1956–1957, but they went on to share many connections, through East Coast poetry centers and the antiwar movement. A Pulitzer Prize Winner for Poetry, he was named Poet Laureate of the United States in 2010.

FRANK O'HARA (1926–1966), American poet at the center of the New York school of poets and painters. He helped Wieners place his first published poem, "With J. R. Morton," at a magazine called *Semi-Colon*. The two remained close friends until O'Hara's death in 1966. Wieners's poignant memoir of their friendship, "Chop House Memories," was published by Bill Berkson and Joe LeSueur in the collage-style *Homage to Frank O'Hara* in 1980.

CHARLES OLSON (1910–1970), American poet and scholar. He worked for the American Civil Liberties Union and then the Office of War Information in Washington, DC, as well as the Democratic National Committee and the Roosevelt campaign, but grew disillusioned, and in 1944 he gave up government work for poetry. From 1951 through 1956 he served as professor and then rector at western North Carolina's experimental Black Mountain College, where he taught and befriended John Wieners. After Black Mountain, Olson settled in Gloucester, except for two years in Buffalo, New York, where he directed the State University's new poetics program, which aimed to be a "Black Mountain II." Throughout these post–Black Mountain years, Olson continued to work on his *Maximus Poems*, which remain unfinished. He died just after his fifty-ninth birthday and is buried in Gloucester.

IRVING ROSENTHAL (b. 1930), American publisher and writer. In the late 1950s he edited the *Chicago Review* and *Big Table*; after the former was censored for printing William Burroughs, the latter was formed in protest. He wrote one novel, *Sheeper* (1967, Grove Press). Though he hadn't been friends with John Wieners prior to Wieners's first hospitalization in 1960, they formed an immediate rapport through correspondence, their experiences as young gay men—and iconoclastic publishers—giving them an instant connection. Rosenthal lobbied friends and Wieners's family for his release, but it was six months before this was effected. He was also a great supporter of Wieners's old friend Edward Marshall's poetry; in the late 1960s, with funding from Panna Grady Rosenthal, he formed Carp & Whitefish, a press whose sole expressed intention was to put Marshall's verse in print. They planned a series of books based around different themes, but only the first of these, *Transit Glory*, themed around travel, was released, in 1967.

MICHAEL RUMAKER (1932–2019), fiction writer, poet, and memoirist, close friend of Wieners, and, along with Wieners and Ed Dorn, one of Olson's most acclaimed students. His trilogy of memoirs, *Black Mountain Days*, *A Day and a Night at the Baths*, and *My First Satyrnalia*, give invaluable and uniquely crafted insight into queer and artistic life in the postwar and early gay liberation years. *Black Mountain Days* shows an especially tender portrayal of young John Wieners, at the point when he and Rumaker were fellow Cold War queers living in the very masculine environment of Black Mountain in its final days. His fascinating and lively book *Robert Duncan in San Francisco* was republished by City Lights with a new interview and selection of letters, edited by Megan Paslawski and Ammiel Alcalay, in 2013.

ED SANDERS (b. 1939), American poet, writer, activist, and musician. Sanders created and edited *Fuck You/ A Magazine of the Arts* from 1962 to 1965, and operated the activist workspace and asylum the Peace Eye Bookstore on the Lower East Side throughout the 1960s. A founding Yippie and Fug, Sanders is pioneer of what he calls "Investigative Poetry," a "history-poesy" movement that pursued traditionally "non-literary" lines of inquiry into history or philosophy using poetic modes[9]; as he wrote in his manifesto for City Lights, the new movement would take its cue from a line of Ginsberg's: "Now is the time for prophecy without death as a consequence."

JAMES SCHUYLER (1923–1991), American poet, artist, and critic. After two years spent in Italy as W. H. Auden's secretary, Schuyler moved into a New York apartment with Frank O'Hara and John Ashbery, with whom he would form the founding trio of the New York school of poets. He met John Wieners back in 1956, when both young poets were working in the Cambridge Poets' Theatre. Like O'Hara he worked as a curator at the Museum of Modern Art, and his art criticism appeared frequently in *Art News*. He won the Pulitzer Prize for his 1980 collection *The Morning of the Poem*.

CHARLES SHIVELY (1937–2017), American poet, activist, teacher, and editor in Boston. His two books on Walt Whitman, *Calamus Lovers* and *Drum Beats*, were both published by Gay Sunshine Press. He worked for many years with *Gay Sunshine*, as well as Boston's *Fag Rag*, two groundbreaking gay liberation publications. He went on to cofound the Good Gay Poets Press, which published Wieners's *Behind the State Capitol or the Cincinnati Pike* in 1975. He became friends with the older poet Wieners while the latter was hospitalized in 1969; their correspondence grew into a lifelong friendship. Shively was with him the night Wieners collapsed in 2002, and later at the hospital when he passed away. Shively later gave their complete correspondence to Boston gay liberation activist and bookstore owner John Mitzel, who made bound copies available for anyone who asked.

GARY SNYDER (b. 1930), American poet, scholar, and translator, longtime Buddhist and deep ecology activist. Snyder was married from 1960 to 1965 to Joanne Kyger, living in Japan and traveling around Asia with Kyger, Allen Ginsberg, and Peter Orlovsky. Snyder was immortalized as the hero of Jack Kerouac's *Dharma Bums*, Thoreauvian Zen trickster Japhy Ryder.

JACK SPICER (1925–1965), American poet, with Robert Duncan and Robin Blaser formed the nucleus of the Berkeley–San Francisco Renaissance. His Poetry as Magic

---

9 Ed Sanders, *Investigative Poetry*, 11.

workshop in 1957 gathered many of the poets—including Joanne Kyger, Helen Adam, George Stanley, and Joe Dunn—who would become Wieners's closest friends when he moved to the city.

ANNE WALDMAN (b. 1945), American poet, publisher, and educator, former director of the St. Mark's Poetry Project in New York, and cofounder of the Jack Kerouac Institute for Disembodied Poetics at Naropa University. Electrified by the 1965 Berkeley Poetry Conference, Waldman came to New York and worked at the nexus of Beat and second-generation New York school poetics, and increasingly engaged with Tibetan Buddhism.

PHILIP WHALEN (1923–2002), American poet known for his deep commitments to Zen Buddhism and ecology in his life as well as his poetics. Whalen served in the army in World War II and afterward attended Oregon's Reed College on the GI Bill, where he befriended Lew Welch and Gary Snyder. An integral part of the San Francisco Beat community, he was one of the Six Gallery readers in 1955, and his poems were published in the San Francisco section of *The New American Poetry*. Dave Haselwood's Auerhahn published two of Whalen's first three books, in the two years after Wieners's *Hotel Wentley Poems* inaugurated the press. His *Collected Poems* were published in 2007 by Wesleyan University Press. A critical edition of his journals, edited by Brian Unger, is forthcoming from the University of Alabama Press.

JONATHAN WILLIAMS (1929–2008), a Black Mountain student of Olson, scion of a wealthy family in the Swannanoa area, and classmate of Wieners. He was founder of the Jargon Society (while he was still serving in the army), a small press that published, among many other books, Olson's *Maximus Poems* 1–10 in 1953, then 11–22 in 1956, and in collaboration with Eli and Ted Wilentz of the 8th Street Bookshop, what became the first volume of *Maximus* (Jargon/Corinth) in 1960.

ROBERT WILSON (1922–2016), American bibliographer, bookseller, publisher, and writer. Wilson owned the Phoenix Bookshop in Greenwich Village, a haven for Beat and other poets, from 1962 till it closed in 1988, later writing a memoir of that time called *Seeing Shelley Plain* (2001). In 1964, with James Carr, Wilson published Wieners's second poetry collection, *Ace of Pentacles*.

Abel, David. "Edward Marshall." *The Text Garage*, May 22, 2013.

Adam, Helen. *A Helen Adam Reader*. Edited by Kristin Prevallet. Orono, ME: National Poetry Foundation, 2007.

Alcalay, Ammiel. *a little history*. Brooklyn, NY: UpSet Press, 2012.

Allen, Donald. Letters to John Wieners, Donald Allen Papers at the University of California at San Diego.

———, ed. *The New American Poetry*. New York: Grove, 1960.

Anastas, Peter. "Olson Is Gone, But We Are Here." *Enduring Gloucester*. December 28, 2014, https://enduringgloucester.com/2014/12/28/olson-is-gone-but-we-are-here-2/.

Angell, Callie. *Andy Warhol Screen Tests*. New York: Abrams in Association with the Whitney Museum of American Art, 2006.

Armstrong, David. *A Trumpet to Arms: Alternative Media in America*. Boston: South End, 1981.

"Archive Catalogue." *The Poetry Center*. San Francisco State University, 2006.

Ballard, Micah. *Negative Capability in the Verse of John Wieners*. Oakland: Bootstrap, 2017.

Baraka, Amiri, and Ed Dorn. *Selections From the Collected Letters: 1959–1960*. Edited by Claudia Moreno Pisano. Lost and Found: The CUNY Poetics Documents Initiative, Series 1, Number 1, Winter 2009.

Beam, Alex. *Gracefully Insane: The Rise and Fall of America's Premier Mental Hospital*. New York: Public Affairs, 2001.

Blake, William. *The Complete Poetry & Prose of William Blake*. Edited by David V. Erdman. New York: Random House, 1988.

Berkson, Bill, and Joe LeSueur, eds. *Homage to Frank O'Hara*. Berkeley, CA: Creative Arts Book Co., 1980.

Bertholf, Robert J. "Robert Duncan's 'The Venice Poem' and Symphonic Form." *Jacket* 28, October 2005, http://jacketmagazine.com/28/dunc-bert-vpessay.html.

Bertholf, Robert J. and Albert Gelpi, ed. *The Letters of Robert Duncan and Denise Levertov*. Stanford, CA: Stanford University Press, 2003.

Birmingham, Jed. "William S Burroughs and John Wieners' *Measure*." *RealityStudio*, October 15, 2016, https://realitystudio.org/bibliographic-bunker/william-s-burroughs-and-john-wieners-measure/.

Blaser, Robin. *The Astonishment Tapes*. Edited by Miriam Nichols. Tuscaloosa: University of Alabama Press, 2015.

Butterick, George F. *A Guide to the Maximus Poems of Charles Olson*. Los Angeles: University of California Press, 1980.

Clay, Steven, and Rodney Phillips. *A Secret Location on the Lower East Side: Adventures in Writing, 1960–1980*. New York: Granary Books, 1998.

Corbett, William. "A letter from William Corbett." *Minutes of the Charles Olson Society* 26 (June 1998), http://charlesolson.org/Files/Corbett.htm.

Creeley, Robert. *The Collected Essays of Robert Creeley*. Berkeley: University of California Press, 1989.

———. Robert Creeley Papers. M0662. Special Collections & University Archives, Stanford University.

Dahlberg, Edward. "Moby-Dick: An Hamitic Dream." *Alms for Oblivion: Essays*. Minneapolis: University of Minnesota Press, 1964.

Dawson, Fielding. *The Black Mountain Book*. Boston: E. P. Dutton, 1970.

D'Emilio, John. *Sexual Politics, Sexual Communities: The Making of a Homosexual Minority in the United States, 1940–1970*. Chicago: University of Chicago Press, 1983.

Dewhurst, Robert. "Measure: A Quarterly to the Poem, 1957–1962." *Let the Bucket Down* no. 1 (2013).

Di Prima, Diane. *Recollections of My Life as a Woman: The New York Years, A Memoir*. New York: Viking, 2001.

Di Prima, Diane, and LeRoi Jones, eds. *The Floating Bear: a newsletter, Numbers 1–37, 1961–1969*. La Jolla, CA: Laurence McGilvery, 1973.

Dorn, Ed. *Ed Dorn Live: Lectures, Interviews, and Outtakes*. Ann Arbor: University of Michigan Press, 2007.

———. "Notes from the fields." *Measure* 2, (Winter 1958): 29–31.

Duberman, Martin. *Black Mountain: An Experiment in Community*. New York: Dutton, 1972.

Duncan, Robert. *The Collected Early Poems and Plays*. Edited by Peter Quartermain. Berkeley: University of California Press, 2012.

———. *The H. D. Book*. Edited by Michael Boughn and Victor Coleman. Berkeley: University of California Press, 2011.

———. Letters to John Wieners. John Wieners Papers, Special Collections Research Center, Syracuse University Libraries.

———. *A Poet's Mind: Collected Interviews With Robert Duncan, 1960–1985*. Edited by Christopher Wagstaff. Berkeley, CA: North Atlantic Books, 2012.

———. *A Selected Prose*. Edited by Robert J. Bertholf. New York: New Directions, 1995.

Ellingham, Lewis, and Kevin Killian. *Poet Be Like God: Jack Spicer and the San Francisco Renaissance*. Hanover, NH: University Press of New England for Wesleyan University Press, 1998.

Fenollosa, Ernest, and Ezra Pound. *The Chinese Written Character as a Medium for Poetry: A Critical Edition*. Edited by Haun Saussy, Jonathan Stalling, and Lucas Klein. New York: Fordham University Press, 2008.

"Found: Charles Olson Gave a Legendary (& Pretty Drunk) Reading at the 1965 Berkeley Poetry Conference." *Harriet* (blog). Poetry Foundation, June 11, 2012. https://www.poetryfoundation.org/harriet/2012/06/found-charles-olson-gave-a-legendary-pretty-drunk-reading-at-the-1965-berkeley-poetry-conference.

Galenson, David W. *Old Masters and Young Geniuses: The Two Life Cycles of Artistic Creativity.* Princeton: Princeton University Press, 2006.

Gilman, Arthur, ed. "Astrological Terms and Divisions of Time." *Poetical Works of Geoffrey Chaucer.* Vol. 1. Boston: Houghton, 1879.

Ginsberg, Allen. "Allen Ginsberg on John Wieners—part one." *The Allen Ginsberg Project,* January 4, 2014, https://allenginsberg.org/2014/01/allen-ginsberg-on-john-wieners-part-one/.

———. *Collected Poems: 1947–1980.* New York: Harper & Row, 1984.

Ginsberg, Allen, and Louis Ginsberg. *Family Business: Selected Letters Between a Father and Son.* Edited by Michael Schumacher. New York: Bloomsbury, 2001.

Ginsberg, Allen, and Neal Cassady. *As Ever: The Collected Correspondence of Allen Ginsberg & Neal Cassady.* Berkeley, CA: Creative Arts Book Co, 1977.

Golden, Eve. *Golden Images: 41 Essays on Silent Film Stars.* Jefferson, NC: McFarland, 2001.

Gooch, Brad. *City Poet: The Life and Times of Frank O'Hara.* New York: Knopf, 1993.

Gosse, Van. *Where the Boys Are: Cuba, Cold War America and the Making of a New Left.* New York: Verso, 1993.

Greene, Robert. Robert Dewhurst unpublished telephone interview with Robert Greene, February 21, 2013. Transcript.

Greetham, D. C. *Textual Scholarship: An Introduction.* New York: Garland, 1994.

Hartley, Marsden. *The Collected Poems of Marsden Hartley: 1904–1943.* Edited by Gail R. Scott. Santa Rosa, CA: Black Sparrow, 1987.

H.D. *Trilogy.* New York: New Directions, 1998.

Holder, Doug. "Interview with Stone Soup Poets founder Jack Powers." *AuthorsDen.* May 23, 2005, http://www.authorsden.com/visit/viewarticle.asp?AuthorID=3792&id=18280.

Hollenberg, Donna Krolik. *A Poet's Revolution: The Life of Denise Levertov.* Berkeley: University of California Press, 2013.

Holt, John. *Instead of Education: Ways to Help People Do Things Better.* New York: Dutton, 1976.

Howard, Richard. "John Wieners: 'Now Watch the Windows Open by Themselves." *Iowa Review* 1, no. 1 (Winter 1970): 101–7.

Jarnot, Lisa. *Robert Duncan: The Ambassador from Venus.* Berkeley: University of California Press, 2012.

Jonas, Stephen. *Selected Poems.* Edited by Joseph Torra. Hoboken, NY: Talisman House, 1994.

Kane, Daniel. *All Poets Welcome: The Lower East Side Poetry Scene in the 1960s.* Berkeley: University of California Press, 2003.

Keats, John. *Selected Letters.* Edited by Robert Gittings. Oxford: Oxford University Press, 2009.

Kerouac, Jack, and Allen Ginsberg. *Jack Kerouac and Allen Ginsberg: The Letters.* Edited by Bill Morgan and David Stanford. New York: Viking, 2010.

Kimmelman, Burt. "The William Bronk-Charles Olson Correspondence." *Otoliths: A Magazine of Many E-Things*. April 2010, https://the-otolith.blogspot.com/2010/04/poet-editors-2-burt-kimmelman-william.html.

King, Basil. *mirage: a poem in 22 sections*. New York: Marsh Hawk, 2003.

———. Unpublished interview with Martha Winston King and Robert Dewhurst, January 2, 2012. Transcript.

King, Martha Winston. "Another Summer of Poverty 1966." *Blazevox* (Spring 2011), http://www.blazevox.org/spring11/Martha%20King%20Spring%2011.pdf.

———. "Seventy Years Ago in the South." *Big Bridge* (2013), https://bigbridge.org/BB17/chapbooks/martha_king/martha_king1.html.

———. "Three Months in 1955: A Memoir of Black Mountain College." *Jacket* (2010,) http://jacketmagazine.com/40/king-martha-black-mountain.shtml.

Knight, Brenda. "Return of the Prodigal Poet—ruth weiss in San Francisco Festival July 24." *San Francisco Examiner*, July 22, 2000.

Kramer, Samuel Noah. *Sumerian Mythology: Study of Spiritual and Literary Achievement in the Third Millennium B.C.* Philadelphia: American Philosophical Society, 1944.

Kruh, David. *Always Something Doing: Boston's Infamous Scollay Square*. Boston: Northeastern University Press, 1999.

Lang, V. R. *Poems & Plays with a Memoir by Alison Lurie*. Edited by Alison Lurie. New York: Random House, 1977.

Lansing, Gerrit. *Heavenly Tree, Northern Earth*. Berkeley, CA: North Atlantic Books, 2009.

LaVigne, Robert. "The Artist's Life as a Work in Progress." *Big Bridge* 6 (n.d.), https://bigbridge.org/issue6/lavigne.htm.

LeSueur, Joe. *Digressions on Some Poems by Frank O'Hara*. New York: Farar, Strauss, & Giroux, 2003.

Levertov, Denise. "To Write is to Listen." *the poet in the world*. New York: New Directions, 1973, 227–30.

Lewis, Joel. "The Lantern on the Wall." *Exquisite Corpse*, January–April 1988. Black Sparrow Papers, Bancroft Library at Berkeley.

Leyland, Winson, ed. *Gay Sunshine Interviews*. Vol. 2. San Francisco: Gay Sunshine, 1982.

Maddocks, Melvin. "The Poets' Theatre Gives Ttself a Curtain Call." *Christian Science Monitor*, October 22, 1986.

Maud, Ralph. *Charles Olson at the Harbor*. Vancouver: Talonbooks, 2008.

———. *Charles Olson's Reading: A Biography*. Carbondale: Southern Illinois University Press, 1996.

Neville, Robert. "A Podium of Poets." *New York Times*, July 25, 1965.

O'Hara, Frank. *Collected Poems*. Edited by Donald Allen. New York: Knopf, 1971.

Olson, Charles. *The Collected Poems of Charles Olson: Excluding the "Maximus" Poems."* Edited by George F. Butterick. Berkeley: University of California Press, 1987.

———. *Collected Prose*. Edited by Donald Allen and Benjamin Friedlander. Berkeley: University of California Press, 1997.

——— . *Letters for Origin*. Edited by Albert Glover. London: Cape Goliard, 1969.

——— . *Selected Letters*. Edited by Ralph Maud. Berkeley: University of California Press, 2000.

——— . *A Special View of History*. Edited by Ann Charters. Berkeley, CA: Oyez, 1970.

"Our History." *Ruggles Street Baptist Church Online*, March 8, 2014, http://www.ruggles baptistchurch.org/history.

Perloff, Marjorie. *Frank O'Hara: Poet Among Painters*. Chicago: University of Chicago Press, 1997.

Pound, Ezra. *ABC of Reading*. London: Faber & Faber, 1934.

——— . *The Cantos of Ezra Pound*. New York: New Directions, 1993.

——— . *Guide to Kulchur*. London: Faber & Faber, 1938.

Rasula, Jed. *The American Poetry Wax Museum: Reality Effects, 1940–1990*. Urbana, IL: United Council of Teachers of English, 1996.

Rimbaud, Arthur. *I Promise to Be Good: The Letters of Arthur Rimbaud*. Translated and edited by Wyatt Mason. New York: Random House, 2007.

——— . *Illuminations*. Translated by Louise Varèse. New York: New Directions, 1946, 1957.

Rosenthal, Irving. Letters from Irving Rosenthal to John Wieners. Irving Rosenthal Papers, M1550. Dept. of Special Collections, Stanford University Libraries, Stanford, CA.

Rumaker, Michael. *Black Mountain Days*. Asheville, NC: Black Mountain Press, 2003.

——— . *Robert Duncan in San Francisco*. San Francisco: City Lights, 2013.

——— . *"like a great armful of wild & wonderful flowers": Selected Letters of Michael Rumaker*. Edited by Megan Paslawski. Lost & Found: The CUNY Poetics Documents Initiative, Series III, Number 6, Fall 2012.

Salmons, Cathy. "He's Still Young: John Wieners Returns to the Local Literary World." *Boston Phoenix*, May 1997.

Sanders, Ed. *Fug You: An Informal History of the Peace Eye Bookstore, the Fuck You Press, the Fugs, and Counterculture in the Lower East Side*. Cambridge, MA: De Capo Press, 2011.

——— . *Investigative Poetry*. San Francisco: City Lights, 1976.

Silverblatt, Michael. "Kenward Elmslie and *The Orchid Stories*." *Paris Review* (October 25, 2016), https://www.theparisreview.org/blog/2016/10/25/kenward-elmslie-orchid -stories/.

Spicer, Jack. *The House That Jack Built: The Collected Lectures of Jack Spicer*. Edited by Peter Gizzi. Hanover, NH: University Press of New England, 1998.

Stewart, Michael Seth. "'The most beautiful and truest': Collecting the Letters of John Wieners." *Jacket2*, December 24, 2012.

Stock, Noel. *The Life of Ezra Pound*. Leeds: Routledge & Paul, 1970.Terrell, Carroll Franklin, *A Companion to the Cantos of Ezra Pound*. Berkeley: University of California Press, 1980.

Wellesley, Dorothy. *Letters on Poetry from W. B. Yeats to Dorothy Wellesley*. Oxford: Oxford University Press, 1940.

Whalen, Philip. *The Collected Poems of Philip Whalen*. Edited by Michael Rothenberg. Middletown, CT: Wesleyan University Press, 2007.

Wieners, John. *Ace of Pentacles*. New York: James F. Carr & Robert Wilson, 1964.

———. *Asylum Poems*. New York: Angel Hair, 1969.

———. *Behind the State Capitol: Or Cincinnati Pike*. Boston: Good Gay Poets, 1975.

———. *A book of PROPHECIES*. Edited by Michael Carr. Lowell, MA: Bootstrap, 2007.

———. *Cultural Affairs in Boston: Poetry & Prose 1956–1985*. Edited by Raymond Foye. Santa Barbara, CA: Black Sparrow, 1988.

———. *The Hotel Wentley Poems*. San Francisco: Auerhahn, 1958.

———. *Invitation*. Santa Barbara, CA: Unicorn Press, 1970.

———. *The Journal of John Wieners Is to be Called 707 Scott Street for Billie Holliday 1959*. Edited by Lewis Warsh. Los Angeles: Sun & Moon, 1996.

———. Letter to Irving Rosenthal, February 24, 1970. Irving Rosenthal Papers, Special Collections & University Archives, Stanford University.

———. "Memories of You." *Fuck You: A Magazine of the Arts* 5, no. 9 (June 1965): 15–16. *RealityStudio: A William S Burroughs Community*, March 17, 2006, https://rspull-supervert.netdna-ssl.com/images/bibliographic_bunker/fuck_you/fuck-you-press-pdfs/fuck-you.05.vol-09.pdf.

———. *Nerves*. London: Cape Goliard Press, 1970.

———. *A New Book From Rome*. Edited by James Dunn. Lowell, MA: Bootstrap, 2010.

———. *Pressed Wafer*. Buffalo, NY: Gallery Upstairs Press, 1967.

———. *Selected Poems: 1958–1984*. Edited by Raymond Foye. Santa Barbara CA: Black Sparrow, 1986.

———. *Stars Seen in Person: Selected Journals of John Wieners*. Edited by Michael Seth Stewart. San Francisco: City Lights, 2015.

———. *Ungrateful City: The Collected Poems of John Wieners*. PhD. diss. University of Buffalo, 2014. Edited by Robert Stuart Dewhurst.

———. *We Were There! A Gay Presence at the Democratic Convention*. Boston: Good Gay Poets, 1972.

———. *WOMAN. Curriculum of the Soul #3*. Buffalo, NY: Institute for Further Studies, 1972.

———. *Youth*. New York: Phoenix Book Shop, 1970.

Wieners, John, and Charles Olson. *"the sea under the house": The Selected Correspondence of John Wieners and Charles Olson*. Edited by Michael Seth Stewart. Lost & Found: The CUNY Poetics Documents Initiative, Series 3, Number 3, Fall 2012.

Williams, William Carlos. *The Collected Poems of William Carlos Williams: 1939–1962*. New York: New Directions, 1966.

———. "On Measure—Statement for Cid Corman." *Something to Say: William Carlos Williams on Younger Poets*. New York: New Directions, 1985, 202–8.

Williamson, George Hunt. *Other Tongues—Other Flesh*. Amherst, WI: Amherst Press, 1953.

Wilson, Robert. Letter to John Wieners, March 28, 1957. R. A. Wilson Ms., Lilly Library at Indiana University.

Wolff, Geoffrey. *Black Sun: The Brief Transit and Violent Eclipse of Harry Crosby*. New York: Random House, 1976.

Zeiger, Arthur. "A Mixed Quartet." *New York Times*, December 3, 1961.

www.ingramcontent.com/pod-product-compliance
Lightning Source LLC
Chambersburg PA
CBHW021750110726
47902CB00006B/1464